# VENICE AND THE MONGOLS

# Venice and the Mongols

## THE EURASIAN EXCHANGE THAT
## TRANSFORMED THE MEDIEVAL WORLD

NICOLA DI COSMO
LORENZO PUBBLICI

TRANSLATED BY
SYLVIA ADRIAN NOTINI

PRINCETON UNIVERSITY PRESS
PRINCETON & OXFORD

Published by Princeton University Press
41 William Street, Princeton, New Jersey 08540
99 Banbury Road, Oxford OX2 6JX

press.princeton.edu

GPSR Authorized Representative: Easy Access System Europe - Mustamäe tee 50, 10621 Tallinn, Estonia, gpsr.requests@easproject.com

ISBN 978-0-691-25624-5
ISBN (e-book) 978-0-691-25622-1

Library of Congress Control Number 2025942956

British Library Cataloging-in-Publication Data is available

Editorial: Priya Nelson and Emma Wagh
Production Editorial: Jill Harris
Jacket Design: Chris Ferrante
Production: Danielle Amatucci
Publicity: Alyssa Sanford and Charlotte Coyne
Copyeditor: Tash Siddiqui

Jacket image: Reproduction of the 1367 Pizigani map from Edme-François Jomard, *Les Monuments de la géographie, ou, Recueil d'anciennes cartes européennes et orientales.* Courtesy of Darlington Digital Library, University of Pittsburgh.

This book has been composed in Arno

Printed in the United States of America

10  9  8  7  6  5  4  3  2  1

# CONTENTS

# ILLUSTRATIONS

## Figures

## Graphs

# Maps

# TABLES

# ACKNOWLEDGMENTS

THE IDEA for writing a book about Venice and the Mongols originated during a meeting we organized in 2009 together with Zvi Ben-Dor Benite, at Villa La Pietra, the Florence campus of New York University. The meeting, titled "The Mongol Empire in World History," brought together key scholars, and we owe heartfelt thanks to Zvi for making the event possible. The participants included Marco Bais, Michal Biran, Marie Favereau, Roman Hautala, Sergej P. Karpov, and Hodong Kim. These discussions offered us the opportunity to engage with the latest Mongol studies and consider a fresh perspective on the historical relationship between Europe and the Mongols. We are deeply grateful for these insightful conversations.

Around four years ago, the project that became this book took shape, focusing on the pivotal role of Venice in this relationship. While this may not be the final word on the subject, we hope it serves as a starting point, as a comprehensive book on Venice and the Mongols has yet to be written. Our sincerest thanks go to the archivists and librarians who helped us access essential documentary sources and rare literature. We are particularly grateful for the dedication and generosity of the staff at the Venice State Archives, especially during the two challenging years amid the COVID-19 pandemic, which tested everyone's patience. We would also like to thank the expert staff at the Historical Studies and Social Science Library of the Institute for Advanced Study, who tracked down elusive studies and documents.

For their invaluable feedback and advice, we wish to thank Sergio Tognetti, who reviewed the section on the economy, and Eugenio Burgio, who helped resolve several questions. Our thanks also go to Tiziana Lippiello, our friend and the Rettrice of Ca' Foscari, for embracing and supporting the idea of writing a book about Venice and Asia from the start.

The Italian edition was curated by the wonderful team at Viella Editore, particularly Cecilia Palombelli and Graziana Forlani, to whom we continue to extend our gratitude. If the present edition has come to light it has been uniquely thanks to the unwavering support of our wonderful editor at Princeton University Press, Priya Nelson, and her team. Without her vision, expert suggestions, and sharp comments this book would not have been possible. Our editorial assistant, Emma Wagh, has been a pleasure to work with from beginning to end. We would also like to thank Rob Tempio for many productive conversations, and Peter Dougherty, formerly director of Princeton University Press, whose experience and wisdom have led the way on multiple occasions. Last but certainly not least, we wish to recognize the efforts of our wonderful translator, Sylvia Notini, who immersed herself in this work with dedication and perseverance. Her keen eye for detail and flair for both languages are chiefly responsible for making the book what it is.

Any errors, omissions, or inaccuracies remain entirely our responsibility.

VENICE AND THE MONGOLS

# Introduction

AS THE thirteenth century dawned in Europe, it was dogged by age-old unresolved conflicts and the emergence of entirely new political configurations. Alongside the enduring conflict between Christianity and Islam, and the power struggles between the papacy and the empire, regional hostilities between cities and communes intensified. Yet, beyond politics, it was the evolution of the economy—particularly the expansion of trade—that opened new horizons, especially for those who had invested heavily in the growth and defense of trade-related sectors.

With the creation of the *Stato da Màr* (Domain of the Sea), Venice, often referred to as the Serenissima, began to shift its focus toward the eastern Mediterranean as early as the thirteenth century, making this region the core of its political and economic ascent. In the wake of the Fourth Crusade (1204), Venice subjugated key territories such as Candia (Crete), Corfù, Modon (Methoni), and other islands, quickly solidifying its dominance in the Aegean. While Christian Europe remained united in its opposition to Islam, internal divisions continued to fracture the continent. The most profound changes of the century, however, were rooted in distant Asia, where new political and economic spaces emerged, enabling increased commercial activity and facilitating the acquisition of new knowledge.

The Mongol conquests, which began in the first half of the thirteenth century, ushered in new political powers ruling Asia, much of the Islamic world, and the eastern fringes of Christian Europe. These shifts radically transformed political relations and, along with them, the commercial landscape. Venetian merchants faced not only an economic and commercial revolution, but also geographical, material, and cultural upheaval. This new reality required them to adapt, testing their entrepreneurial spirit and courage. Of course, this new world also bristled with opportunities tied to a grand vision:

the integration of all trade routes, from the Mediterranean to China, in a single interconnected system, fostered and supported by innovations within the Mongol Empire.

While the full potential of this global trading revolution was only partially realized in select regions, the endeavor nonetheless involved a wide array of participants—states, individual merchants, and cultures across Eurasia. From China to India, Persia to Russia, merchants of various backgrounds— Christians and Jews, Greeks and Armenians, Muslims, Italians, and Tatars— traveled side by side along these new routes. Although we might interpret this period as one of missed opportunities, not only commercially but also politically, such an interpretation would be simplistic. Diplomatic overtures between the Mongols and European rulers, for instance, often failed to produce lasting alliances, but this should not overshadow the achievements of the era.

Venice was a central protagonist in the Mongol ambition to reinvent the world through commerce. While the Mongols provided the infrastructure, the Venetians contributed their knowledge, passion, and financial resources. Alongside their Genoese counterparts, Venetian merchants were instrumental in their wise guidance of fostering and managing these unprecedented relations with the emerging Mongol power. They skillfully employed new tools and strategies to pursue a shared goal, becoming key figures in this transformative chapter of global trade.

While Genoa and Venice were the leading rivals and key players in the European commercial expansion into Asia, their contributions, though intertwined, differed in scope and influence. These differences stemmed from internal factors unique to each city, as well as from diverging positions and objectives in international politics—although their aims were not always directly opposed. Despite their long-standing hostility, the ebb and flow of their influence in the Black Sea, as well as their attempts to expand beyond its borders, were sometimes shaped by political dynamics and historical events unrelated to their rivalry. Therefore, although Venice's relationship with Genoa is an essential part of its history, the true foundation of Venice's presence in the Black Sea lies in its interactions with the Mongols. Even when filtered through other interests and intermediaries, Venice's relationship with the Mongols was its raison d'être for its presence on the Black Sea.

If Venice (like Genoa) had not maintained its foothold on the Pontic coasts, the collapse of the Mongol Empire would likely have spelled the end for its settlements. These outposts would have been severed from international routes and left vulnerable to political turmoil, rendering trade unfeasible. Instead, both Tana, Venice's principal base on the Black Sea, and Caffa, the capital of the Genoese colonial network, managed to endure as vital commercial hubs for decades. Their continued existence attracted investments that would have been unlikely had there been a complete political and economic collapse. Thus, the end of the *pax mongolica* did not mark the demise of Venetian relations with the Mongol and Tatar lords, who vied for the remnants of the Golden Horde. While there was indeed a political retrenchment and a decline in trade, the foundations established during earlier periods proved resilient, and these Venetian and Genoese outposts were only uprooted with the Ottoman conquest of Crimea.

What we refer to as "the plan" is key to understanding the historical role of the Mongol Empire—a role centered on creation and construction, which contrasts sharply with the image of the Mongols as a purely destructive force during their initial invasions. While the devastation caused by their early conquests is undeniable, the simplistic portrayal of the Mongols as an unstoppable and brutal human avalanche that shaped the conquest of Rus', China, eastern Europe, and the Islamic world has been increasingly challenged by historians over the past three decades. This newer perspective emphasizes the Mongols not just as conquerors, but as rulers who facilitated cultural exchanges and drove social and economic transformations across the territories they controlled. Although their arrival was not always welcomed, most regions saw the establishment of new forms of accommodation and mediation. This process often included the Mongols' own religious and cultural conversions, as well as the incorporation of local elites into their administrative and governmental systems. This shift from conquerors to rulers required significant effort and intelligence, and it is reflected in the widespread admiration and respect for the Mongol khans found in European accounts—from the writings of Franciscan Giovanni di Pian del Carpine to the chronicles of Marco Polo and beyond.

The relationship between Venice and the new Eurasian power developed during a mature phase of Mongol governance across various parts of the empire. By this time, the initial shock and apocalyptic fears that had accompanied the Mongols' early conquests were long past. Rather, this relationship was the fruit of positive efforts by European powers to establish diplomatic, mutually beneficial ties, often driven by political calculations. Many diplomatic missions aimed to enlist Mongol military support against Islamic forces, though these attempts ultimately failed. One key reason was the growing internal

divisions within the Mongol political world, which would later become insur-
mountable. Nevertheless, the Mongol rulers shared a common interest in promoting trade, providing merchants with favorable conditions that helped
them to navigate political barriers. Commerce was not just encouraged—it
was essential, as it constituted a major source of fiscal revenue for Mongol
governments.

As mentioned earlier, contemporary historians have re-evaluated the active
role of the Mongols in facilitating the exchange and movements of people,
goods, and ideas within their vast empire. These studies, which we will explore
in greater detail later, suggest that "the plan" inherent to the Mongols' approach to commercial transformation was far more complex than a mere well-
meaning or accommodating attitude. Rather, it was a carefully designed and
far-sighted strategy with multiple layers. Within this framework, we can identify at least four different levels: logistics, finance, production, and legal
structure.

Logistical support for merchants was provided by the extensive network of
postal stations established across the empire, a system already in place during
the initial conquests. Merchants who held special *laissez-passers* were granted
access to these support structures, allowing them to travel efficiently. They also
found market cities that offered hospitality services tailored to meet their specific needs. Additionally, local governments, acting under the authority of the
central Mongol leadership, ensured general safety by removing the threat of
bandits and marauders from trade routes.

From a financial perspective, the large-scale introduction of paper money
in China (and the attempt to extend this innovation to Persia) as a universally
accepted means of exchange, guaranteed by political authority, was nothing
short of revolutionary. Had this system been successfully implemented across
the entire Mongol Empire, it would likely have had a seismic impact on the
global economy. Although this did not come to pass, the quest to develop financial tools capable of supporting commerce between diverse regions and
trading networks became a common endeavor among Mongols, Europeans,
and Muslims alike.

On a productive level, the Mongols greatly incentivized the production of
commercial goods that were in high demand, both within their territories and
internationally, promoting their export. A prime example is the production of
silk in China, a commodity sought by markets across the world, which in turn
stimulated long-distance trade. The Mongols' appetite for exotic and precious
goods, along with the creation of universal standards—which could be termed

a "court culture"—acted as a significant driver and filter for Eurasian trade over vast distances.

Finally, let us turn to the legal frameworks: the treaties and concessions that carefully defined the rights and responsibilities of foreign merchants, including tariffs, duties, and the size of commercial settlements. These agreements were guaranteed by Mongol authorities and upheld by various diplomatic bodies. However, this does not mean that these relationships were straightforward or without friction. While agreements established clear jurisdictions, any perceived violations of these accords was seen by the Mongols as an affront to their sovereignty and often led to diplomatic breakdowns or, in some cases, armed conflict. Despite these tensions, the Mongols often sought to smooth over and limit the reasons for conflicts, a stark contrast to prevailing trends in Europe, where religious wars were more common. In Mongol-ruled territories, such as the Venetian colonies and other European settlements, potential religious conflicts were often diffused through a policy of coexistence. The Mongols' approach to religion was marked by tolerance (or at least indifference), allowing Christian missionaries, for example, to operate freely as long as they did not interfere with other faiths. In general, a pragmatic ethos prevailed, prioritizing compromise over religious zealotry, particularly when commercial interests clashed with papal directives.

The Mongol conquest can be seen as the catalyst that reshaped Eurasian trade, offering European merchants unprecedented opportunities to establish cities, build *fondaci* (warehouses), and turn these into key hubs in foreign territories, allowing access to previously unreachable markets. For European merchants, new horizons opened—both real and imagined—motivating them to invest, explore, and seek common ground with populations and rulers who were no longer considered threatening hordes but reliable intermediaries, business partners, local administrators, and political counterparts. In this transformed landscape, the Venetian experience—perhaps even more so than that of the Genoese—can be divided into two distinct spheres: the state and the merchant. This distinction is crucial to understanding both the limits and objectives of the relationship between Venice and the Mongols.[1]

The Venetian expansion into the Black Sea did not originate from the daring initiative of merchants seeking to discover new shores but rather from the state's pressing need to secure vital supplies of wheat, essential for the survival of the

1. Di Cosmo, "Mongols and Merchants on the Black Sea Frontier," pp. 402–6; Di Cosmo, "Black Sea Emporia and the Mongol Empire," pp. 99–106.

Republic. The damage inflicted on Venetian interests by the combined forces of Byzantium and Genoa, culminating in the Treaty of Nymphaeum in 1261, posed an existential threat to Venice. This challenge demanded a resolute response, leading to the mobilization of military and diplomatic resources to break the blockade imposed by its adversaries, just as the political landscape of the Middle East and Europe was undergoing irreversible changes. From bases in Constantinople and Anatolian ports, Venetian merchants began to explore new routes and territories, while the state pursued a strategy of alliances and warfare on a constantly shifting chessboard involving Catholic and Orthodox kingdoms, Islamic powers, and local potentates—from Italian communes to the kingdoms of Trebizond and Lesser Armenia. The Venetian state was tasked with securing these routes, ports, and markets to ensure the profitability of its merchants, whose activities were the lifeblood of the Republic. Thus, the state's institutions and offices took on the political, strategic, and military leadership of Venice's expansion, defending its interests and guiding its territorial growth.

Venice's political and economic power was significantly influenced by its aristocratic and merchant class; hence, the state was obligated to support commercial activity. This involved outfitting galleys, launching military interventions to defend the Republic's interests, and engaging in diplomacy to expand Venice's influence and secure favorable conditions and protection for its citizens. The Venetian model of state-driven expansion clearly defined the scope and limits of public authority's involvement in managing the community's interests in Mongol territory. This model also justified investments in defense and strong diplomatic presence.

East of Constantinople, the scope of Venice's state intervention was concentrated on the Black Sea, a natural endpoint for navigation, as well as key outlying markets, most notably Tabriz, where Venice set up consular representation. The state did not simply follow the merchants in their efforts to establish relationships with the Mongols and other powers, but rather acted in parallel, often with different priorities. While merchants sought profit, the state focused on defending national interests. Venice's strategic expansion toward Asia was driven by several factors: the loss of its commercial monopoly in Byzantine territory in 1261, the growing political and military threat posed by Genoa, and the increasing vulnerability of its wheat supply, given the politically volatile hinterland.

The Venetian state ensured the stability and protection of its settlements on the Black Sea, but consistently refrained from extending beyond those borders. Public authorities and their representatives rarely ventured farther than the ports where the Venetian ships docked. Merchants who chose to negotiate routes toward Persia, China, or central Asia did so independently, relying instead on the support, assistance, and protection of the Mongols. In practical terms, they entered relationships of dependency, similar to those formed by all merchants operating on Mongol-controlled territory, regardless of nationality. This limited state involvement may explain why so little is known about Venetians' and other Italian merchants' activities beyond the Black Sea. Most of the notarial records, senate decrees, and diplomatic treaties pertain to the Pontic region, beyond which an almost impenetrable curtain falls, and any documentation becomes a precious commodity. However, other sources, such as wills, provide evidence that many Venetians operated beyond Tana and Trebizond, albeit rarely. What is certain is that these merchants, whether traveling alone or in groups, could only rely on their own strength and the protection of Mongol commanders and rulers as they ventured along the Asian trade routes.

The other side of the coin, as we have noted, is represented by the merchant, whose symbiotic relationship with the state is clearly evident. The thirteenth-century Venetian merchant embodied the model of economic development centered on commercial expansion. Many families that rose to prominence in the late twelfth century, such as the doge's nobility, had mercantile origins (for example, the Mastropiero and the Ziani) and were regularly engaged in commerce along with other aristocratic Venetian families (e.g., Morosini, Michiel, Badoer, and Contarini).[2] However, the space occupied by the merchant was defined by private interests that did not always align with those of the state. Merchants often operated in close connection with family and business networks and were the spearhead of Venice's eastward expansion. Ship captains were not only entrusted with vast financial fortunes but also with the responsibility of seeking and exploiting trade opportunities. The dynamism of the Venetian merchant, along with his ability to move, invest, and spend long periods abroad in pursuit of profit, was crucial to the success of the state's strategy—where the merchant was its primary representative. Hence, the success of Venetians on the Black Sea cannot be understood without acknowledging the structural changes that both preceded and resulted from the expansion. The growth of enterprises brought about a qualitative shift in trade activities, which saw the inclusion of new actors such as assistants, accountants, and local agents. This period also saw the emergence of banks, letters of

2. Caravale, "Le istituzioni della Repubblica," pp. 304–5.

exchange, and, by the fourteenth century, the first forms of insurance. In practice, the Venetian merchant increasingly became a modern entrepreneur, at the helm of a complex and multifaceted business operation.

While the Venetian state halted its expansion at the ports of the Black Sea—such as Tana, Trebizond, and as far as Tabriz—individual merchants ventured beyond these limits. These merchants gained new financial knowledge and learned new languages, developing a linguistic and commercial lingua franca that facilitated trade. We know that the Polos communicated in Turkic and Persian, and the *Codex Cumanicus* included a lexicon in Latin, Turkic, and Persian, all essential languages for navigating the routes that extended from the Black Sea. An interesting case is that of Giosafat Barbaro, who, while in Venice, recognized two Tatar slaves by the language they spoke—one he himself knew. Although multilingualism was common in the cosmopolitan spheres of eastern markets, professional interpreters and translators, such as *turcimanni* (interpreters) and *dragomanni* (dragomans), were still indispensable. These figures worked in the chancelleries of Venice, Tana, and other cities, drafting documents, attending legal proceedings, and accompanying ambassadors on diplomatic missions and merchants on their journeys.

As Mongol power collapsed and political authority fragmented, conditions became more difficult for merchants, who could no longer rely on stable structures for support. Faced with new challenges and shifting political configurations, Venice recalibrated its interests and strategies. Although Venetian outposts stubbornly persisted even after the Ottoman conquest of Constantinople in 1453, by this final phase, they had already lost much of the significance they had once held. While this was undeniably a period of decline, culminating in Venice's eventual withdrawal from the Black Sea, the underlying themes of this story—such as the interdependence between the state and merchants, the ability to operate in often hostile territories, and the creation of colonies and trade networks—foreshadowed a new chapter in world history. The Atlantic powers, soon to dominate the oceanic trade routes, would redefine and bring to fruition the unfinished vision of the Mongol Empire—the largest empire ever realized—and the most advanced forms of European trade.

## Historiography

The story of Venice and the Mongol Empire is characterized by historiographical complexity, shaped by several overlapping areas of scholarship. On the one hand, there is the immense bibliography, spanning over a century, that focuses on Italian trade in the Black Sea. On the other hand, in the past twenty-five years, new trends in Mongol studies have shifted away from its conquests to focus on the Mongol Empire's contribution to fostering exchanges, relationships, and international trade. Additionally, there is the figure of Marco Polo and the vast ocean of Polo-related studies. This book lies, if not at the heart, then certainly in dialogue with these three significant historiographical fields. Therefore, it seems appropriate to offer an overview of each, with the understanding that this will not cover every single aspect. The goal is simply to trace their evolution and highlight the most important contributions.

The father of studies on Italian trade in the Levant, including the Black Sea, is undoubtedly Wilhelm Heyd. As early as 1885, Heyd laid the groundwork for subsequent scholarship with his extensive work on medieval trade and its sources. Around the same time, Georg Martin Thomas compiled a collection of documents on "Veneto–Levantine" diplomacy, a project later completed by archivist Riccardo Predelli, who was Trentino by birth but Venetian by adoption. This collection, which spans the years 1300 to 1454, covers not only Venice's relations with Byzantium but also its interactions with powers farther east.

In the first half of the twentieth century, the pioneering studies of Romanian scholar and politician Gheorghe Bratianu shifted the focus of research definitively toward the Black Sea. Two of his most notable works are *Recherches sur le commerce génois dans le mer Noire au XIIIe siècle*, published in 1929, and *Les Vénitiens dans la mer Noire au 14e siècle: la politique du sénat en 1332–33 et la notion de la latinité*, published in 1939. Bratianu famously described the Black Sea in the fourteenth century as the *plaque tournante* (turntable) of international trade—a hub where products from different regions and trade circuits were amassed and redistributed. His research was groundbreaking, establishing the Black Sea as a critical area of historical analysis for understanding the European Middle Ages. Like many scholars of his generation, Bratianu operated in the intellectual shadow of, and in reaction to, the dominant influence of Nicolae Iorga, a politician and intellectual of great stature who had also studied the history of the Black Sea. Additionally, Bratianu was the first to examine Genoese notarial sources from Caffa, which led to the publication of the first series of acts by Lamberto di Sambuceto in 1927 and the masterful posthumous work *La mer Noire* (1969).

In the postwar period, the field of research expanded to include numerous archival and documentary studies. Notably, the French scholar Freddy Thiriet's *La Romanie vénitienne au Moyen Age: le développement et l'exploitation du domaine colonial vénitien, XIIe–XVe siècles* (1959) made a major contribution. Thiriet's surveys in the State Archives of Venice in the 1950s led to the publication of registers of senate resolutions (1958–61) and records of Venetian assemblies concerning Romània (from 1966). Following in the footsteps of Bratianu's research, many other scholars contributed substantially to advancing the study of Venetian and Genoese commerce on the Black Sea. Among them was Charles Verlinden, whose research on medieval slavery directly engaged the Black Sea and Tana. Additionally, the works of Bernard Doumerc and Jean Claude Hocquet on trade and navigation in the eastern Mediterranean remain indispensable for anyone exploring this field.

Research involving the notarial records, such as those of Lamberto di Sambuceto, opened new avenues for reconstructing the organization of Italian trade on the Black Sea and even facilitated early attempts at quantitative analysis. Interest in notarial and economic documents peaked with the work of the Genoese school led by Geo Pistarino, whose influence spurred scholars worldwide to pursue work in this area. Their contributions were crucial. Among these scholars were Anna Balletto, Gabriella Airaldi, and Giovanna Petti Balbi. While studies on individual documents and notarial documents multiplied— sometimes focusing on entire collections, and at other times on a single act— there were also many comprehensive works. French historian Michel Balard completed work initiated by Bratianu on the acts of the Genoese notary active in Caffa during the late thirteenth century (*Gênes et l'outre-mer*, 1973) and published the most thorough study on Genoese Romània (*La Romanie génoise: XIIe-début du XVe siècle*, 1978). Balard's extensive work in the 1970s gave a decisive and lasting impetus to Black Sea studies, breathing new life into many research strands that remain active today.

The Romanian school has continued to produce prominent scholars like Şerban Papacostea and Virgil Ciocîltan, who have made significant contributions to the field. Papacostea authored *La Mer Noire Carrefour des grandes routes internationales 1204–1453* (2006), and Ciocîltan followed with *The Mongols and the Black Sea Trade in the Thirteenth and Fourteenth Centuries* (2016). While Ciocîltan remains firmly rooted in the European tradition of studying Genoese and Venetian presence on the Black Sea, he is one of the few scholars to have expanded the scope of research to include the Asian dimension, particularly the role of the Mongols in the history of international trade.

The Russian school of Black Sea studies is dominated by the figure of Sergej P. Karpov, whose work spans numerous essays and monographs. One notable example is *L'impero di Trebisonda, Venezia, Genova e Roma, 1204–1461*:

*rapporti politici, diplomatici e commerciali* (1986), which provides a detailed analysis of the Venetian and Genoese presence in the Crimea and the major trade routes on the Black Sea. Karpov's contributions also stand out for his publication of previously unseen sources in the series *Pričernomor'e v srednie veka* (The Region of the Black Sea in the Middle Ages) in 1991, such as the acts of Benedetto Bianco, a notary in Tana. The Russian school continues to produce world-class scholars, including Evgeny Khvalkov, a student of Karpov's, whose recent work *The Colonies of Genoa in the Black Sea Region: Evolution and Transformation* (2018) has garnered attention. Another noteworthy scholar is Aleksandr Emanov, whose research focuses on Caffa during the thirteenth and fourteenth centuries.

Alongside archival research, broader studies have been conducted by pioneering scholars such as Roberto S. Lopez, Robert H. Bautier, Benjamin Kedar, David Ayalon, and David Jacoby, among others. These medievalists' works are essential for placing Venetian trade history in a larger economic and cultural context. Over the course of the twentieth century, the study of Italian colonies on the Black Sea emerged as a distinct research field, now occupying a significant place in medieval studies.

Studies on the Mongol Empire and its conquests, largely produced by scholars from the English-speaking world, form the second pillar of our historiographical framework, and this field encompasses various approaches. Traditional historiography has often focused on the theoretical contrast between the Mongol "impact" and the western "response," with much of the research centered on the relations between the papacy and the Mongols, as well as reports on the "Tatars" written by European missionaries and diplomats. Key figures in this area include Paul Pelliot, Jean Richard, Igor de Rachewiltz, Denis Sinor, and, among the most prolific, Peter Jackson. In addition to these excellent scholarly works, there has been extensive research on the Mongols in the Middle East and central Asia, with prominent contributions from Charles Melville, David Morgan, Reuven Amitai, and Michal Biran.

The turning point in historiography that allowed scholars to move beyond the predominantly philological focus of many early studies came with Janet Abu-Lughod's book, *Before European Hegemony: The World System AD 1250–1350* (1989). Without dwelling on the conceptual roots of the book, which places it in a critical dialogue with Immanuel Wallerstein's world-systems theory, Abu-Lughod's work is particularly influential for positioning the Mongol Empire at the heart of pre-existing global commercial networks. Although she did not intend to directly engage with Mongol history, her book reimagines the Mongol Empire as a central hub of a new world order, interpreting it as the driving force behind unprecedented communication and connections between hitherto isolated regions.

Thomas Allsen's studies offer the most precise and insightful historical framework for understanding the global impact of the Mongol Empire. In his landmark works, *Commodity and Exchange in the Mongol Empire: A Cultural History of Islamic Textiles* (1997) and *Culture and Conquest in Mongol Eurasia* (2001), Allsen underscores the active role the Mongols played in what can be termed the "imperialization" of the territories under their rule. This impact, often underappreciated, recasts the Mongols not as passive facilitators of trade but as active agents, shaping and driving global exchanges. They provided vital impulses that had far-reaching effects in the construction of their own empire.

Other scholars have approached the Mongols as a global phenomenon, such as Timothy May, author of *The Mongol Conquests in World History* (2012). The perspective that views the Mongols as agents of change and their imperial vision as a transformative force has influenced much of contemporary historiography. A prime example is the collection of essays in *Nomads as Agents of Cultural Change: The Mongols and Their Eurasian Predecessors*, edited by Reuven Amitai and Michal Biran (2015).

The third and final historiographical area we wish to highlight involves extensive studies on Marco Polo and his *Milione*. Polo studies form a separate strand from those focused on Black Sea trade. While the history of the relationship between Venice and the Mongols has often been overshadowed by the travels of Marco Polo, it is important to clarify that neither Polo nor his work actually played a significant role in shaping Venetian policy toward the Mongols. It is well known that Marco Polo received little recognition upon his return from "Cathay," and the Venetian Republic did not pursue diplomatic or trade relations with China based on the information he provided.

Since the first appearance of the *Milione* (*The Travels of Marco Polo*), and especially following the sixteenth-century edition by Giovanni Battista Ramusio (*Navigazioni e viaggi*), the success of the text has been undeniable. Modern studies on the *Milione*, beginning from the mid-nineteenth century, have primarily focused on two areas: first, the critical reconstruction of the text based on the various surviving versions, and second, the publication of annotated editions. These efforts, led by scholars such as Yule and Cordier, Pelliot, Olschki, Benedetto, and many others, have concentrated on the philological analysis aiming to elucidate the text. However, these are not the aspects we are concerned with. Neither the literary merit of the *Milione* nor whether Marco

Polo actually traveled to China is directly relevant to the broader relationship between Venice and the Mongols.

More recent studies following the publication of Frances Wood's *Did Marco Polo Go to China?* (1996) have been closely linked to commercial and global themes. The doubt raised by the English writer on whether Marco Polo actually traveled to China has sparked various reactions.[3] Today, thirty years after the release of the book, new studies have largely dismissed this hypothesis.[4] The most compelling work that dispels these doubts is Hans Ulrich Vogel's *Marco Polo Was in China: New Evidence from Currencies, Salts and Revenues* (2013), which uses commercial and fiscal data to confirm Marco Polo's presence in China and the reliability of the information contained in the *Milione*. The experiences of the Polos, along with Marco's *Milione* (discussed in chapter 8 of our book), illustrate the depth of commercial knowledge required of Venetians and other Italian merchants who journeyed to unfamiliar lands. However, we present these experiences without framing them as emblematic of Venice's broader relations with the Mongol world.

## The Structure of This Book

We have chosen to structure this book in two parts: a historical-chronological section, and a thematic one. The first part, comprising seven chapters, traces the encounter between Venice and the Mongols, detailing the phases leading up to Venice's withdrawal from the Black Sea. By "Mongols" or "Tatars" we are not referring solely to the Mongol Empire but also to its later expressions, including Tamerlane's kingdom and the various Crimean khanates that emerged after the end of the *pax mongolica*. The political legacy of the Mongol Empire and its successors continued to play an important role in Venice's eastern policies.

Any account of the relationship between Venice and the Mongols could easily be overshadowed by a single theme: Venice's rivalry with Genoa, the major maritime power in Crimea and a perpetual enemy of the Serenissima. To prevent this often-discussed topic from dominating the narrative, we have made a concerted effort to focus specifically on Venice's interactions with the Mongols, highlighting this unique relationship without letting the Genoese rivalry take center stage.

3. See, for instance, the long review by De Rachewiltz, "Marco Polo Went to China."
4. Allsen, "The Cultural Worlds of Marco Polo"; Jackson, "Marco Polo and His 'Travels.'"

The first two chapters explore two parallel movements: Venice's eastward expansion and the Mongols' westward push. Although initially independent of each other, these movements gradually converged. On one side, Venice needed to fight its exclusion from Black Sea trade following the Byzantine–Genoese alliance of 1261. On the other side, the consolidation of the Mongol khanates—specifically the Golden Horde and the Ilkhanate in southwest Asia—reshaped the Eurasian political map, prompting the search for a new balance in the region.

Chapter 3 discusses the first phase of Venetian expansion into the Black Sea, during which Venice remained deeply engaged in its rivalry with Genoa and embroiled in complex Mediterranean politics. This chapter covers the founding of Venice's primary colony in the East: Tana, located on the Sea of Azov—a crucial bridgehead and strategic base. Chapter 4 focuses on Venice's period of greatest expansion between 1320 and 1343, within the Golden Horde. During this time, trade flourished, diplomatic relations advanced, and Venice's rivalry with Genoa entered a new phase, characterized less by the fight for supremacy and more by the necessity of coexistence.

However, the balances established during this period began to falter in the 1340s, leading to the crises discussed in chapter 5, which tracks the eventual collapse of the Mongol Empire as a supranational entity. While relations between Venice and the Mongols maintained their center of gravity in the Golden Horde, the political repercussions of the empire's collapse could be felt on all levels. The fall of the Ilkhanate and demise of the Yuan dynasty in China in 1368 effectively marked the end of Mongol supremacy in Asia.

Following from this, chapter 6 explores Venice's position within this shifting political climate, where new figures emerge in the "Tatar" world, pretenders to the Mongol Empire's remnants, first among them Timur, who attempted to revive the imperial vision of Chinggis Khan. Finally, chapter 7 describes Venice's twilight years in the Black Sea, from the rebuilding of Tana after its destruction by Timur to the eventual Ottoman conquest. This period was not one of inevitable decline, but rather marked by highs and lows that demonstrate Venice's steadfast determination to maintain its presence. However, with the rise of the Ottomans and transformations as profound as those that initially drove Venice toward the Mongol East, Venice ultimately withdrew from the Black Sea.

The second part of the book consists of four chapters that address broader themes. The first of these is devoted to Marco Polo, whose journey to Cathay represents a unique and pivotal moment in the history of Europe's knowledge of Asia. We treat this as a self-contained event, rather than an integral part of Venice's relationship with the Mongols or the wider culture of Mongol and Chinese trade. Special attention is given to the chapters in Polo's book that shed light on the practices and institutions governing trade and finance. As recent economic studies based on Chinese sources have confirmed, the accuracy of Polo's observations is remarkable, due largely to his commercial acumen, which set him apart from other travelers like Ibn Battuta or Odorico da Pordenone. Despite the cultural differences, Marco Polo's keen observations reveal that these worlds were not entire disconnected.

Chapter 9 delves into the evolving geography of trade, innovations in transportation, including routes, ports, and ships, as well as legal and diplomatic frameworks required to formalize relations with the Mongols. Without such frameworks, merchants would have been left to negotiate on their own, without state backing. We also examine the associations between merchants and investors that allowed capital to reach even the most distant corners on the trade route map. Chapter 10 focuses on instruments of exchange, including the essential language skills of merchants. While some managed to learn a smattering of eastern languages, most relied on interpreters and translators. Although Medieval Latin served as the lingua franca in Europe, traveling east from Constantinople meant crossing linguistic borders where multiple trade languages prevailed, particularly Turkic (Cuman) and Persian. This period also saw advancements in financial tools, including the minting of new coins designed to facilitate long-distance trade across non-integrated systems. The issue of standardizing weights and measures was another challenge; while medieval Italian cities used different measures for various goods, the problem became exponentially more complex beyond Italy. Merchants had to rely on equivalency and experience accumulated over many trips to navigate these disparities.

The final chapter discusses the goods exported and imported by Venetian merchants. We take a closer look at key commodities in international trade, such as wheat, silk, and slaves. An overview of the goods transported on Venetian ships is crucial to understanding the shifts in trade over the various phases of Venice's presence in Asia. The accompanying charts, while not exhaustive, illustrate the overall significance of Asian trade in Venice's economy.

The world that the Mongol conquest had created was initially one of fear, apprehension, and a sense of impending disaster. European defenselessness against the devastations visited upon Christians from Rus' to Hungary conjured up apocalyptic visions. Once the dust settled, however, and the "Tatars" turned from conquest to government, new scenarios opened up before the eyes of Mediterranean powers that had long based their fortunes on connecting places and peoples, through commerce and diplomacy. Genoa and Venice, thanks to their maritime supremacy, were uniquely placed to take advantage of the opportunity offered by the Mongol expansion. In the second half of the thirteenth century, both republics began to move into the Black Sea, which became, famously, the turntable of global trade, where goods from the East and the West were loaded on cargo ships or caravans and carried to remote markets across Eurasia. While the story of Italian merchants in the Mongol Empire has been told many times, it has been focused on Genoa, which surely was the main protagonist of the Italian commercial expansion in Asia. Venice was moved by similar interests and goals but its experience was different, bound by special constraints and unique circumstances. Once it extended from the Mediterranean to the Black Sea, their bitter rivalry forced Venetian merchants to carve out their own spaces and, in the process, build a separate relationship with their Mongol partners. Venice on the Black Sea is once again poised between water and land, a familiar stance, but in a much more precarious equilibrium. Venice's strategy, from a position of relative weakness, was one of survival, resistance and constant adaptation to fast-changing circumstances. Its war galleys had to intervene against Genoese threats to protect trade and diplomacy with Mongol rulers. And yet, amidst wars with familiar enemies and fragile partnerships with alien allies, for over a century and a half the economic interests of Venice's commercial class continued to thrive in different forms. Even when the Mongols were no longer powerful, the dream of unfettered access to the richest markets on earth continues to attract merchants, adventurers and travelers. The story of Venice and the Mongols unfolds on the eve of a far more globalized world, which in many ways it anticipates.

# PART I

# A New World Order

# 1

# Venice and the East

## FROM THE ORIGINS TO LANDING ON THE BLACK SEA

## Venice, the East, and the Byzantine Empire up to the Fourth Crusade (1204)

In the second book of *Les estoires de Venise*, Venetian chronicler Martin da Canal (active until 1275) noted that provisions in his city had become more costly. To solve this problem, city authorities sent convoys to the farthest corners of the globe—even as far as the Mongol Empire.[1] Venice's fascination with the East was sparked as early as the city's foundation, and was consolidated over the centuries, thanks especially to its relationship with the Byzantine Empire and its expansion to the islands and ports of the Aegean Sea. This inclination toward the East built the premise of the relationship between Venice and the Mongol khans—yet it was not the sole driving force. To frame Venice's eastward expansion in broader terms, based on its connections to the Byzantine Empire, we will examine the main phases in this chapter.

Throughout the eighth century, Venice remained under Byzantine rule, but the balance of power between the two states began to change as early as the following century, when Venice enhanced its military potential to become Byzantium's armed force in the Adriatic. At the same time, the Frankish Empire extended its control over the city of Venice and the Venetian region; thus,

---

1. Martin da Canal, "La Chronique des Véniciens," II, 152, "*si fu en Venise mult chiere la vitaille; et ne prquant Monsignor li Dus et li nobles Veneciens envoirent lor navie parmi le munde iusque as Tatars.*" Information on the life of Martin da Canal is scarce and almost exclusively limited to the *Estoires*, most likely written between 1267 and 1275.

for decades, Venice was the object of disputes between two great powers.[2] In 809, the Byzantine fleet entered the upper Adriatic to consolidate control of the lagoon city.[3] In 812, the Frankish and Byzantine empires signed a peace treaty in the city of Aachen, in which the former handed over "le Venezie" to its rival. In turn, Byzantium acknowledged the imperial authority of the Frankish Empire's Charlemagne. Having been returned to the Byzantine sphere, Venice now enjoyed complete political freedom. From the middle of the ninth century, the city's government focused on strengthening its navy, using substantial resources to develop long-distance trade. The Venetian navy was essential in stamping out the piracy rife on the Dalmatian coasts, which threatened maritime trade between Venice and Constantinople.[4] In return for its support of the Byzantine fleet, Venice acquired both economic advantages and a privileged position in trade within the empire.

Venice's influence in Byzantine foreign policy continued to grow in the tenth century. With the political stabilization of the Islamic world, new markets were opened to international trade. Venetian merchants routinely traveled to Egyptian ports, then ruled by the Shiite Islamic dynasty of the Fatimids. The Fatimids had invested vast resources to acquire control over the immense flow of goods coming from India, traditionally traded in ports of the Persian Gulf.[5] Venetians, Amalfitans, and Genoese settled in Jerusalem, and were active in the ports of Alexandria, Damietta, Tripoli, and Antioch, even extending their trade to Syria. The Mediterranean's economic and commercial center thus shifted to the coasts of northern Africa, mainly due to investments made by the Fatimids.[6] This facilitated the trade of "light" goods, in particular spices—pepper, ginger, cinnamon, and clove—and raw materials for the

2. The triumph of the Franks over the Lombards in 774 had brought closer to the settlement a rising power that could become a threatening neighbor; this drove Venice to seek support from the Byzantine Empire. Though the empire was heir to the Roman tradition, it was no longer capable of effectively controlling a region as remote as the upper Adriatic. In 771–2, the Venetian Doge Maurizio was still referred to as *consul et imperiali dux Venetiarum provinciae*. Cf. Ortalli, "Il ducato e la 'civitas Rivoalti,'" p. 777; *Epistolae Merowingici et Karolini aevi*, no. 19, p. 713; *Documenti relativi alla storia di Venezia*, vol. 1, no. 30, p. 49.

3. Ortalli, "Il ducato e la 'civitas Rivoalti,'" p. 778.

4. Nicol, *Byzantium and Venice*, p. 31; Curta, "A Note on Trade and Trade Centers," pp. 267–76.

5. Ashtor, *A Social and Economic History of the Near East*, pp. 196–7.

6. Lev, *State and Society in Fatimid Egypt*, pp. 65–79; Brett, *The Fatimid Empire*, pp. 90–94.

textile industry.[7] Venice also opened itself to foreign markets. Due to increasingly frequent relations with the Islamic world, there was an influx of eastern merchants, especially from north Africa and Syria.

The Commercial Revolution of the thirteenth century was the result of a long process that had begun at least three centuries earlier.[8] It was mainly those Italian cities that were best equipped and prepared for innovation that benefited most from this revolution.[9] Maritime trade—and with it the merchant fleet—were at once both the instrument and the consequence of this new course for the European economy, whose growth was mainly determined by its relations with the East. A further development factor was Venice's presence in eastern Mediterranean markets and exposure to Greek–Arab culture; the city not only profited from this, but also played a leading role.[10]

Economic growth was accompanied by demographic growth. Between the end of the tenth century and the early decades of the eleventh century, both urban and rural populations boomed. Of course, as the population grew, so did the need for food, which was matched by an increase in agricultural production. Vast regions of continental Europe were deforested to favor the expansion of agriculture; thus, woods, moors, and uncultivated land gave way to cultivated land. The entire Mediterranean basin required ever more timber for building, heating, industrial, and military uses. Thanks to its network of water transport on the Adige, Piave, Tagliamento, Brenta, and other smaller rivers, Venice had ample access to wood from the surrounding regions.[11] Some of this was traded in the East for precious metals and luxury goods.

Demographic growth also gave rise to a flourishing, proto-industrial economy and to the multiplication of production centers, which in turn led to a rise in exports and a growing reliance on regional and foreign markets. Throughout the tenth century, trade fostered peaceful relations between Venice and the Islamic world. Among the products Venetians purchased from the Islamic

7. Products for the textile industry included dyes, alum used for fixing color, and raw materials such as cotton and silk. Ashtor, *A Social and Economic History of the Near East*, pp. 44–5.

8. Borrowing Lopez's spot-on definition, *The Commercial Revolution*.

9. Petech, "Les marchands italiens" and Lopez, "Venezia e le grandi linee dell'espansione commerciale."

10. Bautier, *Les relations économiques*, pp. 268–9. For more on trade in the east Mediterranean and Venice's role, see the highly informative collection of articles recently published by David Jacoby in *Medieval Trade*.

11. Appuhn, *A Forest on the Sea*, pp. 27–8.

territories were grain, precious fabrics, silk, weapons, and slaves.[12] Nonetheless, trade with Muslims was part of a greater international picture that grew more uncertain in the second half of the 900s. What triggered this uncertainty was a breakdown in relations between the caliphate and Byzantium. Venice remained faithful to the empire, and city authorities forbade the import of weapons and slaves from Islamic markets on two occasions, in 960 and 971.[13] When noble-man Pietro Orseolo (ca. 920–87) became doge, the power balance between Venice and Constantinople began to change. Military campaigns led by Em-peror Basil II (r. 976–1025) against the Bulgarians in the Balkans had called for so great a military and financial effort that the Byzantines had been forced to ask Venice for help in defending and controlling the sea.[14] In 992, the two states ratified a treaty of collaboration that granted Venetian ships freedom of trade throughout the empire.[15] Venice also received advantageous customs duties and trade rights from the Byzantines, most likely based on pre-existing condi-tions, in that they were sealed "according to the ancient custom."[16]

The importance Venice garnered in its relations with Byzantium is evidenced by the fact that only the *logoteta del dromo*, the rank of high officer with close ties to the emperor, had the right to board Venetian ships for inspection.[17] In fact, although Venetians were formally subjects of the empire and therefore foreign-ers (*extranei*), official documents refer to them as loyal allies.[18]

By the dawn of the eleventh century, Venice had become the key link in the chain between western Europe and the Byzantine East. It was the only

12. Nicol, *Byzantium and Venice*, pp. 21 and 37.

13. In 971, a Byzantine diplomatic delegation arrived in Venice to formally protest the com-mercial activity of the Venetians with the Arabs, expressly prohibited by city authorities. Em-peror Giovanni Zimisce (r. 969–976) gave a firm warning: if the Venetians did not cease trading war materials with the Arabs, then the Byzantine fleet would view the Venetian ships as enemies. Doge Pietro IV Candiano thus prohibited the sale of arms, iron, timber, and any other material that might be used to combat the Christians. Tafel and Thomas, *Urkunden*, vol. 1, pp. 25–30; Ortalli, "Il ducato e la 'civitas Rivoalti,'" p. 767; Nicol, *Byzantium and Venice*, p. 37.

14. Nicol, *Byzantium and Venice*, pp. 40–42.

15. Tafel and Thomas, *Urkunden*, vol. 1, pp. 36–9; Ortalli, "Il ducato e la 'civitas Rivoalti,'" p. 776.

16. "Secundum quod ab antiquo fuit consuetudo": Tafel and Thomas, *Urkunden*, vol. 1, p. 38; Pozza and Ravegnani, *I trattati con Bisanzio, 992–1198*, pp. 22–3.

17. Tafel and Thomas, *Urkunden*, vol. 1, p. 38; Pozza and Ravegnani, *I trattati con Bisanzio, 992–1198*, pp. 23–4.

18. Tafel and Thomas, *Urkunden*, vol. 1, p. 37; Pozza and Ravegnani, *I trattati con Bisanzio, 992–1198*, p. 23.

maritime power with a fleet of warships suited to the *basileus* to protect Adriatic trade, not only to the north, which was under the city's direct influence, but also to the south, as far as the Pugliese coast. In 1002, Venetian warships intervened at the sea-facing city of Bari, to protect it from Arab attack.[19] During this time, Venice began its commercial outreach to the ports of Istria and Dalmatia, from which it could gain direct access to the Balkans.

The Norman invasion of southern Italy triggered an acceleration in Venetian expansion to the East. From 1071, led by Robert Guiscard, the Normans had successively conquered Bari, Amalfi, and Salerno, and other crucial Mediterranean ports; in 1081, they headed straight for Durrës (in modern-day Albania), determined to conquer Constantinople.[20]

At the time, the Byzantine Empire was in serious financial and military difficulty. In Italy, Pope Nicholas II (d. 1061) had forged an alliance with the Normans, formally recognizing the duchies of Puglia, Calabria, and Sicily (1059).[21] The Altavilla conquest of Italy's Mezzogiorno forced Byzantium to abandon the peninsula. On the eastern side, in 965, the collapse of the Turkic khanate of the Khazars (spanning between the Caspian Sea and Rus' since the sixth century) fostered the migration of central Asian nomads to eastern Europe.[22] In 1071, the Seljuk Turks completed their conquest of the Anatolian peninsula after defeating the Byzantine army at Manzikert.[23]

The Byzantine Emperor Alexios I Komnenos, who ascended the throne in 1081 and ruled until 1118, asked Venice to come to his aid. Venice had strategic reasons for wanting to stop the Norman advance: many Venetian citizens lived in Durrës.[24] In exchange for Venetian military engagement, Alexios granted Venetian merchants permission to trade throughout the empire and its capital,

19. Nicol, *Byzantium and Venice*, pp. 44–45.

20. Kolia-Dermitzaki, "Byzantium and the Crusades," pp. 62–63; Nicol, *Byzantium and Venice*, pp. 56–57; McQueen, "Relations between the Normans and Byzantium."

21. Nicol, *Byzantium and Venice*, pp. 53–54.

22. On the history of the Khazars, see Golden et al., *The World of the Khazars*. In Italian see Pubblici, *Cumani*.

23. On the Battle of Manzikert and its consequences, see Haldon, *Warfare, State and Society*, in particular pp. 226–28; Bryer and Ursinus, *Manzikert to Lepanto*; Nicolle, *Manzikert 1071*; Cheynet, "Mantzikert: un désastre militaire?" For the Arab perspective, see the essay by Cahen, "La campagne de Mantzikert" (though dated, it is still worthwhile reading).

24. Oikonomidès, "The Medieval Via Egnatia"; Thiriet, *La Romanie vénitienne*, pp. 188–89; Balard, *La Romanie génoise*, p. 475; Curta, *Southeastern Europe in the Middle Ages*, pp. 98, 104, 156 and 273.

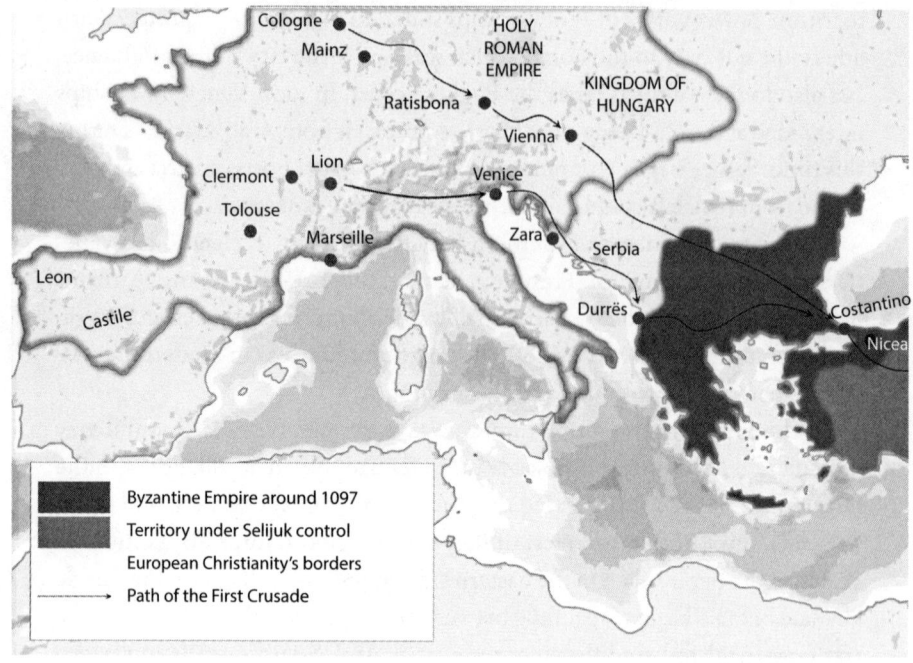

MAP 1. The First Crusade (1096–98)

with no fiscal obligations or other restrictions.[25] In practical terms, the measures issued by Alexios I allowed Venice to establish itself firmly within the empire's economic and financial system, a privilege that no other foreign power had ever had in Byzantium. The Venetians set up a city quarter in Constantinople that was ruled by their own governor, known as the *podestà* (bailiff), with houses, churches, an oven, *fondaci* and a mill.[26] Although the Venetian fleet was defeated by the Normans in 1084, the city did not lose its advantages gained in the Byzantine territory. Quite the opposite, in fact: the following years saw the Venetian presence in Byzantium grow even more thanks to those privileges. In particular, Venetians enjoyed tax exemptions more favorable even than those granted to Byzantine merchants. All these factors created a monopolistic commercial regime.

25. The chrysobull (golden bull) of Alexios I was in May 1082. Tafel and Thomas, *Urkunden*, vol. 1, pp. 43–52 and p. 54; Pozza and Ravegnani, *I trattati con Bisanzio, 992–1198*, pp. 36–45.
26. Pertusi, "Venezia e Bisanzio," p. 12.

The Crusades transformed this international political climate and Venice's position in Constantinople. In 1095, Pope Urban II at the Council of Clermont called for a crusade against Muslims, deeming them a threat to holy sites and all of Christendom. In a climate of renewed religious fervor, news of this crusade to conquer Jerusalem soon spread throughout Europe. After Lent in 1096, throngs of people from every corner of the continent—from bandits to mercenaries, and nobles in search of merit—all headed for Constantinople as a rallying site.

At first, Venice remained on the sidelines to avoid altering the political balance and to protect its interests in the Middle East. Nonetheless, after 1120 it intervened directly in support of Baldwin I of Boulogne, King of Jerusalem (ca. 1058–1118), motivated by the commercial advantages that control of the Holy Land (Acre and Jerusalem in particular) could assure it. In 1123, the Venetian fleet set out for the Palestinian coast and, after facing the Fatimid navy off the shore of Ashkelon, it headed for the kingdom of Jerusalem. The Christian allies then attacked the city of Tyre, which fell after a difficult three-month siege. Baldwin kept his promises to the Venetians; considerable commercial privileges were ratified in a treaty dated August 1126.[27]

This new Venetian militancy, though disguised as crusaders' zeal, was in fact a desire for revenge against Byzantium, following a rift in relations with the Byzantine Emperor John II, who in 1118 revoked the Venetian privileges that had been granted by his father Alexios I in 1082.[28] The Venetian government had initially responded to this with diplomacy, but later resorted to force, driving Byzantium—mired in economic crisis—to surrender.[29] In the peace treaty signed in 1126, John II restored all the privileges that had been granted to Venice in 1082.[30] Although he accepted Venice's conditions, he mitigated the defeat by granting the same privileges to Genoa and Pisa. The Serenissima thus lost its position of monopoly and hegemony. The following years were rife with new treaties, disputes, threats, and conflicts between all parties involved. Overall, however, Italian traders increased their presence in Constantinople.

27. Tafel and Thomas, *Urkunden*, vol. 1, pp. 90–94; Pozza and Ravegnani, *I trattati con Bisanzio, 992–1198*, pp. 51–56.

28. Nicol, *Byzantium and Venice*, pp. 77–78.

29. Angold, "The Byzantine Empire," in particular pp. 226–40; Gallina, *Potere e società a Bisanzio*, pp. 283–85.

30. Tafel and Thomas, *Urkunden*, vol. 1, pp. 95–97; Pozza and Ravegnani, *I trattati con Bisanzio, 992–1198*, p. 51; Nicol, *Byzantium and Venice*, pp. 80–81.

In the Venetian–Byzantine treaty of March 1148, it was established that the city quarter they lived in should be expanded.[31]

Despite competition from the Genoese and Pisans, by the mid-twelfth century, Venetian ships remained mostly unchallenged as they sailed on the East Mediterranean Sea from the Adriatic to the Aegean. Venice's ships regularly sailed into the ports of Halmyros, Durrës, Sparta, and Thebes, and from around 1150, Venetians began to settle in Cyprus, Crete, and Asia Minor: at Arta, Smyrna, and Adramyttion. In cities under Byzantine jurisdiction, the Venetian presence grew year-on-year, integrating with local society via mixed marriages and investments in local businesses.

From the mid-twelfth century, Venetian merchants expanded their reach as the Byzantine economic and political crisis worsened. During the reign of Manuel I (r. 1143–80), the empire went through an unprecedented period of hardship due to the frequent military interventions required to reinforce and pacify its borders, draining its resources. This expansion of Italian merchants' activities in the capital caused much discontent on one hand, and on the other rekindled the rivalry between the Venetians and the Genoese. In 1170, Venetians were blamed for a fire that broke out in the Genoese quarter of Galata, despite no actual proof of this. The emperor ordered Venice to pay for the damages, yet the Venetian authorities threatened military retaliation.[32] In the midst of this tension, on March 12, 1171, Manuel ordered all Venetians living in his empire—over ten thousand in the capital alone[33]—to be arrested and their goods confiscated. The reaction of the Venetian government was immediate. That September, the war fleet set sail from Venice for Constantinople, yet resolution by force of arms failed, and the Doge Michiel was assassinated upon his return to Venice.[34] The events of 1171 fueled Venetian rancor toward Constantinople. An opportunity for revenge was not long in the making.

By 1187, Jerusalem had fallen into the hands of the Ayyubid dynasty of Salah al-Din (or Saladin). After waging a long war against the Latin army, this Islamic commander of Kurdish origin (born in Tikrit in 1137) had also taken Acre, thus

---

31. Tafel and Thomas, *Urkunden*, vol. 1, pp. 109–12 and 113–24; Pozza and Ravegnani, *I trattati con Bisanzio, 992–1198*, pp. 70–75.

32. Nicol, *Byzantium and Venice*, p. 96; Borsari, "Il commercio veneziano nell'impero bizantino," p. 1003; Angold, "The Byzantine Empire," pp. 200–201. See also Tafel and Thomas, *Urkunden*, vol. 1, pp. 150–66.

33. Nicol, *Byzantium and Venice*, p. 98.

34. Nicol, *Byzantium and Venice*, pp. 100–101.

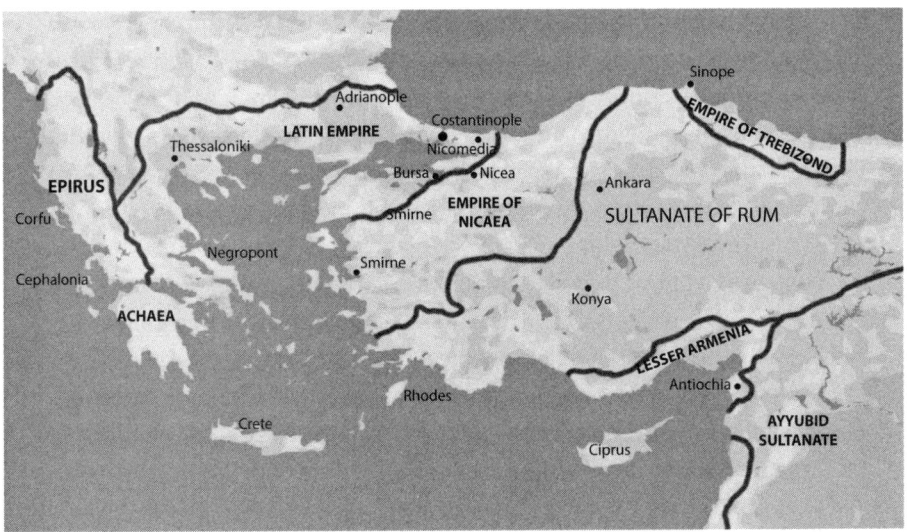

MAP 2. The eastern Mediterranean after the Fourth Crusade

creating a continuous territorial stretch of land from Egypt to Palestine. His control of the key, profitable trade routes in the Middle East was guaranteed. The damage that was done to the European Latins was such that Pope Gregory VIII riled up Christians to join the Third Crusade. Europe's most prestigious rulers, such as England's King Richard the Lionheart and the German Emperor Frederick I, joined the crusade, yet there was no definitive outcome, and the Christian forces failed in their attempt at the reconquest of Jerusalem.

Just thirty-seven years old, Innocent III (1161–1216) was elected pope on February 22, 1198. He was energetic and a proud advocate of papal supremacy over the empire, and the reconquest of Jerusalem became one of his main objectives. From his very first months in office, Innocent III pushed for another crusade against Ayyubid Egypt. This time, preparations were hastened by the tireless work of the itinerant preacher Fulk of Neuilly in France. The prospect of subjugating the Ayyubid infidels, regaining both Jerusalem and Acre, alongside the entire structural complex of the major Egyptian ports, convinced the French aristocracy to accept the pope's invitation. Thus, this crusade was organized by the highest French nobility: the counts of Champagne, of Flanders, and Geoffrey of Villehardouin. All agreed that they would not march directly to Palestine, but rather attack Egypt first. However, the only state that possessed the means to ensure the success of a maritime expedition of that magnitude was Venice.

The crusaders turned to the elderly Doge Enrico Dandolo, an expert on sea routes. Dandolo agreed to give the crusaders the manpower and resources necessary for a war fleet, along with 4,500 armed knights, and nearly 30,000 men. In exchange, he demanded a large payment (85,000 silver marks) and half of all the crusaders' successful territorial conquests. The French delegation accepted Venice's terms, and the pope gave his blessing. The expedition was due to leave Venice on June 29, 1202.

Neither Egypt nor Palestine was the crusade's final destination. Instead, it landed in Constantinople. The reasons for the fleet heading to this Christian—albeit schismatic—city have been subject to debate for many years. There is a lack of sources, and the ones available are not impartial enough for us to reach firm conclusions.[35] It is possible that Doge Dandolo wanted revenge on the Komnenos dynasty due to the events of 1171, to conquer the Byzantine capital and gain control of all the wealth—present and potential—that this would guarantee him. Yet another theory is that the decision to reroute to Constantinople was the result of a series of contingent but unplanned events.

Whatever Venice's initial intentions may have been, two key factors determined the outcome of the expedition: on the one hand, the crusaders' excessive optimism during the early organizational stages, and, on the other, strife within the Byzantine court. Though many took part in the crusade, the money collected was not enough to pay off the debt incurred with Venice, which could now claim rights to the crusade. Political turmoil raged in Byzantium as Emperor Isaac II, backed by Venice, was dethroned, and his own brother, Alexios, ordered that he be blinded. Isaac's son appealed to Latin Christendom for intervention to restore the legitimate emperor back to the throne. In exchange, he promised that once the emperor regained power, he would settle the debt with Venice and accept the supremacy of the Church of Rome. The crusaders debated whether to interfere in Byzantine affairs, but in the end Doge Dandolo prevailed with his strategy to embark for Constantinople.

The crusade's first assault on the city took place in the summer of 1203, achieving its goal. Isaac II, now an elderly man, was restored to power, while the usurper Alexios was forced to flee. However, the real break between western Christendom and the Byzantines occurred in April of the following year, when it became clear that the emperor was actually incapable of settling the debt with Venice. Meanwhile, another usurper had seized power after

---

35. Information on the Crusades comes from very few chronicles: that of Villehardouin, of Robert De Clari, and the monumental work of Niceta Coniate.

removing the emperor: Alexios V Doukas Mourtzouphlos, the son-in-law of the Alexios cast out by the crusaders. Mourtzouphlos had leveraged people's anger against the Latins to secure the throne, promising his subjects that he would not honor the old emperor's pledge to the crusaders. The crusaders, swayed by Dandolo's fury and charisma, decided to attack the city. Now the crusade had turned into the conquest of Constantinople and the destruction of the eastern Roman Empire.

The crusaders breached Constantinople's defenses in April 1204. Its citizens suffered violence at the hands of the crusaders for many days as their emperor was deposed, and their empire carved up. A document was drawn up, the *Partitio Romaniae,* to sanction the new order imposed on Byzantium. Its policies mirror Enrico Dandolo's politics, his first objective being to safeguard Venetian interests. After the capture of Constantinople, four new political actors were born: the East Latin Empire, the empire of Nicaea, the despotate of Epirus, and the empire of Trebizond. All borders to the north and south of the Danube were redrawn. Enrico Dandolo could now boast the title *dux ac dominus quartae partis ac dimidie imperii romani.*[36]

The Sack of Constantinople not only established a new order in which the Byzantine Empire effectively disappeared as a political entity, it also weakened the defensive capacities of the entire Christian East. The victorious West prided itself that it had reunified Christendom and had established a great Latin state at the gates of Asia. Yet, in reality, it was an act of pillaging on a vast scale. Constantinople's immense wealth—its art, sacred relics, and treasures accumulated over centuries—were plundered and dispersed throughout Europe. Venice raked in the bulk of it.

For Venice, the fall of Constantinople was an extraordinary source of material wealth, with the richest city district being occupied by Venetian merchants. The doge was not so much interested in the hinterland as he was in the islands of the Aegean Sea, which, unlike the crusaders, he was very familiar with. He took control of the most strategic isles: Chios, Modon, Crete, and Negropont. The latter became the crown jewel of the Venetian trading system in the Mediterranean, placed in a prime location between Crete and Constantinople. This allowed Venice to create a solid network of islands and footholds on *terra firma* that joined the lagoon city with Constantinople. It is ironic that the conquest of Constantinople reinforced the Byzantine nature of Venetian culture.[37]

36. Pertusi, "Venezia e Bisanzio," p. 20.
37. Pertusi, "Venezia e Bisanzio," p. 21.

## From the Fourth Crusade to the Landing on the Black Sea

Amidst this new political order, new problems rose to the surface. In the years following the conquest of Constantinople, a schism formed between the Republic of Venice and its citizens living in the capital of the former empire. Venetian authorities in the Byzantine capital chose their own representative without consulting the Republic. Marino Zeno was elected as *podestà* and bestowed broad powers over the wealth acquired after the crusade.[38] He took office as early as June 1205,[39] and when the news reached Venice a month later, city authorities feared an independence movement in Romània—that is, the Byzantine Empire and its territory. The new doge, Pietro Ziani, elected on August 5, 1205, quickly adopted a more cautious policy, opting to parley with the mayor of Constantinople, though without shying away from the pre-eminent position of his role, assuming the title of *imperii Romaniae dominator*. From 1207 onward, all Venetian officials in Constantinople—including the *podestà*—were forced to swear loyalty to the doge.[40]

Although the Fourth Crusade seemed to give Venice undisputed rule over the entry routes to eastern markets, opening unexpected horizons for its expansion, it took years to achieve balance in these new circumstances. In this time, the Republic struggled in the face of new responsibilities as well as both internal and external challenges. In part, this explains the long period of stagnation in its expansion beyond the Bosphorus. The city also built a fruitful collaborative relationship with Egypt, where most products from the East were traded; those arriving from the Persian Gulf were imported over land to Damietta and Alexandria, where most Venetian resources in the Mediterranean were concentrated.[41]

At the start of the century, Venetian foreign policy did not prioritize entry of and control over the Black Sea and other major Asian routes. This apparent lack of perspective is actually simple to understand if we consider the fact that the Black Sea at this time was not a territory that guaranteed commercial

---

38. Nicol, *Byzantium and Venice*, pp. 152–53.

39. Tafel and Thomas, *Urkunden*, vol. 1, pp. 558–61; Nicol, *Byzantium and Venice*, p. 153.

40. Nicol, *Byzantium and Venice*, p. 154.

41. In 1208, Venetian diplomacy succeeded in expanding the colony of Alexandria, which had been active since at least the 1160s. Relations between Venice and the Mamluks continued in the thirteenth century with highs and lows, until 1238, when the two states signed an agreement that Venice could keep its commercial privileges and have its own consul in the city. Rösch, "Il gran guadagno," pp. 238–39.

success. Nor could the economic conditions or the political situation of the Pontic hinterland justify the interest of Venetian traders. In fact, it would be the Mongolian conquest (discussed in the next chapter) which would spark new energies to enliven not only the activities of merchants from Genoa, Venice, Pisa, and elsewhere, but above all the investments of Italian republics in the creation and defense of a stable and long-lasting presence in Asia, guaranteed and encouraged by Mongol authorities.

Beyond the dominant position Venice had achieved in the Levant, other factors must be considered alongside the Fourth Crusade that presented new priorities and challenges for the city. First among these is the rivalry between Venice and Genoa, which became the main obstacle to Venetian hegemony. Second, new tensions developed with the Western Empire in a struggle for political dominion over the colonies of the former Byzantine Empire. Lastly, one must also consider Venice's position in relation to the kingdoms that had been formed by the division of the Byzantine Empire. Due to their geographical position and political opportunity, these would later play a major role in Venice's trade expansion on the Black Sea.

## Origins of the Rivalry with Genoa

In the first half of the thirteenth century, both Venice and Genoa aimed to strengthen their presence in territories that could supply them grain and other staple goods. Access to agricultural production in their hinterland was constantly under threat of wars, exclusions, and blockades. To this end, Venice colonized the islands in the Aegean to institute an economic monopoly and a political hegemony. However, this was at odds with Genoese interests.

Unlike Venice, the Ligurian city had secured bases in the eastern Mediterranean since the First Crusade, which it had actively fought in with its own military fleet. Throughout the twelfth century, Genoa had strategically established itself in all the most important cities in Palestine. Saladin's Muslim reconquest dealt a major blow to the Ligurian Mediterranean system. Thus, at the start of the thirteenth century, the interests of the two maritime republics collided. Their alternating conflicts and short-lived ceasefires would last until the end of the fourteenth century.

The Venetian–Genoese rivalry in the Aegean was also exacerbated by the importance of intermediate naval bases for long-range navigation. In the thirteenth century, galleys had to navigate by day, avoiding sailing at night whenever possible. In the wake of the crusade, authorities of the Serenissima focused on defending commercial routes at threat by pirates,[42] as well as defending colonies—especially Corfù—which were exposed to attack by the Genoese.[43] Venice's main strategic objective was to strengthen the commercial system it had acquired in the crusade, based on its control over the Aegean islands, Crete, and the Peloponnese.[44] Moreover, the Venetian Republic was bent on consolidating its predominance in the empire's capital, using it as a hub of commercial flow between East and West.[45]

Aside from the nascent conflict with Genoa, Venetian domination in Romània was put to the test by internal revolts and external threats.[46] In 1214, a popular uprising expelled the Venetians from Corfù, the gateway to the Adriatic Sea. The colony of Crete, a key city for grain supplies, often rebelled against the high taxes levied.[47] It eventually surrendered to Venice in 1218 but only after a fierce fight.[48] In the Peloponnese, the islands of Coron and Modon were left to Venice, while the remainder of the territory fell into the hands of Geoffrey of Villehardouin (d. ca. 1228), a French nobleman originally from Champagne, who founded the principality of Morea in the Peloponnese.[49]

42. Angold, *The Fourth Crusade*, p. 152; Penna, "Piracy and Reprisal."

43. Corfù was of particular concern to Venice. The island was a crucial point in the maritime line connecting the city to Constantinople. In July 1207, Doge Pietro Ziani hoped to guarantee its protection by ceding the *castrum* (fortress) "cum tota insula et perinenciis" to a group of noblemen, including Pietro Michiel, Stefano Foscarini, Gilberto Quirini, and Ottaviano Firmo. These noblemen now had to pay the defense expenses out of their own pockets. Tafel and Thomas, *Urkunden*, vol. 2, pp. 54–59; Angold, *The Fourth Crusade*, p. 153.

44. Crete was not just the biggest island in the Aegean, it was also the epicenter of naval routes connecting Romania to Egypt, Syria, and Palestine. Nicol, *Byzantium and Venice*, p. 171; Jacoby, *The Encounter of Two Societies*, pp. 873–906.

45. Borsari, *Il dominio veneziano a Creta*, pp. 21–25; Borsari, *Studi sulle colonie veneziane nel XIII secolo*, p. 21; Jacoby, *The Encounter of Two Societies*, pp. 873–906; Necipoğlu, "The Byzantine Economy and the Sea"; Karpov, "The Black Sea Region Before and After the Fourth Crusade," pp. 287–88.

46. On the history of the Despotate, Nicol's seminal work *The Despotate of Epiros* remains unrivaled. See also Magdalino, "Between Romaniae," pp. 87–110; Osswald, "The Ethnic Composition of Medieval Epirus."

47. Nicol, *Byzantium and Venice*, p. 172; Angold, *The Fourth Crusade*, pp. 155–56; Gallina, *Una società coloniale del Trecento*.

48. Thiriet, "Sui dissidi sorti tra il Comune di Venezia e i suoi feudatari di Creta."

49. Villehardouin was nephew to Geoffroy (a son of one of Geoffroy's brothers) who authored the *Conquête de Constantinople*. On the principality of Morea, see Shawcross, *The Chronicle of Morea*; Ilieva, *Frankish Morea*; Chrissis, *Crusading in Frankish Greece*; Giarenis, "Nicaea and the West," pp. 206–7.

The loss of Morea, with its rich oil and silk markets, was a serious blow to Venice, which continued making every effort—economic and military—to protect its colonial territories in the Aegean.[50]

Having started at a disadvantage in Constantinople, Genoa implemented a policy of progressive advancement in the eastern Mediterranean, leading to clashes with Venice as part of an undeclared war; the Genoese mainly fought by way of piracy.[51] The first clash arose over control of the island of Crete. In the wake of the crusade, the island had been surrendered to Venice by Bonifacio di Monferrato, who had occupied it during the siege of Constantinople. Venice stalled and the Count of Malta, Enrico Pescatore, supported by Genoa, took possession of Crete in 1206. There were divided reactions from the local aristocracy, with some supporting Venice and others its rivals. The Venetian fleet reconquered Crete in 1211, but it took another two years for the Venetian occupation to stabilize. However, the Cretan population remained hostile to foreign domination and continued to rebel in the decades to come.[52]

In the early thirteenth century, the Venetian–Genoese competition was only getting started. Genoa's expansion was persistent and effective; from the middle of the century, the city asserted itself as the dominant commercial player in Syrian and Palestinian markets.[53] To the East, the Genoese and the Venetians vied for the most profitable markets which were under the control of the Latin kingdom of Jerusalem. Both of them had a quarter in the city of Acre, and their rivalry over these markets—crucial for access to goods coming from Asia—quickly became violent. Relations rapidly deteriorated, and new political configurations and alliances were formed. To gain the advantage, Venice brokered an alliance with Pisa that was openly anti-Genoese (*societatem et compagnam contra Januenses*), which lasted a decade and was then renewed. The treaty, signed in Modena (Ponte Saliceto) in July 1257, quashed the pact of friendship originally forged between the Tuscan city and Genoa, which up to that point had regulated relations between the two parties in Syria.[54] This drastic shift in alliances caused the Venetian–Genoese conflict to explode in

50. Laiou and Morrison, *The Byzantine Economy*, pp. 185, 187, and 205.

51. See the picture traced by Balard, "La lotta contro Genova."

52. Borsari, *Il dominio veneziano a Creta*, pp. 21–22 and 27–36; Ravegnani, "La Romània veneziana," pp. 192–96.

53. Favreau-Lilie [*sic*], "The Fall of Acre"; Origone, "Genoa and Byzantium," pp. 42–46; Balard, "Colonisation and Population Movements," pp. 26–27.

54. Manfroni, "Relazioni di Genova con Venezia," p. 363.

June 1258. The battle in the waters across from Acre was dubbed the War of Saint Sabas by chroniclers,[55] named after the city's monastery. It was the first real clash in a conflict that would last for the next two centuries, alternating between violence and occasional peace treaties and truces.

## Between East and West: Venice and the Empire before the Treaty of Nymphaeum

For centuries, Venice had been the nerve center of western Europe for the trade of eastern goods.[56] This was not only due to its economic–commercial structure and to Constantinople's de facto monopoly, but also by virtue of the continuity and safety of the transit routes in its hinterland, guaranteed by the Germanic Empire. However, the political stability ensured by the Hohenstaufen dynasty descended into a crisis from the mid-thirteenth century, favoring the rise of Italian communes. Venice now had to negotiate with new players, including the cities of Padua,[57] Verona, and Milan, which controlled internal trade routes and those along mountain passes—especially strategic for transporting metals and timber. To secure an outlet at the heart of the continent—crucial for the continued success of the Venetian trade system, which was a combination of long-range traffic and local markets—the city was forced to divert military resources from the political–commercial system of the East.

The conflict between the papacy and the Germanic Empire exacerbated critical issues on the peninsula, making Venice's position more difficult. Although it was not directly involved, it still had to adjust its foreign policy based on the warring Guelph and Ghibelline parties. The Ghibellines supported imperial power and enjoyed dominance over Italian cities thanks to the political machinations of Emperor Frederick II. His death in 1250 dealt a blow to Italian Ghibellinism, further weakened by the defeat of his son Manfred in the Battle of Benevento (1266) by Charles I of Anjou, a supporter of the papacy.[58]

---

55. Musarra, *La guerra di San Saba*; Rösch, "Il gran guadagno," p. 246; Balard, "Colonisation and Population Movements," p. 26.

56. Thiriet, *La Romanie vénitienne*, pp. 141–42.

57. With which Venice had entered the war as early as 1234. Crouzet-Pavan, *Venezia trionfante*, p. 129.

58. On the Battle of Benevento, see Grillo, *L'aquila e il gigli*.

From 1255, the Republic faced another emergency, this time in Negropont, where the Prince of Morea William of Villehardouin (d. 1278) rebelled against the Serenissima's rule, seeking alliances among its rivals.[59] Genoa intervened on Villehardouin's behalf. Although Venice eventually regained control of the island, the immense military effort laid bare the challenges of maintaining the hegemony that Venice had built in 1204.[60] The fault lay with the weaknesses of the eastern Latin Empire, which had never developed into a self-sufficient center of organized power. By 1260, its extent had been reduced to just its capital. The fallout of the crisis favored the new peripheral centers of power that had emerged from the division of the Byzantine Empire.

The ancient city of Trebizond had taken on the designation of "empire" in the aftermath of the Fourth Crusade, having crowned Alexios Komnenos, nephew of the previous Emperor Andronicus (dethroned in 1185 following a palace revolt in Constantinople). In 1204, the crusaders seized the Byzantine capital and Alexios Komnenos found refuge under the protection of the kingdom of Georgia, ruled by Queen Tamara. There, he took the title of *imperatore e autocrate dei Romani* (emperor and autocrat of the Romans). The Komnenos brothers planned to regain Constantinople by controlling the Anatolian peninsula. However, under the leadership of his brother David, their army suffered repeated defeats from three hostile forces: the crusaders, the fledgling empire of Nicaea of Theodore I Laskaris, and the sultanate of Iconium. David perished in battle in Sinope in 1214 and Alexios was forced to focus all his resources on maintaining Trebizond. For sheer survival, he accepted a bond of servitude under the Seljuk Sultanate of Iconium.

The sultanate conquered key cities along the northern Anatolian coast; one of these was Sinope, which it wrested from the control of Trebizond. Nonetheless, formal recognition of the acquired borders kept the eastern portion of the south Black Sea out of the clashes. The Anatolian Seljuks—though hostile—offered a barrier capable of protecting the small empire of Trebizond. The state prospered in relative safety, growing in importance as a political and commercial hub for cities in the Caucasus and Persia. This was all the more vital since the first Mongol incursion of 1220 had caused irreparable damage to the kingdom of Georgia, which had previously been Trebizond's main political point of reference. Without it, the small state was given a growing margin for maneuver. It is precisely this Mongol conquest (analyzed in the next chapter) that

59. Mergiali-Sahas, "In the Face of a Historical Puzzle," pp. 280–81.
60. Tafel and Thomas, *Urkunden*, vol. 3, pp. 1–9.

was another crucial factor for the growth of the Anatolian city. The Trape-zuntine emperors supported the new regime and agreed to become vassals as long as it gave them an advantage and increased their influence in the region. The scheme worked: in 1254, the Trebizond army retook the city of Sinope, a vital strategic trading port in the Black Sea.

The empire of Nicaea was formed as a direct consequence of the fall of Con-stantinople, founded in the Byzantine provinces of northwest Asia Minor by Constantine IX Lascaris, who had fled the capital. The emperors of Nicaea never gave up on the prospect of reconquering the capital and restoring the empire. Due to the geographical proximity, the emperors instantly took up arms against the Latin enemy. The conflict grew more intense from the 1220s, when John III Vatatzes (1192–1254; son-in-law of Emperor Theodore) ascended the Nicaean throne. Venice was among the main adversaries of the Nicaean Empire and their conflict was focused on the Aegean. John Vatatzes's plan to reconquer Constantinople included control of the Aegean's key islands, first among them Crete. In 1233, Vatatzes's fleet attacked the island to support an internal rebel-lion. It was not until 1236 that Venice succeeded in quelling the island's rebel-lion, after a costly conflict both in material resources and loss of lives.

The previous year, in 1235, the empire of Nicaea, backed by the Bulgarians of Ivan II Asen (d. 1241; the conqueror of Thrace to the north), had steered its own military fleet to Constantinople.[61] Venetian forces fended off the siege, aided by a magnificent fleet under order of Latin Emperor of Constantinople John of Brienne (d. 1237). The war lasted until 1241, when the Venetian ships, commanded by John Michiel, defeated the Nicaean fleet off the coast of Tzurullon (modern-day Çorlu), on the Sea of Marmara.[62] Venice's victory quelled tensions with the Nicaean Empire for two reasons: military operations had been particularly costly for both sides, and Vatatzes was under threat by the Bulgarians to the north and by the despot of Epirus to the northwest.[63]

Aware of the troubles in the Nicaean Empire, Venice deployed its diplo-matic channels to pacify relations with both Vatatzes and Genoa. Venice and Genoa agreed to a truce in 1251 that guaranteed a ten-year respite from conflict,

---

61. Giarenis, "Nicaea and the West," p. 212.

62. Akropolites, *The History*, pp. 202–3; Martin da Canal, "La Chronique des Véniciens," I, pp. 511–12. Nicol, *Byzantium and Venice*, p. 171.

63. Theodore, king of Epirus, had for years pursued a policy of expansion in the Balkans. After defeating the Latin Empire in 1217, he gained ground in both Thessaly and Macedonia. Nicol, *Byzantium and Venice*, p. 166.

giving Venice the chance to focus on strengthening its Levantine territories. In the 1250s, the city reinforced its control over its ongoing markets in the Aegean and consolidated relations with new ones. Of these, particular focus was given to the Peloponnese of Villehardouin, which was rich in grains, as well as being the hub of the silk trade.

As the empire of Trebizond asserted its power, the Seljuk Sultanate of Rum, whose capital was Konya (Iconium), suffered an equal territorial retreat due to the growing political stability of the empire of Nicaea, and the weakening of the Latin Empire of Constantinople. The decades-long existence of this crusader state was largely due to its protection by the Venetian military fleet. Vatatzes's successor, the emperor of Nicaea Michael VIII Palaiologos, pursued a policy of expansion, following in the footsteps of his father. He planned to take back Constantinople, seek revenge for the Fourth Crusade, and re-unite the empire—yet, he lacked the military strength to bring his plans to fruition. What he needed was a military power capable of taking on the Venetian navy. Genoa was the ideal candidate. All the conditions for a successful negotiation were at his disposal. On the one hand was the Byzantine hostility toward Venice that, after the events of 1204, was irremediable. On the other, the War of Saint Sabas and the gradual weakening of Latin dominions in the Holy Land had impacted Genoa, which desperately needed a permanent foothold in Romània. To convince the Genoese leaders, the emperor offered the doge of the Ligurian republic those same privileges that in previous centuries had guaranteed Venice its monopoly over trade in Byzantium.

The treaty was signed in March 1261 in the city of Nymphaion (now Nif in Turkey).[64] Genoa promised to provide whatever military aid was necessary to Michael VIII to expunge "the enemies of the empire," as well as a stable naval garrison to defend the capital. It was understood that the enemies in question were primarily the Venetians. The emperor knew that the only way to restore the prestige of the Byzantine Empire and regain control of the region was for the Venetians to be expelled from the Aegean. As well as trade-related privileges, Genoa was granted the pledge that, if Michael reconquered the capital, all of Genoa's rivals would be removed from imperial territory. Constantinople did not fall until July 1261, three months after the Treaty of Nymphaeum. Michael VIII took the city on his own strength, without the aid of the Genoese.

---

64. There is an endless bibliography concerning the Treaty of Nymphaeum. For our purposes, it will suffice to refer to the study by Balard, *1261: Genova nel mondo*.

All the same, the one-sided offer made to his new allies was signed and sealed. The emperor had to honor his commitment.

## Venice and the Black Sea before 1260

At the dawn of the thirteenth century, the Black Sea was still not fully integrated in the Mediterranean trade system, despite having been a crossroads traveled by merchants since antiquity.[65] In the first half of the thirteenth century, there were cheaper alternatives to do trade with the territories around the Black Sea. These were mainly via the Anatolian and Persian routes. Thus, even after 1204, the region of Pontus was not of strategic interest to the Venetians. Not only were the routes unknown, Byzantine emperors had long forbidden entry to the Black Sea, which meant that sailing beyond Constantinople remained treacherous.[66]

There is some controversy around the state and extent of the Venetian presence on the Black Sea before the Fourth Crusade. While there is an abundance of sources on merchants active on the Anatolian coast and in Crimea, the reports are sporadic, suggesting individual initiatives rather than an official policy of the Venetian state. Some Venetians are mentioned in the late twelfth-century Old Slavic epic *Slovo o polku Igoreve* (The Tale of Igor's Campaign), but they may have reached the Rus' territory by land, crossing the Carpathian Mountains.[67] A source from 1206 names the Venetian trader Zaccaria Stagnario, who formed a company with Pietro di Ferraguto of Ancona to trade in present-day Sudak, on the eastern coast of Crimea. Six years later, Giovanni Bianco, another Venetian merchant, set sail on a Provençal ship bound for Samsun, on the southern coast of the Black Sea, not far from Trebizond.[68] At

65. Karpov, "Il Mar Nero come carrefour di cultura," pp. 39–52.

66. Jacoby, "The Venetian Presence in the Latin Empire of Constantinople"; Karpov, "The Black Sea Region," p. 287.

67. *Slovo* describes the battle on the River Kajaly in 1185 between the troops of Igor Svjatoslavič, prince of Novgorod-Sivers'kij (in the principality of Černigov) and the Cumans. The text is seen as controversial, even though recent studies have dispelled any doubts as to the text's authenticity. See the edition listed in the bibliography compiled by Edgardo T. Saronne (*Il cantare di Igor'*, p. 83): "Qui [a Kiev] tedeschi e veneziani qui greci e moravi cantano gloria a Svjatoslav biasimano il principe Igor." (Here [in Kiev] Germans and Venetians, Greeks and Moravi sing the glory of Svjatoslav, and criticize Prince Igor.)

68. Balard, "L'Occident, Byzance et la mer Noire vers 1200," p. 47; *Documenti del commercio veneziano*, nos. 478, 479, 541 and 662, also cited in Cahen, *Pre-Ottoman Turkey*, p. 166.

the time, Samsun was a lively and well-organized market, yet it was peripheral to the main transit routes that led from either the Persian Gulf or the Red Sea to Constantinople.[69]

Sudak was first mentioned in the anonymous seventh-century *Cosmographia* written in Ravenna.[70] For centuries, this city had been subject to the Byzantine Empire, a part of the administrative district (*tema*) of Kherson, however weak the control of the Byzantine state over Pontus may have been.[71] In the late eleventh century, the Cumans (nomads of Turkic origin[72]) attacked Crimea and conquered the city.[73] When the crusaders conquered Constantinople, Kherson came under the rule of the Trebizond Empire, yet Sudak remained under the control of the Cumans until the Mongol attack of 1238–39. Throughout these years, the city was the main hub for traffic between Mediterranean Europe and the markets of Rus', the Baltic, Seljuk Asia Minor, and the Pontic steppe.

The Franciscan missionary William of Rubruck, sent by the pope to the khan of the Mongols in 1253, described Sudak as the terminal at which "all merchants coming from Turkey who intend to travel to the lands of the north arrive," just as "all those who make the reverse crossing, from Russia and the north toward Turkey, arrive there."[74] William of Rubruck goes on to note that in Sudak "those coming from the north bring squirrel furs and other precious hides; those who come from the south bring cotton cloths, silk textiles, and aromatic spices."[75] Sources also tell us that the Italian merchants based in

69. Karpov, *L'impero di Trebisonda*, pp. 74–76.

70. *Ravennatis anonymi cosmographia*, p. 176.

71. Pritsak, "Sougdaia."

72. In recent years, studies on the origins of the Cumans have multiplied. The latest historiography attributes the ethnonym to the most westerly group of the Turkic-speaking Asian population of the Qipchaq. For a complete picture, see Golden, *An Introduction to the History of the Turkic Peoples*; Pubblici, *Cumani*; and Vásáry, *Cumans and Tatars*.

73. Opinions differ regarding the conquest of the cities by the nomads (the Cumans in particular). Most likely it was a way of controlling (a sort of extortion) the main routes of transit that connected a specific city to the most profitable commercial arteries. For a discussion of this controversy, see Golev, "The Cuman-Qïpchaqs and Crimea." In Italian, see the previously mentioned Pubblici, *Cumani*.

74. Rubruk, *Viaggio in Mongolia*, pp. 12–13. Rubruck traveled to these lands in 1253. At the time, Sudak was most likely the last Crimean settlement not under the direct control of the Mongols, as later the Franciscan stated that he had met "the Tatars" only after leaving the city (pp. 18–19). A few years earlier, another Franciscan, Giovanni di Pian del Carpine, had been invited by the pope to explore the people of the Tatars.

75. Rubruk, *Viaggio in Mongolia*, p. 9.

Constantinople spent time in other cities in Crimea and Rus'. The missionary Giovanni di Pian del Carpine cites three merchants—a Genoese, a Venetian, and a Pisan—whom he met in Kiev.[76] And in 1260, the Polo brothers set out from Constantinople to travel toward the Caspian Sea and central Asia (see chapter 8).

In the second half of the thirteenth century, Crimea was considered a nexus where goods arrived from the north, from central Asia via Persia, and lastly from the West, the latter transported by Italian merchants based in Constantinople. However, in the early 1260s, these were still simple individual initiatives carried out by merchants who had settled in Constantinople. It was yet to be the picture of expansion and colonization evident in Venetian trade in the Aegean. Of course, things were about to change—and so would the political order of all the eastern Mediterranean.

76. The Franciscan wrote that among them were Michele, a Genoese, and Manuele, a Venetian. He noted that these men, together with Giacomo of Acre and Niccolò of Pisa, were the most important ones (*isti sunt maiores*). However, he added that there were many others who were *minores*. Pian del Carpine, *Storia dei Mongoli*, p. 332.

# 2

# The Mongols and Europe

## The Birth of the Mongol Empire

Around 1167, a child was born on the Mongol steppe. "He was born clutching in his right hand a clot of blood the size of a knucklebone," while his eyes shone with intense fire. His name was Temüjin, and his appearance already announced an extraordinary destiny. Thus begins *The Secret History of the Mongols*, written around the mid-thirteenth century. It describes the fateful birth of the man who would be known around the world and throughout the centuries as Chinggis (Genghis) Khan.[1]

Son of a local aristocrat named Yesügei, Temüjin was raised in a time marred by growing rivalry between clans and the various Mongol nations. Little is known of this era, apart from the aforementioned and far-from-impartial *Secret History*. The chronicle recounts how Temüjin and his family suffered much hardship after enemy Tatars murdered his father. Temüjin was imprisoned, almost perishing at many points. It was only thanks to his political acumen and courage that he managed to claw his way through the intricate tangle of alliances, vendettas, and infighting that characterized Mongol politics. In 1206, after three decades of war, Temüjin unified the Mongols into a single nation. He was elected khan (sovereign), adopting the title Chinggis Khan.[2]

There is no doubt that Chinggis Khan's rise to power was epic, yet the reasons and means for his conquest were aided by structural changes in Mongol society over the course of at least three generations. The Mongols went from being nomadic shepherds to a world power, and despite their many successes

1. *The Secret History of the Mongols*, vol. 1, p. 13. For the date *The Secret History* was written, see Atwood, "The Date of the 'Secret History of the Mongols.'"
2. Allsen, "The Rise of the Mongolian Empire," p. 343.

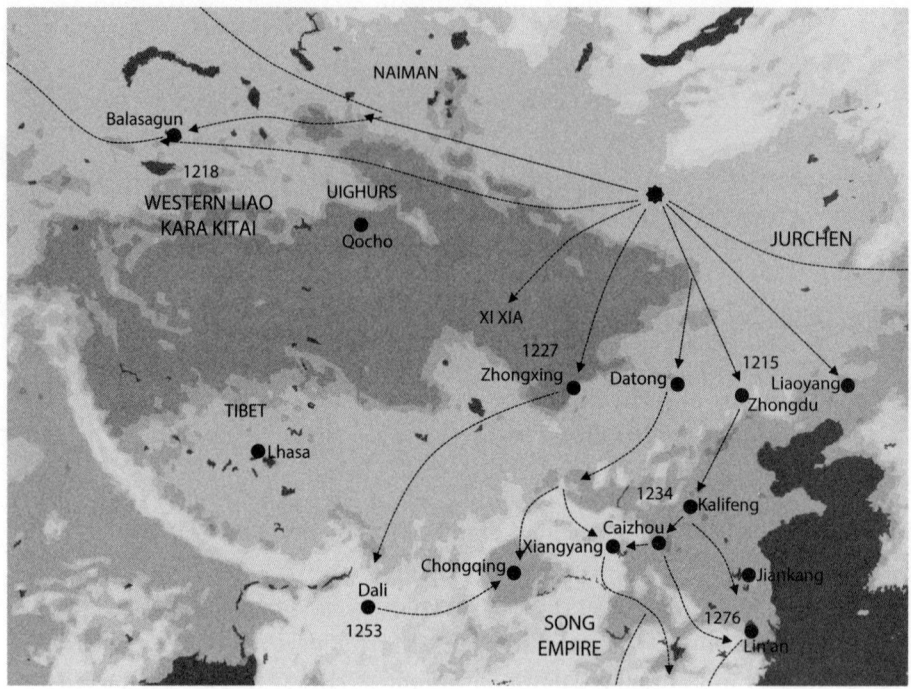

MAP 3. The Mongol invasion of China

along the way, their political and military expansion took over half a century. Moments of crisis and setbacks were overcome only with great difficulty, precipitating radical changes in leadership.

The Mongol conquest first set its sights on bordering states, such as the Chinese Jin dynasty (1115–1236) of Jurchen origin, and that of the Tanguts of Western Xia (1038–1227).[3] Chinggis Khan's main aim in attacking these powerful and populous states was sheer economic necessity. To consolidate the process of political centralization realized by Temüjin and maintain the nation's hegemony, greater tax revenues were needed by way of forced levy of annual payments from the wealthiest neighbors.[4] Hence, the desire for

3. The Jurchen constituted a dynasty of conquest that included all of north China, in addition to Manchuria and Mongolia. For some time, the Tangut people ruled present-day northwest China. On the three dynasties, see Twitchett and Tietze, "The Liao"; Dunnel, "The Hsi Hsia"; and Franke, "The Chin Dynasty."

4. On the relationship between the construction of the empire and taxation, see Di Cosmo, "State Formation and Periodization."

territorial expansion was less urgent. After decades of division and conflict, the unification of the Mongols had created a complex governmental structure with a weak economy. The system was unable to produce fixed income sufficient to maintain an expensive court, a standing army, as well as religious and legal entities. The Mongols required external resources that could only be obtained from the rich agricultural societies of northern China. Like other "imperial" nomads before them,[5] the Mongols wielded a large and disciplined army, led by experienced soldiers. Adjoining states were forced to pay contributions and send military support, thus guaranteeing the stability of the new centralized government.

The Mongol army was a formidable weapon against nearby sedentary states that lacked the means of effective resistance. Even fortified cities could not defend surrounding territory or rural areas. To prevent the Mongols from sacking villages and cultivated land, cities chose to compromise by paying the dues demanded. Although this was essentially giving in to blackmail, it was the only way for these beleaguered states to uphold political order and guarantee peace. The Western Xia were defeated in 1211 and forced to pay an annual duty to the new Mongol state.[6] Next, Chinggis Khan moved against the Great Jin dynasty, devastating and occupying north China. After the capital Yanjing (present-day Beijing) was sacked, the Jin emperor found shelter in the populous and wealthy city of Kaifeng.[7]

Until 1215, the Mongols acted no differently from other nomads who had historically created states and military confederations that had pillaged the Chinese frontiers, imposed taxes, and conquered land. The Jin dynasty was of Jurchen and therefore northern rather than Chinese origin. The Jurchen had conquered northern China after a war with the Kitan, the founders of the Liao dynasty. They were also of "barbarian" origin and were closer culturally to the Mongols than to the Chinese of the Song dynasty, which ruled central-south China.[8] Moreover, during the wars of unification, Mongol military assaults on their enemies led Chinggis Khan to expand west toward Mongolia, to

---

5. This refers to nomadic empires created by Xiongnu (Asian Huns), Turks, Uyghurs, and other nomadic populations of the steppe that emerged in Mongolia and the surrounding areas between the third century BC and the twelfth century.

6. Desmond, "The Mongol Wars with Hsi Hsia."

7. Military aspects of Chinggis Khan's campaigns are described in detail in Desmond, *The Rise of Chingis Khan*.

8. Twitchett and Tietze, "The Liao."

present-day Xinjiang (northwest of today's China) and to eastern Kazakhstan. While the Uyghur realms of the oasis of eastern Turkestan surrendered peacefully to the Mongol invaders, the kingdom of the Kara Kitai fought back,[9] as it was then ruled by Kuchlug of the Mongol Naiman tribe, an age-old enemy of Chinggis Khan.[10] In 1218, the Mongols killed Kuchlug, thus eliminating the last Mongol leader to have resisted Chinggis Khan. Up to this point, the new regime seemed destined to follow in the footsteps of non-Chinese dynasties, such as the Jin, Liao, and Western Xia (Xi Xia).

However, there was one event that radically changed the course of Mongol history, paving the way for the invasion of western Asia: in 1218, Mongol emissaries were massacred by an officer of Khwarazm (or Chorasmia). This vast and wealthy empire encompassed the regions of present-day southern Kazakhstan, Uzbekistan, Turkmenistan, Persia, and western Afghanistan, all ruled by Shah Ala ad-Din Muhammad II, who had ascended the throne in 1200.

Relations between China and central Asia had flourished since the sixth century, thanks to international trade along the "Silk Road." This network of routes linked the most important cities and markets from China to the Middle East, via central and west Asia, and was not only traveled by merchants, but also missionaries, political figures, and ambassadors. International traffic was extremely fruitful for those who could establish political control—and thus a taxation system—over the many goods in transit. From as early as the sixth and seventh centuries, Turkic khans wielded control over this system, in particular over the silk trade and diplomatic relations with the Byzantine Empire.[11] During the Chinese Tang dynasty (618–907), central Asian trade companies of Sogdian origin had created an extensive commercial network that exploited bases in China and the support of another nomadic empire: the Uyghurs (744–840).[12] Most goods flowed through the oases of the Tarim Basin and the Uyghur cities. Thus, after Chinggis Khan conquered these territories, it was a natural step to open to trade with the Khwarazmian Empire

9. On the empire of the Kara Kitai (or Qara Khitai), see Biran, *The Empire of the Qara Khitai.*

10. The Naiman occupied the western part of Mongolia and were among the most powerful political formations at the time of Chinggis Khan's ascent. See Atwood, *Encyclopedia,* pp. 397–98.

11. The Turks were an ancient nomadic people of Mongolia, not to be mistaken for the Anatolian Turks who came later. See Stark, "Türk Khaganate."

12. On the relationship between the Uyghur Empire and the Tang dynasty, see Mackerras, *The Uighur Empire.*

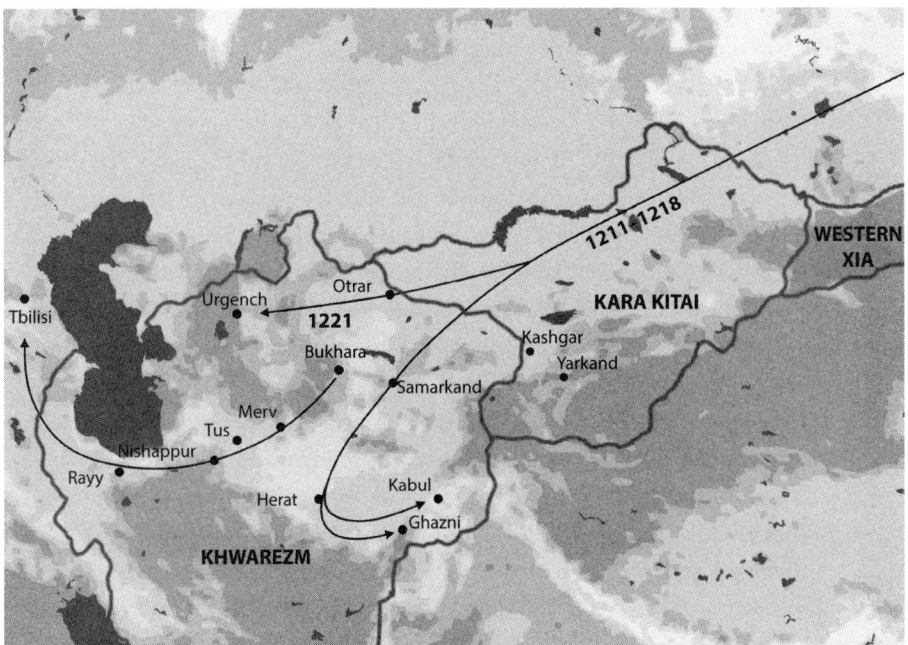

MAP 4. The Mongol invasion of central Asia

to reinforce his hegemony in east Asia. Another decisive factor in consolidating the economy of the fledgling Mongol Empire was the strong partnership between the military power of the nomads and the trade potential of central Asian merchants.

In 1218, a delegation of 450 Muslim traders traveled from Mongol territories to Otrar, a border town in the kingdom of Khwarazm; this was a clear sign of the established relations between the Mongols and the central Asian trading community.[13] However, the local governor accused them of espionage and sentenced them to death. Chinggis Khan intervened by sending Mongol emissaries directly to the shah for an explanation and reparations. He also demanded that the governor of Otrar be punished. Rather than seeking diplomatic reconciliation, the shah had one of the ambassadors executed, with the remaining two sent back after shaving off their beards—an insult equal to death. There was no greater offense in the steppe's political culture than such

13. On the campaign to conquer central Asia, see Allsen, "The Rise of the Mongolian Empire," pp. 354–57.

a violation of ambassadorial immunity. It was tantamount to declaring war—and it was received as such by Chinggis Khan.

In 1219, Chinggis Khan invaded Khwarazm. Although his armies had to navigate uncharted territories, besieging fortified cities and facing an enemy that outnumbered them, it was an unprecedented victory for the Mongols. It is difficult to accurately estimate the number of soldiers, as contemporary sources tend to exaggerate these figures. The Mongols probably had greater mobility and logistical skills and could thus deploy superior forces in each battle, despite being outnumbered by the shah's troops. These were divided between the various cities, while the army directly under the shah's command was probably no greater than forty thousand men. The Mongols, whose forces were estimated at a hundred thousand, whether they laid siege to the city or clashed in the battlefield, could count on a higher number. The Mongols' greatest strength was their knack for war, with ironclad discipline and a coordination of movement unrivaled by any other army at the time, whether Asian or European.

Chinggis Khan's goal was to avenge the offense against his ambassadors by capturing and executing the shah. Over the course of the four-year-long campaign, the Mongols made remarkable strides in asserting their authority across central Asia to the borders of Rus' and the Abbasid caliphate. The khan achieved his goal of exacting revenge on the shah: he died in 1220, having fled to an island in the Caspian Sea. Next, Mongol troops sacked and pillaged Transoxiana and many of its heavily populated cities. Samarkand, Bukhara, and Urgench were besieged and conquered, their populations decimated. The Mongol conquest of Khwarazm guaranteed their dominion over central Asia. Although it remains unclear whether Chinggis Khan intended to annex the region permanently, local officials loyal to the Mongols were appointed to govern these cities and provinces.

Even more significant was the possibility for new conquests. Jebe and Subedei, two of the most experienced Mongol commanders, were ordered to pursue the fleeing shah, with a host of twenty thousand soldiers. They crossed Khorasan in northeast Iran and sailed along the coast of the Caspian Sea to enter the Caucasus in 1220. There, they defeated Armenian and Georgian forces before invading Rus'. Meanwhile, masses of Cuman nomads fleeing the Mongols had sought refuge in Kiev, where they joined the Rus' army to push back the Mongol invasion.[14] In 1223, the Rus' and Mongol armies faced each other in battle on the River Kalka, which exemplified the Mongols' advanced

14. Pubblici, *Cumani*.

military tactics. With a feigned retreat, the Mongols trapped and annihilated the Rus' forces. Not only did this affirm the Mongol military's superiority over European armies, it also gave Mongol leaders vital information on the geography and populations of the Caucasus and Rus', laying the foundations for future invasions.

Chinggis Khan died in August 1227, aged circa sixty years old.[15] The world had now seen the sheer power of the Mongols, and was vulnerable to further invasions. Yet, the Mongol political landscape was a complex web of internal power struggles, focused on succession to the throne when the aristocracy united in a general assembly (*quriltai*) to elevate a potential heir to the rank of great khan. Though the transition to becoming leader of a vast empire was politically charged, it did not cause conflicts between potential successors as might be expected, since this process of accession had a long tradition in the steppe.[16] Upon the death of Chinggis Khan, it seemed that Jöchi, as eldest son, would prevail due to his prestige and rights of primogeniture, yet he died just a few months before his father, in February 1227. Ultimately, it was the third son, Ögödei, who was unanimously elected. Ögödei officially took the throne in 1229 and, after a period of stagnation, Chinggis Khan's children and grandchildren began plotting new conquests.

## The Assault on Europe

It is likely that Chinggis Khan himself had divided the empire into four territories, assigning each to one of his official sons: the east to Ögödei, his third son; the west to descendants of Jöchi, his firstborn, albeit of uncertain paternity; central Asia to Chagatai, his second son; and Mongolia to Tolui, his youngest son and custodian of the family's original patrimony, according to Mongol tradition. This division was solely theoretical; though the capital at the heart of the Mongol Empire, Karakorum, was assigned to Tolui, it remained the imperial seat and Ögödei's residence. The west—and thus Europe—remained the exclusive domain of Jöchi's descendants. In 1235, a general assembly of Mongol commanders planned future military campaigns, including the conquest of north China and the invasion of eastern Europe. Batu, Jöchi's firstborn, had exclusive rights to the latter.[17]

---

15. Ratchnevsky, *Genghis Khan*, pp. 141–44.
16. Fletcher, "Turco-Mongolian Monarchic Tradition."
17. Allsen, "Sharing out the Empire."

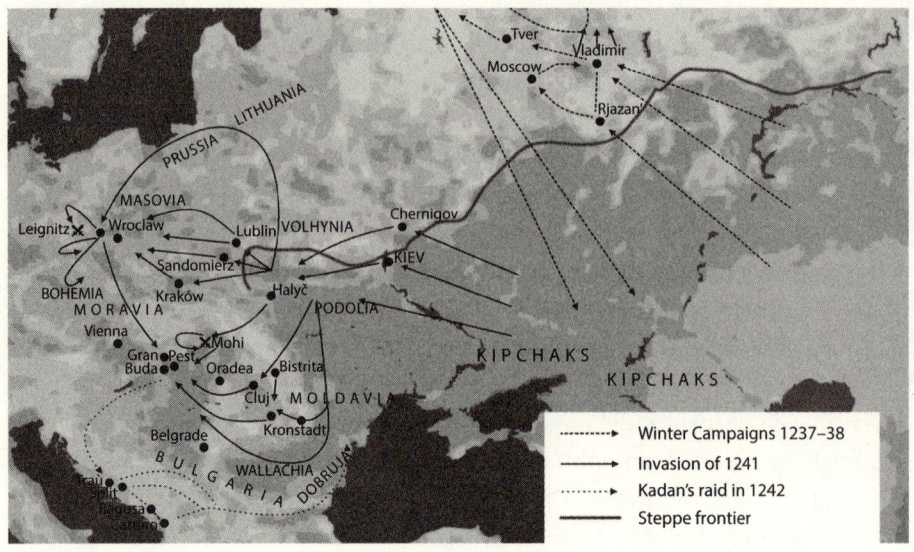

MAP 5. The Mongol invasion of Europe

In 1236, after triumphing over the Jin dynasty, Ögödei and his council decreed a new campaign in the west, entrusted to Batu. The campaign began in 1236–37 and was directed to the regions of the Volga and the Urals, which was then inhabited by Turkic-speaking populations such as the Bashkirs, Bulgars, and Cumans (who had previously been defeated by the Mongols). This first incursion drove the Cumans toward the west, crossing swaths of prairie land that extended as far as the Hungarian *puszta*, where King Béla IV (r. 1235–70) offered refuge to the Cuman chieftain, Koten, and his forty thousand subjects.[18]

The Mongol attack first set its sights on the Rus' principalities, which were divided by internal political rivalries and had detached from Catholic Europe due to the Orthodox schism. Abandoned and at the mercy of the invaders, Rus' put up little resistance. The first cities to fall were those geographically most exposed: Ryazan, Kolomna, Moscow, followed by Vladimir and Suzdal'.[19] Next, Batu marched on Kiev. Here, his demands for complete submission were repeatedly rejected by local authorities who, for good measure, had the Mongol ambassadors executed. As we have seen, the Mongols considered this an unforgivable act, although it seems that their initial aim was

18. Allsen, "Prelude to the Western Campaigns"; Vásáry, *Cumans and Tatars*, pp. 57–58.
19. Lind, "Mongol Invasions of Russia"; Sinor, "The Mongols in the West."

not to destroy the urban and socioeconomic structure of the principalities, but rather to compel surrender so tax and tribute collection systems could be introduced.[20] However, the Russian resistance forced their hand in what can only be described as a grim alternative of the Mongol ultimatum: it resulted in a conquest marked by so much violence that it discouraged any future resistance. The siege of Kiev lasted from November 28 to December 6, 1240. Once the city had fallen, it was ravaged, most of its citizens slaughtered, and its palaces razed to the ground.

Of the Rus' cities conquered between 1238 and 1240, none could resist for longer than a few days. The armies that had been so hastily assembled to head off the Mongol advance were defeated, suffering huge losses. The Mongols' success was down to a series of tactical and strategic advantages. Medieval European armies were commonly made up of a few military professionals— from the chivalric aristocracy—leading poorly armed, inexperienced, and untrained men. In contrast, the Mongols were experts in the art of war, with proven skills in riding, fighting, and archery, as well as in collective tactics. Their combat strategies were based on detailed knowledge of the terrain and precise coordination between the various divisions. On the battlefield, they prevailed with superior weapons, such as the composite (or recurve) bow. This could shoot long-range with the power to pierce through common medieval protections such as shields or armor—which, in any case, only the nobility could afford. Another formidable sight on the open battlefield was the heavy Mongol cavalry charging its enemies. It easily broke the ranks of untrained infantries that lacked suitable defensive weapons. Moreover, the Mongols employed a vast repertoire of ploys to lure the enemy into traps and ambushes. Judging by combat skills, mobility, competence of its commanders, and discipline of its fighters, the Mongol army operated at a level far superior to any European military of its time.[21]

Once the nobility of Rus' had been brought to its knees and its cities destroyed, the Mongols launched a coordinated attack against Poland and Hungary in the spring of 1241. Two decisive battles took place: the Battle of Legnica in Poland on April 9, and the Battle of Mohi in Hungary just two days later. The Mongol army marched across Moldavia and Wallachia, then divided into three columns to cross the Carpathian Mountains. Hungarian grasslands, rich

20. For a comparative analysis of how Russia was treated in the Mongol conquest, see Halperin, "Russia in the Mongol Empire."

21. On the organization of the Mongol troops, see May, *The Mongol Art of War*.

in crops, offered an ideal environment to sustain this nomadic population. The Mongols raided and conquered Hungarian cities, sowing terror among the people, as they had done in Rus'.

Ostensibly, King Béla IV of Hungary had offered a *casus belli*—a cause for war—by extending protection to the Cumans, whom the Mongols considered enemies. At this time, the Cumans had clashed with the local population after their leader, Koten, had been murdered by the Hungarians as a result of ethnic and political tensions. King Béla IV had fled after the Mongols took Mohi, while the Hungarian nobility attempted a brave yet futile resistance. In the winter of 1241, the Mongols crossed the frozen Danube on horseback to enter west Hungary, where they captured Esztergom, the state capital and political center. Meanwhile, a Mongol force commanded by Kadan, son of Ögödei, went in pursuit of the king, who, after seeking aid in Austria, had taken refuge at Klis Fortress in Dalmatia.[22]

The second phase of the Hungarian invasion proved more challenging for the Mongols. Several cities and fortresses resisted their attacks and, finally, between April and May 1242, the Mongols returned to the lowlands of the Volga marching south of the Carpathians across Serbia and Bulgaria. Why they retreated has been the subject of much debate.[23] One of the earliest theories put forward is based on a report by Giovanni di Pian del Carpine (anglicized as John of Plano Carpini), a Franciscan monk sent by Pope Innocent IV to the great khan in 1245. It states that Batu had decided to return to Rus' due to new political circumstances sparked by the death of Ögödei Khan, which required the leading members of the imperial clan to determine his succession. Nevertheless, Batu never went to Karakorum, the capital of the Mongol Empire, choosing instead to remain in Sarai, in the Lower Volga, which was the Mongols' major political hub in the West. One day, Sarai would become the capital of the Jöchi *ulus*—the Golden Horde.

On the other hand, a recent theory attributes the reason for the retreat to the logistical difficulties of the military campaign. In the spring of 1242, thawing masses of ice and snow had accumulated due to a particularly severe and rainy winter, making it more challenging for armies to traverse west Hungary. The Hungarian lowlands turned into a quagmire, trapping Mongol forces and exposing them to possible attack from European troops; ultimately, they were forced to give up their long-term occupation.[24] It is also likely that the pillaging

22. On the Mongol invasion of Hungary, see Jackson, *The Mongols and the West*.
23. Rogers, "An Examination of Historians' Explanations."
24. Büntgen and Di Cosmo, "Climatic and Environmental Aspects."

and violence wreaked upon the population had damaged agricultural production to the point of dramatically reducing available resources. The Mongols never achieved their goal of capturing and punishing the Hungarian king, who was able to return to his country unharmed.

Whatever the reason for the retreat, it is certain that Batu and his generals had extended their lines of communication much beyond what was sustainable, even for an army as mobile as that of the Mongols. The strategic requirements to support the occupation and to control a new territory in a time of growing tensions among the imperial clan probably convinced Batu to concentrate his forces in Rus', where he could better consolidate his power.

Although Europe was saved by the Mongols' unexpected retreat, its armies and all of Christendom had discovered that they were totally powerless in the face of an assault from which there seemed to be no salvation. Having narrowly averted the danger of a wider and longer-lasting invasion, anxiety swept through Europe, though its nations had a chance to reflect.[25] Beyond an understanding of the invasion that drew on prophetic and apocalyptic traditions, Europe's reaction was first and foremost a series of exploratory and diplomatic missions to the Mongols, in order to comprehend their origins, intentions, and strengths.[26] It was this rational and systematic readiness to learn about a greatly feared enemy that marked the shift from a passive and unprepared Europe to an active and aware one.

The Mongol expansion may have gone almost unchallenged, yet the political situation among its leaders deteriorated further. Factions developed among the various lineages, notably between the descendants of Ögödei and Chagatai on one side, and the sons of Tolui and Jöchi on the other. Wives and mothers of the khans also played prominent political roles; these women were highly influential, promoting alliances and maneuvers to advance their husbands and sons. Hostilities between Batu and Güyük (son and successor to Ögödei from 1246) came to a head during the Russian campaign and risked dragging the empire into civil war even before Güyük was designated khan. However, Güyük died just two years after his election. Batu took control of the succession and favored the rise of Möngke, Tolui's firstborn. After three years of negotiations and bloody internal feuds, a new order emerged. In 1251, Möngke was designated the new khan, and with him dawned a new phase in the history of Mongol expansion. His reign was characterized by renewed

25. Bigalli, *I Tartari e l'Apocalisse*; Schmieder, *Europa und die Fremden*.
26. Dawson, *The Mongol Mission*; Richard, *La Papauté et les missions d'Orient au moyen age*; De Rachewiltz, *Papal Envoys*.

military commitment, but also by deep internal divisions—some of which pre-existed his reign, while others were born of the empire's expansion. As a result of these conflicts, the 1260s saw the de facto separation of the empire into four khanates, each of which was independent, though they remained under the formal authority of a single sovereign.[27]

Under Möngke's rule, the Mongols not only continued expanding their territory, but they also learned to govern the newly conquered regions and subject them to their rule. It was a rapid process of transformation involving the army, administrative forces, and the economy. Means and ends thus changed. The Mongol army gained war technology, such as siege machinery imported from conquered states. With this, they could capture even more cities, castles, and other fortified places. Within their dominions, the governing Mongols recruited advisers and local administrators who introduced the principles of taxation to their populations, regularly gathering levies. Moreover, after the destructive rush of the initial invasion, the Mongol leaders sought to preserve economic resources and to foster trade among the empire's many regions. This change in perspective and strategy led the Mongols to build relations with European states, inserting themselves as a new—and powerful—player in the political and diplomatic landscape of the Mediterranean, eastern Europe, and the Islamic Middle East. Meanwhile, Christian Europe had made great strides in accessing knowledge on the Mongols by means of missions and diplomatic encounters. Though it cannot be said that these efforts were successful in political terms, they did facilitate communication between two worlds wholly foreign to each other. This paved the way for further, more fruitful agreements, allowing European merchants to reap rewards that only a few years earlier would have been unimaginable.

## Early Relations between Europe and the Mongols

The first news about the Mongols arrived in Europe as early as 1237, thanks to a Hungarian Dominican friar named Julius, who had traveled to the Volga in search of the native Magyar.[28] While there, he met people who spoke the same language as him, and heard of the destruction wreaked by the Mongols in Rus'. Julius also met noble Mongols who presented him a document on behalf

27. Jackson, "From Ulus to Khanate."

28. The complete text is published in translation by Dörrie, *Drei Texte zur Geschichte der Ungarn und Mongolen*, pp. 125–202.

of Batu, requesting Hungary to submit to Mongol conquest. Julius hastily returned to his homeland to deliver the document to King Béla IV. If the king took the threat seriously, he could then ready the country's defenses. Unfortunately for Hungary, Batu's letter was disregarded.[29]

The devastating impact of the Hungarian invasion meant that the possibility of new attacks on Europe could not be ignored. Pope Innocent IV, elected in 1243, included in the agenda for the First Council of Lyon (1245) the search for a "remedy against the Tatars" (*remedium contra Tartaros*). Even before the Council meeting, the pope had drafted two letters in March 1245 to be sent to the Mongols. In the first letter, the pope explained the fundaments of Christian doctrine, while in the second, he cautioned the Mongols against further attacks on Christendom, as the penalty was divine punishment.[30] These letters were handed to missionaries who would be the pope's envoys. A further aim of the missions to Mongolia was to get to know a people who were believed to come from a hellish place, as suggested by their name *tartarus*, the inferno of Greek mythology. Myths, legends, and prophecies spread throughout a Europe that was still far from the age of modern rationalism. Driven by a desire to not repeat past mistakes, the pope's plan was to gain eyewitnesses and thus a reliable account of the Mongols' true nature, their government, and—above all—their intentions. The newly established mendicant orders of the Franciscans and Dominicans were on the front line in these missions to the Mongol Empire.

The papal letters were entrusted to two Dominicans—Ascelin of Cremona and André de Longjumeau—as well as a Franciscan, John of Plano Carpini. Across two separate missions, the Dominicans made contact with the Mongols of Armenia and Persia, but they did not travel beyond Tabriz. It must be noted that when Ascelin of Cremona stood before Baiju, commander of the Mongol troops in Asia Minor, he risked being executed on the spot for refusing to submit to Mongol protocol, which demanded that he prostrate himself. Perhaps the most interesting outcome of these missions—which were limited and inconclusive—was that they established relations with the Mongol chiefs in the West.[31]

Of greater significance was the mission of the Franciscan John of Plano Carpini, who reached the Mongol court in Karakorum in August 1246. He witnessed the coronation of Güyük, the empire's new khan, who gave him a letter for the pope, essentially demanding he submit to the Mongols. Mongol

---

29. Hautala, "Early Hungarian Information."
30. Aigle, *The Mongol Empire between Myth and Reality*, pp. 45–46.
31. Guzman, "Simon of Saint-Quentin."

diplomacy was not known for its creativity, and interaction with European monarchs brooked no negotiations: the choice was to submit or be invaded. Yet, beyond the diplomatic collapse or the failed attempt to convert Güyük, John presented the pope (residing in Lyon at the time) a report of great detail and accuracy on Mongol traditions, customs, laws, military force, and government. For the first time, Europeans received word not of destruction and violence, but rather of Mongol society, culture, and politics—and, most importantly, it came from a direct and reliable source.[32]

Diplomatic relations with the Mongols were not just the remit of the papacy. In 1247, Güyük Khan sent Prince Eljigidei to the West. Interested in an alliance with the Christians against the caliphate, the prince initiated negotiations with King Louis IX of France. Following these diplomatic overtures, in 1248, Louis IX sent the Dominican André de Longjumeau to Mongolia to deliver a proposal to the khan himself, offering a Mongol–Christian alliance against the Mamluks. Having reached Karakorum just after the death of Güyük Khan (1248), the Dominican was not successful with the regent Oghul Qaimish, wife of Güyük. Rather than the much-hoped-for alliance, he simply received the typical Mongol request for unconditional submission.[33] A likely reason for the failed alliance was the ongoing tension that had grown into open conflict, marking the end of the House of Ögödei and the triumph of the House of Tolui. Outside a Mongol context, these intersections between foreign policy and internal politics were indecipherable, which may explain why the attempts to forge an anti-Islamic alliance between Christian Europe and Mongol Asia never came to fruition. It is a fact that the Mongols' frequent incursions, encounters, and contacts left their mark on Europe, constituting an initial step to understanding a phenomenon that gradually became less terrifying—and even alluring for the opportunities it offered.

Politically speaking, the most successful mission was that of another Franciscan missionary, the Flemish William of Rubruck, sent by Louis IX to Mongolia. Journeying between 1253 and 1255, William found himself in Karakorum before the new emperor Möngke. His is one of the most accurate testimonies; together with that of Plano Carpini, it is a valuable source on Mongol society. The goal of the mission was Catholic evangelization to oppose the spread of Nestorianism among the Asian peoples, and to bring solace to the German prisoners who had been deported to the Mongol territories. William never

32. Dawson, *Mission to Asia*; Pian del Carpine, *Storia dei Mongoli*.

33. On the relationship between the Mongols and European monarchs, see Aigle, "From 'Non-Negotiation' to an Abortive Alliance" and "The Letters of Eljigidei, Hülegü, and Abaqa."

reached these Christian communities, nor did he succeed in converting the khan or any other Mongols to Christianity. However, the mission's significance lies in the relationships he built, and the vital ethnographic, geographical, and religious information he garnered that could help Europe understand Mongol strategy and the characteristics of their society.[34]

The quest for an alliance inspired diplomatic exchanges and missions up until 1262, when Hülegü, brother of Möngke Khan and supreme commander of the Mongol forces in southwestern Asia as well as founder of the Ilkhanate, sent a letter to Louis IX with a further proposal for collaboration against Mamluk Egypt.[35] Reconstructing the exact course of these diplomatic activities is a difficult task as the records are incomplete and a great deal of information has since been lost. Some Christian kings had become supporters and allies of the Mongols, such as King Hethum of Armenia, and were thus committed to an anti-Islamic alliance between the Franks, Mongols, Christians, and pagans. However, this alliance never materialized. We can only speculate as to why: communication issues, internal differences, mutual mistrust, and constantly evolving international circumstances. However, we can say for certain that, by the early 1260s, the perception of the Mongols in Europe had changed. Feelings of impotence and fear after their invasions had almost vanished now that ambassadors and missionaries had gathered information on them. New political maneuvers were dictated by urgent priorities, first among which was the ongoing rivalry between Christendom and the Islamic world. From the European point of view, even though the Mongols were still foreign to them, they were no longer entirely alien. Meanwhile, new divisions had formed within the Mongol Empire, undermining its unity. The accelerating fragmentation led to the creation of separate kingdoms: the Ilkhanate in Iran, the Golden Horde (or Jöchi *ulus*) in Russia, Chagatai's kingdom in central Asia, and the Yuan dynasty in China and Mongolia.

## 1251–66: Expansion, Divisions, and the New Order of the Mongol Empire

In 1251, the *quriltai* was held in Karakorum and two decisions were made that would profoundly shape the future of the Mongol Empire. The first was the election of Möngke Khan, and the second was the continuation of conquests

---

34. Jackson and Morgan, *The Mission of Friar William of Rubruck*; Jackson, "William of Rubruck in the Mongol Empire."

35. Meyvaert, "An Unknown Letter of Hulagu"; Richard, "La lettre de Hülegü à Saint Louis."

to the east in China, and to the west in the Islamic regions of Iran, Iraq, and Syria. Mongol politics were dominated by "parties" that roughly aligned with the lineages of Chinggis Khan's four principal sons. The party of Tolui (the Toluid) were represented by Möngke and his brother Kublai, while the party of Jöchi (the Jöchid) were represented by the powerful western Batu Khan. These two parties were united against the ruling House of Ögödei and his son Güyük. Möngke was elected with Batu's support, as the two already had good relations, having collaborated during the previous western military campaigns. Despite his prestige, Batu was at a political disadvantage due to the sheer physical distance between his capital Sarai in the Lower Volga, and Karakorum in Mongolia (a region that, in theory, was the preserve of Tolui). Batu remained the de facto ruler of the West out of formality, albeit at a lower rank than Möngke. The schism between the East and West was not uncommon for the political traditions of the steppe, as it had precedents in other historical nomadic empires in Mongolia, such as the sixth-century Turks (Göktürks). The divide between Batu and Möngke established the border between East and West to the east of the Aral Sea, between the Talas and Chu rivers.

During the *quriltai* of the summer of 1251, it was also confirmed that Iran, the Caucasus, and Anatolia belonged to Batu's domain (and therefore his expansion), as it was part of the empire's western wing. Nonetheless, there were disagreements over the continuation of campaigns—in particular, the conquest of the caliphate. Here, two positions clashed: on the one hand, it was the prerogative of the khan to determine imperial strategy; on the other, it was Batu's right to conquer the western regions. A further factor was that *noyon* Baiju (Mongol commander in Azerbaijan, Armenia, and Anatolia) was a member of the House of Ögödei, had moved into the service of Batu to avoid the bitter fates that befell many other nobles loyal to Güyük. Batu had established peaceful relations with the caliphate, so continuing the conquest would destabilize the existing political equilibrium. Moreover, it would also prevent Batu and the Jöchids from eventually controlling an economically rich and strategically important region.

The rift between Batu and Möngke led to a stalemate that lasted several years, yet by 1254—the year before Batu's death—preparations began for an expedition under Hülegü's command. This would lead to the conquest of the caliphate, and the foundation of the Ilkhanate.[36] There are speculations that upon Batu's death, Möngke intended to intervene in the internal political

36. Mirgaleev, "The Golden Horde Policies," p. 218.

transition of the Golden Horde to support the candidacy of Sartaq, son of Batu and a close ally of Möngke.[37] Sartaq did indeed succeed Batu, but his reign was short-lived (r. 1256–57); he died during the return journey from the imperial capital, where he had been formally named khan of the Jöchi *ulus*. After his death, Boraqchin, his mother and Batu's widow, briefly reigned as regent before Batu's brother, Berke, took the helm. The crowning of Berke Khan (r. 1257–67) to the throne of the Golden Horde marked not only a shift in the history of the Jöchi *ulus*, but also in the complex network of international relations that involved Venice, Genoa, the Mamluk Sultanate, and Byzantium.

While Batu's succession was underway in the Golden Horde, in 1256, an expedition departed from Karakorum that would result in Hülegü's conquest of Afghanistan, Iran, Azerbaijan, Iraq, and Syria. The Mongol force was an estimated 100,000–150,000 soldiers strong, accompanied by over half a million horses.[38] Two years of planning preceded the expedition, as the Mongols prepared supplies and traced a route that would guarantee the logistical needs of such a large army. Local resources would have to be exploited, and this called for a thorough knowledge of the terrain. The route would have to guarantee sufficient pastures for the horses, as well as protection for the animals and soldiers from freezing temperatures, drought, and other natural perils. The army moved slowly, crossing the Mongolian and Kazakh steppe, then heading southeast to cross present-day Uzbekistan and Afghanistan, before continuing along the towering mountains of Khorasan and north Iran.

Upon reaching the Caspian Sea, Hülegü launched a strenuous winter campaign against the Nizari Ismaili state, a Shiite sect founded in the late eleventh century, also known as the Assassins.[39] The Nizari Ismaili wielded great political influence in Iran, Syria, and Asia Minor, terrorizing both Christian and Muslim heads of state and religious figures. Hülegü demanded the unconditional surrender of their leader, Imam Rukn al-Dīn, who stalled and did not surrender, counting on the security of his fortresses, perched atop mountain peaks. Nevertheless, the Mongol army was guided by Commander Kitbuqa, a skilled

37. Mirgaleev, "The Golden Horde Policies," pp. 218–19; Mys'kov, *Političeskaja istorija Zolotoj Ordy*, pp. 53–54.

38. On the campaign's progress and estimates of the Mongolian troop numbers, timing, and geography, see Smith, "Hülegü Moves West."

39. On the relationship between the Mongols and the Ismailis, see May, "A Mongol-Ismâ 'îlî Alliance?"

Mongol general, Hülegü's right arm, and a leading figure in the campaign. He succeeded in taking Alamut, the main fortress, which brought down the powerful sect. If the caliphate drew a breath of relief over the destruction of the Shiite sect—a mortal enemy of Sunni Islam—then the respite did not last for long.

Hülegü led his troops to spend the winter in the lowlands of north Iran and Azerbaijan, where the Mugham steppe offered sufficient pastures for his troops. During this time, he planned the campaign for the capture of Baghdad, which would destroy the Abbasid caliphate and revolutionize the Islamic world. In the fall of 1257, the Mongol army split up and approached Baghdad from different directions, reaching the city on January 29, 1258. After a short siege, Baghdad fell on February 10. Hülegü was ruthless in his sack of the city. Arab chronicles describe Baghdad's complete destruction and the massacres of its citizens. Caliph Al-Musta'sim (r. 1242–58) was executed.[40] With the downfall of Baghdad, Hülegü had completed his conquest of Islam's major centers of political and religious power—a quest that had begun in the days of Chinggis Khan with the invasion of Khwarazm, and continued during the khanate of Ögödei with his campaigns against the Seljuk Sultanate of Rum, in Anatolia.

Iran, in addition to Azerbaijan, Armenia and Anatolia, had been under the supreme rule of Commander Baiju, who, as previously mentioned, was loyal to Batu. He had governed the province indirectly via control of the local potentates. Hülegü's arrival radically changed the conquest's political geography. Baiju had been ordered to unite his troops with the bulk of the army in the attack on Baghdad, and even before this directive he had been forced to abandon his base in Azerbaijan to make way for Hülegü's troops, and to move to east Anatolia. Subordinate to Kitbuqa (a confidante of Hülegü) during the campaign, Baiju had suffered the future ilkhan's impatience more than once, being accused of dragging his feet. Mistrusted for his past service to Güyük and Batu, Baiju disappeared in 1260 during the Mongol operations in Syria, just two years after the conquest of Baghdad. He was likely executed by Hülegü.

In 1259, operations began to further extend Mongol dominion to the Middle East. The Mongol armadas, strengthened by the Christian forces who were allies of the Georgians, Armenians, and Franks, entered Syria in January 1260. Shortly after, the Mongols captured Aleppo and Damascus, and quickly established a government in collaboration with local emirs. In April or May, Hülegü withdrew the majority of his troops, and retreated toward Azerbaijan and Tabriz. Kitbuqa remained in Syria with a contingent limited

---

40. A chronicle of the conquest can be found in Gilli-Elewy, "Al-awādi al-ǧāmia."

to around ten thousand soldiers.[41] Of course, orders of submission had already been sent to the Mamluk Sultan Qutuz (r. 1259–60), who had only recently risen to power in Egypt, and whose legitimacy was still in question. The Mongols had no reason for concern regarding Qutuz—after all, they had defeated every Islamic army, and now controlled Syria. Qutuz had only ascended the throne in November 1259 with the support of emirs and local governors who, as a rule, proved unreliable. After the fall of the caliphate, the political fragmentation of the Islamic world favored the Mongols, though this gave them a false sense of security. Kitbuqa hastened to consolidate the conquest of Syria, using his contacts with the Franks who controlled several of the region's key cities and fortresses. However peaceful the relations were, the Mongols made their authority felt by sacking Sidon in August 1260.[42] Kitbuqa would replace Baiju as the Mongol governor of the Levant, but he would be much heavier-handed, emulating Hülegü's violence.

Mongol plans for further conquest in the Middle East would soon come to a halt following the success of Qutuz. By mustering emirs and local officials under the Mamluk flag, the sultan was able to push back the Mongol threat. Baybars (r. 1260–77) also joined the effort; famed for his talent and experience as a commander, he had previously guided Islamic troops against Louis IX's crusaders. Comprising twelve thousand well-armed soldiers, the Mamluk army made for Syria, intent on defeating and ousting the Mongols. As soon as Kitbuqa learned of their imminent arrival, he assembled his forces and marched against them. The two armies clashed in Ayn Jalut, Palestine. Qutuz prevailed, while Kitbuqa died, fighting valiantly.[43] In the wake of his victory, Qutuz invaded Syria, wiping out what was left of the Mongols and annexing the region to the territory of the Mamluk Sultanate. However, shortly thereafter, Qutuz was assassinated. Now, Baybars took the throne and re-established the caliphate in Cairo. Berke Khan of the Golden Horde recognized his authority as the head of Islam, and placed him under his formal protection.[44] Thus, Berke and Baybars united against their common enemy: Hülegü's Ilkhanate.[45]

41. Smith, "Ayn Jālūt."

42. Jackson, "The Crisis in the Holy Land in 1260," p. 485.

43. Ayn Jalut has a vast bibliography. Of note are the following: the previously cited Smith, "Ayn Jālūt"; Amitai-Preiss, *Mongols and Mamluks*, pp. 26–48; Morgan, "The Mongols in Syria."

44. Mirgaleev, "The Golden Horde Policies," p. 223. Polyak, "Novye arabskie materjaly," p. 29.

45. Favereau, "The Golden Horde and the Mamluks."

Hülegü vowed to seek revenge. For the next sixty years, the Mamluk Sultanate and the Ilkhanate were beleaguered by recurring battles in which neither
gained the upper hand. Middle Eastern politics were transformed, with new
alliances and conflicts throughout the region. The immediate consequences
of Hülegü's defeat were especially impactful within the Mongol Empire, triggered by a complex situation that had arisen upon Möngke's death in 1259. Two
principal divisions occurred after the old khan's passing: one between the
Ilkhanate and the Golden Horde, which led to a civil war of Hülegü against
Berke, and the second within the Toluids in Mongolia, which led to another
civil war between Arigh Böke and his brother Kublai.[46] The empire did not
stabilize until around the mid-1260s, although hostilities continued between
the various centers of power, such as the war between Kublai and Qaidu,
grandson of Ögödei and a powerful central Asian khan.[47]

After Möngke's death in 1259, his brother Kublai prevailed, with the support
of Hülegü. Kublai was elected khan supreme of the Mongol Empire, yet the
succession was opposed by Arigh Böke, son of Tolui and Kublai's younger
brother. Arigh Böke had first obtained the largest consensus. In this sibling
rivalry, Berke, head of the still mighty Jöchid party, whose hostility against
Hülegü continued to grow, sided with Arigh Böke, who also had the support
of Chagatai's *ulus* in central Asia.[48] Kublai, having returned to Mongolia from
his political and military base in north China, succeeded in bringing the Mongol aristocracy to his side, rebuffing Arigh Böke's challenge. Arigh Böke's defeat sparked a civil war, from which Kublai emerged victorious thanks to superior military resources and strategies. This war reinforced the Kublai–Hülegü
political axis, an alliance that would last throughout Kublai's later conquest of
China and the foundation of the Yuan dynasty (1271–1368). However, this war
also cemented the rivalry between the Golden Horde and the Ilkhanate.

These conflicts were aggravated by religious differences. Berke was the first
Mongol khan to convert to a foreign religion—Islam. Hülegü's violence in the
heart of the Abbasid caliphate resounded around the Islamic world, with all
the faithful condemning his actions. Not only had Hülegü sacked Baghdad
and abolished the caliphate, but he had also executed the caliph (the political
and spiritual leader). Moreover, the loss of Anatolia and Iran from the Jöchid
political orbit was still keenly felt, as was Hülegü's new purge of those local

46. Rossabi, *Khubilai Khan*, pp. 53–62.
47. On the figure of Qaidu, see Biran, *Qaidu and the Rise of the Independent Mongol State*.
48. On the khanate of Chagatai, see Atwood, *Encyclopedia*, pp. 82–88.

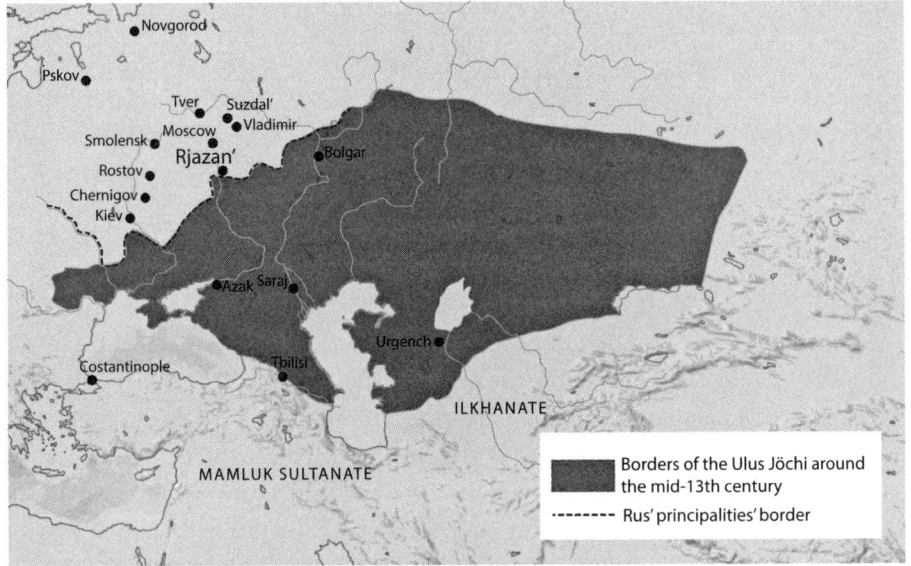

MAP 6. The Jöchi *ulus* or Golden Horde, ca. mid-thirteenth century

elites loyal to Berke in the major cities of the Levant and the Caucasus.[49] In November 1262, two hundred Mongols loyal to Berke left the Ilkhanate and sought refuge under Mamluk protection, begging for asylum from the conflict between Berke and Hülegü.[50]

War broke out in the winter of 1261–62. Jöchid troops, led by the general and *noyon* Nogaï, leader of the right wing of the Golden Horde, attacked the Ilkhanate on the border of the Terek River, in the southern Caucasus, pushing as far as Derbent and Shirvan.[51] Hülegü rebuffed Nogaï with a quick and effective counter-offensive, liberating Shirvan in November 1262. The Ilkhanid army, led by Abaqa, son and future successor of Hülegü, advanced beyond the Terek River, even penetrating the northern Caucasus. In December 1262, it reached Berke's winter camp, which had already been abandoned. Berke mounted a

49. Amitai-Preiss, *Mongols and Mamluks*, p. 79; Mirgaleev, "The Golden Horde Policies," p. 220; Favereau, "The Golden Horde and the Mamluks," pp. 96–97. The report can be found in Al-Dīn, *The Successors of Genghis Khan*, pp. 122–23.

50. Amitai-Preiss, *Mongols and Mamluks*, p. 81.

51. Amitai-Preiss, *Mongols and Mamluks*, p. 79; Jackson, *The Dissolution of the Mongol Empire*, pp. 233–34. According to al-Umarī, both cities were part of the Jöchi *ulus*, at the behest of Chinggis Khan: Mirgaleev, "The Golden Horde State," p. 140.

counter-offensive in January 1263, defeating Abaqa and pushing him back to the southern part of the Caucasus. However, once Berke arrived in Derbent, he withdrew. The war had hurt both sides, and each was incapable of fighting on. The end of this conflict established a new political map of the region, ratified by Kublai Khan in 1263.

To complete the picture, mention must be made of another war between Kublai and the central Asian khanate of Chagatai, which not only included present-day Uzbekistan, but also a large portion of northwest China. Ranging from today's Xinjiang to Ningxia Province, Chagatai thus controlled a large part of the city-oases that were obligatory stopovers of international trade routes. The de facto ruler of the Chagatai khanate, Qaidu, was a thorn in Kublai's side, remaining an element of tension within Mongol politics between 1260 and 1270. In 1264, Kublai began to build a new capital for his empire, Dadu ("great capital" in Chinese), also known as Khanbaliq. Dadu was founded in the location of present-day Beijing, near the old capital of the Jin Empire. From there, Kublai conducted a campaign against the Chinese dynasty of the Southern Song. At the end of a long resistance, the Song were defeated by a Mongol army that was by then multiethnic, and equipped with more modern technology, such as assault weapons and warships, acquired from all its conquests. In 1271, Kublai proclaimed the Yuan dynasty, meaning "origin," which celebrated the dawn of a new era dominated by the Mongols as a universal power. His military operations lasted until 1279, when the last cell of Song loyalist resistance was shattered. China, for the first time in history, was now wholly subject to a foreign people.[52]

## Trade Policies Introduced by the Mongols

Between ca. 1237 and 1260, the major caravan routes of Persia, Transcaucasia, and Anatolia had come under the formal control of the Jöchi *ulus*. By the mid-century, therefore, a territorial continuity had been established between the Mongols and the Latin empires of Constantinople, Nicaea, and Trebizond (a Mongol tributary). The king of Lesser Armenia—a state whose most profitable and strategic trade center was the port of Ayas—was a vassal of the Mongols. Goods leaving from the region's main caravan cities and ports for the coastal and inland markets of the Golden Horde were exempt from paying

52. Rossabi, *Khubilai Khan*, pp. 76–95.

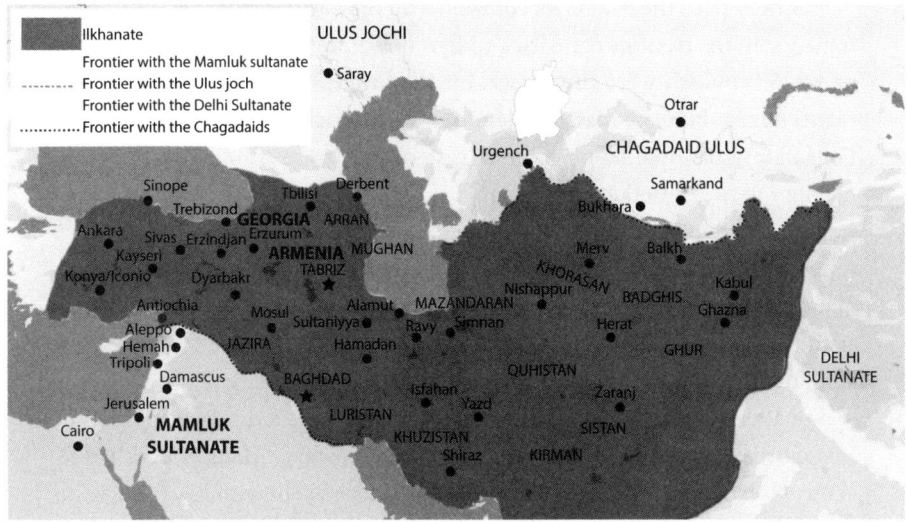

MAP 7. The Ilkhanate in the second half of the thirteenth century

taxes and duties.[53] However, Batu's formal control of the region was complicated by a multifold situation: during the military campaigns, Hülegü had remained the de facto governor of these regions.[54] Thus, Hülegü's power depended on the consent of the Jöchids and the *yarligh* (edicts) issued by Sarai.

Since 1260, Hülegü had assumed control of the main arteries that crossed Iran and Asia Minor from Nishappur to Damghan, all the way to Rayy. From here, it was possible to descend toward Hamadan and Baghdad or climb toward Tabriz, the southern Caucasus, and the great market towns of Dvin and Ani. One could then reach Sivas, a vital trade hub and the city that linked Ayas to the south, and Trebizond to the north. Merchants could continue as far as Konya (Iconium), capital of the sultanate of Rum, and then on to Constantinople and Nicaea. This network of roads, transit stations, cities, and markets allowed for a vast integration of trade, with international merchants and the opportunity to make a fortune, particularly by those who controlled access and transit points.[55]

53. Seyfeddini, *Monetnoe delo i denežnoe obraščenie v Azerbajdžane*, p. 73.

54. Tiesenhausen, *Sbornik*, vol. 2, p. 75.

55. Routes and itineraries are described in detail in Sinclair, *Eastern Trade and the Mediterranean*.

For their part, the Mamluks controlled all the key trading posts, ports, and transit stations from north Africa to Syria traditionally used by the western merchants, which were the reason for the bitterest conflicts among Italy's maritime republics: Damascus, Aleppo, Tyre, Antioch, and Beirut (see map 7). For full international scope, the two systems had to be connected. However, hostility between Berke and Hülegü had severed the links between Sarai and Cairo, preventing traders of the Golden Horde from exporting their products to Egypt. Among these products were the most profitable and in greatest demand by the Mamluks: slaves, in particular young men to be readied for the army. The slave trade was mainly based in the steppe between the northern coast of the Black Sea and the lower course of the Dnieper River.[56]

For this trade to continue, Berke needed to forge a direct link with the Bosphorus, and thus with the Byzantine Empire, which Michael VIII had recently re-established.[57] The effort to reach an agreement with Byzantium was based on the relative convenience of the Alexandria–Constantinople–Crimea–Sarai route, which entailed a return journey lasting almost four months, including stopovers. Michael VIII needed strong allies and secure borders to withstand external threats and to ease the precarious conditions of his army and treasury.[58] In other words, the alliance between the Golden Horde and the Mamluks, originally born of a common enemy in the Ilkhanate as well as commercial necessity, was further fostered by the involvement of the re-established Byzantine Empire, which offered a logical and viable alternative for communication and trade between the two allies.[59]

This new political and commercial order was especially important in relation to Genoese and Venetian activities, insofar as it explained the diverse presence of Italian merchants in Mongol territory. For as long as they could, Italian traders maintained their presence both in the Ilkhanid realm (in the capital city Tabriz, by way of Trebizond), and in the territory of the Golden Horde, particularly in Crimea. Such doubling up was made necessary by the blockade of all direct contact between the two Mongol states. What boosted trade were the innovations brought by the Mongols, who, political divisions aside, had created a homogeneous trading space on an unprecedented scale.

---

56. For a general overview, see Ayalon, *The Mamlūk Military Society*; Amitai, "Diplomacy and the Slave Trade," pp. 350–51.

57. Amitai-Preiss, *Mongols and Mamluks*, pp. 85–86.

58. Bartusis, *The Late Byzantine Army*, pp. 43–62.

59. Korobeinikov, *Byzantium and the Turks*, p. 205.

As mentioned at the beginning of this chapter, the conquest of central Asia was triggered by the massacre of a caravan of merchants under Mongol protection, perpetrated by the ruler of Khwarazm. The Mongols were no different from other nomadic empires in the steppe in their implementation of new policies for commercial expansion. However, given the extent of their empire, and the higher level of production and trade achieved by both the European and Chinese economies in the thirteenth century, the potential they had created was unprecedented. Together with robust commercial structures, the Mongol conquest unified these hitherto separate trade routes into a vast Eurasian mercantile system, which started from western Europe and the Mediterranean all the way to eastern Europe and Russia, to the Middle East, to central Asia, and to China. However limited the Mongols' economic instruments were, it is a fact that they introduced advanced concepts and structures to facilitate trade, limit risks, and grow supply and demand. Let us pause here to consider three aspects: the safety of the routes and markets, specific commercial institutions, and monetary policies.

Records from this period all praise the safety that the Mongol Empire guaranteed merchants. The risk of losing goods at the hands of marauders and pirates was a key reason that discouraged long-distance trade. By reducing risks, investments were incentivized despite the long time between an initial investment and the final profit. Moreover, treaties between the Mongols and European trading powers often included a clause requiring the return of goods and possessions should a foreign merchant die during an expedition. Given the length and danger of these journeys, such guarantees offered by the Mongol states to European investors not only abated risk of losses due to robberies, but also reduced risks caused by a merchant's unexpected death.

Perhaps the most renowned institutions introduced by the Mongols into international trade were the *ortaq* (business partnerships) and *yam* (the network of postal stations). The *ortaq* were perfected throughout the late thirteenth century and involved the partnership of a Mongol investor with a merchant. The merchant was a trade specialist, with knowledge of foreign languages and markets. His task was to invest on behalf of the Mongol partner, as well as to procure specific merchandise.[60] In a sense, this form of Mongol commercial investment was not unlike institutions such as the *commenda* and

---

60. Allsen, "Mongolian Princes and Their Merchant Partners"; Endicott-West, "Merchant Associations in Yüan China."

the *colleganza* of Venice or of Muslim traders.[61] Thus, however much the Mongol and European cultures differed, they were compatible when it came to the relationship between merchant and state. Mercantile language and commercial interests no doubt brought the Mongols and Latins together, overcoming political barriers for the sake of mutually profitable relationships. The Mongol state, represented by the court aristocracy and by the high civil and military ranks, thus became an active partner in international trade, further stimulating markets. In addition, merchants who aligned themselves with Mongol leaders were granted protection and the *laissez-passer*, which guaranteed them privileged access to courts and markets across the entire empire, regardless of political rivalries.

As for the empire's domestic market, khans entrusted tax collection to merchants who were part of the *ortaq*. Not only did these merchants receive a percentage of the duties paid, but they also earned money as moneylenders and usurers, loaning money to those who could not pay their taxes, in the form of silver ingots (which we will return to in more detail in chapter 10). As tax collectors, the *ortaq*—often Muslims from central Asia—took on a prominent role in the fiscal reforms of the Mongol Empire under Möngke and Kublai.

Various European merchants aspired to make contact with the upper Mongol hierarchies, hoping to be granted such privileges. One example of the strategies adopted is found in the notarial archive of Lamberto di Sambuceto. These papers tell us that on May 11, 1290, the falconer Johanes de Rayna was hired to serve a merchant named Pietro de Braino, with a contract valid until the end of August of that same year, to accompany the merchant to the court of Arghun Ilkhan of Persia.[62] The falconer would be paid 800 aspers plus expenses once he had reached the Ilkhanid court. Although the document does not itemize the falconer's tasks, nor why he had been hired, we do know that imperial hunting was a common pastime among influential European and Asian courts. This garnered an international demand for trainers and animals suited to the hunt (birds of prey and felines, in particular) with the various Eurasian aristocracies. We can therefore speculate that the merchant Pietro de Braino aimed to use the falconer to gain invitation to the court, and to employ

61. On the *commenda* in Venice, see Luzzatto, "La commenda nella vita economica dei secoli XIII e XIV." On the *commenda* in the Islamic world, see Udovitch, *Commercial Techniques*, pp. 37–62.

62. Balard, *Gênes et l'outre-mer*, vol. 1, no. 513, p. 192.

his hunting knowledge to establish a trading relationship with members of the Mongol–Persian aristocracy—and perhaps even with the emperor himself.

As for the Golden Horde, not much is known about the specific relations between the Mongol aristocracy and merchants, although it appears that Muslims held the most prestigious role in the *ortaq* system. Nevertheless, khans of the Golden Horde generally held an inclusive and tolerant attitude. The Mongols even continued to uphold a free and open commercial attitude toward the principalities of Rus' that were subject to them. The economic rebirth of Novgorod, which had begun as early as the late thirteenth century, was actually due to the arrival of northern European merchants, drawn in by low tariffs and the flourishing fur trade. Ultimately, a relationship of trust was established between merchants and military authorities, attracting and encouraging investments.

A further aspect that benefited international trade was greater support for transportation and decreased transaction costs. In all territories under Mongol rule, trade flourished due to reduced customs duties, as well as the ease of movement guaranteed by the system of postal stations, where merchants and authorized personnel could find accommodation, spare horses, and pack animals. These stations were also a hub for guides who could help merchants on their journeys. This system, known as *yam*, was originally created to guarantee quick communication over long distances (a kind of pony express), yet it also served as a logistical support system, allowing merchants to calculate the exact amount they would have to pay for the transport of goods. *La Pratica della mercatura*, a merchant handbook written by the Florentine banker Francesco Balducci Pegolotti, is a precious source; beyond the specific information on prices and merchandise contained therein, it gives us a sense of the time required and the costs, all calculated with remarkable precision. The *yam* allowed the merchant to quantify costs and profits with an accuracy unprecedented in European trade history. For example, one could determine the time required to travel from Venice to Tana (between 58 and 67 days), and even from Tana to the capital of China (between 264 and 284 days). By unifying eastern Europe and Asia on a political as well as linguistic level—Turkic and Persian both became lingua francas—and by improving logistical operations (a theme that is discussed further in chapter 9), the Mongols reduced difficulties, costs, and risks. Clearly, they made considerable profits from the transit of goods through their empire. At the same time, a well-informed merchant could carry out his trade seamlessly.

Finally, it is worth mentioning how the Mongols adopted different currencies and, most importantly, increased the circulation of paper money in China. First, they introduced the silver ingot (discussed in chapter 10) as a unified standard of their fiscal policies. The use of this currency allowed the empire to rationalize its fiscal system, a relatively new concept for the Mongols, who did not have a sophisticated governing culture. The transition to a monetary standard, albeit partial and limited to certain areas, thus allowed the various governments to communicate with each other in accounting terms, and markets could rely on a stable system through this convertible means of exchange.[63]

Of course, as mentioned above, the most radical Mongol reform was the large-scale adoption of paper money in China. Kublai was aware of the danger that inflation could cause when money was issued to an extent that surpassed the government's ability to guarantee its nominal value. Through paper money, new mint issuances could be constrained, and banknotes remained convertible into silver at dedicated currency exchange agencies. As we know from Marco Polo (see chapter 8), merchants arriving at the Chinese border from central Asia had to exchange their currencies for paper money, which could then be reconverted prior to their return journey. Although paper money made commercial transactions easier and cut costs, not all Mongol states accepted these reforms. Unlike silver, which was widespread, paper money was not accepted outside of China, and it was wholly rejected when the Ilkhanids attempted to introduce it in Iran in the late thirteenth century.[64]

Overall, we can conclude that, notwithstanding the challenges involved, Mongol monetary policy was the most advanced attempt in the Middle Ages to rationalize exchanges and to introduce standards that were applicable throughout the imperial territories. These policies had a clear objective: to facilitate both trade and tax collection to keep the treasury-draining governments and armies afloat. The Mongols also fostered the access of foreign merchants to markets that had hitherto been unreachable. It is therefore no surprise that from 1260 onward, especially toward the late thirteenth century, a growing number of European merchants were drawn into the orbit of the Mongol Empire. And, as a consequence, rivalries between cities escalated.

63. Von Glahn, *Fountain of Fortune*, pp. 56–58.
64. Jahn, "Paper Currency in Iran."

# 3

# Venice and the Black Sea

## FROM THE TREATY OF NYMPHAEUM
## TO THE FOUNDING OF TANA

### Venice after the Treaty of Nymphaeum

In the 1260s, the main players on the eastern Mediterranean chessboard were the Mongols, the Byzantine Empire, the Mamluks, and the Italian republics. Their relations determined the rhythm and conditions of Venice's commercial penetration into markets controlled by eastern powers. Though alliances were often marred by sudden disruptions, and trade was impacted by political uncertainties, the flow of goods within this circuit remained uninterrupted.

In this second half of the century, the scope of international trade broadened considerably, its center shifting until it completely encompassed the Black Sea territories. Ancient harbors along the coasts were expanded, and new markets were created where traders could sell products manufactured in Europe and buy goods imported from Asia.[1] A key impact of this evolution was the gradual integration of the Black Sea into the Mediterranean and Levantine trade network. The Pontic area became a common space, a nexus between Asia and Europe. Still, this necessary process of political pacification was challenging for all involved. As previously mentioned, new political circumstances had arisen: the consolidation of the Mongol government in the Golden Horde, the conquests of Hülegü, the wars between the Ilkhanate and the Mamluks, as well as the re-establishment of the Byzantine Empire by

---

1. Lopez, "Nouveaux documents," p. 445.

Michael VIII Palaiologos—its ongoing evolution making any future predictions impossible.

Michael VIII had to reckon with the Ilkhanate, which now ruled the Seljuk Sultanate of Rum and almost entirely occupied the Anatolian peninsula, thus controlling the territory's access. Byzantium mitigated this by seeking alliances with other major players in the region: the Mamluks and the Mongols of the Golden Horde, who had already united against the Ilkhanate, their common enemy. The emperor's goal was not only to protect his empire's newfound unity, but to maintain Constantinople as the central hub of the vast commercial network that branched across the Black Sea.[2] In 1261, the Byzantine emperor, Michael VIII, first entered into a treaty of friendship with Berke, khan of the Golden Horde. Then, in the summer of 1262, he received envoys from Baybars, who had recently been crowned ruler of the Mamluk Sultanate; Michael VIII granted the sultanate's Egyptian merchants the right to pass freely through Constantinople without paying customs duties.[3]

As illustrated in chapter 1, the most significant diplomatic initiative for the fate of the Venetian presence not just in Constantinople and the Aegean, but also in its goal to gain access to the Black Sea, was the Treaty of Nymphaeum between Byzantium and Genoa. By allowing the Ligurian city a monopoly over commercial traffic, the treaty punished and excluded Venice. However fragile it may have been, the new Byzantine Empire was the main obstacle to Venice gaining a foothold in the Levant and for its eastern expansion. Only ships from the allied cities of Genoa and Pisa were authorized to pass through the Bosphorus.[4]

Venice reacted by focusing on two aims: the first was to consolidate the system it had built over the last decades, and the second was to affirm its economic and commercial presence beyond the Bosphorus and Dardanelles Straits. Genoa adopted more aggressive tactics. Buoyed by its alliance with Emperor Michael VIII, the city aimed to build a true monopoly over all commercial shipping in the Black Sea. In no time at all, Genoese ships were the

2. Weller, "Marrying the Mongol Khans," pp. 185–86; Amitai-Preiss, *Mongols and Mamluks,* p. 91.

3. Amitai-Preiss, *Mongols and Mamluks,* p. 91.

4. Bratianu, *Actes des notaires génois de Péra et de Caffa,* p. 92.

main carrier of all goods—especially slaves[5]—sailing from the ports of Crimea to the coasts of north Africa.[6]

Losing its dominance in Constantinople was not the only challenge Venice faced. Further adversities were, on the one hand, difficulties in maintaining control over the Aegean islands, which were shaken by anti-Venetian uprisings. The rebellions had never truly been quelled and were rekindled by the Byzantine reconquest of 1261. On the other hand, Venice had to contend with the gradual shift of the political and territorial center of the Seljuks. Since 1220, these had been driven westward by the Mongol invasion of the Caucasus, and the Seljuks now occupied territories close to the Aegean and the Balkans. This further reduced Byzantine room for maneuver in western Asia Minor and made overland travel more perilous for Venetian merchants.[7]

To compound matters, Venice suffered from a grain shortage at the time, caused by a peak in population growth that affected all of western Europe, and Italy in particular, during the thirteenth century. Prices of necessities had grown exponentially:[8] in northern Italy, for example, between 1201 and 1291, the price of grain rose by over 140 percent.[9] From 1250 onward, frequent famines created local and regional crises that also touched Venice.[10] It was these

5. J. J. Saunders's statement that Genoa was the main vector for the transportation of slaves in Egypt and in Syria (Saunders, *Muslims and Mongols*, p. 74) was called into question in a detailed study by Reuven Amitai ("Diplomacy and the Slave Trade," pp. 357–58). However, by no means does Amitai minimize the role of Genoa in the slave trade.

6. Thorau, *The Lion of Egypt*, p. 121; Jacoby, "The Supply of War Materials to Egypt"; and in particular Amitai, "Diplomacy and the Slave Trade," p. 351. In 1263, a Genoese man accompanied Berke's ambassadors from the Golden Horde to the Egyptian court: cf. Amitai-Preiss, *Mongols and Mamluks*, p. 82; Amitai, "Diplomacy and the Slave Trade," p. 356.

7. In addition, outside of the capital of Konya, the sultanate of Rum was a territorial space mostly inhabited by nomads, emigrants, and refugees who had settled in the western lowlands, abundant with grazing pastures. These areas were only under weak control of the central authority, making their crossing a risky endeavor for foreign merchants and diplomats. For more on this topic, see Yildiz and Peacock, *The Seljuks of Anatolia*, in particular the introduction on pp. 1–22.

8. Latimer, "The English Inflation of 1180–1220"; Bridbury, "Thirteenth-Century Prices."

9. See Cherubini, *Agricoltura e società rurale nel medioevo*, in particular pp. 28–31.

10. This, for instance, was the case of the two-year period 1275–77 which encouraged the most populated cities, one of which was Venice, to invest greater efforts in the supply of grain precisely to deal with the inadequacy of local production. See Cherubini, *Agricoltura e società rurale nel medioevo* (chapter 2, "Gli uomini e lo spazio coltivato"); Karpov, *L'impero di Trebisonda*, p. 75. Alfani et al., "Italian Famines," p. 43.

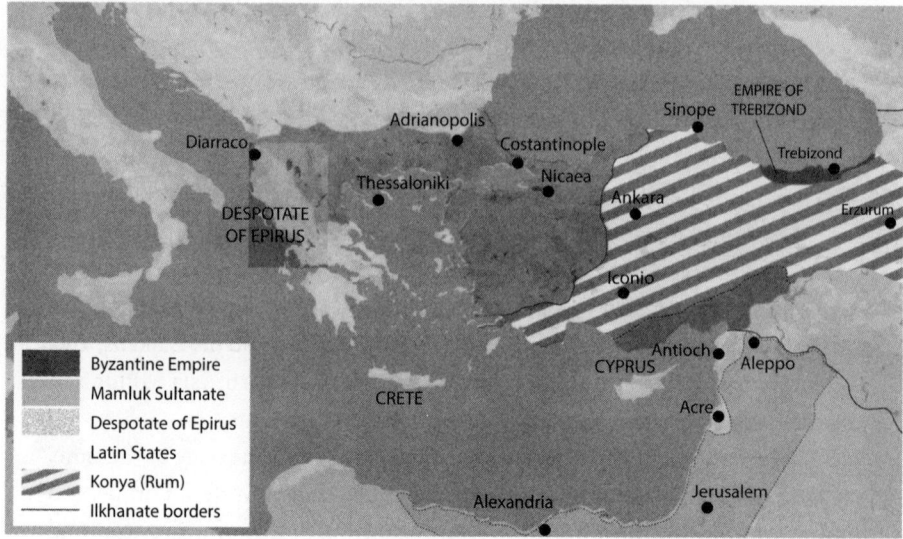

MAP 8. The eastern Mediterranean in the mid-thirteenth century

shortages of grain supplies from the mainland and the Mediterranean colonies—and more importantly, the uncertainties they caused—that drove Venice to seek reliable alternatives. An ideal solution was access to the productive regions bordering the Black Sea, from the plains of the Danube to those of the Dnieper and the Volga. These were now mostly under Mongol rule, yet they had the capacity to save Venice from potential famine, support the city's growth, and grant it independence from political and economic insecurity. Of course, it would be a challenge to set this strategy in motion. Thus, access to the Black Sea became the keystone of Venetian foreign policy. Its success depended not only on developments in the Levantine competition with Byzantium, the western powers, and Genoa, but also on the potential relationship that Venice could forge with the Mongols.

In 1262, Venetian ambassadors reached an agreement with the Prince of Morea, William of Villehardouin, who had long been the vassal of the East Latin Empire and an enemy of Emperor Michael VIII. Villehardouin had been defeated, captured, and imprisoned during the Battle of Pelagonia in 1259.[11] Freed in 1262, he was now eager for revenge. In 1263, after a series of fierce sea skirmishes, the Venetians, with the support of the Principality of Morea,

11. Nicol, *Byzantium and Venice*, pp. 174–6.

clashed with the Byzantine–Genoese fleet near the island of Hydra, in the Saronic Gulf. The Venetian fleet of galleys, commanded by Gilberto Dandolo, gained the upper hand in what would go down in history as the Battle of the Seven Wells.

Venice's victory altered the balance of power and reinvigorated the Byzantine Empire's standpoint; the Ligurian city was no less demanding and intrusive than its rival.[12] If Genoa could not guarantee the empire the military support it needed for a full restoration to its former glory, and if Byzantium was unable to exploit Genoese support to affirm its commercial supremacy in the East, then the resulting imbalance would force Emperor Michael VIII to review the terms of their alliance—or, at the very least, its exclusivity.[13]

Aware of the growing rift in the Byzantine–Genoese alliance,[14] Venice stepped up its diplomatic pressure on Constantinople. In the fall of 1264, negotiations began for a lasting peace treaty, yet these were long and difficult.[15] Venice wanted peaceful cohabitation, but it had no intention of ceding its Levant dominions, as Michael VIII had clear designs on restoring the Aegean to his empire. Despite their diametrically opposed interests, Michael VIII knew that his empire was in a precarious position, as it was still modest in dimensions and resources, not to mention politically weak. Thus, the emperor sought to reduce conflict and protect his borders, rather than risk territorial expansion.

The drafting of the agreement was arduous, but it was eventually signed on June 18, 1265.[16] At first, the Venetian ambassadors—on their own initiative—suggested that the treaty define the alliance as bringing "perpetual peace," yet the Venetian government refused to ratify this declaration, preferring less restrictive wording.[17] The final agreement stated that Venice would renounce any anti-Byzantine initiatives by western powers, and that it pledged to defend the empire in the event of a Genoese attack. In exchange, Venice's territories

12. The Venetians had already defeated the Genoese in Tyre in 1257. Thiriet, *La Romanie vénitienne*, p. 147; Bratianu, "Les origines de la guerre de Curzola," p. 90; Doumerc, "Le dispositif portuaire vénitien (XIIe–XVe siècle)," p. 101.

13. Michael VIII tried to delay the execution of the treaties signed with Genoa in Nif. For more on this topic, see Origone, "Genoa and Byzantium," pp. 46–47.

14. On the shift in relations between Genoa and Michael VIII, see Origone, "Genoa and Byzantium," in particular pp. 46–47.

15. Thiriet, *La Romanie vénitienne*, p. 148.

16. Tafel and Thomas, *Urkunden*, vol. 3, p. 62; Balard, *La Romanie génoise*, pp. 49–50; Nicol, *Byzantium and Venice*, p. 181.

17. Tafel and Thomas, *Urkunden*, vol. 3, p. 62.

in the Aegean were recognized, namely Crete, Negropont, and its fortified possessions in the Morea, notably the ports of Modon and Coron. In all, the agreement meant that Venice would provide limited military support to Byzantium, in exchange for the empire relinquishing its claims on Venetian colonies in the Aegean. However, it was only a temporary truce, not a full-fledged peace agreement.

Venice's goal was to look into the possibility of overthrowing Michael VIII, and restoring Baldwin II (r. 1228–73), the last Latin emperor of Constantinople, deposed in 1261, as he was not only an ally to Venice, but also more easily swayed.[18] The Republic sought the support of Charles I of Anjou (r. 1266–85), signing a pact with him in Viterbo in May 1267.[19] With this agreement, the king of Sicily pledged to recognize the Venetian territories in the Aegean and support the overthrow of the reconstituted Byzantine Empire under Michael VIII and the re-establishment of the Latin Empire in the East under Baldwin II. Venice also pressured Pope Clement IV (r. 1265–68) into supporting a crusade against Michael VIII, declaring him a schismatic enemy of Christianity. However, during this time the political atmosphere had changed due to the rapprochement between the Orthodox and Catholics; Michael VIII had shown he was open to reconciliation, and this reunification of the two churches was also supported by King Louis IX of France. The pope could not support Baldwin II due to his alliance with the then king of Sicily, Manfred (r. 1258–66), an enemy of the papacy. Thus, the Venetians failed to enlist the pope in their anti-Byzantine agenda, and although he did issue an interdiction against Genoa, this move was irrelevant to Venetian plans and was of no consequence to the political balance in Constantinople.[20]

With these setbacks in its ambitious strategy, in 1268 Venice entered a five-year truce with Byzantium and made a non-conflict agreement with Genoa, in which their respective positions and possessions in the Aegean were acknowledged. Via this treaty, the Venetian Doge Ranieri Zeno, who had paid tribute to Michael VIII by calling him *novo Costantino semper augustus*, was granted access to the Black Sea.[21] Venetian merchants could now purchase

---

18. Tafel and Thomas, *Urkunden*, vol. 3, p. 62.

19. Tafel and Thomas, *Urkunden*, vol. 3, pp. 93–100; Thiriet, *La Romanie vénitienne*, p. 149.

20. Balard, *La Romanie génoise*, pp. 47–48. Nicol, *Byzantium and Venice*, p. 180.

21. It is likely that Venice aimed to bring one of its communities back to Sudak, where it had settled in 1253. Balard, *La Romanie génoise*, pp. 113 and 116; Spuler, *Die Goldene Horde*, p. 399; Nystazopoulou, *Hē en tē Taurikē Chersonēsō polis Sougdaia*, p. 30.

grain, provided they did not trade with Byzantium's enemies.[22] However, they were still forbidden access to the Sea of Azov and to land in Tana.[23] Meanwhile, the Genoese settled in Pera, which was destined to become their main overseas trading base until the Ottoman conquest.[24]

While Venice worked on re-establishing good relations with the House of Palaiologos, Byzantine–Genoese relations suffered a setback after several incidents that angered Constantinople, halting Genoese commercial expansion within the empire.[25] The intense diplomatic efforts that had begun in 1272 led to a final treaty being drafted in July 1278; this restored relations between the two states, defining the terms for Genoa's presence in Byzantine territory.[26]

## The Struggle for Access to the Black Sea

Although Venice had gained access to sail east of Constantinople, its position was still weak. After the truce of 1268, both Venice and Genoa had carved out autonomous areas of influence in the eastern Mediterranean.[27] Venice prevailed in the western waters of the Aegean, while Genoa controlled the eastern zone and the straits. This clearly put Venice in an inferior position since the center of trade—particularly the strategic and profitable trade in grain, slaves, and spices—had shifted to the Black Sea ports under Mongol rule. Thus, even though its treaty with Michael VIII had granted Venice tax-free grain exports, Genoa had grabbed the largest market share.[28]

22. Tafel and Thomas, *Urkunden*, vol. 3, pp. 96–98.

23. Cessi, "La tregua fra Venezia e Genova," p. 10; Papacostea, "'Quod non iretur ad Tanam'"; Papacostea, "The Genoese in the Black Sea," p. 19.

24. Balard, *La Romanie génoise*, p. 51.

25. The first incident between Genoa and the empire probably occurred in late 1272 or early 1273, when a Genoese citizen murdered a resident of Constantinople in Galata after a quarrel; another incident was provoked by the Genoese opposition to Michael VIII's decision to cede the rich alum mines in Phocaea to the Zaccaria brothers. Balard, *La Romanie génoise*, p. 53 and Origone, "Questioni tra Bisanzio e Genova," p. 624.

26. Bertolotto and Sanguineti, *Nuova serie di documenti*, p. 507. Balard, *La Romanie génoise*, pp. 52–53. For an analysis of the treaties, see Origone, "Questioni fra Bisanzio e Genova."

27. Venice signed another treaty with Genoa and Pisa on August 22, 1270, which decreed a break in hostilities; see Manfroni, "Relazioni di Genova con Venezia," p. 372.

28. Nevertheless, in March 1278, Venetian authorities brought suit against Michael VIII because some merchants had been taxed by the Byzantine authorities in Eraclea, in direct violation of the accords. Karpov, "The Grain Trade," pp. 58–59.

The papacy was also leaning toward good relations with Byzantium, if only for the purpose of healing the schism between the Catholics and the Orthodox. At the Second Council of Lyon (1272–74), Gregory X (r. 1271–66) achieved such a reunification—albeit briefly. Abaqa Ilkhan (r. 1265–82) had sent a delegation to Lyon that included David of Ashby, chaplain of the papal legate of Palestine, Tommas Agni.[29] The Ilkhanid's openness to an alliance with the Christian West, though it was of no actual consequence, is evidence of the growing closeness and mutual visibility of the two worlds: the Christian and the Mongol. Between these two giants, Venice would attempt to carve out an autonomous position to its own advantage.

This climate of tension between Venice and the Byzantine Empire overshadowed the entire second half of the thirteenth century. It was only interrupted by five-year truces in 1268, 1273, and 1277. In contrast to the Byzantine–Genoese alliance, Venice once more turned to the Angevin Empire, which, as early as 1271, had begun threatening Constantinople again. On July 3, 1281, in Orvieto, the parties signed a pact of collaboration, by which Venice pledged naval assistance to the Angevin army for the conquest of Constantinople.[30] However, the plan was abandoned after the anti-French revolt of the Sicilian Vespers forced the Angevins to leave the island on March 30, 1282.[31] This setback convinced Venice that it was time to give up the idea of restoring the Latin Empire of Constantinople, and to resume relations with the Byzantine Emperor instead.

Meanwhile, the papacy's position radically changed once it was clear that Michael VIII would not honor his pledge to bring the Orthodox Church back to Rome—mainly due to strong internal opposition. Thus, in October 1281, he was excommunicated by Pope Martin IV (r. 1281–85). The loss of papal support and the threat of the Venetian–Angevin alliance made Byzantium even more dependent on Genoa's support. In turn, Genoa played this to obtain near monopolistic privileges, including full rights to navigate the Black Sea. It was now restored to its former position that it had won with the Treaty of Nymphaeum two decades earlier.[32] Venice was weakened by these events. The presence

---

29. To everyone's surprise, some members of the delegation accepted to be baptized. On David Ashby, see Aigle, "The Letters of Eljigidei, Hülegü, and Abaqa," p. 154 and no. 29; Jackson, *The Mongols and the West*, pp. 167–68.

30. Balard, *La Romanie génoise*, p. 53; Thiriet, *La Romanie vénitienne*, p. 152; Tafel and Thomas, *Urkunden*, vol. 3, pp. 287–308.

31. On the Sicilian Vespers, see Benigno and Giarrizzo, *Storia della Sicilia*, vol. 3, and Runciman, *I Vespri Siciliani*.

32. Balard, *La Romanie génoise*, p. 55.

that it had fought so hard for on the Pontic coast—however modest—was now in jeopardy. Combined with problems caused by revolts in Crete and other colonies,[33] it is evident that the struggle for access to the Black Sea would soon enter an even more critical phase.

Meanwhile, Genoa had consolidated its position in Crimea. The regions of the mainland, particularly the area around Caffa, were major grain supply centers. From 1275, the Ligurian authorities had turned the east coast of Crimea into the epicenter of their trade. According to acts drafted in Caffa by the Genoese notary Lamberto di Sambuceto between 1289 and 1290, the Genoese export of various types of grain (wheat, millet, rye) from Crimea to other Black Sea ports totaled over 1,300 tons.[34]

In 1285, Venice signed a new treaty with Michael VIII's successor, Emperor Andronicus II (r. 1282–1328) to renew the privileges of the 1277 truce. This treaty included exemption from all state taxes for Venetian merchants and those they traded with, the restoration of the Venetian quarter in Constantinople to its size before the Fourth Crusade, extraterritorial rights, and the Venetian bailiff's exclusive jurisdiction over the entire area granted to it. The agreement allowed Venice to consolidate its position in the empire's capital and on the straits. Perhaps this is the reason Venice remained neutral while armed conflict erupted between Genoa and Pisa in the early 1280s.[35] The two Tyrrhenian republics warred in the Mediterranean, the final battle occurring in August 1284 just off the Pisan port. The Battle of Meloria saw Genoa destroy the rival fleet, inflicting such a heavy defeat on Pisa that it marked the end of its presence on the international scene.[36]

The Genoese settlement in Crimea and the strengthening of Caffa's position did not discourage Venice's presence in the region. In 1287, the great council of Venice resolved to send a new consul to Sudak, expected to remain in office for one year; he was accompanied by a notary, an assistant (*famulus*), and two horses.[37] We do not know if this was the first such consular appointment, but as

33. Rösch, "Il gran guadagno," pp. 234–35.

34. Balard, *Gênes et l'outre-mer*, vol. 1, nos. 7, 107, 184, 404, 409–12, 417, 419, 423–24, 430, 502, 505, 703; Karpov, "The Grain Trade," pp. 60–61.

35. Venice's ambiguous policies in those years have sparked much interest from scholars in this past century. For further information, see the classics by Canale, *Della Crimea*, vol. 2, and Manfroni, *Storia della marina italiana*, as well as Thiriet, *La Romanie vénitienne*, and Balard, *La Romanie génoise*. For a more recent overview, see Karpov, "The Black Sea Region," pp. 285–94.

36. Ceccarelli Lemut, "Pisa nel Mediterraneo durante il XIII secolo."

37. Canale, *Della Crimea*, vol. 2, p. 441.

this official was referred to as the "consul of Gazeria,"[38] it is likely that Sudak was the main Venetian base in Crimea in the late 1280s. Indeed, the presence of a consul suggests a stable settlement, routinely frequented by merchants, such as the Polo family, who had a *fondaco* in the city of Crimea.[39] In a resolution dated April 1287, the official was given a salary of 100 lire, plus 50 lire and 20 *soldi* to pay his notary. When his post ended in April 1288, the consul received a salary of 100 lire, yet the fee allowance to pay his retinue was doubled from one to two *famuli*.[40]

During this time, Venetian expansion to eastern markets was also facilitated by the minting of high-value currency that had a wider international circulation (see more on this in chapter 10). The 1280s saw the steady growth of Venice's economy, and in 1284, city authorities decided to mint a new gold coin: the ducat. Genoa and Florence had already minted their own gold coins since 1252, the *genovino* and the *fiorino*, respectively. In the second half of the thirteenth century, Venice was also committed to expanding its presence in northern European markets, particularly in the Baltic states and Germany. Proof of this effort lies in the sheer size of the Fondaco dei Tedeschi on the Grand Canal: conceived between 1222 and 1225 as a center for metal import, this warehouse developed and grew throughout the end of the century.[41]

In the Baltic region, better equipped cities were opening to the international market, exporting products in high demand in Europe, such as furs, wax, copper, and iron. Northern European merchants exploited these Baltic trade routes and their ancient ties with Russian cities like Novgorod to procure luxury goods, especially spices and silk, via the cities of Lviv and Thorn.[42] Thus, in addition to being a source of grain supplies, Sudak took on an important role in northern imports from Rus'.[43] Throughout the thirteenth century,

---

38. Gazaria (or Gazeria) is the Genoese name for Crimea after the Treaty of Nymphaeum. The term stems from the khanate of the Khazars, who, from the seventh century, controlled a vast territory, ranging from the Dnieper to the west to the Aral Sea in the east, including the peninsula of Crimea, with the exception of the Chersonesus, tenaciously preserved by the Byzantine Empire. See Pubblici, *Cumani*, pp. 67–75.

39. Polo, *Il Milione*, ed. Ronchi and Segre, 2.2 and 2.3, pp. 4–6.

40. Canale, *Della Crimea*, vol. 2, p. 441; *Deliberazioni del Maggior Consiglio*, vol. 3, p. 201. These conditions were confirmed a year later, as recorded in a resolution of the Great Council dated May 1290 (*Deliberazioni del Maggior Consiglio*, vol. 3, p. 261).

41. Barbon, "I segni dei mercanti a Venezia."

42. Martin, *Treasure of the Land of Darkness*, pp. 61ff.

43. Jahnke, "The Baltic Trade," p. 201.

Venice remained the key nexus for distribution and trade, despite the fact that Venetian merchants were a rare presence in the trading circuits of northern Europe. There are few sources that mention Venetian traders at markets in the French Champagne region, indicating the eastward shift of the Republic's economic and commercial interests.

For all these reasons, the Black Sea remained the subject of intense competition and growing tensions. Genoa fiercely continued to oppose Venetian advancement in Crimea. Yet, Venice could neither forgo defending the strongholds that it had established—however weak—nor could it retreat. In 1293, the Venetian Republic began forging a network of alliances to encircle its rival, by seeking support from the papacy, the Byzantine Emperor, the Mamluks, the kingdom of Cyprus, and of Bulgaria, where the Venetians already held a strategic hub in the port of Mesembria.[44]

Genoa's move was to approach the Ilkhanate. Between April and May 1290, a Genoese ship, armed by Vivaldo Lavaggio on behalf of Arghun Ilkhan, sailed to northern Pontus, between the Kerch Strait and Ciscaucasia, to recover goods that had been stolen by pirates from Armenian merchants operating in Caffa.[45] During those same months, Pietro de Braino (as mentioned toward the end of chapter 2) was at the court of Arghun.[46] Furthermore, Arghun's Minister of Finance, Saad-Ad-daula (d. 1291) was fully aware of the Mongol army's limitations in seafaring, and thus summoned Genoese builders to Baghdad to build two galleys for the battle against the Mamluk naval blockade in the Gulf of Aden, the main port linking the north coast of Africa and the Indian Ocean.[47] It is likely that the Genoese naval assistance for the Ilkhanate was intended to patrol the eastern coastline of the Black Sea, from the Kerch Strait to the southern Caucasus—an area exposed to Jöchid raids.

The Venetian–Genoese rivalry intensified in the 1290s, coming to a head with armed conflict in 1294 with the Second Venetian–Genoese War. Cities of the Venetian and Lombard mainland, such as Mantua, that were under Venice's direct control, paid an extra customs duty for goods transiting through

44. Delegations were organized for each of these destinations. Giomo, "Regesto dei Misti del Senato," p. 134.

45. Bratianu, "Les origines de la guerre de Curzola," p. 94; Paviot, "Les marchands italiens," pp. 83–84.

46. Bratianu, "Les origines de la guerre de Curzola," p. 94; Ciocîltan, The Mongols and the Black Sea Trade, p. 158.

47. Bratianu, "Les origines de la guerre de Curzola," p. 94; Bratianu, Recherches sur le commerce génois, p. 257; Richard, "An Account of the Battle of Hattin," p. 174.

the city to contribute to the war effort.[48] A first skirmish between the Genoese and Venetian fleets took place off the island of Coron in 1293, but the first real battle was fought by the port of Ayas in 1294, in which the Genoese attacked the Venetian fleet, inflicting substantial damage.[49] On July 22, 1296, the Venetian counterattack saw the Genoese quarter of Pera set ablaze. The Genoese reaction was swift: all Venetians living in Constantinople were slaughtered.[50] Emperor Andronicus now found himself embroiled in a war he had not wanted but had been unable to avoid.

The Black Sea was not spared. In 1295, after devastating Focea, a Venetian fleet under order of Admiral Giovanni Soranzo (d. 1328) attacked and pillaged Caffa. However, the reckoning between Genoa and Venice took place on the Adriatic Sea, near the island of Curzola on September 8, 1298. The Venetian fleet suffered a heavy defeat despite outnumbering the Genoese armada, with ninety ships to Genoa's eighty. Most Venetian galleys were sunk in battle and eighteen captured. Loss of life was great on both sides. Now too exhausted for a protracted war, on September 22, 1299, the two cities signed a peace treaty in Milan under the mediation of Charles II of Anjou, Pope Boniface VIII, and Matteo I Visconti, the *capitano del popolo* of Milan.[51] The treaty stated that all prisoners of war would be released, damages compensated for, and the spheres of influence clearly defined—without the Byzantine Emperor being able to change the terms of the agreement (*nec Imperatori aliquid peti possit*). To avoid a new *casus belli*, any individual act of hostility would be judged as such, rather than as a state's political act of aggression. Genoa pledged not to intervene in the conflict between Venice and the Byzantine Empire in the waters of the Adriatic Sea.[52] To the same extent, Venice pledged not to intervene in the event of war between Genoa and Pisa.

1299's peace of Milan marked the beginning of a new phase in the Venetian–Genoese rivalry. Despite its defeat, Venice could once again cross the straits, enter the Black Sea, and defend its territories.[53] On the other hand, Genoa had no intention of giving up its supremacy on the Black Sea. The Byzantine

48. Giomo, *Libri commemoriali*, vol. 1, no. 21, p. 8.

49. Ciocîltan, *The Mongols and the Black Sea Trade*, p. 160; Bratianu, "Les origines de la guerre de Curzola," p. 94.

50. Balard, *La Romanie génoise*, p. 60.

51. Tafel and Thomas, *Urkunden*, vol. 3, no. 390, pp. 391–92.

52. "Quod durante guerra, quam Veneti habent cum Imperatore Grecorum, Januenses non possint navigare ad aliquam terram, quam teneat Imperator intra Culfum." Tafel and Thomas, *Urkunden*, vol. 3, no. 390, p. 391.

53. Papacostea, "The Genoese in the Black Sea," pp. 20–21.

Emperor Andronicus II, who was excluded from the peace negotiations, refused to recognize the treaty, therefore continuing hostilities between Constantinople and Venice. These years saw constant sabotage and piracy on Venetian ships in the Aegean, up to October 1302, when, after long and difficult negotiations, the two states signed a truce. After significant resistance by the emperor, he finally ratified the truce in March of the following year.

## Political Developments in the Mongol Empire

### The Ilkhanate

From 1260 to 1300, relations between the Golden Horde and the Ilkhanate were marked by constant hostility. Various internal factors were at play for the two dynasties, alongside alliances in which all European and Asian powers intervened at different levels. The years after the establishment of the Ilkhanate were especially turbulent. In February 1265, the Ilkhan Hülegü died and was succeeded by his son Abaqa (1234–82). To take advantage of the dynastic transition, the Jöchid Berke Khan launched an offensive in the Caucasus, led by General Nogaï. However, he was defeated by the Ilkhanid army, commanded by Abaqa's brother, Yoshmut.[54] The war continued for some months, until 1266: Berke Khan died under mysterious circumstances. The war came to an end, and Abaqa secured the border on the Caucasus line, leaving a permanent military garrison for its defense.

Meanwhile, a new threat loomed in the east, this time triggered by aggression from Baraq (d. 1271), khan of the Chagatai *ulus*. In the spring and summer of 1270, his army crossed the Amu Darya but was soundly defeated by Abaqa near Herat.[55] To the west, in 1277, the death of the powerful Mamluk sultan Baybars in Damascus prompted Abaqa to launch a diplomatic offensive. Although he aimed to bring western powers on his side to isolate his Mamluk enemies, the maneuver turned out to be a failure.[56] Meanwhile, the ilkhan continued exerting military pressure, carrying out raids in Syria in 1280. Baybars's successor, Sultan al-Mansur Qalawun (r. 1279–90), defeated the Ilkhanid army in the Second Battle of Homs in 1281, thus strengthening the Mamluks' position.[57]

---

54. Amitai-Preiss, *Mongols and Mamluks*, p. 87.
55. Amitai-Preiss, *Mongols and Mamluks*, p. 88.
56. Amitai-Preiss, *Mongols and Mamluks*, pp. 103–5; Jackson, *The Mongols and the West*, p. 168.
57. Amitai-Preiss, *Mongols and Mamluks*, pp. 187–201.

Abaqa died in 1282, and was succeeded by his brother, Tegüder (also named by sources as Ahmad), who was converted to Islam. During his short reign (1282–84), it seemed as though relations between the Ilkhanate and the Mamluks could be defused. Tegüder proposed an alliance with Sultan Qalawun in the name of their common faith; however, his letter struck the wrong tone for a reconciliation and negotiations never got off the ground.[58] Tegüder was assassinated by his nephew in 1284; Arghun (r. 1284–91) then claimed the throne for himself. A Mongol traditionalist who had not converted to Islam, Arghun restored contact with the papacy and the kingdoms of Latin Europe. In all, the ilkhan sent four diplomatic missions to the west: in 1285, 1287, 1289–90, and the last in the summer of 1290.[59]

Relations with the Ilkhanate were essential to Venice's strategy to access Black Sea markets and reach Asian trade routes. Within this network, the cities of the Ilkhanate were crucial hubs: all the main caravan routes left from Tabriz to reach central Asia, the Caucasus, Asia Minor, and the Palestinian coastline. In Arghun's letter to Pope Honorius IV in 1285, three Venetians are listed as interpreters to the ilkhan.[60] In 1286, there is evidence of other Venetians present in the ilkhan's court: Pietro Viadro and Simeone Avventurato, who both brought precious gifts (though received little in return).[61] Nevertheless, the Venetian presence within Ilkhanate borders was still sporadic and only the result of individual efforts.

In 1289, the Mamluk Sultan Qalawun conquered Tripoli. That same year, the Golden Horde and the Ilkhanate once again went to war with each other. This time the aggressor was Nogaï, the Mongol general and commander of the Jöchid army, who invaded his southern rival by attempting to cross the Derbent Pass, near the western coast of the Caspian Sea. The Ilkhanid army confronted Nogaï near the Karasu River (western Euphrates) on May 11, 1290,

58. Jackson, *The Mongols and the West*, pp. 168–69.

59. The second of these missions is recorded in the remarkable memoirs of the Nestorian monk Rabban Sauma, who visited Pope Nicholas IV in 1288, as well as King Philip IV of France and Edward I of England. Jackson, *The Mongols and the West*, p. 169.

60. These were Pietro da Molin, Gerardo da Ca' Turco, and Giorgio Zuffo. The Latin version of the letter was published in Lupprian, *Die Beziehungen der Päpste*, pp. 245–46. See also Morozzo della Rocca, "Sulle orme di Marco Polo," p. 120. For an analysis of the correspondence between the Mongol ruling class and the papacy, see Aigle, "The Letters of Eljigidei, Hülegü, and Abaqa."

61. Petech, "Les marchands italiens," p. 562; Morozzo della Rocca, *Fonti per la storia del commercio veneziano*, p. 120; Paviot, "Les marchands italiens," p. 74. On September 6, 1307, Simone Avventurato is said to have been a Venetian bailiff in Famagosta. He is likely the same person (Giomo, *Libri commemoriali*, vol. 1, p. 78).

inflicting a heavy defeat.[62] On May 18 of the following year, Acre fell into the hands of Qalawun's successor, al-Ashraf Khalil (1262–93), with the aid of the Genoese.[63] The fall of Acre had grave consequences, as it was the nerve center of the Venetian trade system in the eastern Mediterranean. Its defeat closed the most important access point to Venice's Asian routes. A further blow to Venice's relations with the Islamic East was the papal ban on conducting trade with the Mamluks.[64] However, the Mongol conquest did open new and viable alternatives to the routes that had been closed by the expulsion of westerners from Palestine—making it necessary to access the Black Sea.[65]

Venice's gradual opening to Mongol Persia must be understood within this complex geopolitical framework. Venetian diarist and historian Marin Sanudo pointed out that the ilkhan was a natural ally of the Latin crusaders, as he was a "sworn enemy of the sultan and of the khan of the Tatars of the North."[66] Even though political relations with the Ilkhanate were not a part of formal diplomatic initiatives, from the late thirteenth century onward, Venice sought a dialogue with the Mongols. It is evident that a Venetian merchant community was established in Tabriz in 1305, although the city's conversion to Islam by Ghazan Ilkhan (1271–1304) had made it difficult for western traders to settle in Mongol Persia.[67] After his death in 1304, Ghazan was succeeded by his stepbrother Oljeitu, who was far more tolerant. In 1306, Oljeitu sent a diplomatic mission to Venice, granting the Republic's merchants protection and freedom of movement (*vadant et veniant salvi et secure*) in Tabriz and throughout the Ilkhanate; these rights were extended to Venice's citizens (*vestri mercatores et vestra gens*).[68] Via this same measure, Venetian merchants had all their financial debts pardoned within the kingdom's territory,[69] and Venetian authorities were allowed a bailiff with a

62. Bratianu, "Les origines de la guerre de Curzola," p. 97.

63. On the 1290 truce between Genoa and the sultanate, see Bauden, "Mamluk Diplomatics," p. 85; Holt, "The Mamluk Institution." See also Holt, *Early Mamluk Diplomacy*, pp. 92 and 146–51; Ciocîltan, *The Mongols and the Black Sea Trade*, p. 85 and no. 114.

64. Jacoby, "The Supply of War Materials to Egypt"; Karpov, "The Black Sea Region," p. 286.

65. Ciocîltan, *The Mongols and the Black Sea Trade*, p. 160.

66. Bratianu, "Les origines de la guerre de Curzola," p. 97.

67. Lane, *Early Mongol Rule*, p. 57.

68. *Diplomatarium veneto-levantinum*, vol. 1, p. 47: "exemplum privilegii quod nuncius domini Tartari portavit . . . illustri domino duci Venetiarum."

69. *Diplomatarium veneto-levantinum*, vol. 1, p. 47: "ne propter aliquod ebitum, ne propter aliquam rem retroactam hinc inde nemo possit vobis petere aliquid, ne dare brigam de ulla re: et ita est meum preceptum."

military garrison in Tabriz.[70] Finally—just like Genoa—Venice could boast its own permanent consul in the capital of the Ilkhanate.

## The Jöchi Ulus

The rift between western Christianity and the Mamluk Sultanate had made Middle Eastern routes impassable; thus, the Pontic region was now the prime destination for access to impracticable Middle Eastern routes.[71] This was in the Jöchid *ulus*, which was firmly under the rule of Toqta (r. 1291–1312) and which extended from the northern basin of the Black Sea to the central Asian steppe, being a necessary link for European mercantile states. After supporting Nogaï, who had been defeated by Toqta, Venice sought to smooth over its relations with the new khan of the Golden Horde to garner a permanent settlement on the Black Sea.

The 1280s had seen a major political shift within the Golden Horde's ruling class. In 1283, the new Jöchid khan Töde-Möngke (r. 1280–87; successor to Möngke Temür), once again approached Kublai after decades of latent conflict caused by the struggle for the throne of Karakorum in 1260. It signaled a truce between the Ilkhanate and the Jöchids.[72] The pause in hostilities with the Ilkhanate gave the Jöchid ruling class the energy it needed to organize an invasion of eastern Europe in the 1280s.[73] New campaigns of conquests and military successes often altered the balance of power within Mongol aristocracy; by the end of that decade, war erupted over the succession of Möngke Temür. On one side was Nogaï, the head of the Jöchid *ulus* right wing, who had settled on the Danube, declaring his independence from Sarai. On the other side was the reigning khan, Talabuga (or Tole-Buqa, r. 1287–90), great-grandson of Batu. Nogaï prevailed, and installed Möngke Timür's son and his own cousin, Toqta, on the throne, thus maintaining his sphere of influence independent of Sarai in the western region of the Golden Horde, between the Dnieper and Danube Rivers.[74]

70. *Diplomatarium veneto-levantinum*, vol. 1, pp. 47–48.

71. On the pope's reaction to the Mamluk conquest of Acre, see Ashtor, *Levant Trade*, pp. 42–46; Ortalli, "Venice and Papal Bans"; Jacoby, "L'expansion occidentale."

72. Tegüder's letter to Qulawun of 1283 underscores the renewed unity among all the Mongols. Jackson, *The Mongols and the West*, p. 198 and no. 11.

73. Jackson, *The Mongols and the West*, pp. 198–99.

74. See Atwood, *Encyclopedia*, pp. 79 and 206.

Möngke Temür had allowed the Genoese to settle in Caffa, their first consular presence dating back to 1284.[75] In addition, he had stabilized relations with the Chagatai khanate and continued Berke's policy of alliance with the Mamluk Sultanate—all while continuing contact with the Latins. Strife within the Golden Horde forced Venice and Genoa to take sides, in the hopes that the chosen faction would gain the upper hand. Venice supported Nogaï, which later led to frictions with Toqta. Genoa, though in favor politically, was unable to exploit its advantage, and ran into conflict with the khan in later years, as we shall see.

In 1291, the Venetian senate sent an envoy to Nogaï, whom the sources name *imperator noqa*.[76] Unfortunately, no records of this mission have survived, and therefore we cannot say for certain what relations emerged between Venice and Nogaï. Nonetheless, if we consider that Venice's aim was to replace Genoa as the prime trading partner to the Golden Horde, we can hypothesize that the envoy was sent with a request for the grant of land to settle on, as well as tax advantages, and perhaps even an alliance against the Genoese in Caffa. We can assume that this diplomatic mission used Genoa's traditional alliance with the Ilkhanate as leverage. In any case, the envoy's strategic goal was to strengthen the Venetian presence in Crimea, at that time under Nogaï's control.[77]

A direct descendant of Jöchi, and nephew to Berke, Nogaï had distinguished himself as the commander of the Jöchid army in the war against the Ilkhanate. Previously, Batu had passed on to him direct control of the Golden Horde's most western portion—the region roughly corresponds to today's Romania, Bulgaria, Moldavia, and Ukraine—essentially, all the lands between the Don and the Danube rivers. Later, a somewhat less extensive territory,

75. Ciocîltan, *The Mongols and the Black Sea Trade*, pp. 156–57.

76. This document, dated April 15, 1291, states: "Capta fuit pars quod ambaxator iturus ad imperatorem noga debeat habere equos dcem et imperperos IIII in die pro expensis et si avanzarent deveniant in Cumune": Manfroni, "Relazioni di Genova con Venezia," p. 384. Although he was a nobleman, a general, and cousin of Toqta, Nogaï was not the khan elected by the Golden Horde, and yet he was the most influential person among the Jöchids in that time. For more on Nogaï and Toqta, see Uzelac, "Echoes of the Conflict"; Bratianu, *Recherches sur le commerce génois*, pp. 256–57; Ciocîltan, *The Mongols and the Black Sea Trade*, p. 160.

77. Bratianu, "Les origines de la guerre de Curzola," p. 93. The Venetian delegation to Nogaï on April 15, 1291, was preceded five days earlier by instructions from the senate to the envoys. These included the proposal to install a consulate in Crimea. The consul should remain at his post for three years, with an annual salary of 400 *hyperpyrons*, with a servant, three horses, and a notary priest. Manfroni, "Relazioni di Genova con Venezia," pp. 384–85 and no. 3.

from the Dnieper to the lower course of the Danube, became Nogaï's economic and political base, and he exercised sovereign control over it. Although he never proposed himself as khan of the Golden Horde, Nogaï did, in fact, have enormous power, with direct influence over the politics of the state.

When Möngke Temür died, his legacy naturally passed to his successor, Tode-Möngke. However, he proved to be a weak and inefficient monarch. In 1284–85, Nogaï and Talabuga invaded Hungary once more, but the expedition was met with fierce resistance, with the Mongols defeated. In 1287, Nogaï forced Tode-Möngke to cede his crown to his nephew, Talabuga. However, Nogaï did not give up any of his own power—in fact, he increased it. During this period of co-regency, Nogaï forged several relationships with foreign states, thereby boasting his sovereign prerogative. Talabuga resented his power; the resulting struggle ended with Nogaï capturing his nephew and delivering him to his enemy, Toqta, who executed him in 1291.

To better define and expand their respective areas of influence, the two Mongol leaders, Toqta and Nogaï, interfered in the internal affairs of their neighbors (both the Balkans and the Rus' principalities) by supporting one or the other faction according to their own convenience. Nogaï's aim was to keep an iron hold on his political privileges and weight. Toqta, however, saw this as a way to exercise his legitimate power as sovereign of the Golden Horde. Between late 1293 and the beginning of 1294, Toqta Khan asserted his authority over the principalities of northern Rus', rescinding the privileges enjoyed by the local aristocracy (both Rus' and Mongol) who were loyal to Nogaï.[78] In a clear challenge to Toqta's imperial power, Nogaï began having coins minted that featured his likeness (at least from 1296). The move was considered a declaration of war, and soon the two sides faced each other in battle. The first clash took place in 1297 on the Aksai River, near the delta of the Don; Nogaï emerged victorious and decided to extend his control to the trade bases in Crimea.[79]

---

78. Uzelac, "Echoes of the Conflict," p. 511; Veselovskij, *Trudy po istorii Zolotoj Ordy*, pp. 120–25.

79. A great deal has been written about the war between Nogaï and Toqta. The most recent works include Uzelac, "Echoes of the Conflict"; Mys'kov, *Političeskaja istorija*, pp. 131–41; Veselovskij, *Trudy po istorii Zolotoj Ordy*, pp. 177–84; Počekaev, *Tsari ordynskie*, pp. 65–71; Sabitov, "Voennoe protivostojanie." The most reliable source on the conflict is the Mamluk historian al-Manṣūrī, in Tiesenhausen, *Sbornik*, vol. 1, pp. 110–19 and 122–23. A further—albeit less accurate—reference on the succession of the events is *Rashiduddin Fazlullah's Jami'ü't-Tawarikh—Compendium of Chronicles*, pp. 257–59 and 441.

In late 1298 (or early 1299), Nogaï attacked and conquered Sudak.[80] Next, he set his sights on Caffa, which was besieged, raided, and set ablaze.[81] He justified the attack on Caffa as retribution for the murder by the Genoese of one of his nephews who had been sent to the city to collect taxes.[82] Despite this incident triggering his attack, a probable underlying cause was Nogaï's intention to take possession of Crimea's ports, colonized by the Genoese. There are no sources that confirm the existence of a formal contract between Venice and Nogaï, but—if we consider the aforementioned envoy and their strategic convergence—there was most likely an agreement to weaken Genoa's position.

Following the battle on the Aksai River, the tide turned in Toqta's favor. Nogaï could no longer rely on support from the military aristocracy, and thus sought help from Ghazan of the Ilkhanate; a Muslim like him, Ghazan was also an enemy of Toqta.[83] However, rather than accept Nogaï's offer, Ghazan entered into an agreement with the Jöchid khan, promising not to intervene in the Golden Horde's internal affairs.[84] Another possible reason for Ghazan's decision was an intervention by Genoa, which was the ilkhan's necessary trading partner, and which had suffered under Nogaï's attack in Crimea.

80. Tiesenhausen, *Sbornik*, vol. 1, p. 184; Ciocîltan, *The Mongols and the Black Sea Trade*, p. 161 and no. 79.

81. It is unclear which sector of the city Nogaï actually conquered. The available documents suggest that the Genoese emerged unscathed by the Mongol attack, perhaps because they had already fortified a substantial part of their settlement. Nonetheless, there is some doubt on the exact sequence of events, which has still not been resolved. Tiesenhausen, *Sbornik*, vol. 1, pp. 101, 153 and 272–73.

82. Uzelac, "Echoes of the Conflict," p. 510; Ciocîltan, *The Mongols and the Black Sea Trade*, p. 162.

83. From this perspective, of particular interest is the brief mention made by the Lucchese Bishop Tolomeo of the conflict between the two Mongol leaders in *Historia ecclesiastica*. He describes Emperor "Theca" as a good man and a friend of Christians, and the Emperor "Nocha" as an evil, destructive pagan. Tholomeus von Lucca, *Historia ecclesiastica nova*, p. 234. See also Spinei, "Les Mongols dans Historia Ecclesiastica Nova" and Uzelac, "Echoes of the Conflict," p. 514. In his correspondence with the pope, Giovanni da Montecorvino also wrote on several occasions that Toqta was a friend of Christians, and that the safest road to Cathay was that controlled by the khans. Rubruc, *Itinerarium*, in *Sinica Franciscana*, vol. 1, pp. 349 and 351.

84. Uzelac, "Echoes of the Conflict," p. 511; Tiesenhausen, *Sbornik*, vol. 1, p. 196. According to Rashid ad-Din, Ghazan affirmed that he would intervene between the two of them to *non trarre vantaggio dalla situazione* (so as not to take advantage of the situation), recommending peace. To prove his intentions, he "did not spend the winter in Arran, but rather in Baghdad and Diyabekir": *Rashiduddin Fazlullah's Jami'ü't-Tawarikh—Compendium of Chronicles*, pp. 258–59.

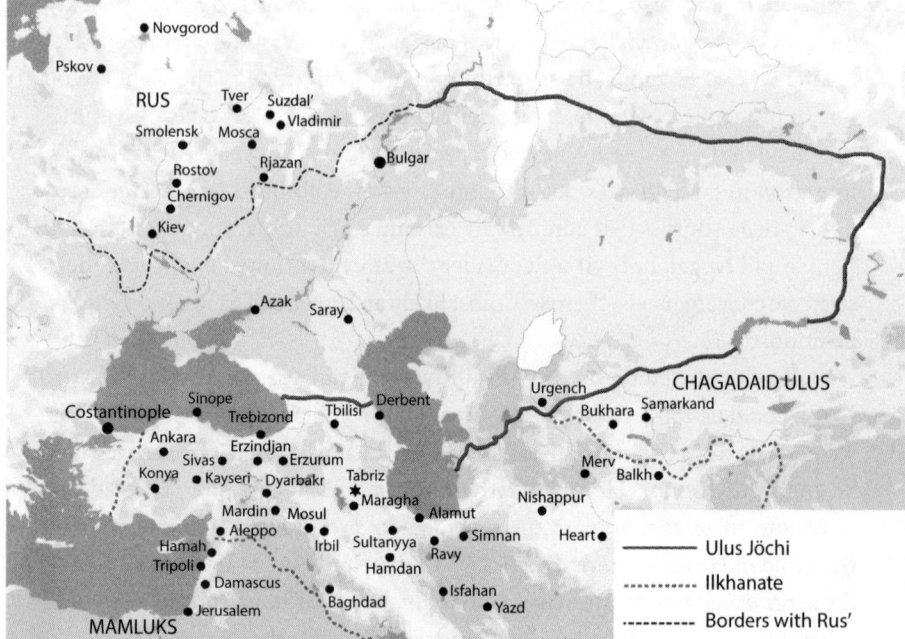

MAP 9. The Jöchi *ulus* or Golden Horde and the Ilkhanate
at the end of the thirteenth century

At the turn of the century, Toqta and Nogaï reached a final reckoning. Their armies clashed in the fall of 1298 on the lower course of the Don, while Nogaï was still engaged in Crimea. The decisive battle came late in 1299 and continued into the following year, held on the plains of Kukanlyk, at the mouth of the Dniester River.[85] Here, Nogaï met his fate: taken prisoner by a Rus' contingent of Toqta's army, he was executed on the spot by a common soldier.[86]

The end of the civil war did not bring about a stabilization of the Golden Horde's politics. Pockets of resistance continued for at least two years, particularly in the Balkans along the course of the Danube, where Nogaï's son, Chaka (d. 1300), was in command, with many men still loyal to the cause.[87] The conflict

85. Perhaps in the Odessa region, on the banks of a tributary of the Dniester, the Kogilnikin. See Uzelac, "Echoes of the Conflict," p. 512 and "War and Peace in the Pontic Steppes," p. 66.

86. Uzelac, "War and Peace in the Pontic Steppes," p. 66; Tiesenhausen, *Sbornik*, vol. 1, pp. 113–15 and 122; *Rashiduddin Fazlullah's Jami'ü't-Tawarikh—Compendium of Chronicles*, p. 258.

87. In the wake of Nogaï's defeat, the three children of the Mongol *noyon* clashed over whether to continue fighting Toqta or to accept his authority. The conflict continued for over a year, until,

had wreaked havoc on the Pontic region's economy, causing extensive suffering on the populations between the Dnieper and Danube rivers. Genoa and Venice found themselves juggling the Horde's erratic politics to maintain their positions in the northern and eastern Black Sea, as well as on the banks of the Danube.

### Venice, Genoa, and the Mongols on the Black Sea and in Persia in the Early Fourteenth Century

Amid the vast network of relationships between the dominant powers of the eastern Mediterranean and the Black Sea, the rivalry between the two Italian republics continued to roil. Such is the context for the peace treaty between Venice and the Byzantine Emperor Andronicus II in 1302. In the early fourteenth century, Venice had pacified its most restless colonies in the Aegean, and had stabilized its relations with Byzantium and Genoa. Finally, the Republic could focus on exploring beyond the straits. Venice's desire and need to establish itself as the center of international routes prompted its authorities to promote new diplomatic efforts with the Golden Horde. Its primary goal was to secure a foothold in Tana at the mouth of the Don River.

Tana, a part of the populous city of Azaq, owed its commercial success both to the wealth of local production and to its role as a terminus for goods coming from central Asia and the northern regions of Rus' (which roughly corresponds to modern-day Ukraine, Belarus, and European Russia). These goods were then distributed to western and north African markets.[88] The archives of the aforementioned Genoese notary Lamberto di Sambuceto, who lived in Caffa between April 23, 1289 and August 12, 1290, is one of the main sources to illustrate the city's activities on the Sea of Azov.[89] In this time, the notary drew up 133 *commenda* contracts out of a total of 903, and an additional 54 contracts pertained to *commenda* that had been concluded earlier.[90] These figures—albeit related to a single notary and a limited period—show that trade between Caffa and Tana totaled 340,354 aspers (almost 7,500 ducats).[91]

---

between the end of 1300 and the beginning of the following year, the khan sent an army to repress the forces of the firstborn Chaka. Uzelac, "War and Peace in the Pontic Steppes," pp. 67–68.

88. Balard, *La Romanie génoise*, p. 151.

89. Balard, *Gênes et l'outre-mer*, vol. 1, p. 68, no. 376.

90. Balard, *Gênes et l'outre-mer*, vol. 1, p. 36.

91. Karpov, "Black Sea and the Crisis of the Mid XIVth century," pp. 71–72; Balard, *La Romanie génoise*, p. 853.

This is the largest volume of trade ever mentioned in documents regarding the Pontic commercial centers.[92] While sources attest to the presence of Latin merchants in Tana, they do not establish the actual scope and size of the settlement's population.

In Tana—as throughout the entire Black Sea basin—beyond conflicts and diplomatic efforts, it was, in fact, individual travelers and merchants who dictated the pace of Venetian expansion. Often acting independently and anticipating state initiatives, they took advantage of the spaces created by Mongol governments and were unrestrained by diplomatic protocols. In other words, toward the end of the thirteenth century, Venetian expansion mirrored Genoa's in that the "flag followed the trade": commercial interests led state policies and the gradual establishment of colonies.

It is worth noting that Latin Christendom had little sway over the Mongols in terms of culture or religion. Instead, Mongol courts absorbed elements of Islamic and Chinese culture, converted to Islam in the Golden Horde and the Ilkhanate, and to Buddhism in China. Europe had no significant impact on the Mongol elites, who were primarily drawn to and influenced by Asian civilizations and religions.[93] It was trade that helped Europeans gain increasing influence in the Mongol Empire. International trade was the primary economic resource for the khanates facing the West, and it would not have been possible without the development of merchant colonies on the Black Sea. These acted as crucial hubs for a more extensive trading network that spanned the whole Eurasian continent.

Mongol diplomacy made no differentiation between the various European states and monarchies. Although the Mongols drafted treaties with different political entities, they rarely took interest in their rivalries and disputes. Diplomatic correspondence tells us that the intricate political relationships between European states seemed impenetrable even to a people accustomed to tribal divisions and intense interethnic conflicts. A prime example was the ongoing tension between Genoa and Venice, which featured prominently in diplomatic relations with the Mongols, since Venice repeatedly sought protection from violence at the hands of the Genoese. However, while the Mongols acknowledged their differences, they simply maintained equidistant relationships. At other times, the Mongol reaction to alleged violations affected both

92. These notarial acts have been previously published by G. I. Bratianu (*Actes des notaires génois*) and then again, in a complete version, by M. Balard (*Gênes et l'outre-mer*).

93. DeWeese, *Islamization and Native Religion*, pp. 81–90.

republics, regardless of whether the Venetians or the Genoese were at fault. This had tangible consequences, especially in legal terms. If a "Frank" committed a violation, the Mongols punished the entire Latin community, regardless of citizenship. Although one might expect this to foster a spirit of coalition and aligned interests among Latins operating on the Black Sea, and despite frequent calls by the two doges for Christian solidarity, the spirit of competition was stronger than any impetus for unity. Moreover, these tensions were often the result of broader conflicts outside the Pontus, which reverberated at the local level for the two cities. Conversely, conflicts arising in the Black Sea spilled over to other arenas. That said, notwithstanding the republics' mutual hostility, there is evidence of trade agreements and transactions between the Genoese and Venetians.

The experiences of the Polo brothers exemplify the open-minded attitude held by the Mongols toward foreign merchants, yet they were not an isolated case. Other Europeans had preceded them, albeit with different methods and intentions.[94] Some Venetians exploited the southern route, particularly the ports in the Middle East. They were active in Tabriz from the early 1260s, around the same time as the arrival of Hülegü. In December 1263, a Venetian merchant, Pietro Vilioni, drew up a will in Tabriz,[95] which provides at least two important facts: the absence of other Venetians among the deed's witnesses, and the significant commercial activity of Vilioni himself.[96] We can assume that Tabriz in 1263 had no settled Venetian community, yet merchants passing through to the East benefited from the presence of other established Italian communities, such as the Genoese or Tuscans, as can be inferred from the document's Pisan and Lucchese linguistic characteristics.[97]

94. Morozzo della Rocca, *Fonti per la storia del commercio*, p. 120. The first was the Hungarian Dominican friar Giuliano who traveled to Rus' via the Volga, in 1235, just before the Mongol invasion: Sinor, "Un voyageur du treizième siècle." The missions of John of Plano Carpini in 1245 (Pian del Carpine, *Storia dei Mongoli*) and William of Rubruk in 1253 (Rubruk, *Viaggio in Mongolia*) are more famous.

95. Pietro Vilioni's will was published for the first time by Cecchetti, "Testamento di Pietro Vioni." Stussi, "Un testamento volgare." The document is currently held in the collection of the Procuratori di San Marco of the Venetian Archivio di Stato. See also Jacoby, *Medieval Trade*, pp. 131 and 159.

96. Also noted by Morozzo Della Rocca, *Fonti per la storia del commercio*, p. 120.

97. Müller, *Documenti sulle relazioni delle città toscane*, pp. 95–107; Malanima, "Pisa and the Trade Routes." Tabriz, like the entire eastern sector of Mesopotamia, attracted the commercial flow rerouted there after the Mongol conquest of Baghdad in 1258.

Vilioni traveled with a substantial amount of precious goods entrusted to him by his compatriots. Crystals, gemstones, pearls, silver, chessboards, a saddle "wrought in crystal," and "green silk"; these are just a few items mentioned in his will, which lists the names of all those who had entrusted these to him. Among these names were the Venetians Maffeo Migiano, Leonardo Minio, and Marco Eviso. Another Venetian merchant, Paolo Dandolo, is listed as the owner of pearls and gemstones.[98] The German and Venetian "white" cloths belonged to Agnese Bogio, and other Venetian cloths to a *ser* Stefano di Luglano. In contrast, products purchased in Tabriz that were to be brought to Venice were all owned by Vilioni himself. This clearly indicates he was member of a broader commercial network with interests in Acre. However, this single case cannot show that the Venetians held a prominent position in the Ilkhanate. They were newcomers, preceded by Genoese, Armenians, and Byzantines.[99] It was not until the beginning of the fourteenth century that Venice established a permanent presence in Tabriz, Trebizond, and Tana.

## Venice and Tana: From Merchant Harbor to Stable Settlement

As we have seen, Venice was initially denied the establishment of a stable settlement in Crimea due to Genoa's dominance in the region. Venetians were limited to frequenting the key ports in the peninsula, but also pushed beyond the Kerch Strait, as far as the mouth of the Don, in search of space for permanent operations. Here, it is challenging to determine the exact chronology of events. Though we have abundant sources, they lack continuity and do not establish when the Italian merchants reached Tana. What we do know for certain is that the Genoese had arrived and settled there many years before. Heyd's studies, based on the oldest cartographic records, including one by Pietro Visconti in 1318 and another by the Pizigani brothers in 1347, show us that the settlement was first built on the left shore of the southern arm of the Don's delta.[100] Heyd also states that Tana first appeared on a map of 1306 by Giovanni, curated by the

---

98. Stussi, "Un testamento volgare," p. 28.

99. Preiser-Kapeller, "Civitas Thauris."

100. Heyd, *Storia del commercio*, pp. 748–49; Skržinskaja, "Storia della Tana," p. 22; also in Berindei and Veinstein, "La Tana-Azaq," p. 110.

church of San Marco di Genova.[101] The settlement also appears in the Luxoro Atlas (early fourteenth century) under the name "Tanna."[102]

The first western travelers to venture into the steppes north of the Black Sea were Catholic missionaries between the 1230s and 1250s—none mention Tana. The previously cited Dominican Julius, who had reached as far as the banks of the Volga, makes no mention of Tana.[103] In 1246, the Umbrian Franciscan John of Plano Carpini wrote that he had met a group of Italian merchants in Kiev; they had arrived in the city by crossing the "territory of the Tatars" after leaving Constantinople.[104] William of Rubruck, who visited Crimea in 1253, also makes no mention of Tana, though he did write that "to the east of that province [Sudak], furthermore, there is a city called Matrica where the Tanai River [the Don] enters the sea of Pontus through a delta some twelve miles across. . . . However, merchants coming from Constantinople who reach the previously mentioned city of Matrica send their boats as far as the Tanai River to buy dry fish, especially sturgeon."[105]

The first mention of a merchant presence in Tana dates to the 1270s, naming the Genoese merchant Oberto de Serra in possession of "Tana silk" on October 1276, which he sold to Puccio Ronchini of Lucca "for 656 lire."[106] As mentioned previously, the 1270s marked a break in hostilities between Venice, Genoa, and the Byzantine Empire. It is plausible that the Venetians had gone on to trade in the territory of the Golden Horde during this period, yet there are no reliable sources on the matter.

In the 1280s, Tana overtook Sudak as the most important trading port on the Black Sea after Caffa—not because of the number of merchants living there (which was high), but for its geographical position. Considering the time it took for the two communities in the region to grow, it is likely that the Genoese settlement originated and developed from the late 1260s onwards, and that the

101. Heyd, *Storia del commercio*, p. 750.

102. Nordenskiöld, *Periplus*; Kretschmer, *Die italienischen Portolane*; Fomenko, "Nomenklatura," p. 68.

103. Friar Giuliano traveled to Rus' twice: first in 1235, then in 1238. See Sinor, "Un voyageur du treizième siècle"; Jackson, *The Mongols and the West*, pp. 16–17; Hautala, "Catholic Missions in the Golden Horde."

104. Pian del Carpine, *Storia dei Mongoli*, p. 332.

105. Rubruk, *Viaggio in Mongolia*, p. 32 and the translation on p. 33. Matrica is Matrega, south of the Kerch Strait, on the east coast.

106. Ferretto, *Codice diplomatico*, p. 99.

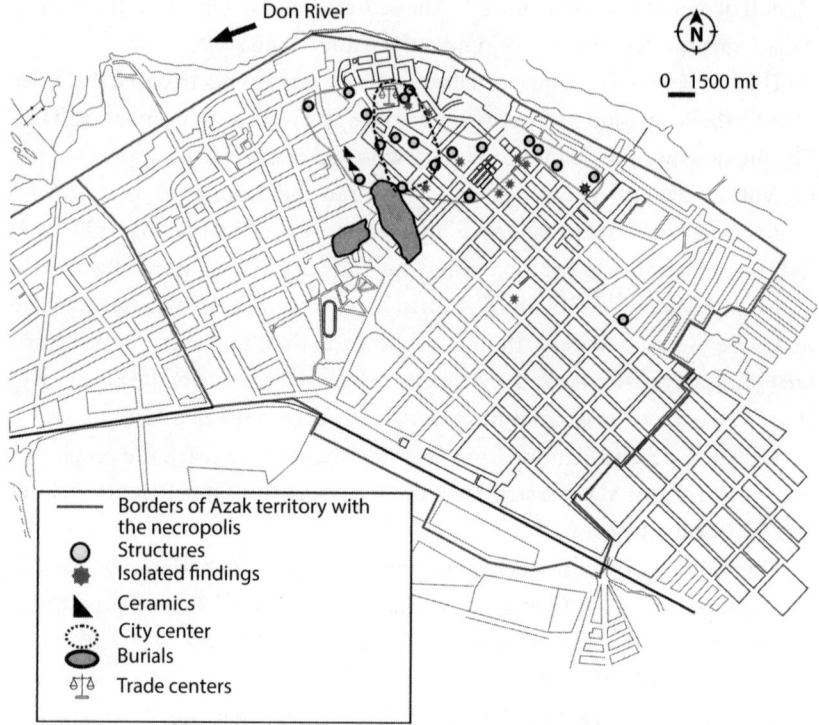

FIGURE 1. Topographic map of Tana in the 1290s. From the excavations of
A. N. Maslovskij (based on Karpov, *Istorija Tany*).

Venetians did not arrive until the end of the century,[107] by which time Tana was
already a thriving hub of international trade.[108] A wide variety of goods passed
through the city, the most important being textiles, fish, wine, and grain. Goods
were not just transported to Constantinople and the Mediterranean basin, but
also to other Black Sea ports, proof of the ever-growing role of European merchants in local trade and the integration of regional economic spaces.

By the early fourteenth century, the Genoese settlement in Tana had already created an administrative structure. From 1304, the consul Ansaldo

107. On the different hypotheses and the chronology, see Karpov, "On the Origin of Medieval Tana," pp. 228–30.

108. Bratianu, *Recherches sur le commerce génois*, pp. 275–76; Balard, *Gênes et l'outre-mer*, vol.
1, p. 183, no. 467; pp. 316–17, no. 788; pp. 378–79, no. 903.

Spinola was working in the city,[109] and in October 1307, the notary Francesco di Saliceto drafted deeds in the consul's home. Records show that Obertino di Pontenure and Oberto di Pasamorte, both from Piacenza, entered into a limited partnership agreement as witnessed by this notary.[110] Though the Venetians also frequented Tana at the time, they did not have their own institutional presence there yet.

The Jöchids favored and encouraged the settlement of Italian merchants; like all Mongol rulers, they were keen on driving trade. However, the growing and organized presence of Latins and their economic power became overbearing and therefore difficult to regulate. Western merchants were accused of kidnapping and trafficking children and young "Tatars" for the slave trade.[111] There is some credence to this accusation, as the Genoese were, in fact, responsible for the perpetual flow of slaves into Mongol territory, who were then sold to the Mamluks in Egypt. This slave trade was a source of great tension, leading the khan to implement punitive measures in an effort to curb it.[112]

The slave trade was expressively forbidden by the law of the Horde, justifying Toqta's strong reaction to the trafficking of young Mongols. However, it is also true that Caffa's growing economic and political clout further needled the khan's irritation. As we have seen, Toqta did not defeat his key enemy Nogaï until 1299, and it had been a challenge for him to bring a degree of political stability to his realm. Thus, it was the sum of all these factors—the slave trade, the Latin invasion of the empire, and the challenges of political consolidation—that threatened his power as sovereign.

In response to the Latins' overreaching—though perhaps more to impose the weight of his authority—Toqta had all Genoese merchants operating in Sarai arrested in 1307, and laid siege to Caffa. On May 21, 1308, after strenuous resistance and more than eight months of siege, the citizens set the city on fire and escaped by sea.[113] The Mongols sealed their victory by imposing a total ban on all westerners from any city in their dominion. The economic damage

---

109. Balard, *La Romanie génoise*, p. 151; Lopez, "Nelle terre dell'Orda d'Oro," p. 463.

110. Bautier, *Les relations économiques*, p. 326.

111. Heyd, *Storia del commercio*, p. 740, states: "Toqtai, the khan of the Horde, having come to know that the Genoese of Caffa and other westerners kidnapped Tatar children to sell them as slaves to the Muslims"; see also Balard, *La Romanie génoise*, p. 151.

112. Golubovich, *Biblioteca bio-bibliografica*, vol. 3, p. 173; Berindei and Migliardi O'Riordan, "Venise et la Horde d'Or," pp. 245–46.

113. Heyd, *Storia del commercio*, pp. 739–40; Golubovich, *Biblioteca bio-bibliografica*, vol. 3, p. 173 (who states the date as May 20); Balard, *La Romanie génoise*, p. 152.

to Genoa, and subsequently Venice, was immense. From the early thirteenth century, the Latin presence, particular the Genoese, had grown without bounds, cosseted by the Golden Horde, which was hampered by its weak central government. Toqta's show of strength now had a regulatory impact. The Mongols were determined to control the Latin presence in their territory, and future treaties between Venice and the Golden Horde show how careful the khans were to establish clear legal boundaries for foreign settlements on their land.

After abandoning their settlements on the northern Black Sea, Italian traders deserted the Golden Horde for several years. The Genoese did not return to Caffa until 1311, evidenced by the notarial activity of Riccobono Palmerio in Tana.[114] However, Toqta's sudden death in 1312 radically changed things. The new ruler to ascend the throne, Uzbek (r. 1313–41), was in favor of reopening Latin–Mongol relations.

The new khan was a devout Muslim, and from the very start of his reign, he faced opposition from the Mongol aristocracy who were against the advance of Islam among its ranks.[115] Uzbek ushered in a new political stance that included a more open and benevolent attitude toward Latin merchants, seeing the need to boost trade once more.[116] The Genoese took advantage of this, organizing themselves so they could return to the cities in Crimea on a permanent basis. In 1313, Ligurian authorities established a new magistracy, the *Octo sapientes constituti super factis navigandi et maris majoris*, later simply referred to as Officium Gazarie. This new body office operated locally and was in charge of Crimean affairs. The Officium had legislative powers and was made up of eight magistrates, each elected for a six-month term, who were assisted by a "major" council (composed of twenty-four members, both noble and common Genoese citizens), as well as by another restricted council (composed of six members elected by the major council).[117]

114. Balard, *La Romanie génoise*, p. 152. There is no information on what damages the settlement in Tana suffered during Toqta's attack. It is likely that both the Genoese and Venetians used the city at the mouth of the Don River as a base where they could return to and reorganize in Crimea. Karpov, "On the Origin of Medieval Tana," pp. 233–34.

115. DeWeese, *Islamization and Native Religion*, pp. 93–94; Sinor, "Nekotorye latinskie istočniki," pp. 23–25; Hautala, "Pis'ma franciskancev."

116. Uzbek also opened up to Christian missionaries, in particular to the mendicant orders, even though it was not a simple coexistence in the cities of the Golden Horde. Hautala, "Latin Sources."

117. Sauli, "Imposicio Officii Gazarie"; Forcheri, *Navi e navigazione a Genova*.

After resettling in Crimea, the Genoese worked to return to Tana as well. Though the city appears in maps of the Officium Gazarie from 1313, these references are sporadic. It is only from 1315 that we see a regular presence of Ligurian merchants in Tana, though they could only reside in the city for limited periods.[118] Sources of the Officium tell us that, in 1316, Genoese traders and their traveling companions were forbidden to winter in Tana or to purchase real estate there. Violators were fined 500 gold *hyperpyrons*.[119]

The return of Latin merchants to the Jöchi *ulus* was a precious resource for the Mongols, too. From the start of his rule, Uzbek invested vast resources to build a complex administrative machine, and to strengthen his army. Regarding his relations with Latin Christianity, Uzbek favored missionary activity, particularly that of the Franciscans, whom Nogaï, also a Muslim, had largely supported. For example, in 1314, Uzbek issued an edict (*yarligh*), guaranteeing many privileges to the Friars Minor.[120] To finance this grand reform, Uzbek invested in international trade and supported the construction of new foreign settlements on Mongol territory. It was the dawn of a new era, the first page of a fresh chapter of what has been called *pax mongolica*, somewhat reductively. Despite the fragile balance of relations with the Mongols and its rivalry with Genoa, Venice would rise to take a leading role.

118. Sauli, "Imposicio Officii Gaziarie," col. 306.

119. Sauli, "Imposicio Officii Gaziarie," col. 381: "quod aliquis ianuensis vel qui pro ianuensi distringatru vel appelletur seu beneficio ianuensis gaudeat non audeat vel presumat aliquo modo vel ingenio yemare seu sivernare in Tana seu habere tenere vel acquirere in Tana aliquam habitacionem vel domum seu habitaculumæ"; this section of the "Imposicio" of September 1341 also states that "in Tana in itinere differre ibi diebus decem et non ultra sub pena predicta [librarum quingetarum]": col. 346; Heyd, *Storia del commercio*, p. 751.

120. Kovács, "The Franciscans and Yaylaq Khatun," p. 58; Hautala, "Jarlik xhana," pp. 34–35.

# 4

# Venice and the Mongols

## YEARS OF CONSOLIDATION (1319–43)

## The Political Landscape of the 1320s

By the early fourteenth century, Venice had achieved a lasting peace with the Byzantine Empire, allowing it to explore new alliances and strategies in its relations with the Mongols.[1] Its enemy republic, Genoa, which had firmly opposed the opening of Venetian trading bases on the Black Sea, had entered a period of political crisis that reverberated across its colonies. In 1321, Ghibelline supporters in the community of Pera rebelled against the Genoese motherland where the Guelph party had taken power.[2] Venice exploited Genoa's weakness by reinforcing its own position on the Black Sea, intensifying its diplomatic efforts with all other states in the region.

These efforts were largely successful; in 1319, Venice signed a treaty of collaboration with Emperor Alexios II of Trebizond. Next, in 1320, Venetian ambassadors renewed their formal pact of friendship with the Armenian Kingdom of Cilicia, allowing the Republic's merchants to trade in the port of Ayas and on the caravan routes connecting the Anatolian city to Tabriz. That same year, Venice renewed its 1306 agreement with the Ilkhanate, convincing Abu Said Ilkhan (see below) to amend certain clauses in its favor. Venice gained permission for free movement around the empire, for its merchants to live in Tabriz and establish a *fondaco*, and have consul representation, as well as exemptions and other fiscal privileges. Venice then reinforced its presence in the Aegean and entered into agreements with local lords of the larger

---

1. The peace treaty between the two powers was signed in 1310.
2. Thiriet, *La Romanie vénitienne*, p. 162; Balard, *La Romanie génoise*, pp. 67–69.

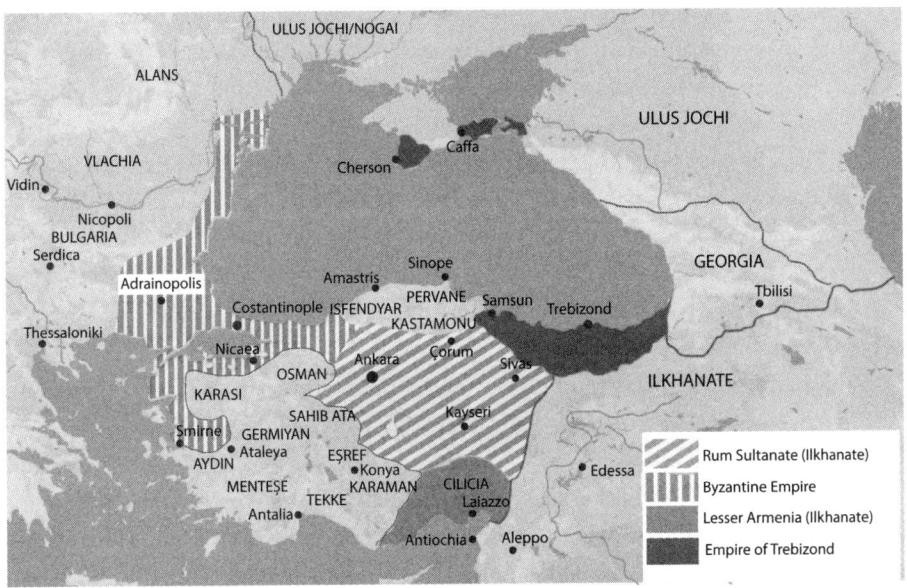

MAP 10. The Black Sea at the beginning of the fourteenth century

islands, including Negropont and Crete, as well as strengthening its links with smaller ones. The senate also authorized negotiations with Uzbek Khan of the Golden Horde so Venice could install itself in Tana. This ambitious goal was finally realized in 1332, when the khan granted Venice a piece of land at the mouth of the Don, for the Republic's establishment of its own quarter that it could fortify and manage independently.

It is evident that the Venetian consolidation of dominion over the Black Sea basin was made possible by an evolving political landscape, characterized by friendships, alliances, and by an easing of hostilities between powers—which, not too long ago, had been deadly enemies. Yet, another significant factor was the emergence of new players who pressed to secure themselves space in the political and economic system of the eastern Mediterranean. Venice exploited these opportunities, nurturing and reinforcing its presence in the East. The Republic itself became a decisive factor in this process of supra-regional economic and commercial integration.

The fourteenth-century international political picture had evolved on other fronts as well: foremost among them was the conflict between the Ilkhanate and the Mamluks. These two states controlled the caravan routes and key hubs scattered from the northern coast of Africa to the very heart of Persia, and their hostilities slowed or even obstructed trade flows. To fully understand the evolution of events and the scale of changes that took place in those years, we need to retrace the steps leading up to the Ilkhanid–Mamluk conflict, in which both Genoa and Venice were involved—albeit indirectly.

The war between the sultanate and the Persian *ulus* had raged for decades in fits and starts, from the very first armed conflict in 1260 in Ayn Jalut, Palestine. This first phase of conflict lasted a decade, ending in the Second Battle of Homs (October 1281), which saw the heavy defeat of the Ilkhanid army. The following years were marked by declared hostilities, espionage, raids, and border violations, as well as trade blockades. At the Battle of Ayn Jalut, the Mamluks had faced a modest and ill-prepared Mongol force, yet in Homs, Abaqa Ilkhan stood ready with a full army, prepared to avenge the affront to the notorious Mongol military pride.[3]

In the aftermath of the Second Battle of Homs and the death of Abaqa (1282), the two sides sought a truce. Abaqa's successor, Tegüder Ahmad Ilkhan, reigned for just over two years and failed to complete peace negotiations with Sultan Qalawun (r. 1279–90). The new ilkhan, Arghun (r. 1284–91) made no significant changes to the policies of his predecessor, yet did intensify diplomatic efforts to further rouse the anti-Mamluk front by involving the papacy and with it the powers of Christian Europe. This did not lead to a détente.[4] Rather, relations deteriorated further. In his wake came the brief rule of Geikhatu (r. 1291–95), during which border violations and skirmishes resumed. Tensions led to open war during the first years of Ghazan's reign (r. 1295–1304), who attacked the Mamluks in Syria three times, with a victory in 1299 in Homs, followed by two bitter defeats (1300 and 1303). During preparations for a fourth offensive, the ilkhan died (1304) and the expedition was canceled. Ghazan was succeeded by Oljeitu (r. 1304–16), who sought to reconcile with the sultan, though he never stopped negotiating with the western powers to ally against him. Although relations remained hostile, there was a pause in armed conflict for almost a decade. Instead, the ilkhan grew closer to the papacy in an anti-Mamluk alliance, though there was no formal agreement. In late 1312, the Mongols attacked Syria on the course of the Euphrates River at al-Rahba—it was yet another failure.[5]

---

3. Amitai-Preiss, *Mongols and Mamluks*, pp. 187–201.
4. Amitai, "The Resolution of the Mongol-Mamluk War," pp. 359–60.
5. Amitai, "The Resolution of the Mongol-Mamluk War," p. 361.

During this period, Uzbek Khan of the Golden Horde initiated diplomatic contacts with the Mamluks, by virtue of their common rivalry with the Ilkhanids. In the spring of 1314, the first Jöchid diplomatic mission reached Cairo,[6] and over the years, an alliance was forged with Mamluk Sultan al-Nasir (d. 1341). The pact was sealed with the betrothal of the sultan to Uzbek's niece, Tulambay Khatun,[7] and they wed in early May 1320.[8] It is interesting to note that the betrothed's entourage included the Genoese slave trader Segurano Salvaygo, confirming just how important this particular trade was for Genoa and the entire economy of the region, from the Black Sea to Egypt.[9]

A state of latent conflict remained; there were minor clashes on both sides, expressed in incursions and raids urged on by military commanders who sought to compensate their troops.[10] For example, in the spring of 1315, Mamluk forces attacked Asia Minor, taking advantage of the conflict between the Ilkhanids and the Chagatai khanate that had erupted the year before.[11] More skirmishes affected the Aleppo region the following year, with the Mongols trying to force the borders and the Mamluks counterattacking. Oljeitu even went so far as to support an attempted coup to install an Arab pretender to the Cairo throne.[12]

Upon Oljeitu's death in 1316, his successor was his twelve-year-old son Abu Said, who settled in Tabriz under the protection of the powerful emir Chuban (d. 1327). This was a period of increasing political instability, with threats on all borders: in 1318, Yasa'ur (d. 1320), the Chagatai governor of Khorasan, launched

6. Favereau, "The Golden Horde and the Mamluks," p. 104; Ciocîltan offers the date April 14: Ciocîltan, *The Mongols and the Black Sea Trade*, p. 175.

7. The bride was Toqta's daughter. Ciocîltan, *The Mongols and the Black Sea Trade*, p. 176.

8. Or in April: Ciocîltan, *The Mongols and the Black Sea Trade*, p. 189.

9. On the figure of Segurano Salvaygo, see Kedar, "Segurano-Sakran Salvaygo"; Amitai, "Diplomacy and the Slave Trade," p. 355 and no. 32; Balard, "Le transport des esclaves," p. 363; Stello, "Caffa and the Slave Trade," p. 378; Amitai, "Between the Slave Trade and Diplomacy," p. 408; Judkevich, "The Nature and Role of the Slave," pp. 428–31 and 435.

10. Morgan, "The Decline and Fall of the Mongol Empire," pp. 430–31.

11. The Chagatai khanate of central Asia was geographically between Yuan China and the Ilkhanate. For years, it tried to strike up diplomatic relations with the Mamluks to balance the axis of the alliances. In 1315, the Chagatai khan Asen Buqa (r. 1310–18) received a lavish delegation from Cairo. For more on this subject, see Biran, "Diplomacy and Chancellery Practices," p. 376.

12. To this end, he sent a delegation to Mecca: Amitai, "The Resolution of the Mongol-Mamluk War," p. 363.

a revolt against the Tabriz government,[13] and a few months later, the Jöchids attacked in the Caucasus.[14] Tensions between the Ilkhanid aristocracy and Chuban's rule further aggravated the Ilkhanid government's gradual decline.[15]

Aware of the enemy's weakness, the Mamluks attacked Asia Minor with the aim of taking the port of Ayas (1318). Perhaps this is what inspired Ilkhanid diplomats to initiate an end to hostilities.[16] After months of negotiations, a peace treaty was concluded in 1321, though it was not ratified until early 1323 in the mosque of Tabriz.[17] In a letter sent to Sarai, the Mamluk sultan openly declared that he would no longer attack the kingdom of Abu Said, as he and his court had finally converted to the "true faith."[18] Although we cannot underestimate the strength of the religious motives for this peaceful resolution, what really underpinned the rapprochement of these historical enemies were motives of a political and commercial nature. Unsurprisingly, both sides were committed to keeping markets open and protecting the merchants who frequented them.[19]

Thus, there was a major shift in the political balance among the Mongol states. In late 1320, Uzbek tested the new system of alliances by inviting the Mamluks to join Jöchid forces against the Ilkhanate. However, the Mamluk sultan, who was about to reach an agreement with Abu Said, flatly refused and ordered Uzbek to cease hostilities.[20] The closeness between the Ilkhanate and the Mamluks damaged the Jöchids, as the sultanate could now import slaves and other Asian goods via Tabriz. The Pontic alternative, which started from Tana and Caffa to reach the Mediterranean, was managed by Genoa.[21] The

13. Amitai, "The Resolution of the Mongol-Mamluk War," p. 364. Yasa'ur was the great-grandson of Chagatai Khan.

14. Ciocîltan, *The Mongols and the Black Sea Trade*, pp. 188–89.

15. Kamalov, *Otnošenija Zolotoj Ordy c Chulaguidami*, p. 75.

16. Amitai, "The Resolution of the Mongol-Mamluk War," pp. 365–67. The port of Ayas became a major naval hub for the entire Anatolian and Middle Eastern commercial network, especially after the Mamluk conquest of Acre, as we shall see further on. Sinclair, *Eastern Trade and the Mediterranean*, p. 25.

17. Amitai, "The Resolution of the Mongol-Mamluk War," pp. 362 and 371.

18. Ciocîltan, *The Mongols and the Black Sea Trade*, p. 190.

19. The agreement shows, among other things, that the times of the Mongols' more universal leanings, as sanctioned by the Yasa, the legal code supposedly collecting the edicts of Chinggis Khan, were long gone. Amitai, "The Resolution of the Mongol-Mamluk War," p. 368.

20. Favereau, "The Golden Horde and the Mamluks," p. 104; Ciocîltan, *The Mongols and the Black Sea Trade*, pp. 189–90.

21. Despite papal prohibitions, Venice maintained relations with the Mamluks, balancing on the fine semantic line of what the pope had expressly prohibited (items related to strategy,

khan of the Golden Horde had every interest in expanding his hegemony over Black Sea trade, but to do so, he would have to curtail Genoa's power. It was amidst this atmosphere of political earthquakes that Venice entered the stage as a major player in Mongol trade policies.

## Venice between the Trebizond Empire, the Kingdom of Lesser Armenia, and the Ilkhanate (1319–23)

Political fluctuations had an impact on trade routes, which shifted accordingly—albeit gradually—as each route required various facilities, such as the caravanserais (roadside inns), postal stations, bridges, checkpoints, and accommodation.[22] Venetians frequented the most familiar and best equipped arteries, such as the Anatolian and Middle Eastern routes that had been traveled since the days of the Crusades. Between 1319 and 1322, there was frenetic activity from the chancelleries of all states involved in eastern trade. While Mongol diplomacy was engaged in peace negotiations with the Mamluks, Venice moved on several fronts. In July 1319, Ambassador Pantaleone Michiel successfully completed a mission entrusted to him by the senate to Emperor Alexios II of Trebizond.[23] Among the many concessions he garnered, he ensured that Venetian ships could dock in the city's harbor, just as the Genoese did (*sicut faciunt Januenses*). All Venetians—whether noble or not (*tam parvi quam magni*)—could circulate freely. Overall, he secured beneficial fiscal conditions: 20 Trebizond aspers for every cargo (*soma*) intended for sale and 3 percent *commerchium* on the weight of goods or on the total income. If both seller and buyer were Venetian, the percentage was halved. Gold and silver paid nothing, except for the 20 aspers required per load. Caravans coming over land from Constantinople, Ayas, and Tabriz were subject to a tax of twelve aspers per load, while sales were charged 1 percent on the proceeds. Venetians obtained land on which they could build homes, a governmental loggia, and a church. They could elect a bailiff with a retinue (*precones*, or heralds), accredited by local authorities, who would administer justice in the

---

military, and construction) and what was tacitly allowed. The treaty of 1317 expressly mentions gifts, cloths, and spices, which the sultan Naser Mohammad sent to the doge, along with the announcement that he had freed all Venetians imprisoned in Alexandria (Giomo, *Libri commemoriali*, vol. 2, no. 75, p. 186).

22. Sinclair, *Eastern Trade and the Mediterranean*, pp. 22–23.

23. *Diplomatarium veneto-levantinum*, vol. 1, pp. 122–24; Thiriet, *La Romanie vénitienne*, p. 162.

Venetian quarter. This treaty with Trebizond was a crucial step for Venice's Black Sea expansion as it created the vital infrastructures needed to reach Asian markets by land (via the caravan routes that connected the Anatolian port to Ayas and to Tabriz) and by sea (via the route to Crimea and the Sea of Azov).

Less than a year later, the Venetian chancellery organized a mission to the ilkhan to obtain a renewal of its privileges in Tabriz. In December 1320, they forged a treaty with Abu Said, in which the ilkhan guaranteed the Venetian community all the prerogatives established in 1306, along with a few new ones. He also granted formal protection to all those who operated in his empire under the flag of Saint Mark. The document reflects the political air of the time, particularly the growing tension between Venice and the papacy. After Acre—a trade market of crucial strategic importance—was conquered by the Mamluks in 1291, the Holy See took great strides to isolate the infidels and prohibit Christian states—including Venice—from any relations with Muslims.[24] The ban was respected to varying degrees,[25] and Venice chose to violate this order whenever its interests outweighed the ban or when the pope's attitude was suitably lax.[26] However, it was precisely due to these violations that, in 1304, Pope Benedict XI (r. 1303–4) confirmed the resolutions underwritten at the Council of Lyon, which excommunicated anyone transporting building materials, weapons, or provisions in Mamluk ports.[27] Despite this resolution, the slave trade continued. That same year, a Genoese galley with a cargo of

---

24. The pope's ostracism of the Mamluks was a consequence of the Crusades, and intended to damage the economic interests of the Egyptian sultanate. The first bans on docking at Alexandria's port and of any commercial relationship with the sultan's subjects date to at least the Third and the Fourth Council of Lyon, 1179 and 1215: Ortalli, "Venice and Papal Bans," pp. 242–43; Jacoby, "L'expansion occidentale."

25. For example, in 1292 the senate banned all Venetian merchants from buying and selling slaves *ad terras Soldani*, but in 1302 it recommended that ambassadors living in Rome should persuade the pope to ease the ban and allow travel to Alexandria. At the same time as lobbying the pope, Venetian diplomats negotiated with the Mamluks. That same year of 1302, Venice signed a treaty with the sultan, clearly stipulating that Italian merchants could invest their profits from the sale of "banned" products for the purchase of new goods, without paying any taxes. *Diplomatarium veneto-levantinum*, vol. 1, pp. 5–9; Ashtor, *Levant Trade*, pp. 17–44; Ortalli, "Venice and Papal Bans," p. 245 and no. 11; Jacoby, "La Venezia d'Oltremare nel secondo Duecento."

26. Ortalli, "Venice and Papal Bans," p. 243.

27. Giomo, *Libri commemoriali*, vol. 1, no. 169, p. 39. While it is true that military and construction material was expressly prohibited in the papal papers, it is also true that other goods, such as textiles, were not mentioned: Ortalli, "Venice and Papal Bans," p. 246.

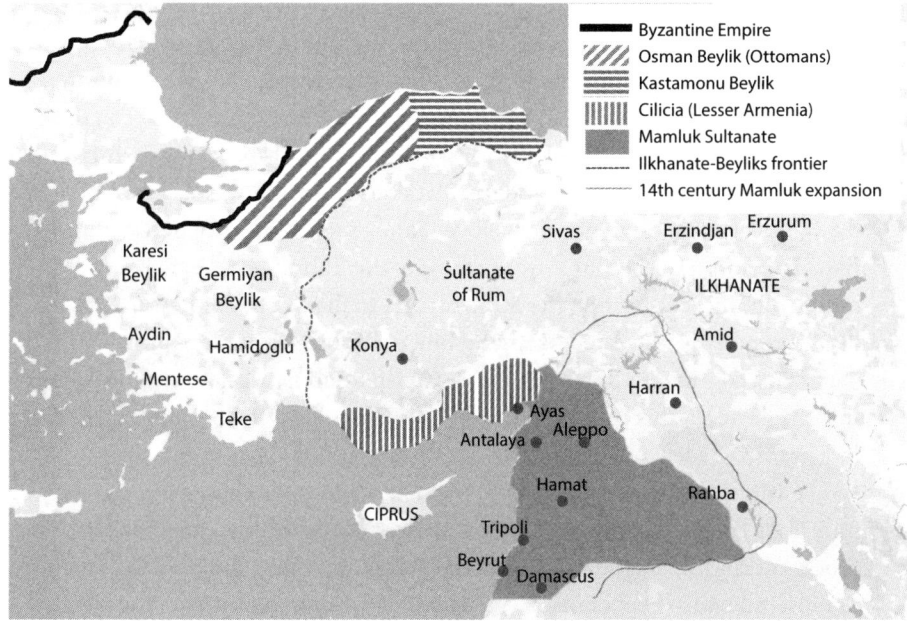

Byzantine Empire
Osman Beylik (Ottomans)
Kastamonu Beylik
Cilicia (Lesser Armenia)
Mamluk Sultanate
Ilkhanate-Beyliks frontier
14th century Mamluk expansion

MAP 11. The southern Black Sea between 1320 and 1350

slaves sailed for Alexandria, where they had been purchased by the local merchant Salomon Macomet.[28] The galley had to divert to Candia (Crete) due to pursuit by Turkish pirates.[29] In 1308, the new Pope Clement V (r. 1305–14) ordered the bishop of Venice to publish the papal constitution on the doors of San Pietro in Castello Cathedral, which underscored the ban on exports to the Mamluks; not only weapons, horses, and war materials were prohibited, but any kind of merchandise (*alia quecunque mercimonia*), punishable by excommunication and the loss of civil rights.[30]

For Venice, all that could be done was to obey the pope's orders—at least officially. In 1313, the senate forbade its captains from going to Egypt and

28. Giomo, *Libri commemoriali*, vol. 1, no. 216, p. 47.

29. The Duke of Candia confiscated the material, causing great financial damage to the Genoese merchants, which was then refunded: Giomo, *Libri commemoriali*, vol. 1, nos. 176 and 187, pp. 40 and 42.

30. Giomo, *Libri commemoriali*, vol. 1, no. 381, p. 89. On the pope's politics regarding the Mamluks in the thirteenth century, see Purcell, *Papal Crusading Policy*. On the period in question and on Venice, see Stantchev, *Spiritual Rationality*, pp. 133–44.

Syria.[31] The closure of Acre and prohibition of Egypt caused enormous damage to the Republic, driving the authorities to rethink their trade network. Hence, Venice chose to focus its efforts and investments on Ayas, Cyprus, Constantinople, and especially on the Black Sea. Although the papal ban did not entirely sever all contact with Egypt and Syria, it did cause a shift in European trade toward Persia and the Black Sea. This shift was also driven by the political changes mentioned above. Following the détente between the Ilkhanate and the Mamluks, from ca. 1320, the Tabriz–Ayas caravan route resumed traffic, connecting the Mongol state to their vassal of Lesser Armenia.[32] From Ayas, the direct overland link to Trebizond made it possible to maintain a continuous flow to and from Constantinople at relatively low cost. In no time at all, this route replaced the Persian Gulf–Red Sea path for the Indian spice trade.

The Mongols themselves realized the damage to trade caused by ongoing wars.[33] As far as we know, the Mongol aristocracy never boycotted the peace process during the negotiations between Tabriz and Cairo. This indicates that its most influential exponents—a generation now far removed from the ideology of universal conquest that had driven thirteenth-century expansion[34]—understood that peace was more profitable than war. In this light, the treaties stipulated by Venice with Alexios II and Abu Said acquired a clear significance; they were influenced by the need for guaranteed protection of citizens' free and safe movement between the Indian Ocean and Constantinople.

In December 1320, the Venetian ambassador Michele Dolfin signed such a treaty with the ilkhan Abu Said, and its translation from the Venetian vernacular reveals the Mongols' desire to welcome and protect western merchants.[35] The treaty's clauses are generous as well as precise; they regulate every aspect of cohabitation between western merchants and the local population, clearly establishing customs duties and taxes due to the local authorities for conducting their business, and how the merchants were still subject to Mongol rule should they commit crimes in the territory of the Ilkhanate involving local

---

31. "Ad terras soldani scilicet a Damiata usque ad portellam Armenie": Giomo, "Le rubriche dei Libri Misti," p. 317.

32. Sinclair, *Eastern Trade and the Mediterranean*, pp. 22–26.

33. Amitai, "The Resolution of the Mongol-Mamluk War," p. 374; Amitai, "Northern Syria between the Mongols and Mamluks," pp. 146–49.

34. Amitai, "The Resolution of the Mongol-Mamluk War," pp. 381–83.

35. *Diplomatarium veneto-levantinum*, vol. 1, pp. 173–76.

citizens. This also proves the degree to which local authorities were themselves active in trade activities, encouraging and supporting them—but only as long as foreign traders respected certain conditions and limits.

The opening of the charter is explicit: *questo sie lo exemplo deli comandamenti de Monsayt imperador.*[36] It was the Mongols who dictated conditions, even if the agreement was evidently the result of a negotiation by Venetian ambassadors. Abu Said granted Venetians freedom of movement throughout his empire, free from taxes and levies that were not included in the formal agreements.[37] Venetian merchants were not subject to any charges on imports and exports within the kingdom's cities, yet based on the treaty's stipulations, they had to pay an unspecified percentage of their profits.[38] Moreover, all transactions were regulated and protected by state laws. Of course, however effective the central authority's control over outlying areas was, the ilkhan knew that the local nobility enjoyed a de facto autonomy, allowing it to impose arbitrary charges on merchants. The treaty clearly shows Abu Said's desire to limit such profiteering, and explains why the text specifies that Venetian merchants had free movement throughout the empire with their caravans, only having to pay a protection duty or fee (*solamente el so drito lialmente*).[39] In addition, Venetian merchants were provided with guards for protection and guidance while traveling through areas under the ilkhan's jurisdiction. Should thefts occur in regions subject to Ilkhanid sovereignty, local authorities were charged with finding the perpetrators and recovering the loot. If the cargo could not be found, the victims were compensated.

Merchants were also entitled to graze their draft and pack animals (mostly horses and mules) without further payment (*senza alguna chosa*) for up to three days; this regulation also protected subjects of the ilkhan who leased such animals.[40] Religious figures (friars and priests) were authorized to profess

36. "Monsayt" refers to the ilkhan Abu Said.

37. It is interesting to note how an official *pactum*, among other items translated from Venetian, contains Mongolian terms for fiscal matters (*tamtaulazo, tomaga*) as well as for many other things, such as the guards overseeing transit routes within districts (*tatauli*).

38. Neither *tamtaulazo* nor *tomaga*. This was a success for Venetian diplomacy, since the document states that prior to this, Venetians had to pay just to stay in Tabriz and throughout the Ilkhanid territory.

39. *Diplomatarium veneto-levantinum*, vol. 1, p. 174. The fact that this point had to be specified indicates that such violations were the norm.

40. It was stipulated that they could not be diverted from their activity, even if found to be guilty of serious crimes, until they had completed their service for which they were hired by Venetian merchants.

their religion freely under protection of Mongol authorities in every city or region in the state.[41] In the event that a Venetian citizen died, no one could take possession of their goods; the bailiff or the eldest among the *nobili viri* (noblemen) had to deal with the matter. For instance, when the ambassador Dolfin signed the treaty with Abu Said, he was also given back all the goods that been taken by a certain Badradrin Lulu and had belonged to Francesco da Canal, who had recently died in Erzindjan.[42]

The treaty also recognized the right to limited extraterritoriality for Latin citizens who had committed crimes among their own people. The limitation of consular jurisdiction for the Latin community (*da franco a franco*) was a principal that we regularly observe in treaties between Venice and the Mongols. The Venetian bailiff had the power to judge the offender of a crime *secondo la soa usanza*. Alternatively, the Venetian charged with a crime could choose to be tried by a local court. In any case, criminal responsibility was always exclusive to the individual; relatives or associates could not be held accountable for crimes they had not committed. Otherwise, if the court case involved non-western citizens, then the jurisdiction came under Mongol law, even if the accused was Venetian. This legal pluralism, which linked legal practices to one's culture and nationality, was common throughout the Mongol Empire.

## Conflicts and Agreements in Asia Minor

From 1322, Venice's interest in Tabriz and the markets of the Ilkhanate continued to grow. While in 1291 Venice had managed to sidestep (on and off) the papal ban on trade with Egypt, this became impossible from 1322. Pope John XXII's policies regarding the Mamluks became firmer and prohibitions stricter, to the point that the Venetian senate had to order merchants not to frequent Alexandria or any place under the sultan's authority (*vel ad alias terra Soldano subiectas*).[43] As in 1308, there were no exceptions to the goods allowed for trade (*cum aliquibus rebus vel mercibus*). There was no way to loosen the strictures of the papal ban; thus, in April 1324, Venice closed its consulate and the entire Venetian community in Alexandria left the city.[44] Venetians would not return until 1345.

---

41. The treaty article, specifically 19, is also in Golubovich, *Biblioteca bio-bibliografica*, vol. 3, p. 209.

42. *Diplomatarium veneto-levantinum*, vol. 1, p. 176.

43. Ortalli, "Venice and Papal Bans," pp. 244–45; Ashtor, *Levant Trade*, pp. 44–63.

44. Ortalli, "Venice and Papal Bans," p. 247.

As a result, Tabriz and Ayas became even more central to Venetian trade strategy in the East. After securing its privileges in the capital of the Ilkhanate, Venice also sought stability for its community in the kingdom of Lesser Armenia. This was in the early 1320s; although a formal agreement signed in 1307 was technically still in force between the two states,[45] Venice had not had a chance to exploit its rights. A few months after the treaty had been signed, Andrea Sanudo's galleys had stormed and seized the castle in the port of Ayas, causing extensive damage to the infrastructure and triggering formal protest from the king. Since then, relations between the states had cooled and the clauses in the 1307 treaty had fallen into disuse. To renew its privileges in the Anatolian Kingdom, Venice resumed negotiations with the Armenian authorities, led by Ambassador Michele Giustiniani.

Young King Leo V had just ascended the throne (r. 1320–41)[46] and now offered Venice very favorable terms: he permitted Venetian ships to unload their goods in any port in the kingdom. In addition, he exempted certain goods—such as leather, hides, and silk—indicating that these were exchanged in large quantities. As for silver and gold, the former had to be transported directly to Ayas, where there was a royal mint. Half the silver was destined to pay the customs duties to the Mamluk Sultanate.[47] Gold could be traded freely (*ad suum libitum sine aliquo obstaculo*).[48] Venetian merchants and their goods also enjoyed freedom of movement, a right that was contingent on ongoing peace with the Mamluk Sultanate (*tempore quo cum Saracenis habebimus*

---

45. Giomo, *Libri commemoriali*, vol. 1, no. 319, pp. 75–76.

46. Son of Oshin I (r. 1307–20), he is sometimes referred to as Leo IV. See Dashdondog, *The Mongols and the Armenians*, pp. 208ff.

47. After the Mamluk attack on Ayas in 1322, the Armenian Patriarch Constantine IV Lampron (r. 1322–26) was sent on a mission by Sultan Muhammad al-Nasir to negotiate peace. In the resulting treaty, the Mamluks formally promised that they would abstain from any hostile act against the Christian state for the next fifteen years. However, it was a costly concession, and the Armenian treasury was forced to hand over half of all revenues from the sale of salt to the sultan. Hence, the "duty" mentioned in the document was none other than a tax paid by the king of Lesser Armenia to the sultan, guaranteeing his country's independence. On the other hand, as mentioned above, the papal bans on trade with the Mamluks had rerouted Venetian commercial traffic to the Anatolian port, which both Egyptian buyers and merchants flocked to, transforming Ayas into the "legal" meeting point for supply and demand, which could not be met directly for fear of violating the pope's ban. See also Ghazarian, *The Armenian Kingdom*, p. 73.

48. *Diplomatarium veneto-levantinum*, vol. 1, p. 176. The empire of Trebizond needed silver to make coins.

*pacem*).[49] Lastly, Venice obtained full jurisdiction over its own quarter (except for citizens of the kingdom, who were subject to state law), and that no Venetian indigents could be harassed by local authorities. The treaty was ratified in March 1321.[50]

Having established its own quarter in the kingdom of Lesser Armenia, Venice found itself in a politically precarious position. In 1321, Ayas remained a major target of Egypt's foreign policy. On more than one occasion, the Mamluks had tried and failed to invade the small Anatolian kingdom and capture its main port. For example, in 1322, Muhammad al-Nasir's army attacked and destroyed the city before retreating.[51] In March 1322, the Venetian senate asked the bailiff of Trebizond to report on the "news" of events in the Anatolian city. Venetian merchants had been attacked and robbed on the road to Tabriz, and authorities of the motherland ordered the bailiff to compensate the victims.[52]

The pro-western policies of this small Christian state, formally the vassal of the Ilkhanate since the days of Hethum I (r. 1226–70),[53] encouraged Pope John XXII to ask Abu Said Ilkhan directly to step in to protect Lesser Armenia—yet to no avail.[54] Though the Mamluk attack on Ayas did not result in the city's conquest, it had exposed its vulnerabilities. Controlling the Armenian city would have given the sultan direct access to trade routes with Asia, guaranteeing a regular influx of slaves, and independence of the Italian merchants who dominated the Bosphorus route.[55]

The political situation was constantly evolving, and these changes also affected relations between the Ilkhanate and the Golden Horde. The peace between the Ilkhanate and the Mamluks was echoed by Abu Said's initiative—in 1323, he launched negotiations with Uzbek's Golden Horde.[56] Perhaps the

49. *Diplomatarium veneto-levantinum*, vol. 1, p. 180.

50. *Diplomatarium veneto-levantinum*, vol. 1, pp. 178–81.

51. Stewart, *The Armenian Kingdom and the Mamluks*, p. 185; Ghazarian, *The Armenian Kingdom*, p. 73.

52. Paviot, "Les marchands italiens," p. 75; Giomo, "Le rubriche dei Libri Misti," pp. 327ff.

53. On this topic, see Pubblici, *Mongol Caucasia*, pp. 144–45 and 164–66.

54. The pope had written to the ilkhan in 1321, counting on the fact that there were emirs who had converted to Christianity at the court of Tabriz. See Richard, *La Papauté et les missions d'Orient*, p. 175 and no. 159.

55. Favereau, "The Golden Horde and the Mamluks," pp. 105, 56; Kamalov, *Otnošenija Zolotoj Ordy c Chulaguidami*, p. 78.

56. Kamalov, *Otnošenija Zolotoj Ordy c Chulaguidami*, p. 78.

Ilkhanate initiative should be read in the following context: between the end of 1324 and the start of the following year, it assembled an army on the border between the two states in the Caucasus, most likely to quell a local revolt.[57] In those months, Jöchid diplomacy also worked to re-establish good relations with the Mamluks. Mongol ambassadors reached Cairo and were received with full honors. In turn, the khan received the sultan's envoys at the end of the year or in early 1325.[58] Thus, from a standpoint of potential isolation, the Horde had once again integrated itself into a large trading system.

## Venice and the Ilkhanate between 1324 and 1335

In the mid-1320s, Asia Minor's trade routes were under threat by the small peripheral Turkic emirs who wished to expand their power, encroaching on both the Byzantine Empire and the Ilkhanate. From correspondence between Venice and its representatives in Persia, it appears that by 1324 Tabriz was no longer safe. The bailiff made an official plea to the motherland for an intervention, to ensure the safety of the traders residing there.[59] The Mongols were no longer able to garrison all the roads, and merchants were suffering from the gradual closure of transit routes, yet it was mainly the peripheral authorities (who were more difficult for the central powers to control) who perpetrated the abuses.[60] Added to this were the tensions within Tabriz's Venetian community. In a letter dated June 6, 1324, the consul Marco da Molin wrote to the doge to complain about the violence that had been unleashed in the city by Francesco Querini, a Venetian citizen.[61] Querini had partnered with Candiano Sanudo to purchase spices from a Mongol citizen who had previously been banished from the Venetian community for reasons unspecified in the letter. For this infraction, Querini was sued by several of his fellow countrymen—possibly competing

57. Kamalov, *Otnošenija Zolotoj Ordy c Chulaguidami*, p. 79.

58. Ciocîltan, *The Mongols and the Black Sea Trade*, p. 192.

59. *Diplomatarium veneto-levantinum*, vol. 1, pp. 192–94.

60. This was most likely encouraged by the Genoese and their trading partners, who could no longer keep their rivals out of the Black Sea by either diplomacy or war. Instead, they ostracized their rivals by bribing local officials. Thus, the 1320 treaty with Abu Said reiterates that no one may demand anything of the Venetians outside of the terms set in the agreement; on the contrary, all must ensure the protection of Venetian merchants. On this subject, see Ciocîltan, *The Mongols and the Black Sea Trade*, pp. 133–34; Petech, "Les marchands italiens," pp. 568–69.

61. Petech, "Les marchands italiens," p. 568; *Diplomatarium veneto-levantinum*, vol. 1, pp. 192–94; Paviot, "Les marchands italiens," pp. 75–76.

merchants: Gian Michiel, Marco Dandolo, Niccolò Contarini, and Andrea Gradenigo. Querini was a well-connected man in Mongol aristocratic circles, and sought revenge by turning to the entourage of the ilkhan's mother, who ensured all his rivals were arrested. Eventually, the quarrel was settled, but the bailiff had to pay 260 bezants to free the Venetian citizens. Nevertheless, da Molin states in his letter that the city had become dangerous for his country-men.[62] In October 1325, the bailiff of Constantinople also informed Venice that the situation in Tabriz had become challenging.[63]

In late 1325, news reached Venice that more of its citizens in Tabriz had been arrested and imprisoned for debts. The senate sent an envoy to settle the matter, even though the bilateral pact of 1320 should have provided the legal framework for such a situation. As we shall see further on, conflicts regarding jurisdiction—especially those of a criminal nature—were more difficult to resolve. Ambassador Marco Corner was assigned a stipend of 600 *lire di grossi* (the equivalent of 5,000 bezants), and a large retinue (notary, cook, inter-preter, armed guards, and an accountant), as well as money to buy gifts for the ilkhan. Corner was also asked to arrange the funeral of Francesco da Canal, a Venetian citizen who had recently died in Tabriz. We do not know the out-come of Corner's mission, although there is evidence that the tensions con-tinued. In June 1332, Hazi Suliman Taibi of Tabriz and his Venetian partners, Giovanni di Andrea Sanudo and Giovanni di Niccolò Sanudo, entrusted a shipment of goods to another Venetian merchant, Niccolò Giustiniani, in the city of Erzerum. For reasons unspecified in the sources, the shipment was lost, and the partners demanded compensation.[64] That July 17, the Vene-tian senate ordered the bailiff of Trebizond to procure 4,000 bezants for these reparations.[65]

The death of the ilkhan Abu Said in 1335 marked the end of the Hülegü lineage. His successor was Arpa Ke'ün (m. 1336), a descendant of the Toluids; he ruled for just over a year until May 1336, when he was killed in a battle against troops of the governor of Baghdad. The Ilkhanate fell into a state of anarchy. Civil war raged among the Mongol aristocracy, making further

62. Giomo, *Libri commemoriali*, vol. 1, pp. 256–57; *Diplomatarium veneto-levantinum*, vol. 1, pp. 192–94.

63. Giomo, "Le rubriche dei Libri Misti," p. 332.

64. Giomo, *Libri commemoriali*, vol. 2, p. 43; *Diplomatarium veneto-levantinum*, vol. 1, pp. 222–23.

65. Paviot, "Les marchands italiens," p. 77; Thiriet, *Régestes des délibérations*, no. 60, p. 35.

diplomatic and trade relations impossible. The Venetians not only found it more challenging to conduct talks with the Mongols, but also struggled to organize their own *fondaco* in Tabriz. There was no longer a system in place that saw to the maintenance and safety of roads, and the administrative chain that had once guaranteed conditions for trade activities had fallen apart. Moreover, it was no longer clear whether the armed forces stationed along routes were aware of or abided by the treaties between Venice and the ilkhan—or if they were now out of the state's control and therefore a threat to traders. The dissolution of the Ilkhanate was compounded by the Mamluk conquest of Ayas in 1337; it was the same year that the 1322 peace treaty between Lesser Armenia and the sultan expired. This fatal blow to the organized presence of westerners in Tabriz forced both Venetians and Genoese to drastically reduce their investments in Persia.

In the face of this crisis, Genoa abandoned Tabriz and boycotted trade with the entire city.[66] The repercussions were so heavy that the emir Hasan Kuçek (r. 1338–43), who had recently taken control of Tabriz and its region, sent his ambassadors to Genoa with an offer of compensation for the damage they had suffered. However, the revival of relations between Genoa and what remained of the Ilkhanate was short-lived, as we shall see in the next chapter. Venice, on the other hand, acted more slowly, playing for time to see how political events would unfold. The Venetian senate entrusted the bailiff of Constantinople to manage the crisis, yet did not allow a new consul to be appointed in Tabriz. It took at least two decades for Venice to resume a dialogue with the Persian authorities. By the mid-1320s, Venice was diversifying its diplomatic efforts to secure alternatives; its most coveted market was still Alexandria, but the papal ban remained firmly in place.[67] These circumstances indirectly made the Sea of Azov and Tana more attractive alternatives.

## The Expansion of the Venetian Community in Tana (1332–43)

The Genoese had returned to Caffa in 1313, and the city rapidly became a crucial hub for trade going from central Asia through Azaq, a populous city at the mouth of the Don, inhabited by numerous merchant communities of all

---

66. Ciocîltan, *The Mongols and the Black Sea Trade*, p. 138; Bautier, *Les relations économiques*, p. 277.

67. Jackson, *The Mongols and the West*, p. 302; Ashtor, *Storia economica e sociale*, pp. 314–15.

backgrounds. Genoa had built a monopoly in northern Pontus that worried the Mongols as it threatened their sovereignty. After years of undisputed Genoese presence in Crimea and Tana, Uzbek Khan sought alternative merchant communities that would cause no harm to trade, but that would weaken Genoa's supremacy in the region. Venice rose to accept the role and expand its reach.

Until the mid-1320s, Venetians had not established their own community on Golden Horde territory. Instead, they owned businesses in Constantinople and maintained their commercial bases (warehouses and *fondaci*) in Sudak and Caffa, from which they could reach the Sea of Azov. The Byzantine capital was in dire straits, torn asunder by the struggle between Andronicus II and his nephew Andronicus III, who was supported by a large swath of the military under order of John Cantacuzenus. The situation allowed for abuses perpetrated by local authorities in blatant violation of treaties signed between Venice and the emperor. The Genoese in Pera took advantage of the Byzantine weakness to grow their influence in Constantinople.

In March 1320, complaints reached Venice from its citizens living in Constantinople. The bailiff Marco Minotto protested their treatment at the hands of both local authorities and the Genoese, sending a list of the damages his fellow citizens had suffered. The hostility was so great that Venetians could neither conduct their own business nor gain justice—their only recourse was to buy it. Moreover, it had become difficult to sell the grain imported from the Black Sea due to extortion by imperial officers.[68] Beyond the many bureaucratic challenges, Venice was banned from working and selling hides and leather imported from Crimea, and was also prohibited from exporting timber. Equally problematic was the local recruitment of sailors, as each hiring was taxed. Lastly, the city's interpreters favored the Genoese and refused to serve the Venetians. Minotto's letter to the senate states that many Venetians were forced to pretend they were Greek just to be able to work.[69] Further demands for compensation were for a fire that occurred in the summer of 1319, raging through the *contrada* (district) of San Pietro dei Pisani in Constantinople and damaging numerous homes. Unfortunately, Venetians were forbidden from repairing their homes.[70]

68. Giomo, *Libri commemoriali*, vol. 1, p. 215.

69. *Diplomatarium veneto-levantinum*, vol. 1, p. 167.

70. Giomo, *Libri commemoriali*, vol. 1, pp. 214–15; *Diplomatarium veneto-levantinum*, vol. 1, pp. 164–66.

In late 1320 (or early 1321; the source is undated), both Venice's official complaint to the Byzantine Emperor and his reply to Minotto's accusations arrived. Andronicus II granted the Venetian requests—in part—and allowed them to work safely in Constantinople, and to sell their goods in line with the treaty signed by Venice with John III Ducas, emperor of Nicaea, in the first half of the thirteenth century.[71] However, Andronicus II turned on Venice, protesting to the doge about the Venetian treaty violation and encroaching on his areas of influence in the Aegean. These disputes made an agreement impossible and stoked tensions between the Venetian community and the Byzantine authorities.

Wary of direct conflict, the Republic intensified its diplomatic efforts, ushering in the highly advantageous renewal of the truce in October 1324.[72] Among many other concessions, Venice was no longer restricted in its grain purchases within the empire.[73] Venice's goal of permanently easing its relations with Andronicus II was twofold: on one hand, it guaranteed protection for its citizens in Constantinople, while on the other hand, it reinforced the anti-Turkic front in Asia Minor. The capital of the Byzantine Empire was a necessary command center for directing trade with Black Sea ports, allowing the management of overland traffic that passed through territories suppressed by the ever-growing Ottoman power (see chapter 6) and the restlessness of small emirates scattered around the major Anatolian centers.

The previous chapter showed that after Toqta's expulsion order, western merchants returned to Crimea and Tana (the Latin name for the area in Azaq occupied by western traders). The Genoese were in Tana as early as 1313, while the Venetians probably came in the 1320s. Fragmented and ambiguous records suggest that the Venetians were already present in Tana in 1320, however.[74] A senate resolution dated that same year states that the seven armed galleys for the journey to Romània, under order of Romano Morosini, could go as far as the Sea of Azov but not dock in Tana.[75] After this mention, the earliest certain proof of a Venetian presence at the mouth of the Don dates to 1322: it indicates Uzbek Khan's desire to counter Genoa's trade monopoly. Nonetheless, a

71. *Diplomatarium veneto-levantinum*, vol. 1, pp. 164–65.

72. Renewed in 1332. *Diplomatarium veneto-levantinum*, vol. 1, pp. 230–34.

73. *Diplomatarium veneto-levantinum*, vol. 1, pp. 200–203; Thiriet, *La Romanie vénitienne*, p. 160–61.

74. Berindei and Migliardi O'Riordan, "Venise et la Horde d'Or," pp. 246–47.

75. Giomo, "Le rubriche dei Libri Misti," p. 328.

decade would pass before the Republic would settle its own permanent community in Tana, headed by a stable consul-run administration.[76]

In August 1322, and again in January 1323, the Mongol governor, residing in the Crimean city of Solgat,[77] Tuluk Timur, carried out a punitive raid on the Byzantine community living in Sudak. No doubt this violence was ordered by Uzbek. The reasons for the raid are unclear, but it was driven in part by the khan's desire to subjugate a settlement that was becoming increasingly independent. A further reason was the strained coexistence between the Christian and Islamic communities, where the former dominated.[78]

The expeditions against Sudak[79] were to Caffa's advantage, which had always been a trade rival of the nearby city. At the start of the fourteenth century, Caffa had confirmed its commercial supremacy along the Crimean coast. The Genoese had formally boycotted the port of Sudak since 1316, greatly impacting the city and its trade communities—including the Venetians.[80] The Serenissima made diplomatic overtures with Uzbek to remedy this. As we have seen, the khan was well disposed toward Venice. Furthermore, the Jöchid treasury was in constant need of cash to fund an ever-increasingly complex administration and its ambitious plans for reform. Venice's permanent entry to the Sea of Azov meant securing a large slice of the continental demand via the foremost European trading partner, fostering a supply path that had shifted toward the central Asian route, whose western terminal was Tana.

---

76. Archivio di Stato di Venezia (hereafter ASV), Senato Misti (hereafter SM), VII, fols. 66r and 86r, VIII, fol. 62r; Stöckly, *Le systéme de l'incanto*, p. 106; Karpov, *Drevnejšie postanovlenija*, p. 17, doc. of September 22, 1322.

77. The governor of Solgat (today's Staryi Krym) was the highest Mongol officer in Gazaria.

78. Ciocîltan, *The Mongols and the Black Sea Trade*, pp. 193–94 and especially Hautala, *V zemljach "severnoj Tartarii,"* pp. 37–39 and Vasil'ievskij, *Trudy*, vol. 1, pp. cxciii–xciv. Sources indicate that a pretext for the attack was the sound of bells from Christian churches, which offended devout Muslims. In 1318, Pope John XXII wrote to Uzbek Khan, urging him to welcome Christians in his kingdom with kindness, and to allow them to carry out their missionary work. On September 23, 1323, the pope wrote the khan of the Golden Horde once more, complaining that he had driven Christian soldiers out of Sudak, that all bells had been removed from churches, and that these had been converted into mosques.

79. Evidently, the Mongol raids had the hoped-for effect: when Ibn Battuta reached Sudak in the spring of 1334, he noticed that the city was mainly populated by Turks: Gibb Hamilton, *The Travels of Ibn Battuta*, pp. 471–72. See also Hautala, "Comparing Eastern and Missionary Sources," p. 39; Vasil'evskij, *Trudy*, vol. 1, p. cxcv.

80. Balard, *La Romanie génoise*, p. 158, who proved that the city disappeared from Genoese documentation until the mid-century.

Negotiations reached a turning point in the early 1330s. In 1332, the senate organized ten galleys to be armed for the Romània–Black Sea voyage, which left in March with Andrea Geno, the ambassador whom the senate had sent to Tana to meet with the khan and ratify the terms of the settlement. The mission was successful, and Venice gained its first important concession from Uzbek. The treaty, signed on August 7, 1333,[81] was a generous one: it gave Venice leave to settle a community in Tana, the right to build houses, conduct business,[82] and dock in the port for up to ten days.[83] The Venetian quarter extended from the riverbed to a hospital (though sadly, we have no further information on this). A 5 percent duty (*commerchium*) was imposed on all transactions by Venetian merchants, yet precious stones, silver, spun gold, and pearls were exempt.[84] Venice was also allowed its own consul as administrator and diplomatic representative. Tana never obtained an extraterritorial status on the level of Caffa's, but Venetian citizens remained subject to the consul's jurisdiction and would not be judged by local officials unless their disputes were with Mongol subjects. The document does, however, mention earlier agreements between the khan of the Golden Horde and Venice, showing that diplomatic overtures had been underway for some time, preparing the necessary steps for settlement to be authorized. Having been granted its own quarter, Venice set out to turn Tana into a key hub in its Levantine trade system—though this was still a role that required testing. It is for this reason perhaps that the senate left it to the captain of the galleys that had left in March of that year to decide whether to sail to Tana; in any case, a stop in the city's port could not exceed five days.[85]

81. *Diplomatarium veneto-levantinum*, vol. 1, pp. 243–44; Heyd, *Storia del commercio*, p. 751; Tafel and Thomas, *Urkunden*, pp. 243ff. Ibn Battuta also wrote a vivid description of Tana in the Uzbek era; the traveler reached the city on the River Don in the spring of 1332, together with a Mongol emir, and was able to visit it, noting its remarkable liveliness and diverse population.

82. "Domos hedificarent oltre che faciendum mercationes suas": *Diplomatarium veneto-levantinum*, vol. 1, p. 244.

83. "Aplicantesque navessuas in Tanam, in quibuscunque civitatibus contingat eos facere mercationes": *Diplomatarium veneto-levantinum*, vol. 1, p. 244; Heyd, *Storia del commercio*, p. 752.

84. The document probably confirms that Venetians had frequented Tana in the past, since Uzbek waived taxes on precious goods for them *ab antiquo*: *Diplomatarium veneto-levantinum*, vol. 1, p. 243. Pegolotti, *La pratica della mercatura*, p. 24: "Oro e argento e perle non pagano né comerchio né tamuga né nullo diritto alla Tana." These goods were highly prized by the Mongols, who encouraged their trade.

85. Thiriet, *Régestes des délibérations*, no. 19, p. 26.

Having reached an agreement with Uzbek, Venice moved to strengthen its friendship with the kingdom of Lesser Armenia, which had averted the Mamluk threat. On November 10, 1333, Ambassador Giacomo Trevisan declared a successful conclusion to his diplomatic mission with Leo V, from whom he had obtained permission for Venetian merchants to travel, stay, and return *in nostra Dei custodiata terra*. Trevisan also negotiated an allowance for Venetians to export every type of good (*portare extra terram nostram vel quascumque mercationes*) from the port of Ayas.[86] As we have seen, this port was directly connected to Trebizond, where Venice had an established community and a bailiff since 1319. The aim was to use the city as a commercial hub of the Pontic system, receiving goods by land from Ayas and by sea from Tana, thereby avoiding direct shipping from the mouth of the Don to Constantinople, still a treacherous route.

Niccolò Nanni[87] was Tana's first consul, nominated on February 28, 1333, yet it was not until Marco Soranzo's arrival in 1334 that Tana's administration took on a more structured nature. The consul received a salary of 30 silver *lire del grosso*. It was a substantial stipend, yet a necessary sum for the construction of a residence and to lay the foundations of his activity. Upon completion of the building, his salary dropped to 25 silver *lire del grosso*, although he was given permission to "trade."[88] He was also assigned the sum of 1000 aspers for any administrative expenses related to Venetian residents (*pro honore nostro et bono mercatorum nostrorum qui erunt ibi*).[89] The consul could count on a large retinue (*familia*): a notary priest (*presbiter*), an interpreter, four *famuli*, four horses, two town criers (*precones*), and two advisers.[90] The fact that the consul was given two advisers tells us just how important his administrative work was. Advisers were elected from among Tana's noble residents after the consul's inauguration, and all those over the age of twenty were eligible.[91] Necessary

86. Alishan, *L'Armeno-Veneto*, pp. 38–39, no. 14. Leo V had granted Venice a similar privilege when dealing with the delegation of Michele Giustiniani, sent at the behest of Doge Giovanni Soranzo (Canestrini, *Documenti spettanti al commercio*, pp. 41–44). Shortly before, the Venetian ambassador Pantaleone Michiel had obtained a similar privilege with Trebizond: Canestrini, *Documenti spettanti al commercio*, pp. 44–48.

87. ASV, SM, XV, fol. 67r, March 15, 1333; Karpov, *Istorija Tany*, p. 73.

88. *Diplomatarium veneto-levantinum*, vol. 1, pp. 249–50 (the act is dated February 9, 1334).

89. *Diplomatarium veneto-levantinum*, vol. 1, p. 250.

90. ASV, SM, XV, fol. 57; *Diplomatarium veneto-levantinum*, vol. 1, p. 249; Karpov, "Venecianskaja Tana po aktam kanclera Benedetto B'janko," p. 10.

91. ASV, SM, XXV, fols. 9v and 10, April 6, 1349. See also Karpov, "Enforced Councilor," p. 266.

social attributes to become an adviser were very strict. The senate ruled that if no nobles within the city could be found to take on the role, then the consul would operate on his own, much like the bailiff of Trebizond, who was also assisted by two advisers.[92] Those elected were given free accommodation (*non solvendo aliquam pensionem*) but could not refuse office, under penalty of a fine of 300 aspers.[93] Advisers were tasked with helping the consul manage the Venetian community and settle any quarrels, distribute houses for rent to merchants docking in the port, and manage land for cultivation.

Having gained this concession, Venetian authorities decided to fortify the settlement. The consul asked the senate for permission to build a first defensive structure over a perimeter of 379 *passi* (paces). However, the permitted extension was significantly smaller at no more than 160 *passi*.[94] As a Venetian *passo* corresponds to just over 1.7 meters (1.738674 to be exact),[95] the land Uzbek had granted to Venice had a total perimeter of 659 meters, while the permitted fortification measured just over 278 meters—most likely due to part of the area being marshland and thus unsuited for construction.

In April 1339, just as in 1332, the senate armed ten galleys for a voyage to Romània. Three were headed for Tana (followed by Trebizond) where they could remain docked for seven days.[96] Tana's supreme importance in these years is confirmed by a document issued by the great council on July 4, 1339, which expressly states that trade in distant lands (Tana and Trebizond are both mentioned) is the main activity of Venetian citizens and those they work with, making it of utmost importance to protect them.[97] In fact, these galleys left the following July for Romània once more, all three directed to Tana, where they again remained for a week.[98] The Venetian settlement was not tolerated by the

92. "Si vero in Tana non essent nobiles qui possent esse consiliarii, tunc consul per se solum exequatur et facia regime suum et sibi commissa, ut facit baiulus Tapessonde": *Diplomatarium veneto-levantinum*, vol. 1, p. 250.

93. *Diplomatarium veneto-levantinum*, vol. 1, p. 250. Since all noble residents of Tana—with some rare exceptions—were merchants, it was often an onerous task to aid the consul in his work, diverting those elected from their business in a region which the Venetian authorities themselves considered very dangerous.

94. ASV, SM, XV, fols. 57v and 58r; *Diplomatarium veneto-levantinum*, vol. 1, p. 251. Both dates recorded by Thiriet (1333) and Thomas (1334) are incorrect. See Karpov, "On the Origin of Medieval Tana," p. 235, no. 64.

95. See Martini, *Manuale di metrologia*, p. 817.

96. Thiriet, *Régestes des délibérations*, no. 91, p. 41.

97. Thiriet, *Délibérations des assemblées vénitiennes*, vol. 1, pp. 193 and 308–9.

98. Thiriet, *Régestes des délibérations*, no. 105, p. 43.

Genoese, rekindling their historic rivalry; this time, its epicenter was in Tana. That same year, 1340, the rift escalated to the point where a group of Genoese merchants attacked the Venetian quarter.[99] Tensions soared and the Venetian senate demanded that the Tana consul lodge a formal complaint with the governor of Solgat, as the abuses were too many and too frequent to be tolerated. On July 5, 1340, the senate asked the khan for a settlement further away from the Genoese, as well as a reduction in the *commerchium* to just 3 percent of the value of goods.[100]

The brawl reached the highest diplomatic levels. After complaints by the Venetian doge against his Genoese counterpart, Genoa's authorities replaced their consul in Tana and charged him with causing the disorder.[101] Simone Boccanegra (Genoa's doge) sent Bartolomeo Gradonico (Venice's doge) two letters (dated June 24 and July 12, 1342) in which he apologized for the damage done to the Venetian residents of Tana.[102] In the second letter, he noted that he had mandated a new consul, Beltramino Merello, so that the two communities might coexist in peace.[103] In 1342, while the Venetians and Genoese sought to heal their differences and realign their respective diplomatic efforts, and simultaneously negotiating more favorable conditions with the khan, a transformative event occurred: Uzbek died.[104] This man, more than any other, had guaranteed the Golden Horde's political continuity and had opened the empire to a western presence; his death led to a period of great uncertainty. Relations among the various Latin communities in Crimea and the Azov became precarious. Diplomatic initiatives with the governor of Solgat grew apace.[105]

Uzbek's long reign had ushered the Golden Horde into the peak of its power and wealth. Upon his death, the empire entered a period of political and

99. Heyd, *Storia del commercio*, p. 755.

100. Thiriet, *Régestes des délibérations*, no. 111, p. 44.

101. Canale, *Della Crimea*, vol. 2, pp. 449ff.

102. *Diplomatarium veneto-levantinum*, vol. 1, pp. 259–61.

103. "Quod nedum de cetero fraternitas et cara unitas inter vestrates augeatur et preterita enormia puniantur et corrigantur per eum, sed amici gaudia gaudijs cumulent et inimici vestri et nostri ad dolendum tristissime provocentur": *Diplomatarium veneto-levantinum*, vol. 1, p. 260.

104. Thiriet, *Régestes des délibérations*, no. 138, p. 49. The document is dated March 16, 1342, not 1341, as erroneously written by Thiriet (ASV, SM, XX, fol. 41).

105. To avoid clashes with the Genoese, on March 17, 1343, the Venetian senate asked the consul of Tana to accept the land (*teradego*) offered by the Mongols. Thiriet, *Régestes des délibérations*, no. 151, p. 51.

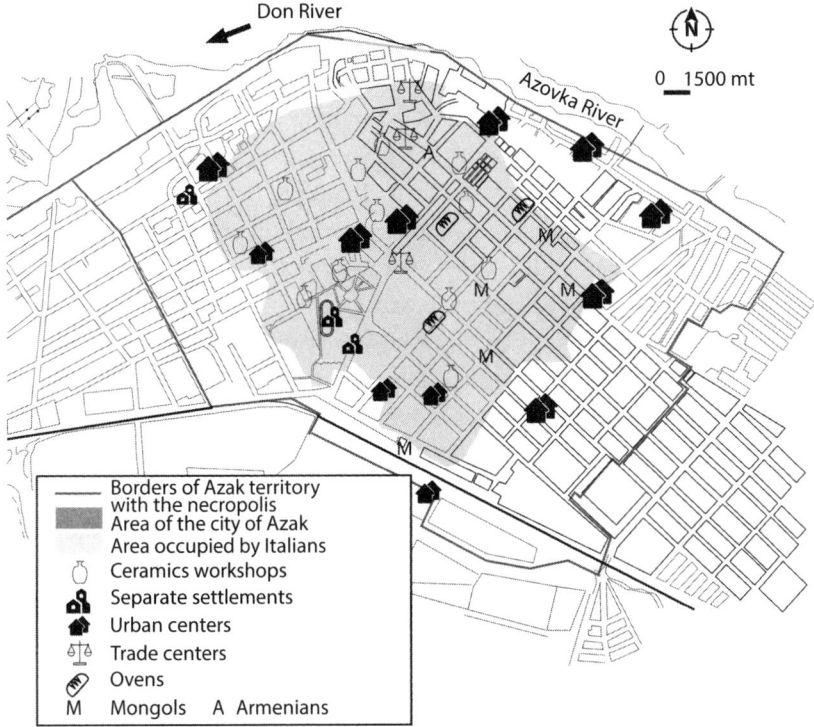

FIGURE 2. Topographic map of Tana in the 1340s. From the excavations of
A. N. Maslovskij (based on Karpov, *Istorija Tany*).

economic decline. His son Jani Beg (r. 1342–57) succeeded him; an ardent
Muslim, he is described in Islamic sources as an indefatigable supporter of the
Muslim religion and culture. He encouraged the construction of mosques,
attracted scholars from various regions of Islam, but was never hostile to the
presence of Christians, at least in the early years of his reign. Moreover, flourishing trade with westerners remained an indispensable source of income for
the Mongols.[106]

In 1342, the ambassadors Giovanni Quirini and Pietro Giustiniani negotiated an advantageous agreement with Jani Beg. The khan granted Venice a new

---

106. The *commerchium* varied, as we have seen, between 3 to 5 percent based on the goods
and on the agreements signed with the khans of the Horde. Pegolotti writes that the Venetians and
the Genoese were the only ones to pay 4 percent on products like wine, sturgeon, leather,
and horse hides, while all the other merchants paid 5 percent. Pegolotti, *La pratica della mercatura*, pp. 24–25.

piece of land and allowed its fortification. Moreover, he confirmed the concessions made to Venice by his father in 1332, and authorized Venetian merchants to inhabit and conduct business in Tana, separately from the Genoese.[107] As part of this agreement, Venice gained the right to freely administer justice in its own quarter, and to oversee the movement of goods at their own expense, taking whatever measures they saw fit.[108] Thanks to this pact with Jani Beg at the start of the 1340s, Tana remained the main hub of the northern route, which Pegolotti deemed the "safe" path to China. However, circumstances were changing—and not all for the best.

In early 1343, disturbing news reached Venice of events that would jeopardize its relations with the Mongols. Many merchants in Tana were evading the duties owed—or were trying to. On July 22, 1343, the senate issued an order based on a report of these activities, which most likely came from the outgoing consul. The resolution confirms that many merchants were defrauding the *commerchium*, and it expresses the grave concerns of the Venetian authorities, both in the motherland and *in loco*, concerning this illegal behavior. The authorities ordered the consul to force all merchants active in the settlement to swear an oath that they would respect the tax obligations set down in the treaties.[109]

Tensions now simmered between the various communities that lived and worked in Tana.[110] Every effort to control individual misdeeds failed. Very soon an incident would occur in this settlement on the mouth of the Don that would spark unprecedented violence.

107. "Cum eorum mercationibus possint stare et habitare secure in dicta terra Tane, separatim a Ianuensibus Franchis": *Diplomatarium veneto-levantinum*, vol. 1, pp. 261–63, in particular p. 262.

108. *Diplomatarium veneto-levantinum*, vol. 1, pp. 261–63.

109. Thiriet, *Régestes des délibérations*, no. 157.

110. After new tensions arose on July 12, 1343, the Genoese doge wrote to Venice, guaranteeing that he had instructed Beltramino Morello, the consul, to punish the excesses committed by his citizens to the detriment of the Venetians, and asking the Ventian doge to do the same: Giomo, *Libri commemoriali*, vol. 2, p. 103.

# 5

# Venice and the Mongols

## YEARS OF CRISIS (1343–60)

## The Crisis of 1343: Origin and Consequences

Tana was a settlement built specifically for trade; hence, local traders were anything but a minority there. Many had regular business relations with Italians, with whom they shared *fondaci*, stores, and taverns. Local merchants entered different types of contracts with Italians, and even partnered in companies. They were active in the slave trade, and brought luxury goods to Tana that Venetian merchants—who were rarely able to procure such items directly—could purchase for resale either locally or for transport back to their homeland. It was in this climate of daily interactions that violence flared: the most savage clash to have ever erupted between Mongols and westerners residing in the empire. The conflict was triggered in Tana in the late summer of 1343 and quickly spread to Caffa and the Black Sea, involving all Venetian and Genoese settlements, with immediate consequences for the delicate system of Latin–Mongol relations.

In early 1343, life in Tana had a peaceful ebb and flow. The new Jöchid khan, Jani Beg, had visited the settlement a few months before and was welcomed with honors by the consul Filippo Michiel.[1] Yet, by late summer, the mood had shifted drastically due to a sudden and violent incident: in September, a fight broke out between a Venetian citizen and a Mongol merchant. There are a great many sources that tell us about this event and its causes.[2] Though some describe it in great detail, accounts are contradictory. The most detailed

---

1. Karpov, *Istorija Tany*, p. 218.
2. Karpov, "Génois et Byzantines face à la crise de Tana."

contemporary account is that of the Swiss Franciscan John of Winterthur (d. ca. 1348). He recounted that a rich and powerful Muslim trader (*pagano*) assaulted a noble Venetian by punching or whipping him (*pugno vel flagello*).[3] Although he does not specify the cause for the aggression, members of the Venetian senate were absolutely certain that the blame lay with *un homo insido dentro di nuy, lo qual à fato mal* (an evil man among us who caused harm).[4] The man in question was Andreolo Civran, a Venetian merchant living in Tana, who decided to avenge the affront he had suffered by gathering a group of compatriots, going to his attacker's home, and murdering him along with his entire family.

A briefer version is given in *Chronicon* by Lorenzo de Monacis (1351–1428), written around 1420. A diplomat, humanist, and well-informed writer, de Monacis simply states that the Venetian Civran (*de Civrana prole*) was slapped by a Mongol and reacted by murdering the man with his sword.[5] De Monacis also writes: "per lo mal che aveva fato questo homo (il Civran), lo imperador Zanibech sì se corozà"—Emperor Jani Beg was enraged by the evil deeds wrought by this man (Civran).[6] Indeed, the Mongols were enraged and demanded Civran be turned over to them. At that point, a large group of Tatars attacked Tana's Latin quarters, forcing both Venetians and Genoese to flee by sea.[7] A version of events provided by another Venetian chronicler, Morosini (ca. 1368–ca. 1433), has a more laconic tone but is faithful to those accounts by Winterthur and de Monacis. According to Morosini, an unnamed noble Venetian suffered an offense at the hands of a rich Mongol. A group of Venetians then broke into the attacker's home and murdered him and members of his family. Morosini confirmed that the Mongols' reaction was swift and violent, forcing all Latins, regardless of nationality, to flee Tana by sea. However, only a few managed to escape; those who remained were helpless at the hands of the Mongols' vengeance.

Historiography has been fascinated with this incident since the nineteenth century. According to Canale's reconstruction (later also discussed by

---

3. *Die Chronik Johanns von Winterthur*, p. 219.

4. Morozzo della Rocca, "Notizie da Caffa," p. 267.

5. Monaci, *Laurentii de Monacis Veneti Cretae Cancellarii Chronicon*, p. 207.

6. Morozzo della Rocca, "Notizie da Caffa," p. 267; Archivio di Stato di Venezia (hereafter ASV), Senato Misti (hereafter SM), XXI, fol. 83v.

7. Monaci, *Laurentii de Monacis Veneti Cretae Cancellarii Chronicon*, p. 207; *Diplomatarium veneto-levantinum*, vol. 1, p. 268.

Heyd),[8] the Venetian Andreolo Civran was alleged to have killed the Mongol Khodja Omar in a fight.[9] Omar was not just any citizen—he was a Mongolian fiscal officer (a *beg*). As we have noted many times over, the privileges that the Mongol khans afforded Venice and Genoa were imperial concessions. Every agreement was underpinned by clear definitions of the respective jurisdictions, which outlined that if a subject of the khan was the victim of a crime, or somehow involved in criminal deeds, the case was to be judged under Mongol law. However, Civran had evaded the khan's justice. Perhaps out of a sense of solidarity or because Civran was under protection, the Venetian representative did not hand him over to the local authorities. Once Civran had succeeded in returning to his country, he was put on trial there and sentenced. His punishment was relatively light, however: he was exiled from Venice for five years, and received a lifetime ban from working in any markets under Mongol rule.[10]

Although Civran emerged unscathed, the consequences of his actions were seismic, forcing Genoa and Venice to redefine their respective strategies and alliances in the Levant. There was immediate and substantial material damage caused by the clashes between the local population and the Latins.[11] Many European residents lost their lives, others their property, goods, and all that they had invested.[12] Many were robbed in their homes or while fleeing. Merchants were desperate to avoid bankruptcy and broke the papal ban by transporting their goods to Mamluk-controlled ports. However, the Venetian authorities proved to be tolerant of this, and either reduced or condoned any

8. Canale, *Della Crimea*, vol. 2, p. 458; Heyd, *Storia del commercio*, p. 757; Skržinskaja, "Storia della Tana," p. 10.

9. Venezia–Senato, *Deliberazioni miste*, vol. 22, no. 205, p. 105.

10. To fully understand why Civran's sentence was so light, we must consider the web of kinships between all the members of the Venetian patriciate directly involved in Tana's trade. These ties were so tight that when legal proceedings were instituted against Civran, it was impossible to find a judge who was not a blood relative of the merchants involved in the 1343 incidents.

11. Recent archeological excavations have revealed traces of fires in Tana that can be dated to this period. Karpov, *Istorija Tany*, p. 100; Maslovskij, "Podval kupečeskogo doma."

12. According to Villani, these would amount to 300,000 *fiorini d'oro* for Venice and 350,000 for Genoa: Villani, *Nuova Cronica*, vol. 3, p. 368. From a communiqué issued by the captain of the galleys of Romània, Marco Morosini, the Mongols "arrogantissimus Scitha sive Tartarus, orto privato litigio, alapam dedit cuidam Veneto de Ciurana prole ... Tartari conglobati in multitudinem insurgunt furioso impetu in Christianos": *Diplomatarium veneto-levantinum*, vol. 1, p. 268; Balard, *La Romanie génoise*, p. 154; Karpov, "Krizis Tany."

sanctions that were owed. By turning a blind eye, they acknowledged just how exceptional this crisis was.[13]

Jani Beg's reaction was in line with that of the local population. Alongside the attacks on Venetian property, he ordered that Tana should come under siege, soon forcing all westerners to flee for shelter in Caffa, a well-fortified city that was difficult to conquer. Caffa was less fallible to siege thanks to its position on the coast; this gave it both a means of escape and a route to reprovision and receive reinforcements. It must be noted that Genoese authorities welcomed Venetian citizens to Caffa, demonstrating solidarity in the face of a common enemy. There were several factors underlying Jani Beg's reaction. The oldest sources emphasized the khan's ire.[14] Despite its simplicity, this reason should not be underestimated, since the murder of a Mongol aristocrat was a grave crime that could not go unpunished. In addition, the Caffa Genoese had become openly independent, and were therefore a threat to the Mongols. For years, the Ligurian merchants considered the Crimean city not as a concession but as an extension of their motherland, and as such autonomous. As had been the case in the past, the time had come for Jani Beg to reassert his authority.[15]

News of the clashes spread quickly and soon reached Italy. On October 25, 1343, the Venetian senate elected five *savi* (wise men) tasked with carefully examining the facts and evaluating the damage done by their community. On November 10, an arrest warrant was issued for those responsible for the violence, most likely Civran's six accomplices (*illos qui sibi viderentur culpabiles de homicidio vel homicidiis perpetratis in Tana terra*); their torture and interrogation was ordered.[16] Meanwhile, the senate sent two ambassadors to Jani Beg's court to "set things right": Nicoletto di Raynerio and Zanachi Barbafella.[17] However, the appeasement failed, and the road to Tana remained firmly shut.

In the aftermath of the Mongol attack, those who could escape had either reached Caffa, where they had Genoese protection, or Constantinople, where they found protection in the Venetian quarter. Yet not everyone had escaped. Citizens who were trapped in Tana had to be evacuated, and any lost goods

---

13. In fact, Pope Clement VI even allowed Venice to send its own merchant galleys to Alexandria in the spring of 1344. *Diplomatarium veneto-levantinum*, vol. 1, pp. 277–78.

14. Heyd, *Storia del commercio*, p. 187.

15. *Diplomatarium veneto-levantinum*, vol. 1, pp. 329–31.

16. Venezia–Senato, *Deliberazioni miste*, vol. 21, p. 311.

17. Sanudo, *Vitae ducum Venetorum*, col. 611; *Diplomatarium veneto-levantinum*, vol. 1, pp. 266–67; Karpov, *Istorija Tany*, pp. 101–2.

needed to be recovered. Another problem had arisen: among the chaos, several Venetians committed acts of pillage and theft. Unsurprisingly, Venetian authorities warned those responsible to return the ill-gotten goods within eight days of any complaints. To deal with this, the magistrate of the *extraordinarii* (created in 1302 to collect freights from communal galleys) was tasked with investigating the robberies committed by Tana's "foreign" residents.[18] Their primary objective was to heal the rift with Jani Beg as quickly as possible, so Venice could resume sailing on the Black Sea.

Nonetheless, events took a turn. After expelling the "Franks" from Tana, the khan set his sights on Caffa. The Mongol siege was thwarted by Genoese resistance: in February 1344, the city's inhabitants emerged from its fortifications in an offensive that broke the siege. Although the Mongol army was forced to retreat, Jani Beg did not abandon his goal of conquering the Genoese colony. For their part, having averted the fall of Caffa, Genoa and Venice embarked on two diplomatic paths: the first toward the Mongol court, and the second toward each other. Between January and February 1344, Venice's senate carefully considered the grave news coming from Tana. It was decided that another envoy should be sent to the khan, and that Venetian merchants should be banned from trading with the Golden Horde. The penalty was set at a fine of 500 *grossi* plus half the value of the goods transported. Venetian authorities tasked the bailiff of Constantinople with executing these measures.[19]

During the clashes in Tana, the Mongols had arrested several Venetian merchants; according to the chronicle by Giovanni Villani, these numbered sixty in total.[20] At a subsequent senate session, held on March 12, 1344, ambassadors were authorized to ask for the release of these Venetians, whom "l'imperatore dei Tartari detiene fra tormenti e privazioni" (the emperor of the Tatars is holding in custody amid torment and deprivation), as well as for the recovery

18. Venezia–Senato, *Deliberazioni miste*, vol. 21, pp. 300–305.

19. Thiriet, *Régestes des délibérations*, no. 162, p. 54.

20. This number appears regularly in the sources with different references. Winterthur, for instance, writes that there were sixty Venetian victims of the Mongol retaliation after Civran killed Omar and his family. Even as the months went by, the situation did not improve. Villani, *Nuova Cronica*, vol. 3, pp. 367–68: "In questo tempo essendo cominciata una grande zuffa alla città della Tana nel Mar Maggiore in Romania tra' Viniziani e Saracini della terra . . . e presono poi da LX mercatanti latini, che a romore non furono morti, e tenolli in prigione da II anni." A resolution of the Venetian senate confirms the information reported by the Florentine chronicler: that the merchants arrested, according to the voices coming from down there (*a romore*), would still be alive (Thiriet, *Régestes des délibérations*, no. 169, p. 55).

of their goods.[21] Before authorizing further action, the senate awaited more specific information, presumably delivered by a merchant who was expected to arrive in Venice shortly, and by the crew of a Genoese galley arriving from Caffa.[22] Venetian envoys had been organized in February 1344 and now received permission to leave in the spring; thus, on May 10, two galleys were readied for the journey.[23] That June, the senate established the terms of the treaty to be presented to the khan in person and in the usual manner.[24]

Meanwhile, negotiations with Genoa continued. On June 18, 1344, the Genoese ambassador Corrado Cigala reached Venice and proposed to the doge that they join forces (*unio sive compositio*) to organize a joint diplomatic action to pressure Jani Beg, demanding that he release all prisoners, compensate for damages, and allow the merchants of the two cities to return to the Gazaria (the Genoese colonies in Crimea).[25] The strategy was ambitious: the two republics agreed to refuse any accord should Jani Beg attack Caffa again. To coerce the khan, Venice and Genoa resorted to an embargo of all the Horde's markets; however, this move would generate further friction because, as we know, Genoa believed that the "Horde's markets" did not include Caffa, while Venice believed it did.[26]

At first, Venice accepted Genoa's proposal, and the agreement was ratified on July 1.[27] The treaty specifically mentions the many casualties—both Genoese and Venetian—who were involved in the clashes in Tana. Diplomatic delegations were arranged to be sent to Crimea and, if possible, directly to Jani Beg. Venice sent two ambassadors to Caffa, Marco Ruzzini and Giovanni Steno, who were to meet their Genoese counterparts, hired by Corrado Cigala,

21. "Personarum nostrorum qui per imperatorem Tartarorum Zanibech in duris tormentis miserabiliter detineri dicuntur": *Diplomatarium veneto-levantinum*, vol. 1, p. 320.

22. Thiriet, *Régestes des délibérations*, no. 165, p. 54; *Diplomatarium veneto-levantinum*, vol. 1, p. 321.

23. In a resolution of May 31, the terms of the journey were established: the galleys could not transport any goods without explicit authorization and the fine for such actions was equal to 50 percent of the value transported (ASV, SM, XXII, fol. 24; *Diplomatarium veneto-levantinum*, vol. 1, p. 326).

24. *Diplomatarium veneto-levantinum*, vol. 1, p. 278.

25. Morozzo della Rocca, "Notizie da Caffa," pp. 281–82.

26. Ciocîltan, *The Mongols and the Black Sea Trade*, p. 207; Morozzo della Rocca, "Notizie da Caffa," pp. 290–92.

27. Karpov, *Istorija Tany*, p. 108 and n. 90; *Diplomatarium veneto-levantinum*, vol. 1, pp. 279–84; Morozzo della Rocca, "Notizie da Caffa," p. 294.

plenipotentiary of doge Simon Boccanegra. Together, the delegation would journey to the khan.[28] They were tasked with conducting joint negotiations, in a treaty of alliance, and not to negotiate separately unless strictly necessary. The delegation should ask Jani Beg to free their fellow citizens, and to return the seized goods. They were also to enter a treaty of friendship with the khan, offering him compensation for damages.[29] Should this attempt at peace with Jani Beg fail, Genoa and Venice would commit to calling off all trade relations with the Golden Horde for one year starting from July 1, 1344. Violation of the ban would incur a fine equal to 10,000 ducats.

However, it was clear that the union was entirely in Genoa's favor, and things soon came to a head. Having landed in Caffa in late August 1344, the Venetians Ruzzini and Steno informed the senate that, despite the agreement not to do business in Gazaria, the Genoese were regularly loading goods in the port of Caffa as they did not believe it to be subject to Mongol authority.[30] This loophole would remain controversial. For Venice, the area known as Gazaria included all the territory subject to the authority of the khan; Genoa, on the other hand, disagreed and believed that Caffa was an extension of its mother-land and Genoese in all respects. Genoa thus believed it should be excluded from the naval blockade.

On November 20, 1344, the senate sent Niccolò di Freganesco on a diplo-matic mission to Genoa to investigate whether there was a violation of the trade ban with the Golden Horde via Genoa's use of Caffa's port. The Genoese doge insisted this was not a breach as Caffa was not a territory subject to Jani Beg's authority. He pointed out that if Genoa closed Caffa to all commercial traffic, its inhabitants would not have had the resources to resist the Mongol siege, and this would have harmed the two republics more than the Mongols themselves.[31]

Venice likely swallowed this bitter pill. In such a perilous situation, it was safest to accept the conditions set by its rival and to join forces so as not to risk losing Caffa. In fact, the Venetians were using the city while they hoped for a return to Tana.[32] Venetian ambassadors managed to garner agreements that

28. Giomo, *Libri commemoriali*, vol. 2, p. 139.

29. Giomo, *Libri commemoriali*, vol. 2, p. 139.

30. Morozzo della Rocca, "Notizie da Caffa," p. 270; Venezia–Senato, *Deliberazioni miste*, vol. 22, pp. 268–69.

31. Morozzo della Rocca, "Notizie da Caffa," p. 271.

32. *Diplomatarium veneto-levantinum*, vol. 1, p. 282. Genoa and Venice signed a treaty impos-ing an embargo on the markets of the Horde, and promised not to negotiate separate peace treaties with the Mongols.

rebalanced the union, allowing their merchants to enjoy the same conditions in Caffa as the Genoese. Moreover, while it is true that the commercial embargo blocked economic activities on both sides, the greatest damage was actually being done to the entire region. Reports from Venetian ambassadors in Caffa feature complaints from local merchants about the situation.[33]

Despite the joint diplomatic efforts that continued until early 1345, the two cities gained nothing from Jani Beg. To step up the pressure on the Mongols, the terms of the union (which were due to expire in March 1346) were redefined on July 1.[34] This time, the terms were more favorable to Venice, as Genoa agreed to exempt Venetians from paying trade duties, allowing them to frequent the district of Pera as well as Caffa, along with a bilateral promise to boycott Tana.[35] In reality, these advantages were a smokescreen: the agreement was made in late summer and would not come into effect until the fall, when Black Sea shipping would be at a standstill anyway.[36]

The conditions of the alliance also included promises from both parties not to enter agreements either with Jani Beg or his subjects and successors.[37] Genoa and Venice agreed not to sail either on their own ships or on the ships of others to the east and north of Caffa. On this point, the document was peremptory: one could go to Constantinople and to Pera with armed or unarmed ships,[38] but merchants from both republics were banned from traveling to or remaining within the borders of the Golden Horde (*ad aliquas terras vel loca dicti imperatoris Ianibech*) for as long as the union was in effect. It was also forbidden to travel to Tana with or without goods. Naturally, Caffa was once

---

33. "Tutti i mercanti e gli abitanti di Solgat desiderano la pace così come tutto il popolo dei Tartari (omnes mercatores de Sorgati et omnis populus multum dexiderat habere pacem et similiter populus Tartarorum habere pacem dexiderat)": Morozzo della Rocca, "Notizie da Caffa," pp. 277–78. See also Papacostea, "'Quod non iretur ad Tanam,'" p. 206.

34. *Diplomatarium veneto-levantinum*, vol. 1, p. 299. The document expressly states that the league with Genoa is constituted "pro factis ac negotijs Maris Maioris et imperii Gazarie et occasione guerre, dissensionis et discordie."

35. *Diplomatarium veneto-levantinum*, vol. 1, pp. 303–5. Morozzo della Rocca, "Notizie da Caffa," pp. 283–84.

36. Morozzo della Rocca, "Notizie da Caffa," p. 271; Venezia–Senato, *Deliberazioni miste*, vol. 23, pp. 18, 22, 30–32.

37. "Non faciet . . . pacem, condcordiam vel remissionem cum dicto imperatore Ianibech vel eius curia, officialibus vel subditis seu imperio suo, vel aliquo successore suo": *Diplomatarium veneto-levantinum*, vol. 1, p. 302.

38. *Diplomatarium veneto-levantinum*, vol. 1, p. 302.

again excluded from the embargo.[39] Genoa was committed to guaranteeing access to Caffa to all Venetian traders who, with their goods and ships, could cover the sea between Caffa and Pera (*salvo ad locum et civitatem Caffa, et ab inde infra versus occidentem sive versus Peyram*).[40] Thus, the Venetians could use the port of Caffa to unload the goods they had brought from Tana. Even more important was Genoa's concession regarding the consul: a Venetian officer could settle in Caffa and assume legal responsibility for the Venetian community for as long as the alliance with Genoa lasted.[41] It was up to two *boni viri*—one Venetian and one Genoese—to establish how much rent Venetians had to pay for houses and the *fondaci* granted to them by the authorities. Nonetheless, as "human nature is irremediably wicked,"[42] it became necessary to establish clauses for the event of any breaches to each and every rule contained in the treaty. Anyone who sailed to the East or as far as Tana was subject to a fine as high as 10,000 gold ducats, plus damages caused by any Mongol retaliation and, finally, a variable sum for each violation of other points in the treaty. The agreement would remain effective for a year, but it could not be used as a legal basis for future disputes.[43]

Meanwhile, on the Black Sea, things remained as normal despite the alliance with Genoa and the activity of ambassadors who had gone to Tana once again. On November 13, 1345, after examining the letters *ambaxatorum nostrorum Tane* and consulting the three *savi* (wise men), Genoa's senate concluded that there was no hope of reaching a peace treaty with the Mongols. The republic ordered its envoys to return by the expiry date of the union with Venice, April 1, 1346.[44] Indeed, in the winter of 1345–46, Jani Beg—who still believed he could prevail over Caffa's resistance—assaulted the city walls once more. The khan failed, but the consequences rippled across the entire continent.

39. On this matter, see also Papacostea, "'Quod non iretur ad Tanam,'" p. 207.

40. *Diplomatarium veneto-levantinum*, vol. 1, p. 303: "liberi et immunes in dicta civitate [Caffae] ab omnibus drictibus, cabellis, introytibus, comercij, seu exactionibus, que in ipso loco colliguntur." See also Papacostea, "'Quod non iretur ad Tanam,'" p. 208.

41. "Regere possit Venetos et homines Venetiarum ibidem existentes, conversantes et morantes": *Diplomatarium veneto-levantinum*, vol. 1, p. 303.

42. "Quia naturam humana, malicia hoinum crescente, opportuit jure et iusticie esse totaliter subiugatum ... et sic necessarium esse dignosctiru, quod prave agentes penis debitis puniantur": *Diplomatarium veneto-levantinum*, vol. 1, p. 304.

43. *Diplomatarium veneto-levantinum*, vol. 1, p. 303; Giomo, *Libri commemoriali*, vol. 2, p. 148.

44. Morozzo della Rocca, "Notizie da Caffa," p. 274. Since "non apparet spes aliqua possendi habere concordium cum imperatore Zanibech": Venezia–Senato, *Deliberazioni miste*, vol. 23, p. 126.

Jani Beg had carefully planned the siege by readying a fleet and organizing an attack by sea. Nonetheless, the Genoese navy easily defeated the Mongols. Their counteroffensive launched in early 1346, and the Ligurian galleys occupied the port of Cembalo (modern Balaklava).[45] At the same time, the Mongol army found itself facing an enemy even more dangerous than the Franks: the plague. The most detailed source on the 1345–46 siege of Caffa is in the chronicle of the Piacentino notary Gabriele de Mussi (or de' Mussis), who recorded many details of how the epidemic affected the ranks of the besieging army.[46]

The plague that swept across Europe from 1348 onward was already endemic in Asia in the 1330s.[47] In 1345, it struck the cities of the Golden Horde, particularly Sarai and Astrakhan. Between the spring and summer of 1346, the disease spread in the Volga region, and in early 1347, the first clusters appeared in the Caucasus, reaching Tana and Caffa that spring.[48] De Mussi's account survived in a copy dated to the late fourteenth century, and provides details of the siege of Caffa where the Mongols used catapults to launch plague-ridden bodies inside the walls to infect their enemies.[49] Although there are no documentary sources that confirm this, the presence of plague in Crimea no doubt played a decisive role in its transmission across Europe.[50]

De Mussi's chronicles greatly influenced the historiographical debate on the origin of the plague in Europe. Due to his ties to Genoese and Venetian affairs in the East, de Mussi most likely witnessed these events firsthand. However much some elements may seem exaggerated, he is generally reliable as a

45. And they would never leave. Ciocîltan, *The Mongols and the Black Sea Trade*, pp. 211–12; Petti Balbi, "Caffa e Pera a metà del Trecento," p. 226.

46. De Mussi, "Historia de morbo."

47. The origin of the plague in east Asia is still being debated, but initial reports on the widespread and inexplicable death rate in China were already appearing in sources of the time about the Mongol conquest of the Xi Xia empire, in 1226–27. For a complete picture and new hypotheses, see Hymes, "Epilogue," pp. 287–88. Centers of the epidemic in China during the Yuan dynasty had already emerged in 1307 and after that in 1344–45. Ibid., pp. 299–300; Favereau, *The Horde*, p. 253.

48. Karpov, "Black Sea and the Crisis," p. 67; Favereau, *The Horde*, p. 256.

49. This has also been cited as the first example of biological warfare: Wheelis, "Biological Warfare."

50. There are endless sources on the Black Death in the fourteenth century. For an overall picture, alongside the previously mentioned classics, see Cohn, *The Black Death Transformed*; Cantor, *In the Wake of the Plague*; Pamuk, "The Black Death and the Origins"; Green, "Taking 'Pandemic' Seriously"; Green, "The Four Black Deaths."

source, and there is little doubt that, although the Mongols and their siege tactics were not in themselves responsible for the spread, the plague did indeed arrive in western Europe aboard Genoese ships sailing from the Black Sea.[51] However, it did not arrive as a consequence of the 1346 siege of Caffa, but rather in the following years, aboard ships transporting grain. In the *fondaci* (warehouses) of Tana, Caffa and all the region's cities, large quantities of grain had been amassed; as rats and grain go hand in hand, it is highly likely that the end of the war between the Italians and Jani Beg saw shipping routes reopened, carrying both grain and flea-infested rats, a vector for the plague bacillus to humans. In Rus', on the other hand, the main vectors for plague were parasites of fur-bearing animals, such as marmots. Though the trade differed, the mechanisms were similar.[52]

Recent studies confirm the theory put forward half a century ago by Ruggero Romano that the epidemic was directly related to the famines that had struck at a local level across continents.[53] For example, from 1341 to 1347, the Byzantine civil war had reached its peak,[54] causing enormous damage to agricultural output, resulting in a grain shortage throughout western Pontus.[55] We can therefore exclude the theory of bacteriological warfare and accept the more realistic theory of fleas as vectors of this infectious disease. The fact remains that the plague wreaked devastation on populations not just in Europe but in the entire Black Sea basin and in Asia. Among the many accounts from that time, events are summed up best in the Sienese chronicle attributed to Agnolo di Tura, as well as in the account of the Florentine chronicler Matteo Villani. Very little is known about the Sienese chronicler, but he described burying five children who had died of plague. In a passage of his *Cronaca senese*, di Tura wrote that the Genoese galleys "tornaro d'oltremare . . . con molta infermità e corutione d'aria la quale era oltremare. . . . E così gionti a Gienova di fatto v'attaccaro il morbo grandissimo e morivavi molta gente." (They came back from overseas with many diseases and breathing problems . . . and so

51. "Partes aquilonaris": Karpov, "Black Sea and the Crisis," pp. 68–69.

52. Langer, "The Black Death." See also Favereau, *The Horde*, p. 256; Schamiloglu, "Preliminary Remarks," pp. 449–50.

53. Romano, "La storia economica"; Schamiloglu, "The Impact of the Black Death," p. 326. Winterthur noted in his chronicle that he witnessed a great famine strike Germany in 1343, forcing the population to adapt to eating grass and roots for survival (*Die Chronik Johanns von Winterthur*, pp. 200 and 205).

54. Nicol, *The Last Centuries of Byzantium*, pp. 219–20.

55. Karpov, "Black Sea and the Crisis," p. 68.

upon landing in Genoa they spread the terrible disease and caused the deaths of many people.)[56] The Florentine chronicler Matteo Villani, brother of the more famous Giovanni, who also died of the plague in 1348, wrote:

> cominciossi nelle parti d'Oriente, nel detto anno [1346], in verso il Cattai e l'India superiore, e nelle altre provincie circustanti a quelle marine dell'Oceano, una pestilenzia tra gli uomini d'ogni condizione di ciascuna età e sesso, che cominciavano a sputare sangue e morivano chi di subito, chi in due o in tre dì. . . . E nell'ultimo di questo tempo s'aggiunse alle nazioni del Mare Maggiore, e alle ripe del Mare Tirreno, nella Soria e Turchia, e in verso lo Egitto e la riviera del Mar Rosso, e dalla parte settentrionale la Rossia e la Grecia, e l'Erminia e l'altre conseguenti provincie.[57]

Nevertheless, in April 1346, with the Mongol army still encircling the walls of Caffa, Venice enforced the decision it had made months earlier and ordered its diplomats to return, unless "new hope should arise"—perhaps with the aid of Genoese ambassadors.[58]

## Peace with Jani Beg

Undoubtedly, the plague was a major crisis in Europe and Asia in the fourteenth century, yet it struck the Christian West with a particular vehemence as it exacerbated an already difficult economic situation.[59] Italy had

---

56. Agnolo di Tura continued to write the chronicle that Andrea Dei had begun. The latter recorded the history of his city from 1186 to April 1348. After this came the beginning of Agnolo's story and also, according to the chronicler, of the pandemic that struck Siena. *Cronaca senese*, pp. 122–3 and Benedictow, *The Black Death*, p. 244.

57. "The plague began in the East, in the aforementioned year (1346) around China and northern India, and in the surrounding regions as far as the ocean. It spread among men of every condition, and age, who began to spit blood and die, some right away, others within two or three days. . . . And in recent times [the disease] reached as far as the people of the Black Sea, as far as the Tyrrhenian Sea, Syria, Turkey, and toward Egypt and the Red Sea shores, northwards, to Russia, Greece, Armenia, and the neighboring provinces." Matteo fell victim to the disease during the second wave that struck Florence in 1362. Matteo Villani, *Cronica*, vol. 1, p. 5.

58. Meanwhile, Venetian galleys sent to Romània were authorized to enter the Black Sea only after the bailiff of Constantinople expressed his opinion. The homeland lacked reliable information as the situation was constantly evolving and could change from one minute to the next. Thiriet, *Régestes des délibérations*, no. 185, p. 58; Venezia–Senato, *Deliberazioni miste*, vol. 23, p. 128.

59. Cherubini, "La 'crisi del Trecento'"; Romano, "La Storia economica." On the consequences of the crisis on international trade, see Tangheroni, *Commercio e navigazione*; Kedar, *Mercanti in crisi*; Karpov, "Black Sea and the Crisis," pp. 65–66.

suffered poor mid-decade harvests, forcing Venetian authorities to import grain from the Jöchid *ulus*, despite the embargo established by the 1345 treaty with Genoa.[60]

From a political perspective, the mid-fourteenth century saw the situation in the Black Sea basin worsen. As outlined in the previous chapter, by 1338, Venice had abandoned the markets of the Ilkhanate because the Chobanids, who had come to power in Tabriz when the emir Hasan Kuçek took charge, could not guarantee adequate control of the territory. Soon after this decision by the Venetian authorities, Genoa also forbade its merchants from traveling to Persia, first in 1340 and then in 1342.[61] On the second occasion, the Chobanid leader Malik Ashraf (d. 1357) renewed the offer his predecessor Hasan Kuçek had made to the Genoese, promising a *fondaco* in Tabriz. Genoa accepted, but the first of their caravans headed to Tabriz was attacked and pillaged by marauders.[62]

The political climate in Asia Minor was also at boiling point. Byzantium and Trebizond were engaged in ongoing conflicts. From 1321 to 1354, the fragile Byzantine Empire of the Palaiologos was torn asunder by a seemingly never-ending civil war.[63] The Ottomans laid siege to Trebizond in 1341 and in 1348.[64] The second siege saw the Venetian quarter set ablaze, causing great damage. Between 1348 and 1349, Genoa and the empire of Trebizond went to war; Genoa prevailed, destroying the wealthy city of Kreasous (modern Giresun).[65]

Both the events of 1343 and the Mamluk conquest of Ayas in 1337 forced western markets to resume their investments in Alexandria, as there was no other way to reach Persia. Venice noted the stalemate in negotiations with Jani Beg and its dangerous alliance with Genoa, which had made the Republic highly vulnerable. Thus, Venice decided to protect itself by reopening trade channels in the Levant. To this end, it officially asked Pope Clement VI

60. "Non obstante strictura contenta in parte predicta, cum ista condicione, quod cum navigiis, cum quibus navigabunt ad partes predictas, redeant Venecias caricati frumento vel blado, vel vacui exeant de terris et partibus Zanibech." Venezia–Senato, *Deliberazioni miste*, vol. 24, pp. 46–47; *Diplomatarium veneto-levantinum*, vol. 1, p. 336; Thiriet, *Régestes des délibérations*, no. 196, p. 60. See also Karpov, "Black Sea and the Crisis," p. 68.

61. Karpov, "Black Sea and the Crisis," p. 69; Balard, *La Romanie génoise*, p. 720; Bautier, *Les relations économiques*, p. 277; Lopez, "Nouveaux documents," p. 454; and Ciociltan, *The Mongols and the Black Sea Trade*, p. 200.

62. Karpov, "Black Sea and the Crisis," p. 69 and n. 8.

63. Nicol, *The Last Centuries of Byzantium*; Ostrogorsky, *Storia dell'impero bizantino*, especially chapter 8; also Pertusi, *Fine di Bisanzio e fine del mondo*.

64. Karpov, "Black Sea and the Crisis," pp. 68–69.

65. Karpov, *L'impero di Trebisonda*, pp. 152–54.

(r. 1342–52) to suspend the trade ban with the Mamluks; his answer was positive.[66] On the Persian front, in 1344, the Venetian bailiff of Constantinople, Marco Foscarini, made contact with the authorities of Tabriz—but with no results.

While the colonies of Caffa and Tana had developed as an alternative to other routes, the war with Jani Beg threatened these bases that housed the majority trade and investments. This harmed everyone, but especially Venice, which could not regain possession of Tana. After its treaty with Genoa expired (in April 1346), Venetian authorities resumed diplomacy with Jani Beg—but independently this time. Sources are silent on these last months of 1346, but we know the situation remained in flux, as the galleys that were auctioned off in September could only cross the straits after carefully evaluating the situation.[67] Diplomatic relations with the Jöchids re-emerge in the sources in the spring of 1347, when Genoa and Venice signed separate peace treaties with Jani Beg. War had crippled the Mongol economy, and the khan could not afford to continue hostilities. Evidently, negotiations between Venetian envoys and Jani Beg were successful, for on May 16, 1347, a merchant from Candia (Crete) reported that peace had been restored and trade with Tana could resume.[68] For its part, Genoa immediately mobilized, not wanting to be excluded; it ended its embargo and gained permission to return to Mongol ports from June 1347.[69]

In their peace negotiations, Venice asked Jani Beg to renew the concessions it had enjoyed before the crisis. On June 19, 1347, the senate sent two ambassadors, Giovanni Quirini and Zulfredo Morosini, to the khan; a third ambassador was added, nominated by the bailiff of Constantinople.[70] The initiative was successful,[71] and on December 26 of that year, Jani Beg signed a treaty that

66. In February 1345, the ambassador Niccolò Zeno stipulated a contract that stated that the sultan al-Salih (r. 1342–5) gave the Venetian merchants permission to return to Alexandria and to all the ports in the state. The treaty was renewed by al-Salih's successor, al-Kamil (r. 1345–46) that August. *Diplomatarium veneto-levantinum*, vol. 1, pp. 289–98. From then onward, Venice would gradually regain its dominant position over markets controlled by the Mamluks.

67. Thiriet, *Régestes des délibérations*, no. 192, p. 60; Venezia–Senato, *Deliberazioni miste*, vol. 22, p. 184.

68. Morozzo della Rocca, "Notizie da Caffa," p. 274; *Diplomatarium veneto-levantinum*, vol. 2, pp. 336–38; and Papacostea, "'Quod non iretur ad Tanam,'" p. 208.

69. Morozzo della Rocca, "Notizie da Caffa," p. 275; Karpov, *Istorija Tany*, p. 119.

70. Thiriet, *Régestes des délibérations*, no. 201, p. 61; Morozzo della Rocca, "Notizie da Caffa," p. 275.

71. According to the senate resolution of June 19, 1347: "quoniam nova habemus quod Imperator Zanibech cum Ianuensibus est concordatus." Venezia–Senato, *Deliberazioni miste*, vol. 24, p. 72. And in another paper dated July 14, the Senate revealed that it had finally decided to

granted Venetians a separate area to the Genoese quarter.[72] The khan granted a *paiza* (an imperial *laissez-passer*) to all those sailing on Venetian ships. Moreover, the jurisdiction of the Venetian consul in Tana was also confirmed, but his power was only within the Venetian quarter and over its Latin residents. Anyone who committed an "outrage" or violence against Mongols or Muslims would be arrested to face the khan's justice.

The Mongol governor of Tana handed over the land that had been granted to the Venetians. It was modest in size but large enough for a *fondaco*, measuring approximately 170 meters in length and 120 in width, for a total area slightly over two hectares, and it extended all the way to "the riverbank."[73] The agreement also specified tax terms: Venetian merchants would pay 3 percent of all transactions, while all others paid 5 percent.[74] Gold and silver were exempt from taxation. Everything that was measured in *cantari*, a unit applicable to both weight and volume that varied over time, had 5 percent added to it, and was to be weighed at the entrance and exit of the city by officers of the Venetian consul.[75] The consul's salary was set at 70 *lire di grossi*, compared with the 60 that he had been paid before the 1343 crisis. The increase was most likely a compensation for the risks that the position involved; however, by 1348, this had been reduced to 40 *lire di grossi*, though he was granted permission to conduct business.[76] The consul could also demand a 1 percent levy on commercial transactions from all Venetian traders or from those working on their behalf to meet the budget allocated by the senate. With these earnings, the consul had to cover all expenses for the city administration, and

use a different strategy by forgoing "totaliter a facto compositionis." Venezia–Senato, *Delibera-zioni miste*, vol. 24, pp. 103–4; Morozzo della Rocca, "Notizie da Caffa," p. 275.

72. "a li nostri Franchi Venitiani sia dado luogho diviso da quello de Zenoessi, da poder far le suo mercadantie": *Diplomatarium veneto-levantinum*, vol. 1, p. 311.

73. Calculation based on the fact that, in those years, the Venetian *passo* was equal to five *piedi*, and one *piede* measured around 0.34 meters. *Diplomatarium veneto-levantinum*, vol. 1, p. 311: "In ver levante per longheza passa C, et per larcheza passa LXX in fina su la riva del flume."

74. On the conditions for citizenship in Tana, see Pubblici, "Venezia e il mar d'Azov." The *cives* of the documents was a temporary legal condition reserved for those working within the area in Tana, pertaining to the Venetians in order to profit from the benefits conceded to Genoa and Venice.

75. Pegolotti, *La pratica della mercatura*, pp. 24–26; *Diplomatarium veneto-levantinum*, vol. 1, p. 312.

76. The consul could conduct trade, but he had to abstain from the role of *sensale/pesatore* (agent/weigher) in order to avoid conflicts of interest. *Diplomatarium veneto-levantinum*, vol. 1, pp. 340–41.

if the funds were insufficient, he would have to pay the difference out of his own pocket, after which he could request reimbursement from Venice.[77]

## The Veneto–Genoese War

The Venetians' return to Tana upset Genoa, which had hoped to eliminate its rival, or at least make it wholly subordinate, during the war with Jani Beg. As we have seen, the war had ruined business for everyone, but of all the parties involved in the conflict, Genoa had lost the least. On the contrary, Caffa had come out stronger, as it had not been touched by the embargo on Gazaria that had weakened Tana. Furthermore, Genoa owned a whole sector of Constantinople—the area of Pera/Galata—and had expanded its reach into the Aegean. While the Genoese and the Venetians jointly resisted the Mongol siege, within Caffa's walls the two republics vied for their respective spheres of influence in the Aegean. Genoese fleets had managed to conquer Chios on June 15 and Phocaea on September 20, 1346, alarming both Venice and the Byzantine Emperor John VI Cantacuzenus. Genoa had grown its political clout throughout the eastern Mediterranean despite major pushback from Venice, but now—after weathering Mongol attacks and the devastating consequences of the plague—the political and economic balance between the two powers was once again in question.

When Genoa welcomed the Venetians in Caffa, a precarious situation arose, exposing Venetian residents to various abuses, to which they responded with a litany of complaints.[78] Venice's return to Tana did not in the least undermine Caffa's supremacy on the Black Sea; rather, it rekindled the rivalry. On September 1, 1347, the Venetian senate rejected Genoa's request to "share" the port of Caffa provided they abandon Tana.[79] In 1348–49, tensions escalated between the two communities in Tana, aggravated by the wider international context of a crisis between Byzantium and Genoa. Genoa's conquest of Chios and Phocaea with Simone Vignoso at the helm had not only been a tough setback for Venice's influence in the Aegean, but also a humiliation for Emperor John Cantacuzenus. By the end of the decade, diplomatic relations had reached a stalemate and conflict was inevitable. The rivalry, once dormant but

77. "Remittendo residuum Venecias per incantum dominio vel officialibus furmenti": ASV, SM, XXIV, fol. 114; *Diplomatarium veneto-levantinum*, vol. 1, pp. 340–41.

78. ASV, SM, XXIV, 35; *Diplomatarium veneto-levantinum*, vol. 1, p. 340.

79. *Diplomatarium veneto-levantinum*, vol. 1, p. 340.

unresolved during the joint resistance against the Mongols, was needled again after peace was brokered with Jani Beg; the Genoese were fiercely determined to maintain their own dominant position and felt threatened by Venice resuming trade in Tana. On the one hand, Genoa was growing more aggressive in its dominance in the Aegean and the Black Sea, and on the other hand, Venice and Byzantium were growing closer in an effort to curb Genoa's power.

Before conflict could erupt, diplomatic activity grew frenetic but was ultimately ineffective. On May 19, 1348, the Venetian senate ordered Giustiniano Giustiniani, captain of the Romànian galleys, to take his convoy to safety.[80] The galleys were auctioned in December 1348 and were sold for an average of 49 *lire di grossi,* compared with the price of 80 for those in Cyprus—a clear sign that the situation was worsening beyond the straits.[81] On April 5–8, 1350, the auctioned Romània–Black Sea galleys were forbidden from crossing the straits.[82] In the summer of 1350, tensions between Genoa and Venice came to a head on the Black Sea. On July 18, Doge Andrea Dandolo sent an envoy to Genoa in protest: Marin Faliero was sent with the mandate to demand complete reparations for the harassment the Venetians had suffered, and to defend the rights of the Republic in Tana.[83] The senate lamented the constant Genoese oppression in Caffa and Tana, as well as their attempt to block Venetian ships from entering the mouth of the Don. Faliero was also to demand an end to the Genoese abuse of Venetians in Constantinople.[84] We have no details on the outcomes of this mission, but subsequent events prove that the diplomatic overture failed. Venice prepared for war.

On August 28, 1350, the senate ordered the consul of Tana to warn all merchants still in Caffa to seek refuge in ports under Venetian jurisdiction.[85] This

---

80. Thiriet, *Régestes des délibérations*, no. 211, p. 63. Proof of the tension can be found in another document, dated November 1349, in which Pietro Tagliapietra, captain of the galley of Bitici Niddo, was sentenced in Venice for having wrongly accused the Tatars of the port of Varango (Varangolimen in western Crimea) of stealing his ship (Karpov, *Latinskaja Romanija*, p. 181).

81. Thiriet, *Régestes des délibérations*, no. 217, p. 64; Venezia–Senato, *Deliberazioni miste*, vol. 24, pp. 440–41.

82. Thiriet, *Régestes des délibérations*, no. 239, p. 69; Venezia–Senato, *Deliberazioni miste*, vol. 24, p. 47. The resolution to arm the galleys of Romània did not pass, with eight votes against, and two for.

83. Thiriet, *Régestes des délibérations*, nos. 244 and 245, pp. 70–71.

84. Thiriet, *Régestes des délibérations*, no. 245, p. 71.

85. Thiriet, *Régestes des délibérations*, no. 247, p. 71. On the Veneto–Genoese war, see ASV, Procuratori di San Marco, Commissarie, busta 2. This contains the letters and receipts of Marco

war did not just involve the Byzantine Empire and the Ottomans, but also the Catalans, the crown of Aragon, and—albeit indirectly—the kingdom of Hungary.[86] All these states had a vested interest in carving out their own spheres of interest in the eastern Mediterranean.

The Venetian–Genoese war lasted five years in alternating phases. Venice, worn out by the plague, resorted to compulsory conscription to fit out and arm thirty-five galleys under order of Captain Marco Ruzzini. The first real clash between the two fleets took place in front of Negropont. Venetian galleys attacked and confiscated fourteen Genoese galleys loaded with goods. Soon after, Genoa counterattacked: a fleet reached the Aegean island and sacked it, catching the Venetian fleet off-guard. Venetian authorities grasped that they could not win the war, and considered forcing an alliance with the crown of Aragon. The Catalan–Aragonese seemed ideal allies, as they had forever been at war with Genoa over control of Sardinia. Thus, on January 16, 1351, the two powers signed a formal agreement. A few months later, in May, the Byzantine Emperor John Cantacuzenus joined the alliance and promised twelve galleys to the league's fleet. If Genoa was defeated at sea, they would be forced to the negotiation table. The main goals of this new anti-Genoese alliance were the restitution of the island of Chios and the Pera district in Byzantium, and above all to reduce Genoa's presence on the Black Sea.[87]

The war lasted for months. Characterized by mild skirmishes and clashes, violence did not escalate until the alliance's fleet arrived off the coast of Constantinople in February 1352, eagerly awaited by the Byzantine Emperor. The Battle of the Bosphorus was fought between February 13 and 14, and ended in a terrible massacre.[88] Although the Venetian doge Andrea Dandolo celebrated the alliance's "great success" in a letter to King Peter VI of Aragon,[89] the battle had no real victor. Both sides suffered substantial losses in human lives and vessels, to the point that the Venetian–Catalan–Aragonese fleet was forced to retreat, leaving Cantacuzenus to deal with Genoa's

---

Nani, which are worthwhile reading since Nani, a merchant with interests in Cyprus, captained the galley of Pancrazio Giustiniani during the war.

86. The agreement between Venice and the crown of Aragon was signed on January 16, 1351. Costa, "Sulla battaglia del Bosforo," p. 198. See also Balard, "A propos de la bataille du Bosphore"; Werner, *Die Geburt einer Grossmacht*, p. 140.

87. Kyrris, "John Cantacuzenus"; Costa, "Sulla battaglia del Bosforo."

88. Kyrris, "John Cantacuzenus"; Costa, "Sulla battaglia del Bosforo"; Balard, "A propos de la bataille du Bosphore."

89. Costa, "Sulla battaglia di Bosforo," pp. 208–10.

vengeance alone. The emperor had no choice but to surrender, with direct repercussions for Venice's strategy on the Black Sea. On May 6, 1352, Genoese and Byzantine diplomats signed a peace treaty that ended Byzantium's participation in the league. Genoa regained full control of Pera and demanded that all its privileges that had been granted almost a century ago in the Treaty of Nymphaeum be confirmed *en bloc*. It inflicted further humiliation on the fragile emperor by forcing him to ask Genoa for permission to send Byzantine ships all the way to Tana.[90]

In the middle to the end of 1352, the theater of war shifted to the Aegean, though it remained a conflict that mostly consisted of skirmishes and looting. Having defeated Byzantium and reduced the ambitions of the league, Genoa allied with the Angevins of Hungary, who longed to expand into Venetian Dalmatia. The final act of the conflict took place in 1353, in Porto Lungo, near Modon in the Peloponnese. Here, the Genoese admiral Paganino Doria crushed the Venetian galleys of Niccolò Pisani. It seemed like an easy triumph for Genoa, but just as it appeared that the war had turned in Genoa's favor, Venetian diplomacy managed to bring its rival to the negotiation table for peace. This was not the result of a clever diplomatic maneuver, but rather a practical outcome. All parties were wrung out by war, having lost too many resources fighting battles that benefited no one. Moreover, Genoa was in severe debt and relied on the Milanese *signoria* (lordship) of Giovanni Visconti (d. 1354), who had no interest in pursuing the war against Venice. Thus, a peace treaty was signed in Milan on June 1, 1355.[91] The terms penalized Venice, but it was a better option than military defeat. Venice and Genoa pledged to refrain from hostilities, to free all prisoners of war, and not to frequent Tana for the next three years, until 1358.[92] Apart from the *devetum Tane*, the peace treaty had no substantial impact on the balance of power.

Genoa and Venice respected the conditions of the peace treaty and refrained from sending their ships to Tana, even though it was an onerous burden. Both republics had made substantial investments in the region to guarantee an adequate infrastructure system. This fact, along with the tantalizing profits generated by trade, motivated them to re-establish contacts with

90. Lock, *The Franks in the Aegean*, pp. 158–59. The full text of the treaty is published in Medvedev, "Dogovor Vizantii I Genui."

91. Thiriet, "Venise et l'occupation de Ténédos," pp. 224–25; Thiriet, *La Romanie vénitienne*, pp. 176–77; Balard, *La Romanie génoise*, pp. 85–86.

92. Thiriet, *Délibérations des assemblées*, vol. 1, p. 233.

Mongol authorities and to take back possession of their emporia as soon as possible. Jani Beg mirrored their desire, as he had been heavily damaged by the war.

In March 1356, Venice made the first move and organized a delegation to the governor of Solgat, the Mongol *noyon* Ramadan who was responsible for all of Crimea. The delegation asked Ramadan whether they could return to Tana, re-settle in Sudak, and keep the *commerchium* at 3 percent. Perhaps to ensure a direct dialogue at the highest levels, or perhaps because it did not entirely trust the Mongol governor, the Venetian senate ordered Ambassador Andrea Venier to go directly to Jani Beg to convey the same requests, along with the demand to free two Venetian merchants who had just been arrested in Sudak.[93] The khan's reply was cold: Venetians could only settle in the port city of Provato, a settlement near Caffa that was decidedly modest compared to Sudak, both in terms of size and infrastructure.[94] Venetian ships could also go to Solgat, but were to be inspected by both a Mongol and Venetian officer before departure, to verify that no fugitive slaves were kept aboard. This new concession was also dependent on Venice paying compensation for damages suffered by a group of Mongol merchants who, while traveling on a large Genoese ship, had fallen prey to theft during the Venetian–Genoese hostilities. Ramadan told the Venetian ambassadors that their consul's jurisdiction remained limited to Latins, and that if Venetian merchants cheated on their customs duties, their goods would be confiscated.[95]

Although the agreement was restrictive, Venice had no choice but to accept the terms. The captain of the Romànian galleys, Niccolò Pisani, was sent to inspect the territory of Provato where the new Venetian settlement was to be established. However, that same year of 1357, the senate did not authorize the galleys of Romània—auctioned in May—to enter the Black Sea. Most likely, Venice did not believe this to be a sound investment, especially since the ban on returning to Tana would soon expire in 1358. For the first time since the peace of Milan, Venetian galleys were once more allowed to sail for Black Sea ports.[96]

93. Thiriet, *Régestes des délibérations*, no. 273, p. 77; Giomo, *Libri commemoriali*, vol. 2, p. 24.

94. Thiriet, *Régestes des délibérations*, no. 299, p. 82. The concession is dated 1356. Ramadan renewed Venetian access to the port of Provato, which was called New City; see also *Diplomatarium Veneto-levantinum*, vol. 2, p. 25.

95. Giomo, *Libri commemoriali*, vol. 2, p. 242.

96. Thiriet, *Régestes des délibérations*, no. 328, pp. 88–89.

## The Political Crisis of the Golden Horde (1356–59)

By the early 1350s, peace had been restored with the Italian republics and Jani Beg could focus on domestic problems as the Ilkhanate found itself in crisis. The state only had a nominal existence, and there were opportunities for expansion that were supported by some of the Ilkhanid aristocracy. Persian sources describe the pleas from Muslim noblemen to Jani Beg, asking him to march on Tabriz and to free the realm from the turmoil and injustice of its new rulers.[97] Jani Beg saw a chance to annex Azerbaijan, a region of great geopolitical importance. The fertile plains of Mughan not only represented one of the most advanced economies in the Caucasus, but could host a vast number of horses and troops in the event of war. Moreover, the region's main cities of Barda, Nakhchivan, and Beylagan had sophisticated textile industries, especially silk. Wine and oil production were exceedingly profitable, as was grain production, thanks to a vast irrigation system that connected to the rivers Kura and Aras. As we have seen, the Chobanid dynasty had proven incapable of guaranteeing safety on caravan routes. The resulting loss of long-distance trade prompted the local aristocracy, together with the religious institutions (who derived the biggest profits from it), to appeal to Jani Beg that he incorporate the Ilkhanate territory in the Jöchi *ulus*.[98]

Between late 1356 and December 1357, the khan of the Golden Horde advanced south with his army, aiming straight for the Caucasus. The clash with Malik Ashraf's Chobanids took place on the Ugaiansk lowland, where, in 1357, Jani Beg achieved a clear victory. The Jöchids absorbed Azerbaijan into the Golden Horde, then conquered Tabriz and restored a centralized power in Persia—yet this was temporary and uncertain.[99] After this success, it seemed that the Jöchid *ulus* might expand ever farther, but events took an unexpected turn. That year, Jani Beg set out for Sarai, leaving his son Berdi Beg (r. 1357–59) as governor of Tabriz. During his return journey, Jani Beg died.[100] Berdi Beg

97. Broadbridge, *Women and the Making of the Mongol Empire*, p. 161; Grekov and Jakubovskij, *L'Orda d'Oro*, p. 221; Spuler, *Die Goldene Horde*, p. 100. Favereau, *The Horde*, p. 245.

98. Ciocîltan, *The Mongols and the Black Sea Trade*, p. 200 and no. 234.

99. In the year 757 of Hagira (1356) the mint in Tabriz minted coins with Jani Beg's effigy. See Smith and Plunkett, "Gold Money," pp. 290–93; Grekov and Jakubovskij, *L'Orda d'Oro*, p. 222.

100. Doubts remain as to the cause of Jani Beg's death. It is uncertain whether he died of natural causes, the plague, or was assassinated by one of his *beg* due to the Horde's frequent dynastic disputes. The most convincing theory is that his own son, Berdi Beg, ordered his

had to leave Tabriz to take his father's throne, and his departure left Azerbaijan prey to the local aristocracy, which had only formally—and for too short a time—submitted to the Jöchid khan.

Jani Beg's death ushered in a period of rapid decline for the Golden Horde. Internal and external problems culminated in an all-out civil war in the 1360s. Consequences for the Venetian settlements on the Black Sea soon followed. To fully understand this process, three factors must be stressed that played out in concert and contributed to the acceleration of political disarray: the bubonic plague, the Ottoman advance in the West, and the end of China's Yuan Dynasty. We have already discussed the plague; assuming the numbers cited in sources are accurate, in 1346–53, a quarter of the Golden Horde's population succumbed to the disease. In Tana, the victims were even more numerous: some estimates state that almost half the residents in the Venetian quarter died during and after the epidemic.[101]

The second factor was the Ottoman advance to the south of the Balkans in the 1350s. This was consolidated in 1354, when the troops led by Suleyman Pasha (d. 1357), the son of Sultan Orhan Bey (ca. 1281–1362), conquered the Byzantine stronghold of Gallipoli. In the following decades, the Ottomans continued their triumphant march in the Balkans to take control of the straits. At the same time, at the other end of Asia, a rebellion led by a Chinese general in 1368 swept aside the Yuan dynasty, ending Mongol rule and establishing the Ming dynasty. The Ming (as we shall see in chapter 7) adopted measures that not only made trade relations conditional on political relations, but they were also—at least initially—more interested in maritime exploration and trade than in the reopening of continental routes. These two events, though geographically distant, had major consequences on Eurasian trade—in particular on Venetian trade in the Mongol Empire. An entire mercantile class was affected by these ongoing transformations, which rapidly altered the established political and economic fabric of the world, involving not only the Venetians and the Genoese, but also Armenians, Arabs, Jews, and Mongols.

Without a doubt, a further external factor was Berdi Beg's disruptive behavior. Having returned to Sarai after his father's death, and having appointed a trusted governor in Tabriz, the new khan found himself facing further

father's murder, instigated by the emir Toglubai, so that he could take his place. This version is given in the chronicle of Nikon (*Letopisnyj sbornik*, p. 229). See also Favereau, *The Horde*, pp. 261–62.

101. Chajdarov, "Épidemija čumy," pp. 49–51.

infighting among the aristocracy.[102] Berdi Beg had ascended the throne under mysterious circumstances, and it was believed that he had ordered his father's assassination. He could only count on the support of a portion of the nobility, including his grandmother Taydula, Uzbek's principal wife and a major figure in Mongolian politics.[103] Such court conflicts were common at times of succession in nomadic societies, yet they set dramatic events into motion. To reinforce his position and guard against opposition, Berdi Beg began to purge potential rivals to the throne: namely, any male descendants of Uzbek and Jani Beg, his uncles and brothers.[104]

This wave of terror had the opposite effect to Berdi Beg's intentions. Much of the nobility became hostile toward him, destabilizing his already shaken base of power. Perhaps this is why in the first months of his reign he restored the privileges that Venice and Genoa had once enjoyed, in an effort to revive the economy and rake in resources via taxes. On September 24, 1358, Berdi Beg entered a new pact with the Venetian ambassadors Giovanni Quirini and Francesco Bon in which he renewed the concessions that Uzbek and Jani Beg had once offered.[105] Berdi Beg granted Venice a separate area within the Genoese quarter (*desparte dali Zenoesi*), and confirmed the levy on trade (*commerchium*), yet increasing it from 3 to 5 percent, and calculated according to the weight of the goods.

The size of the Venetian settlement remained unchanged from previous agreements: 100 paces (*passi*) in length times 70 in width, all the way to the shore: "lo bagno de Safadin inver levante per longeza passa cento, per largeza difina la riva delaqua passa LXX" (the Saffadyn bath 100 paces in length toward the Levant and 70 in width as far as the riverbank). Entry of ships to port was also carefully regulated. A tariff of three *sommi* per ship was to be paid to the Mongol governor of Tana, Toghulubeg, collected by his officers (*messi*), and destined for the personal coffers of Empress Taydula.[106] That same governor

102. See Broadbridge, *Women and the Making of the Mongol Empire*, especially chapter 5, pp. 155–57. Even the recent conquests in the southern Caucasus were lost, then reconquered by the anti-Jöchid revolt of the local nobility led by the Hülegü dynasty of the Jalayirids as early as 1358.

103. For more on the empress, see Favereau and Geevers, "The Golden Horde," pp. 469–70.

104. According to some sources, Berdi Beg could also have ordered the murder of his own son. Favereau, *The Horde*, pp. 261–62.

105. *Diplomatarium veneto-levantinum*, vol. 2, pp. 47–51; Balard, *La Romanie génoise*, p. 154; Thiriet, *Régestes des délibérations*, no. 311, p. 85.

106. *Diplomatarium veneto-levantinum*, vol. 2, p. 50.

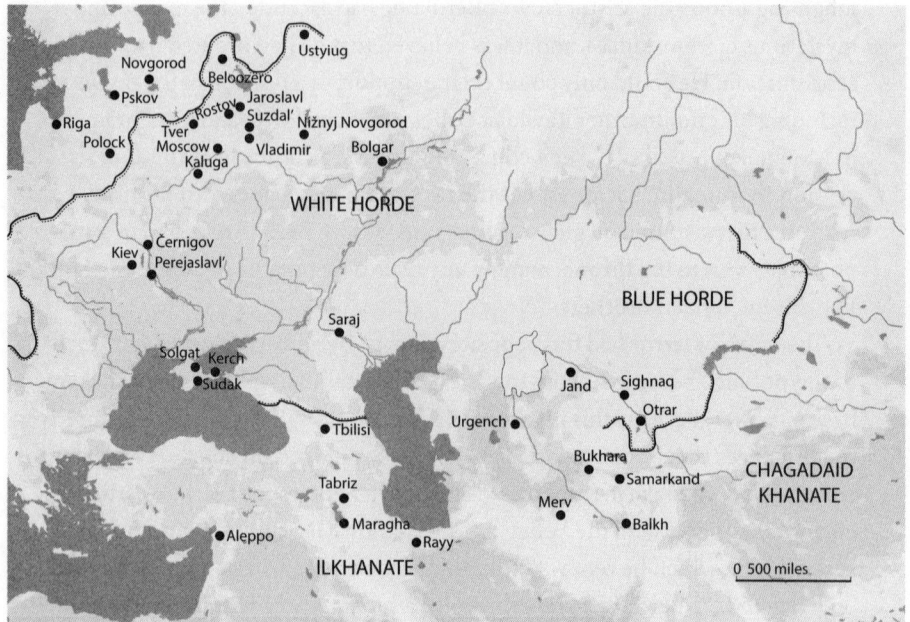

MAP 12. The border between the White Horde and the Blue Horde

was personally charged with the safety of the Venetians. If a ship was damaged in Tana, no one could touch it without it first being examined by Venetian officers.[107] Any disputes and crimes committed in the Venetian quarter remained within the consul's powers, while the weighing of goods was to be carried out by officers on both sides. Memories of the 1343 violence were still fresh, and Berdi Beg took precautions against any possible abuse, ordering that Venetians guilty of crimes against Muslim or Mongol citizens should be immediately handed over to local authorities, to be tried under the laws of the khan.[108]

Two days later, on September 26, 1358, the Venetian ambassadors signed the agreement together with Cotlug Timur, *noyon* of Solgat and Ramadan's successor. The treaty confirmed their privileges in other ports of the Sea of Azov and of Crimea: Provato and Caliera (a minor port between Sudak and Caffa),[109] and also gave them permission to permanently frequent Sudak.

107. It is worth noting that the document expressly refers to the Genoese as the most imminent threat: *Diplomatarium veneto-levantinum*, vol. 2, p. 50.

108. *Diplomatarium veneto-levantinum*, vol. 2, p. 50.

109. Heyd, *Le colonie commerciali*, pp. 113–14.

Transit fees remained unchanged from the March 1356 agreement, and the Mongol governor, as before, remained responsible for the merchants' safety.[110] However, Berdi Beg's concessions were contingent on Venice paying for any damage that its galleys may have caused by acts of piracy to Mongol merchants during the years of conflict, up to 1353.

Previously, Venetian authorities had promised Ramadan that they would pay for damages, but they had not kept their word. For this reason, on September 26, Berdi Beg issued a decree that all concessions would only be granted in exchange for adequate compensation for damages: these included over 2,300 *sommi* of stolen goods, the death of two Mongol subjects, and the over two-year-long imprisonment of two Mongols captured during the conflict.[111] It was the Empress Taydula (d. 1361) who advanced a part of the sum from her personal treasury (*de nostra propria cassena*) to allow the Venetians to operate once more in the region without having to wait for the transfer of funds from the motherland.[112] Taydula was a charismatic and highly influential figure, who had remained at the center of politics for two decades, favoring the election of Jani Beg, and subsequently of Berdi Beg. Her power stemmed not only from her position as wife and mother of a khan, but from her prestige among the most influential *noyon*—and of course from her vast personal wealth. She remained a devout Christian and never converted to Islam; perhaps this also explains her intervention in favor of resuming trade with the Latins, beyond mere personal interest.[113] In late September 1358, once the new treaties had been signed, Venice sent Pietro Caravello to Tana as the new consul, with funds equal to 80 *sommi d'argento*, earmarked for the construction of a house.[114] The Romània–Black Sea galleys were auctioned, and the shipbuilders' response was positive: the average amount invested was 160 *lire di grossi*, compared with 50 *lire* on average during the years of crisis.

However, just when it seemed that Venice had found a reliable champion, Berdi Beg was assassinated by his brother Qulpa in 1359 in a fight for succession. Qulpa, as *noyon*, wielded control over what the Mongols referred to as

---

110. *Diplomatarium veneto-levantinum*, vol. 2, p. 51; Giomo, *Libri commemoriali*, vol. 2, p. 289.

111. *Diplomatarium veneto-levantinum*, vol. 2, no. 26, pp. 52–53.

112. This is further proof of just how important and independent the empress was, even after her husband's death. *Diplomatarium veneto-levantinum*, vol. 2, no. 28, pp. 53–54.

113. Favereau, *The Horde*, pp. 262–63.

114. Thiriet, *Régestes des délibérations*, no. 335, p. 90; ASV, Cancelleria Inferiore (hereafter CI), Notai, busta 19, fasc. 7, reg. 1, fols. 7r, 9r, 13v and 14r; Pucci Donati, *Ai confini dell'Occidente*, nos. 51, 62, 85, 87, pp. 32, 36, 41–42.

*Ak Orda* (the White Horde), which was the western part of the Jöchi *ulus*.[115] When the *ulus* was formed, it was originally entrusted to Batu, Jöchi's firstborn son, while the left side (the Blue or Oriental Horde, since Mongols oriented from north to south) had gone to another son, Hordu (*floruit* 1225–52),[116] encompassing the territory between the right shore of Syr Darya, as far as the city of Sighnaq, and the eastern coast of the Aral Sea, in present-day Kazakhstan.

There were no major cities in the region, which was primarily inhabited by nomadic populations of Turkic origin, who outnumbered the Mongols.[117] What we commonly refer to as the Golden Horde (a term that was never used by the Mongols themselves) was nothing more than the combination of the two territories, East and West, into a single political entity at the center of which was the imperial stronghold (*ordo*), Sarai. Although it was formally subject to the authority of the Jöchid khan, the Blue Horde of Hordu maintained its relative independence, even during times of great turbulence, sometimes aligning with the Jöchids and sometimes at odds with them.

Berdi Beg's death spurred the disintegration that was already underway and that favored the westward advance of the Blue Horde. However, the assassination did not quell internal dissension in the ruling clan; in 1360, Qulpa was murdered by another brother, Nawruz (d. May or June 1360). Sources are unclear on these events and are mainly based on numismatic finds that are not supported by written evidence. Judging by certain coins minted in Sarai, Berdi Beg is believed to have ruled until 1361 and not until 1359.[118] However, this is refuted by the papers of the priest Benedetto Bianco, who settled in Tana as the consul's notary in 1358. In a document notarized on September 1, 1359, Bianco affirmed that when he took office, the khan of the Golden Horde was Berdi Beg (*regnante Berdibech, serenissimo imperatore tartarorum*), but that four days after his death, Qulpa rose to power (*creatus fuit alius imperator nomine Colbadinus Can*). In turn, Qulpa was dethroned and put to death together with

---

115. On the confusion between the Blue Horde and the White Horde, see Atwood, *Encyclopedia*, pp. 41–42.

116. *Rashiduddin Fazlullah's Jami'ü't-Tawarikh—Compendium of Chronicles*, pp. 335–36; Grousset, *The Empire of the Steppes*, p. 469.

117. Grekov and Jakubovskij, *L'Orda d'Oro*, pp. 251ff. Recent excavations have revealed a great number of peasant villages around Lake Alakol (on the modern-day border between Kazakhstan and China).

118. See Grekov and Jakubovskij, *L'Orda d'Oro*, pp. 227–28.

his two sons in February 1360 during a coup d'état led by Nawruz.[119] This indicates that Nawruz was already on the throne in early 1360, and that, according to Benedetto Bianco, he claimed to be a descendant of Uzbek without foundation (*sine aliqua meritione*).

The political instability that followed Berdi Beg's death forced Venice to act in haste to prevent the power vacuum from leading to a new stalemate in political and trade relations, and to prevent a hostile reaction from the Mongols, as had happened after Uzbek's death in 1341. It was deemed necessary to dispatch a delegation to the new khan as a diplomatic custom. However, it was also an essential step in defending the privileges that Venice had so recently restored not only in Tana but also in other areas under Mongol rule. On January 13, 1360, Giovanni Quirini and Francesco Bon set out once more to Sarai with the aim of convincing the khan to renew the tariffs granted by Berdi Beg, and, if possible, to reduce the *commerchium* from 5 to 3 percent (or at least 4 percent).[120] They were given 500 ducats to spend on gifts (the document refers to precious objects) and anything else that may have been necessary to ensure the mission's success.

The months that passed between Berdi Beg's and Nawruz's respective deaths were heated. Sarai lost its position as the political center, which it had maintained since its foundation. Since the reign of Toqta, Jöchid politics had been marked by their tendency toward centralization and the strengthening of the imperial clan, which had systematically reduced the aristocracy's political space. At the same time, the khan had granted the leaders of the local aristocracy considerable independence in managing their provinces, as well as a share of tax revenues from trade. This did not resolve the latent conflict between central and peripheral interests, which imploded after Berdi Beg's death, followed so soon by that of Empress Taydula.

Thus, in 1360, the Jöchid dynasty came to an end. The deaths of Batu's descendants exacerbated rivalries and drew the nobility of the Blue Horde to the west, paving the way for a relentless fragmentation of power. Political instability grew. To maintain its own position within the Golden Horde's markets, Venice was forced to embark on new diplomatic maneuvers.

---

119. This version is confirmed by the Russian sources. Karpov, "Načalo smuty v Zolotoj Orde," p. 531.

120. Thiriet, *Régestes des délibérations*, nos. 355 and 358, p. 95.

# 6

# Venice and the Mongols in the Years of the Jöchid Crisis (1360–95)

## The Crisis of the Horde and the Venetian Response

### The End of Political Unity in the Golden Horde

Berdi Beg's death in 1359 ended Batu's lineage. Throughout the next two decades, a fierce and frenetic power struggle played out. Ever since the days of Uzbek, who had risen to the top of the khanate thanks to support from the aristocracy, regional political power had always been in the hands of the local nobility. This consisted of *emirs, beg,* and *noyon* (depending on whether they used Arabic, Turkic, or Mongol titles) and their power was based on the forces they could deploy in case of war and on the alliances they could forge.[1] The highest ranks of the nobility were made up of governors of large administrative areas; Crimea was of foremost importance thanks to its vast agricultural resources and substantial fiscal revenues generated by trade. Berdi Beg's death exacerbated the internal political crisis that was already well underway. The Horde fractured into two political divisions, each dominated by one or more clan. While the White Horde occupied the west of the Volga all the way to the principalities of Rus', thus also controlling Sarai, the capital, the Blue Horde stretched east, occupying the territories on the other side of the Volga and in central Asia. This political division was based on hegemonic claims, which—as we shall explore in this chapter—often came into conflict, marking the

---

1. Spuler, *Die Goldene Horde,* p. 116; Favereau, *The Horde,* pp. 268–72.

second half of the century by chaotic twists and turns of infighting. Ultimately, this led to a long and devastating conflict between Timur and Tokhtamysh. The history of the Italian settlements on the Black Sea was directly affected by these never-ending political storms. Among the tumult, Latin authorities could only play a passive role, limited to diplomacy and defensive strategies.

After the deaths of Berdi Neg and Empress Taydula, the khans of the Horde who lived in Sarai lost control of most of the territory. Their positions were under constant threat, throwing the empire into instability. The political process that guaranteed legitimacy (albeit partial) to the current khan developed into a kind of protectorate of the White Horde, which claimed the right to elect a khan thanks to its military superiority, as long as he was a Chinggisid. In order to ascend the throne, a khan had to be a descendant of the great conqueror, but by then, any descendants who could boast this lineage had lost the political clout of their ancestors. From the end of 1360 to October 1361, coins were minted bearing the effigies of five different khans, including Berdi Beg himself, who had died a year before.[2] The two halves of this empire—the West, or White Horde, whose center lay in Crimea, and the East, or Blue Horde, whose capital was the city of Sighnaq—had mirror-image problems: they both lacked dynastic prestige. The ripple effects were felt across the empire; Khwarazm, for example,[3] was ruled by the Sufi-Qonggirat dynasty, a powerful Turkish–Mongol clan that had arisen around the Mongol tribe of Börte, consort of Chinggis Khan, which had long since converted to Islam.[4] The Qonggirat ruled northern Khwarazm with the blessing of the khan of the Golden Horde, but after the collapse of the central authority they occupied the major city of Urgench, and from 1364 declared themselves formally independent of Sarai. From Urgench, a strategic trading city, the Qonggirat could expand into central Asia over the territory of the Chagatai khanate, which was also weakened by infighting.

### The Growth of the Western Wing and the Rise of Mamaï

Soon after Nawruz took control of Sarai, he was assassinated by a group of conspiring noblemen who supported the eastern wing (the Blue Horde), and who favored the rise to power of the Shaybanide Kidyr (d. 1361) in the Volga

2. Grekov and Jakubovskij, *L'Orda d'Oro*, p. 227; see also Favereau, *The Horde*, pp. 262–63 and 267.

3. Favereau, *The Horde*, p. 267.

4. Favereau, *The Horde*, p. 267; Sabitov, "Emiry Uzbek-Chana," pp. 128–29.

region.[5] Russian sources describe him as a man of great strength, determined to re-establish the central power of the Horde and to reassert Mongol authority over the vassal states.[6] Nonetheless, that same year, 1361, Kydir was the victim of a conspiracy himself, most likely betrayed by his son, Timur Hogja who ruled for just a few weeks[7] before he was also overthrown by another emir at the head of the Horde's western wing: Mamaï (d. 1381).[8]

Born in Crimea around 1335, Mamaï was a member of the Mongol military aristocracy that had benefited enormously from Berdi Beg's weak rule and the ensuing succession crisis. Between 1357 and 1359, Mamaï rose to the highest ranks of the Horde's bureaucratic and military structure, holding successive posts as minister of justice, chief of staff, and governor of Crimea. From 1359 onward, he supported Abdul Khan, a pretender to the throne and enemy of Qulpa (Berdi Beg's brother and murderer). Mamaï was also Berdi Beg's son-in-law, having married his daughter Tulunbek (d. ca. 1386).[9] He eventually became commander-in-chief (*beylerbey*) of the Horde's western wing, which included Crimea and the northern basin of the Black Sea. There was no way for Mamaï to become a legitimate khan, as he was not a Chinggisid; elevation to the throne would have made him a usurper. Instead, he took on the role of "great elector" and kingmaker, backing several khans. However, none of them were able to reunify the Jöchid *ulus*.

Alongside turbulent and unpredictable Mongol politics, Venetians in Tana found themselves facing internal crisis. The peace of Milan may have silenced arms, but it had not healed divisions. Though the conflict had ended some years earlier, resentment still simmered and coexistence with the Genoese in

5. Russian sources describe Kidyr as *oglan*, the crown prince of the Blue Horde. Kidyr was the son of the khan Sasi Buqa (r. 1313–21). Kidyr was legitimately a Jöchid as he was of Shaybanid origin, that is, a descendant of Shībān (d. 1266), the fifth son of Jöchi.

6. In Sarai, he received Dmitry Ivanovich, Grand Prince of Moscow, as well as Vladimir Andrei Konstantinovich of Nizhny Novgorod, and the dukes of Rostov and Yaroslavi. Grekov and Jakubovskij, *L'Orda d'Oro*, pp. 229–30; see also Favereau, *The Horde*, pp. 270–71.

7. This is according to Russian sources from August to September 1361. Coins have been discovered that were minted in Sarai that same year. Grigor'ev, "Zolotoordynskie chany."

8. On Mamaï, see the much-discussed yet always original Gumilev, *Drevnjaja Rus' i Velikaja step'*, in particular pp. 422–50, then the chapter on the White Horde (Белая орда); Trepavlov, *Gosudarstvennyj stroj Mongol'skoj imperii*, pp. 62–67; Krivošeev, *Rus' i Mongoly*. The Massaria di Caffa of 1374 tells us that Mamaï was in Caffa (Balard, *La Romanie génoise*, p. 457). See also Prochorov, "Etničeskaja integracija."

9. Tulunbek was of Qyiat origin, that is, the Borjigid (Borjigin) from which Chinggis himself was descended. Atwood, *Encyclopedia*, pp. 44–45.

Tana was causing concern for Venice. In late 1359, tensions between the two communities escalated once more. Venetian authorities sent an official letter to the Genoese doge to protest the violation of Venetians' rights in Constantinople, and especially in Pera. The Venetian community there was strategically crucial due to all the goods coming and going from Black Sea ports. The Genoese authorities in Constantinople boycotted Venetian trade, in particular obstructing the trade of necessities, as well as grain and wine.[10] To counter Genoese hostility, on February 27, 1360, the Venetian senate sent two ambassadors to Tana, tasked with convincing the new khan to renew the pacts and all allowances.[11] However, as we have seen, it was at this point that Nawruz ended Qulpa's brief reign, triggering political crisis in the Golden Horde.

Even the most challenging years had seen a constant hegemonic power, albeit unstable and weaker than in the past. Now, rapid political changes had built an atmosphere of uncertainty. Before Mamaï took full control of the White Horde, Venice was without a stable interlocutor; the Republic needed someone whose authority was acknowledged and who could guarantee that the agreements would be honored. Thus, Venice was forced to resort to new diplomatic strategies. First and foremost, Venice sought to settle its rivalry with Genoa.

On January 13, 1361, the Venetian doge Giovanni Delfino and the Genoese doge Simone Boccanegra agreed that the inhabitants of Tana must abstain from fights and quarrels to live together in peace.[12] This agreement gave special powers to the consuls of both cities to sanction their citizens in proportion to the seriousness of the crime (*secundum enormitatem delicti*). The use of weapons was limited and subject to the exclusive authority of the consul, fining offenders as much as 200 ducats or *genovini*.[13] Furthermore, should the consuls or bailiffs in Tana or Constantinople themselves break the agreement, the doge would intervene.[14] In two letters, dated February 1 and 4, 1361,

---

10. Giomo, *Libri commemoriali*, vol. 2, no. 169, pp. 307–8.

11. "Pro honoranda persona novi imperatoris Tartarorum et pro obtinenda franchitate, libertate et pactis nostri [...] elligantur in maiori consilio due solempnes ambaxatores." Archivio di Stato di Venezia (hereafter ASV), Senato Misti (hereafter SM), XXIX, fol. 49; Venezia–Senato, *Deliberazioni miste*, vol. 29, p. 228; Thiriet, *Régestes des délibérations*, no. 358, p. 95.

12. "Vivere et se habere pacifice et quiete et in bona fraternitate ac caritate et dilectione sincera, et se abstinere a rixis et brigis quibuscumque invicem inferendis": *Diplomatarium veneto-levantinum*, vol. 2, no. 37, pp. 66–8 and no. 38, pp. 68–70.

13. Giomo, *Libri commemoriali*, vol. 2, nos. 227–28, p. 318.

14. *Diplomatarium veneto-levantinum*, vol. 2, no. 38, p. 68.

Simone Boccanegra and Giovanni Delfino ratified the agreements in a peace treaty for Crimea and Tana (*per totum imperium Gazarie*).[15] Peace with Genoa gave Venice the valuable breathing space it needed to continue its activities on the Black Sea.

## The 1360s

In the early 1360s, various tensions had developed in the eastern Mediterranean, mainly caused by the climate hostile to Venice that was brewing on Crete.[16] This led to a direct decrease in the number of galleys auctioned: in 1361, only four of five galleys were able to find a shipowner.[17] These new complications compounded an already poor commercial environment: due to bad relations with Trebizond and the collapse of the Ilkhanate, by the 1340s commercial shipping already favored Tana.[18] Moreover, the death of Emperor Basil of Trebizond in April 1340 triggered a crisis of succession, which quickly degenerated into a civil war, interrupting trade relations. A few years later, the Venetian settlement was struck by the plague, after which the Veneto–Genoese war and the *devetum Tane* completely excluded Trebizond from all major trade on the Black Sea until 1358.

From the early 1360s, relations improved due to events within Trebizond politics. In 1349, John Komnenos rose to the throne at the tender age of eleven, taking the name Alexios III (1338–90). After some years, he achieved maturity and inaugurated a series of reforms that brought Trebizond back to the center of Pontic traffic. Political stability allowed for a recovery in trade relations and, from 1363, relations between Trebizond and Venice were re-established, as were the voyages of Venetian galleys on the Black Sea. In 1364, the captain of the Ròmanian galleys, Domenico Michiel, received instructions to continue on to Trebizond with the ambassador Guglielmo Michiel.[19] Alexios III granted the ambassador a Golden Bull that guaranteed Venetian traders access

15. Giomo, *Libri commemoriali*, vol. 2, no. 228, p. 318.

16. Thiriet, *La Romanie vénitienne*, p. 174.

17. ASV, SM, XXIX, fol. 120r–v; Thiriet, *Régestes des délibérations*, no. 375, p. 98; Venezia–Senato, *Deliberazioni miste*, vol. 29, pp. 568–69.

18. On these problems and on the relationship between Venice and the empire of Trebizond in general, see Karpov, *L'impero di Trebisonda*, in particular chapter 2, pp. 71–139.

19. ASV, SM, XXXI, fol. 70v; Thiriet, *Régestes des déliberations*, no. 419, pp. 108–9.

to the ports, free circulation, and the protection of local authorities.[20] Relations between Venice and the empire of Trebizond were formally resumed from May of the following year.[21] From 1359 to 1366, Venice regularly sent galleys to the Sea of Azov,[22] the sole exception being 1364, when, according to the resolution of the Venetian senate dated July 21, the road to Tana was closed.[23] During this time, the number of galleys and auction prices remained very low, the latter gravitating to around 60 *lire di grosso* compared with the 122 *lire di grosso* for the galleys headed for Cyprus and the over 170 *lire di grosso* for those headed for Alexandria and Beirut.[24] On May 21, 1366, five galleys sailed to Romània, docking in Tana and Trebizond.[25]

Meanwhile, a power that would soon become a major player in Mediterranean and Middle Eastern politics was growing stronger: the Ottoman Empire. Having arisen from one of the many Turkish emirates that followed the division of the Seljuk Empire (a result of the mid-thirteenth century Mongol conquest), the Ottomans quickly gained control over east Anatolia, even threatening the Byzantine Empire. In 1354, after conquering Gallipoli, they entered Europe and continued their advance in Thrace, before conquering Adrianople (modern-day Edirne) in 1366 (or 1369).[26] Venice considered the Ottoman expansion in the Balkans to be a threat to navigation in the Aegean.

20. Karpov, *L'impero di Trebisonda*, pp. 86–87; Karpov, *The Empire of Trebizond and Venice*, pp. 1–8; Karpov, "Il problema delle tasse doganali."

21. ASV, SM, XXXI, fols. 95v and 97; Thiriet, *Régestes des délibérations*, no. 424, p. 110. On May 8, 1364, the four merchant galleys headed to Tana and Trebizond were auctioned for 55, 63, 63, and 64 *lire di grossi* respectively.

22. Thiriet, *Régestes des délibérations*, no. 419; ASV, Cancelleria Inferiore (hereafter CI), Notai, busta 117, carta 120, in which, on October 3, 1362, Bartolomeo di Firenze sold a Tatar slave to Lorenzo Quirino of Santa Maria di Venezia for 400 aspers; ASV, CI, Notai, busta 134f., Notai Diversi, slave contracts dated July 11, 1366; ASV, SM, XXX, fols. 73r and 74r; Fenster, "Zur Fahrt der venezianischen Handelsgaleeren," pp. 165–66.

23. ASV, SM, XXXI, fol. 70v; Thiriet, *Régestes des délibérations*, no. 419, pp. 108–9.

24. ASV, SM, XXXI, fols. 59v–61v; Thiriet, *Régestes des délibérations*, no. 417, p. 108.

25. ASV, SM, XXXI, fols. 138v–139; Thiriet, *Régestes des délibérations*, no. 433, p. 112; ASV, CI, Notai, busta 117, perg. 133 dated July 1, 1366; perg. 134 dated July 17, 1366.

26. The Ottoman conquest of Edirne has been studied most exhaustively, not only due to its historical importance, but because the sources offer a contradictory timeline. Undoubtedly, the city fell into Turkish hands between 1361 and 1371. Recent studies cite a probable date of between 1366 and 1369. See Vatin, "L'ascesa degli ottomani," p. 49; Inalcik, *The Ottoman Empire: The Classical Age*, pp. 36–38; Wittek, *La formation de l'empire ottoman*; Zachariadou, *Romania and the Turks*.

To oppose the Ottomans, Venice attempted to create a broad anti-Turkish alliance that would include Byzantium, the kingdoms of Bulgaria and Cyprus, and the Knights Hospitaller of Rhodes. Venice led this diplomatic initiative to form a crusade in 1366, headed by Prince Amedeo of Savoy, that would reconquer Gallipoli and other recent Ottoman conquests.[27] The coalition was successful in weakening the young state led by Murad I (r. 1362–89) for a few years. However, victory was short-lived; they could not stop the Ottoman expansion.

Although relations with the Trebizond Empire had been re-established and the Ottomans had been hit hard by the crusade, trade routes were still not entirely safe. In 1368, the Venetian senate ordered the consul of Tana to send 200 *sommi* to the bailiff of Trebizond to fortify the settlement. That same year and the next, fewer galleys were bound for Romània and the Black Sea: if in 1368 they went from six to five, in 1369, of the planned five only four were awarded—proof of the persistent state of danger. Although the Anatolian region and its caravan routes had also become unsafe, Venice never completely abandoned contact with Tabriz.

We have seen in chapter 3 how the collapse of Hülegü's dynasty led to the Ilkhanate's division into several emirates. The largest and most influential of these was ruled by the Jalayirid, a local dynasty founded by the emir Uwais (r. 1356–74).[28] As commander of the Mongol troops in Azerbaijan, Uwais had occupied a vast region, including Tabriz, Azerbaijan, a portion of Iraq including Baghdad, and several regions of western Iran. In May 1369, Uwais wrote to the Venetian bailiff of Trebizond, requesting that "all Venetian merchants of Trebizond and the other merchants" return to Tabriz, where they would be guaranteed protection and reduced taxes.[29] On August 22, the bailiff replied that he was ready to resume relations,[30] as a large caravan (*magna caravana*) had been stuck in Trebizond for two years waiting to leave for Tabriz, unable

27. Amedeo of Savoy took the cross in Avignon on April 1, 1364. Thiriet, "Una proposta di lega antiturca," p. 332; Karpov, *L'impero di Trebisonda*, p. 85.

28. Uwais was the son of the first Jalayirid emir Hasan Buzurg (d. 1356) and of the Chobanid princess Dilshan Khatun (d. 1351), formerly the wife of Abu Said from 1333 until the death of the ilkhan. Atwood, *Encyclopedia*, p. 236; *Ta'rīkh-i Shaikh Uwais*.

29. Giomo, *Libri commemoriali*, vol. 3, no. 485, p. 81; *Diplomatarium veneto-levantinum*, vol. 2, pp. 158–59.

30. *Diplomatarium veneto-levantinum*, vol. 2, pp. 159–60; Giomo, *Libri commemoriali*, vol. 3, no. 522, p. 86.

to move due to unsafe conditions.[31] Instability in the Golden Horde and the shift of trade flow toward the ports of Alexandria and Beirut probably encouraged Venice to accept the emir's proposal, who offered sufficient reassurances. However, Uwais was unable to keep his promises. In late 1371, the first reports of Venetian merchants being robbed in Iran reached Venice, and in November 1372, the bailiff of Trebizond, Francesco Giustiniani, sequestered goods of merchants arriving from Tabriz as compensation, ending any further attempts at trade in the territory of the former Ilkhanate.[32]

## Venice between Mamaï and the Rise of Tokhtamysh

### Mamaï, the Russians, and the Grand Duchy of Lithuania

From the 1360s onward, regional political entities that had been subject to Mongol domination for decades took advantage of the Horde's division and subsequent weakening to free themselves of its power and supplant it. The main players in this transition were Grand Prince Dmitry Ivanovich of Moscow (1350–89) and of Vladimir (from 1363), Prince Mikhail of Tver (r. 1368–82), and Grand Duke Algirdas of Lithuania (r. 1345–77). Lithuania had managed to expand into the most exposed Rus' principalities (in the southwest) during the years of conflict between Nogaï and Toqta, a period in which the Mongols had been too busy fighting among themselves to intervene in defense of their allies. In the 1320s, the Baltic grand duchy had conquered Kiev (which was later lost), and two decades later, it conquered Galicia and Volhynia.

With the end of the Mongol hegemony, the grand duchy of Lithuania continued to expand, aiming for the Black Sea and its highly desirable trade network. In 1362, Algirdas's troops occupied Chernigov and Perjaslavl, eventually reaching Moscow. At the end of the year, his troops attacked the wealthy region of Podolia, the gate to the Pontus. Podolia was protected by Mamaï; the clash was inevitable. In the winter of 1362–63, the two armies faced off near the Syniukha River in what the chronicles recorded as the Battle of the Blue

---

31. *Diplomatarium veneto-levantinum*, vol. 2, pp. 158–59; Karpov, *L'impero di Trebisonda*, p. 92.

32. *Diplomatarium veneto-levantinum*, vol. 2, p. 163. The sequestered goods were then returned to the Persian merchants, perhaps because Giustiniani did not receive instructions from the homeland about how to proceed with the indemnity. See Karpov, *L'impero di Trebisonda*, pp. 92–93.

Waters; the Mongols were defeated.[33] This victory guaranteed the Lithuanians control of Kiev and Podolia, but the time was not yet ripe to release Mamaï from the alliance.

Inserting himself in the internal struggles of the principalities of Rus', Algirdas backed Mikhail of Tver from the outset against Dmitry of Moscow, who was in turn a vassal of Mamaï, and thus was drawn into the Rus'–Lithuanian conflict. For his part, Mamaï was pragmatic; by changing sides, he opposed Dmitry Ivanovich, who was a far greater threat to Mongol authority due to Moscow's strategic position. Mamaï chose to back Lithuanian ambitions, offering the Baltic state recognition of its conquered lands in exchange for loyalty. Algirdas secured himself a privileged position among the vassals of the khan, thereby enhancing his own political stature.[34]

Mamaï had gained what he wanted, but at the start of the following decade, his relations with the Rus' princes deteriorated. Exploiting weakness within the imperial clan, Dmitry had stopped paying taxes and duties (or he chose to underpay). In response, Mamaï declared him disgraced, and granted the principality of Moscow to Mikhail of Tver. To avoid conflict, Dmitry paid tribute to Mamaï by bringing him gifts and money for the unpaid duties. Yet it was an artificial peace, destined to end. Dmitry's ambitions were in stark contrast to Mamaï's hegemonic aims: if the grand duchy of Moscow continued to expand, he would become an inconvenient antagonist for the Mongol emir.

Anti-Mongol revolts arose in various cities of Rus'; though they may have been spontaneous, they cast a harsh light on the fragility of this political balance.[35] In 1374, the city of Vladimir arrested and sentenced to death Mamaï's tax collectors. The protest spread to other cities and Mongol troops were sent to Nizhny Novgorod and Moscow, where they were repelled. A long war ensued. In 1376, the Russians attacked Kazan, southeast of Moscow, where a modest Tatar garrison was located. For the first time ever, it was the Russians who pursued the Mongols. Dmitry's forces intercepted and defeated enemy troops along the course of the Vozhan River in August 1378.[36] Two years later,

33. Kozyr, "Syn'ovods' ka bytva 1362"; Uzelac, "Tatary v Dunajsko-Dnestrovskom Meždureč'e"; Mykhaylovskiy, European Expansion, pp. 43–48.

34. Favereau, The Horde, p. 270 and n. 47.

35. Grekov and Jakubovskij, L'Orda d'Oro, pp. 235–38; Halperin, Russia and the Golden Horde, p. 55 and "The Six-Hundredth Anniversary of the Battle of Kulikovo Field."

36. Favereau, The Horde, p. 271; Martin, Medieval Russia, p. 213; Pelenski, The Context for the Legacy of Kievan Rus', p. 144; Fennell, A History of the Russian Church, p. 152.

on September 8, on the plain of Kulikovo and the confluence of the Don and the Nepradva, the Rus' army once again defeated the Tatars in an epic battle that earned Dmitry the nickname Donskoy (of the Don).[37]

However, the Russian victories were not enough to free them of the "Tatar yoke" once and for all. Instead, the principality formally remained subject to Sarai, though the political balance had shifted. First, the Russian display of strength had nipped Lithuanian ambitions over Moscow in the bud, limiting Baltic influence to the region of Podolia.[38] Second, Mamaï emerged weakened, which meant that both the Mongol aristocracy and their trading partners (the Genoese and Venetians) no longer saw him as a reliable interlocutor. Lastly, Mamaï's defeat showed that, in order to keep the flow of trade active, it was necessary to invest in relations with local authorities. For instance, in the late 1360s in Tana, Mamaï demanded that the Venetians pay a 4-percent tax and the Genoese a 3-percent tax on sales. To rectify this disparity, on June 3, 1369, Venice passed a resolution to send a delegation to the emir, led by the consul of Tana, with gifts worth 100 silver *sommi*.[39] We do not know whether this mission was successful but, a decade later, the picture had changed: rather than send costly diplomatic delegations all the way to Sarai, Venice chose to consolidate relations with the local Mongol aristocracy.

## Venice and the Blue Horde

From 1361, divisions within the western horde had at least in part been mitigated by Mamaï's authority. However, the situation to the east was a different story. The Blue Horde had its political center in the city of Sighnaq (in today's

37. There is a vast bibliography on the Battle of Kulikovo and its historical significance. For the purposes of this book, it is sufficient to mention the most recent and significant studies. For the perspective of the Russian sources, see Garzaniti, "Le origini medievali della 'santa Russia.'" For an overall picture and an in-depth analysis, see Halperin, "The Battle of Kulikovo"; Halperin, "A Tatar Interpretation of the Battle of Kulikovo Field."

38. For more information, the picture offered here is the most informative, though old: Grekov and Jakubovskij, *L'Orda d'Oro*, chapter 6, pp. 193–205; see also Prochorov, "Etničeskaja integracija." Furthermore, it is difficult not to acknowledge the importance of Tamerlane's work in helping Moscow against the Golden Horde and Lithuania in the final years of the fourteenth century. See also Halperin, *Russia and the Golden Horde*, p. 57 and Halperin, "The Russian Land and the Russian Tsar," pp. 48–52.

39. ASV, SM, XXXIII, fol. 19v; Thiriet, *Régestes des délibérations*, no. 476, p. 121. Vásáry, "The Beginnings of Coinage," p. 382.

Kazakhstan) and drew resources from the rich agricultural and urban economy of the Volga region. From 1360, it was governed by Qara Nogai (d. ca. 1364), a descendant of Toqa Timür (the youngest son of Jöchi), and was elected thanks to the support of Mongol nobility.[40] His cousin Urus (d. 1377) rose to the throne in 1362,[41] while Mamaï was expanding eastward, and Kidyr was enthroned in Sarai—the khan who had only recently dethroned Nawruz.

The Blue Horde was already politically independent of Sarai, and had gained this privilege during the khanate of Uzbek, that is, when Sighnaq was dominated by Mubarak Khwaja (r. 1320–44), who had already begun minting his own money in 1327–28.[42] Uzbek's successor, Jani Beg, had intervened to re-establish his own authority over the Blue Horde, and in 1344 had enthroned Sighnaq Chimtay (r. 1344–60), son of Mubarak Khwaja. When Chimtay died, Urus (or Muhammad Urus) rose to power in 1362, coming into open conflict with Mamaï. Urus's expansionist politics were successful, and he managed to usurp Mamaï's influence over various cities; of these, the most vital were Astrakhan and the capital itself, Sarai, both of which fell in 1375. These and many other events had direct repercussions on Venetian business in Tana.

Until 1376, traders had regularly sailed to the Sea of Azov. Each year, Romànian galleys had been equipped based on the usual itinerary.[43] However, starting in 1376, voyages were interrupted for almost a decade as the political situation degenerated.[44] In this time, the senate allowed captains of these galleys to anchor at Black Sea ports for a few days longer. From 1365 to 1373, Romànian galleys could stop in Tana for no more than seven to eight days; in 1374 and 1375, they were authorized to stop for twelve days; and in the two-year period of 1386–88 a stopover of more than fourteen days was permitted.[45]

40. Vásáry, "The Beginnings of Coinage," p. 382.

41. Atwood, *Encyclopedia*, p. 42.

42. Grekov and Jakubovskij, *L'Orda d'Oro*, pp. 261–62.

43. Thiriet, *Régestes des délibérations*, no. 463, p. 119 (May 13, 1368); no. 474, p. 121 (May 7–8, 1369); no. 486, pp. 123–24 (May 28–32, 1370); no. 498, p. 126 (May 19, 1371); no. 508, pp. 127–28 (May 20, 1372); no. 523, pp. 130–31 (June 21, 1373); no. 540, p. 134 (June 8, 1374); no. 561, p. 139 (May 24–29, 1375); and no. 579, pp. 144–45 (June 5, 1376).

44. Sailing did not resume until the summer of 1384: Thiriet, *Régestes des délibérations*, no. 676, p. 164; Karpov, *La navigazione veneziana*, pp. 46–47.

45. ASV, SM, XXXV, fols. 16, 24r–24v and 26v; Thiriet, *Régestes des délibérations*, nos. 540 and 561, p. 139; Stöckly, *Le système de l'Incanto*, pp. 110–11 and the tables on pp. 371–74; Karpov, *La navigazione veneziana*, p. 91, table 7.

The crisis that struck the basin of the Sea of Azov throughout the 1370s also forced Venice to increase its defense spending in Tana. In July 1370, the senate established *provvisiones* to be passed to the consul, which provided for the supply of weapons and money to repair the loggia (*lobia*) where the notaries operated, and to restore the settlement's fortifications. The consul also received 36 *sommi* to pay a full-time interpreter.[46] In April 1374, the senate ordered the consul to consult with his government, the Council of Twelve, to consider the purchase of a piece of land separate from the Genoese quarter (*a parte Januensium*) and its eventual fortification.[47] The response from Tana's *noyon* was positive, and the land was purchased and fortified. However, a few months later, the consul reported that the Genoese had not accepted the expansion of the settlement, and now threatened retaliation. It was further proof that the two communities were chronically unable to coexist.

## Tokhtamysh

Ongoing power struggles between rival branches of the imperial clan and the defeats suffered in the decade of 1370–80 forced Mamaï to withdraw. This facilitated the advance of the Blue Horde from the east, though its leadership was anything but solid. In 1376, violent clashes broke out within the upper echelons of the aristocracy. This period saw the rise of Tokhtamysh, a young commander and son of Tuli Kwhadja (Toy Khoja), a high officer of the court.[48] The defeat of the Golden Horde, championed by Urus in 1374 and discussed at the *quriltai* of his coronation, had been opposed by a section of the aristocracy that Tokhtamysh's father was a member of; for this reason, he was sentenced to death by Urus himself.[49]

Tokhtamysh was born around 1342 and could claim rights to dynastic legitimacy as he was a direct descendant of the Jöchid clan on his father's side, and a Qonggirat on his mother's side.[50] After witnessing the murder of his father, Tuli Kwhadja, by order of his uncle, Urus, he developed a deep hostility toward Urus, whom he could not yet openly defy. The young emir spent years

---

46. ASV, SM, XXXIII, fols. 64v–65; Thriet, *Régestes des délibérations*, no. 488, p. 124.

47. ASV, SM, XXXIV, fol. 102; Thriet, *Régestes des délibérations*, no. 537, p. 133.

48. DeWeese, "Toḵtamish"; Jackson, *The Mongols and the West*, p. 219 and no. 174; see also Favereau, *The Horde*, pp. 278–80; Grekov and Jakubovskij, *L'Orda d'Oro*, p. 264.

49. Grekov and Jakubovskij, *L'Orda d'Oro*, p. 264.

50. Favereau, *The Horde*, p. 278.

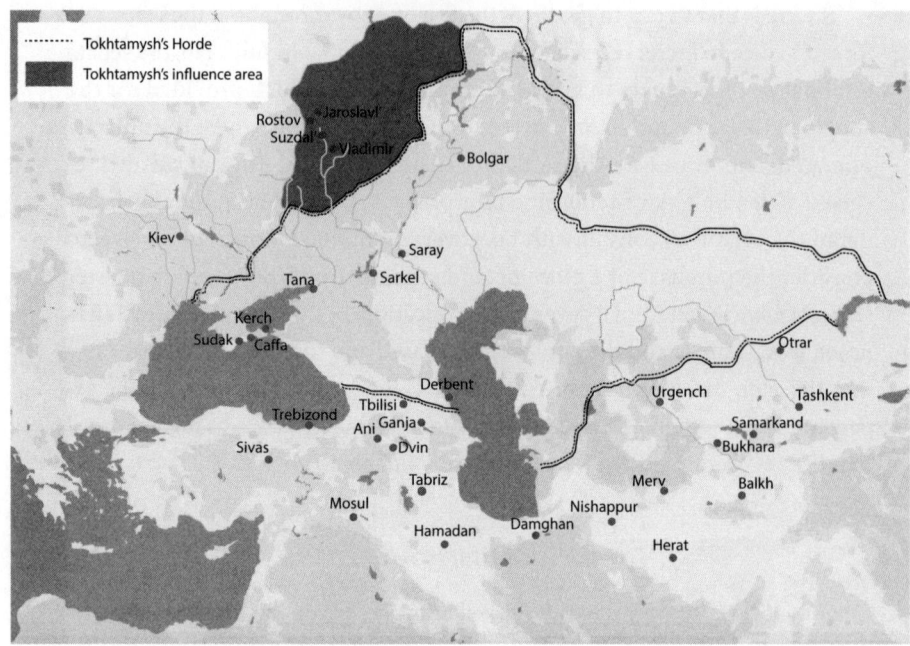

MAP 13. The Golden Horde after the rise of Tokhtamysh

gathering resources by attacking villages and plundering the countryside. Urus soon realized that his nephew was a threat, as Tokhtamysh was undermining his prestige and authority. Perhaps because he felt the encroaching enemy or out of strategic calculation, Tokhtamysh took refuge in Samarkand in 1376. At the time, the region was already under the control of the young Timur (or Tamerlane), whom we will discuss in more detail later. Timur controlled Transoxiana (west of Syr Darya) and was apprehensive of Urus expanding the reach of the Blue Horde. Tokhtamysh's arrival was an ideal opportunity to stop Urus's advance.[51] Timur thus took him under his wing and gave him resources, land, and government responsibilities, particularly in Otrar, not far from Urus's capital, Sighnaq.[52]

Military fortunes soon turned in Tokhtamysh's favor: in late 1377 or early 1378, he took over Sighnaq.[53] Having seized power over the Blue Horde, he

51. Favereau, *The Horde*, p. 280.

52. According to some authors, Timur also gave the city of Sighnaq to Tokhtamysh, which he had not yet conquered. Grekov and Jakubovskij, *L'Orda d'Oro*, p. 265.

53. Grekov and Jakubovskij, *L'Orda d'Oro*, p. 267.

confronted Mamaï directly, who had been busy maintaining control of Rus' and Lithuania.[54] Tokhtamysh's political aim was the reunification and the reconstitution of the Jöchi khanate, and to this end he sought and gained the support of much of the regional aristocracy, which handed him the khanate's capital, Sarai, in 1380.

In October 1380, the two armies clashed on the River Kalka, which had once been the stage of the historic battle between the Mongols and the Rus'–Cuman troops over a century and a half before. Mamaï's army was decimated. The defeat led to the first defections among the aristocracy loyal to Mamaï. He took refuge in Caffa, a city formally in his territory, so that he could reorganize. Nevertheless, a few days later he was murdered by the Genoese under mysterious circumstances. For some time, the *beg* of the White Horde had turned their back on Mamaï, convinced he would lose the war. It is likely that the *beg* of Solgat had asked the Genoese to get rid of Mamaï.[55]

At the start of the decade, it seemed as though Tokhtamysh was succeeding where Mamaï had failed, namely in the reunification of the Jöchid *ulus*. Within months, and with the support of most of the local emirs, he had conquered Astrakhan, the Volga region, the northern Caucasus, and Crimea. For the first time in over two decades, a consistent power had returned to be hegemonic on both sides of the Volga. For his part, Timur maintained control of Transoxiana.

## Venice, Genoa, and the War of Chioggia

War and the involvement of the territorial nobility, as well as political adjustment within the Golden Horde, had immediate consequences on Venetian politics in the Black Sea—not just to the north, where the clashes had a direct impact, but to the south as well, where the political landscape was in constant flux. Starting in 1375, relations between Venice and the empire of Trebizond were once again in crisis. This clash had old roots, and Venetian merchants were the victims of continuous harassment by the local population. Emperor Alexios III did not defend them and even incurred debts with the Venetian merchant community that he could not—or did not want to—repay. To make matters worse, he had cut their privileges. As the situation reached a boiling

---

54. Favereau, *The Horde*, p. 280.

55. Balard, *La Romanie génoise*, p. 457; Spuler, *Die Goldene Horde*, pp. 126–27. According to Balard's calculations, Mamaï died in Caffa between March and November 1381.

point in Tana and with the consequent need to consolidate its presence in Trebizond, Venice had no choice but to react. It did everything it could to dethrone the problematic emperor. Marco Giustiniani, an experienced admiral, was hired to sail to Constantinople with ten armed galleys, and then continue on with six galleys to the gates of Trebizond, to intimidate the emperor and force him to negotiate.[56] Venice's show of strength was successful and led to an agreement signed in July 1376, in which the emperor's authority was recognized in exchange for his commitment to guarantee the security of the trade activity, and to drastically reduce—by half—the fiscal duties on all transactions, except for customs duties on incoming goods.[57]

At this time, Black Sea navigation was characterized by tension and a subsequent slowdown in trade throughout the region. Naturally, this had repercussions on ship auctions, a system which collapsed in 1374–76.[58] Tana and Trebizond were the two nerve centers of the Venetian Pontic system. As had always been the case, external crises triggered extreme reactions in Venetian–Genoese relations, in one direction or another. In 1376, the Venetian galleys of Romània had to be escorted to Tana by the armed ships of Marco Giustiniani, who then awaited their return to Constantinople. It was during these months—September to October—that the *casus belli* emerged that would cause the fourth conflict between the two cities: the War of Chioggia. It began with a dispute over the control of Tenedos, a small and strategic island in the northeast part of the Aegean Sea, south of the colony of Chersonesus. However, the real motive lay once again in the competition to dominate Black Sea trade, a constant factor in the complex web of relations between these two states in the east Mediterranean.

In 1369, a few years after the anti-Venetian revolt in Crete, the Byzantine Emperor, a weakened John V Palaiologos (d. 1391), had conceded the island of Tenedos to Venice to pay for a portion of the vast debt he had amassed. Thanks to its strategic position, Tenedos allowed Venice to control the Hellespont and thereby all transit to and from Constantinople. Genoa reacted by stepping in and taking advantage of the crisis in Byzantium in an attempt to mitigate Venice's power. Emperor John V Palaiologos was under attack on two

---

56. Venice attempted to solve the negotiations peacefully, but records tell us that it was also planning an insurrection. For an accurate reconstruction, see Karpov, *L'impero di Trebisonda*, pp. 99–101.

57. *Diplomatarium veneto-levantinum*, vol. 2, pp. 249–50.

58. Karpov, *La navigazione veneziana*, p. 102; for an overall picture of the events in these years, see Karpov, "Veneciansko-trapezundskij konflikt."

fronts: by the Ottomans, who had already taken Gallipoli and controlled the Dardanelles, and at court where his son and heir to the throne, Andronicus IV, had been conspiring against him. In 1376, the situation worsened when Andronicus IV, helped (or pushed) by the Genoese of Pera, had his father imprisoned and formally gave Tenedos to his allies. This meant expelling the Venetians, who busied themselves with fortifying the island.[59]

The ensuing Veneto–Genoese war was the last great conflict between these two cities—and perhaps the hardest for them both. This time the conflict was global, as the extent and weight of Genoese and Venetian interests in the East now involved most bordering countries. King Louis I of Hungary had allied with Genoa to consolidate his dominions in Dalmatia, thus cutting off timber supplies for Venice. The patriarch of Aquileia also took Genoa's side, as did the seigneury of Padua, da Carrara, who had already been at war with Venice for some time. The Byzantine Empire, as mentioned, entered the war due to dynastic struggles. The Ottomans, by then integrated in the region's politics, also sided with Genoa. Venice found itself increasingly isolated, facing a test with evermore uncertain results.

The war's main theater was in the western Mediterranean, but battles extended to the Romànian seas, in particular off the shores of Tenedos. As the war raged on, navigation in the Black Sea came to a standstill, causing major economic damage to both Genoa and Venice. In June 1377, during the Rialto auction of Romànian galleys, only three were armed; of those, only two found a buyer. Ultimately, on August 7, the senate decided not to grant them passage due to the high risk.[60]

Finally, the peace in Turin, signed in August 1381, confirmed an abundantly clear fact: neither Genoa nor Venice could stamp out the other's presence in the Levant. The treaty reinforced the knife-edge compromise that had allowed the two republics to live side by side to this point. The main beneficiary of the War of Chioggia was the Ottoman Empire of Murad I, an emerging power that had already taken western Anatolia from Byzantium, had entered the Balkans, and was there to stay.

Genoa and Venice stipulated that Tana would be excluded from navigation for two years.[61] In 1382, two galleys armed by the Venetian state headed to the Black Sea but did not reach the mouth of the Don. It was not until 1383 that

59. Balard, "La lotta contro Genova," pp. 114–15.

60. Thiriet, *Régestes des délibérations*, nos. 592 and 593, pp. 146–47; Chinazzo, *Cronica*, pp. 19–20.

61. Chinazzo, *Cronica*, pp. 209–10.

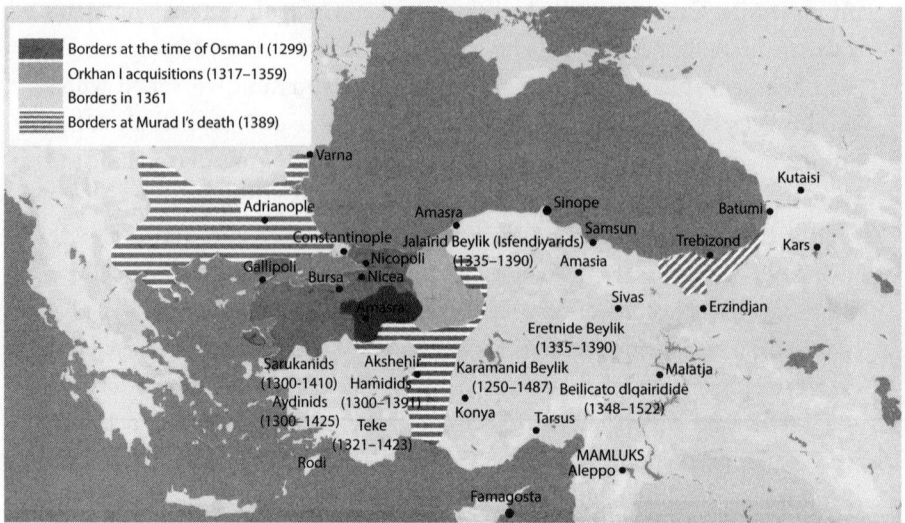

MAP 14. Ottoman expansion between 1300 and 1389

regular journeys to Tana resumed,[62] and on July 24, Doge Antonio Venier (d. 1400) sent two ambassadors to the Tatar governor of Crimea (*excellentissimum dominum Imperatorem Tartarorum*) to request confirmation of the agreements in force. Evidently, Venice feared that taxes on trade would be raised. The diplomats were tasked with ensuring that the *commerchium* remained at 3 percent; if this was not possible, it should be fixed at a maximum of 5 percent.[63] After the peace of Turin, Tana enjoyed another brief period of prosperity that lasted until the mid-1390s. Travel was regular, and auctions showed that there was considerable interest in trade. However, conflicts within the Golden Horde had not been placated by Tokhtamysh's victory over Mamaï. A new conflict would soon wreak havoc upon the delicate political equilibrium, once again tipping the scales of power and forcing Venice to batten down the hatches.

## The War between Tokhtamysh and Timur

Timur was born in April 1336 in Kesh, a city south of Samarkand. His father was Taragai, leader of the nomadic Barlas clan, Mongols who had become Turks and converted to Islam. His mother was Takina Khatun, of whom little

62. ASV, SM, XXXVIII, fol. 34v; Thiriet *Régestes des délibérations*, nos. 648 and 649, p. 158; Karpov, *L'impero di Trebisonda*, p. 101.

63. *Diplomatarium veneto-levantinum*, vol. 2, pp. 188–90.

is known, but who may have been an indirect descendant of the Chinggisid clan.[64] As a young man, Timur entered the service of the emir Qara'una Qazaghan, the undisputed lord of Transoxiana.[65] Timur took advantage of this opportunity and earned the goodwill of Qazaghan, who entrusted the young man with ever-increasing military responsibilities. However, in 1358, this powerful emir of Transoxiana was murdered in a plot organized by his own son. Eighteen months later, the Qara'una had to contend with an onslaught of legitimate heirs to the Chagataid throne: the Mongols of the Moghulisan of Toghluk Timur (d. 1363),[66] who had governed the eastern part of the khanate for decades in open conflict with the hegemonic power of Transoxiana. Much of the aristocracy that controlled the clans and tribes of the region allied with Toghluk Timur, facilitating his advance. So did the young Timur (Tamerlane), who welcomed enemy troops without resistance. He even went to meet them with gifts and offered his services.

Still only twenty-five years old, Timur's strategy was successful. Toghluk Timur entrusted him with the defense of Transoxiana and of an entire *tümen* (10,000-men unit). However, conquest of such a vast area, inhabited by such diverse clans and tribes, could never be fully assured. In 1361, the population

64. Tamerlane derives from Timur *leng* ("lame" in Persian), a nickname he was given as an adult when he lost the use of one leg. Upon Timur's birth, just as when Chinggis Khan was born, legend has it that the child was born clutching a clot of blood, which—according to *The Secret History of the Mongols*—represented an imperial destiny. The Barlas were connected to the Chinggisid clan of the Borjin. The bibliography on Tamerlane is vast. Russian sources describe him in great detail: *Moskovskij Letopis'nyj*. Of particular interest, even though it is slightly fictionalized, is the description offered by Grousset, *The Empire of the Steppes*. Albeit dated, a good biography by Prawdin: *L'empire Mongol et Tamerlan*. However, the best monograph on Tamerlane remains the one by B. Forbes Manz, *The Rise and Rule of Tamerlane*. All of Jean Aubin's writings on the matter are essential reading, but they are not collected. Among the less recent works, see Kehren, *Tamerlan* and Roux, *Tamerlano*, with an updated bibliography. One of the most interesting and instructive narrative sources on the Mongol commander is no doubt Clavijo's mission (Markham, *Narrative of the Embassy of Ruy Gonzalez de Clavijo*). Another excellent critical edition is the one edited by Anna Spinelli, *Dal Mare di Alboran a Samarcanda*. A privileged observation of the Mongol commander, in that it was written by a firsthand witness to the events, remains *La storia* by the Armenian T'ovma Metsobets'i, trans. as *The History of Tamerlano and His Successors*.

65. In 1346, Qazaghan had succeeded in rising to the head of the tribal aristocracy in the Chagataid *ulus*, exploiting the years-long power crises. Without a direct blood tie to the Chinggisids, he governed indirectly, selecting which khans should be enthroned and controlling their activity closely. Forbes Manz, *The Rise and Rule of Tamerlane*, pp. 157–58 and 160.

66. It is likely that Toghluk Timur was a direct descendant of Chagatai, thus enjoying greater prestige than his western counterpart Qazakhan. Grousset, *The Empire of the Steppes*, p. 344.

openly rebelled against oppression by a rapacious government, and Toghluk Timur returned to quell the revolt. Timur then chose to join the rebels against the Chagataid, betraying their support of him. It was a difficult and risky choice. At the time, Timur could count on a handful of loyal figures and the support of a small part of the military nobility of Transoxiana.

Thus began the flight of the future grand emir, pursued by Toghluk Timur's men, who sought to punish his betrayal by making an example of him. Yet in 1363, the khan died and was succeeded by his son, Iljas Khoja (d. 1368). He continued to hunt for Timur and his loyalists, who fled to the region of Nishappur.

Timur had now joined forces with his brother-in-law Hussayn (whose sister was Timur's wife), and Iljas Khoja feared that they might reunite the forces of Transoxiana and lead to a renewed division of the state that his father had re-unified. Meanwhile, Timur and Hussayn had gained fame among the population and the troops by serving as officers in internal disputes in the more remote regions of Transoxiana. When Khoja's Chagataid army met Timur and Hussayn's forces for the first time, thousands of men had joined them. The first battle took place in 1363, in what sources call the Battle for the Stone Bridge (*Pul-i Sengi*)—probably a bridge over the River Wakhs. The Chagataid army suffered a bad defeat. This was merely the first of Timur's many military successes, and his right leg had already been maimed by an arrow injury that had been poorly treated. In the spring of 1365, the two armies clashed once again near Tashkent, on the high course of the Syr Darya. Although there are no details of how the battle unfolded, Iljas Khoja prevailed, forcing the Timurid army to retreat to Samarkand. Chagataid forces besieged the city, but failed miserably, perhaps partly due to a virulent outbreak of horse flu that decimated their horses. It was a coup de grâce for the khan, who was forced to abandon his goal of bringing Transoxiana back under Chagataid control. For Timur, it was just the beginning of a rapid rise to power, but the moment had come to deal with the relationship with his brother-in-law. Hussayn's ambitions had made him an uneasy ally.

These two men who had fought side by side against a common enemy now fought against each other in early 1368 in Balkh, where Hussayn had taken refuge. The city surrendered and though Timur spared his brother-in-law's life, Hussayn would be murdered under mysterious circumstances only a few months later. Timur was now free of all obstacles, and in April 1370, he was proclaimed grand emir, the undisputed sovereign of all of Transoxiana. He made Samarkand the capital, a city with a glorious past and geographically

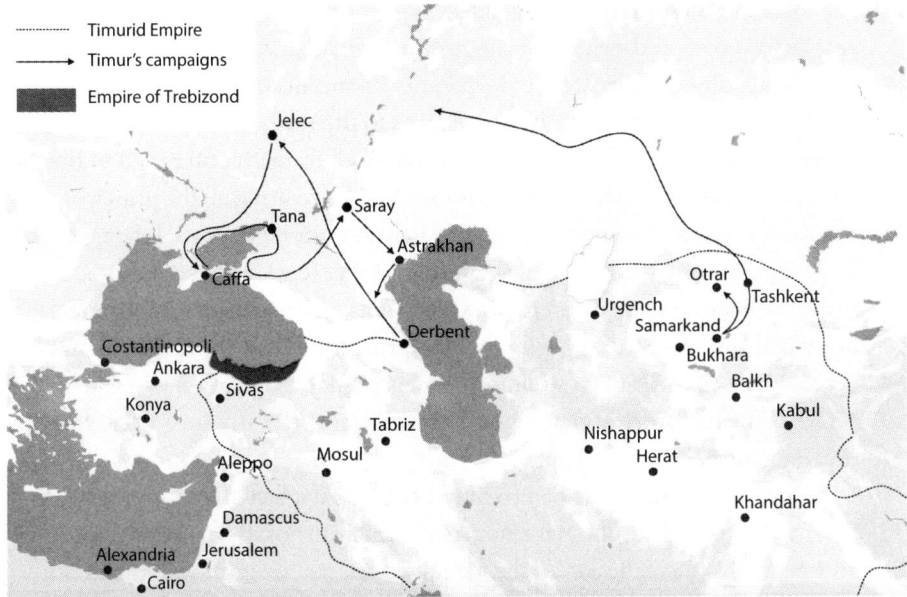

MAP 15. Timur's campaigns against Tokhtamysh (1388–91 and 1395)

well placed in the valley of the Zaresfhan, midway between Bukhara and Tashkent. From there, Timur organized his new state: he fortified the city, elimi-
nated hostile nobility, empowered those he trusted, and reformed the administrative system, focusing on trade as the main resource. To this end, he began
a vast reform to uniform weights and measures, invested in the safety of the
caravan routes, and ensured that tribes settled near oases did not rob traveling
merchants. For a few years, he managed to avoid conflict, fully focused on
internal stabilization and building an efficient army.

From 1371, Timur launched a series of military campaigns that soon led to
the considerable expansion of his already vast territory. The first initiatives
were directed toward the interior, to force the rebel tribes of Transoxiana into
submission. In 1372, he attacked Khwarazm, which had resisted for years. In
1379, he lay siege to Urgench, and after defeating the city's resistance, he completed his conquest of Khwarazm. After Khwarazm, he invaded Khorasan, a
crucial step in the direction of Azerbaijan, the gate to the Caucasus. The
Timurid campaign of Khorasan was long and demanding, but it ended in 1385,
after which Timur planned to attack the Iranian Jalayirids.

It was in this context that the break with Tokhtamysh occurred. After defeating Mamaï and taking control of almost all the territory that had once been

the Jōchi *ulus* in the days of its greatest expansion, Tokhtamysh hastened to reassert his own authority over the princes of Rus' and the grand duchy of Lithuania. After all, consistent government also meant administrative and fiscal reform. Tokhtamysh quickly sent envoys to the Russian Prince Dmitry of Moscow and the grand duchy of Lithuania. Both formally submitted to the khan, but Tokhtamysh had planned for some time to bring all the principalities of Rus' under his direct control, a formal and substantial vassal state with large fiscal obligations. Prince Dmitry of Moscow aspired to greater independence and refused to pay tributes. Thus, in August 1382, the Mongol army laid siege to Moscow, aided by the princes of Nizhny Novgorod and Ryazan. The city fell after a strenuous defense and its population was slaughtered. Thus, both the victory of Kulikovo and the dream of Russian independence were wiped out.

Tokhtamysh and Timur had risen to become established leaders, with efficient armies and substantial resources at their disposal—and they would soon clash. Numismatics reveal the nature of their rivalry: in 1383, Tokhtamysh minted coins in Khwarazm, which had just come under the control of the Timurid. It was a clear challenge to the grand emir's authority.

In 1385, Timur attacked the Jalayirid to occupy the southern Caucasus, but although he won several battles, he retreated without completing the conquest, possibly due to the death of his daughter. Tokhtamysh took advantage of this to attack Tabriz, near the end of 1384 or the beginning of 1385. The city fell in the winter of 1385. Tokhtamysh also forged diplomatic relations with the Mamluks, sending a delegation to Cairo in early 1385.[67]

A clash between the two khans was nigh. Their first battle took place in Dagestan in 1386–87, ending without a victor. The following year, Tokhtamysh attacked Khwarazm and won several battles against the Timurid troops near Otrar and Bukhara. Tokhtamysh pillaged the countryside and villages in the districts, but failed to take the central cities. In those months, Timur was in Iran. The counterattack on Tokhtamysh started in Urgench, which was overwhelmed by Timurid armadas in the freezing winter of 1388. Again, Timur bided his time and returned to Samarkand rather than pursuing Tokhtamysh's forces en route. In the spring of 1389, having amassed a large army, Timur crossed the Syr Darya and ventured into the steppe to annihilate the rival khan once and for all.

---

67. Perhaps Tokhtamysh sought allies because he was concerned about Timur's reaction to the conquest of Tabriz. Favereau, *The Horde*, p. 284.

The campaign was long and exhausting. Some sources state that Timur even contracted malaria. In early April, several deserters of Tokhtamysh's army were intercepted near the Ural River; with their help, Timur determined where the majority of enemy troops were located, encamped a few miles away near present-day Orenburg. It was there, along the course of the Kondurcha River in the Volga basin, that the two armies faced each other in their first real battle. Timur won, but it was not a decisive victory as the battle had taken place on enemy territory, without logistical support. Tokhtamysh was defeated, but not conquered.[68]

Over the next three years, Tokhtamysh reorganized and turned to local lords for help, garnering support from the *beg* to the tribal chiefs. Above all, he sought an alliance with the Mamluks and the grand duchy of Lithuania. He also had the support of Moscow, which he had besieged and conquered only a few years earlier. Grand Duke Vasily (d. 1425), son and successor of Dmitry Donskoy, never forgot the atrocities perpetrated in 1382 by Tokhtamysh's troops, but saw the advantage in supporting him. Indeed, accepting the bond of vassalage meant immediately obtaining control of Nizhny Novgorod, Gorodets, and Murom, the great plains east of Moscow and the midcourse of the Volga.

Soon after defeating Tokhtamysh, Timur had to intervene in Azerbaijan and in Iran to repress the uprisings provoked by local clan leaders who refused to submit. Timur's military campaign, known as the Five Years War, was long and extended over a vast territory. Begun in the summer of 1392, operations were focused on Luristan, and in the spring of 1393, Timur conquered Shiraz, before attacking and conquering Isfahan and Hamadan a few weeks later. That August, Timurid troops entered Baghdad, then in the hands of Ahmad Jalayir (d. 1410), the Jalayirid emir banished from Tabriz during the 1382 Tokhtamysh raid. Once again, Ahmad fled to safety before Timur's troops entered the city.[69]

Military operations ended in the Caucasus, with the conquest of the kingdom of Georgia near the end of 1394. After many years of war, Timur had reconstituted a semblance of the Ilkhanate, in addition to Transoxiana, which was now almost entirely under his control. Yet, just as Timur was in the Caucasus, Tokhtamysh broke through with his forces in Shirvan, passed Derbent, and arrived a few miles from where the bulk of Timurid forces were stationed. A clash between the two armies became inevitable, but rather than engage, Tokhtamysh withdrew. Sources are unclear on the reasons for his decision, but it is likely that the khan had counted on the support of the local populations—support which

---

68. See Forbes Manz, *The Rise and Rule of Tamerlane*, pp. 71–72.
69. Forbes Manz, *The Rise and Rule of Tamerlane*, pp. 70–73.

he never received. In the first months of 1395, Tokhtamysh settled in the lowlands along the course of the Terek River, not far from the western coast of the Caspian Sea, while Timur passed the Caucasus. In April, Timur met Tokhtamysh's army, which was still deployed in the valley of the Terek River.

The battle of April 15, 1395, was one for the ages. Timur risked death in combat, but the final outcome was all in his favor, with Tokhtamysh's troops forced to withdraw in disarray. In hot pursuit, the Timurid army invaded what remained of the Golden Horde. Timur conquered Bolghar, devastated the countryside of the Kiev district, then turned south, headed to the Sea of Azov, where he searched for Tokhtamysh. The khan had taken refuge with the Grand Duke of Lithuania, hoping to regroup in safety.

## The Timurid Attack on Tana

In the late 1370s and early 1380s, the region's political instability directly affected life in Tana. The khanate of Tokhtamysh (1380–95) had re-established some political order and had encouraged a return of the Venetian galleys to the Sea of Azov, building a fragile economic recovery. However, his centralist policies for the Golden Horde were incompatible with the independence that the Latin settlements in Gazaria had carved out for themselves. Thus, in 1385 and 1386, the khan attempted to bring Crimea back under his control. From the city of Solgat, the Mongols advanced upon the richest and most independent city in the region: Caffa. Although Latin diplomacy worked hard to avoid a siege, every attempt failed. On May 31, 1387, the Genoese doge Antoniotto Adorno wrote to his Venetian counterpart, Antonio Venier, announcing that all attempts to find a compromise with the Mongols had failed.[70] Genoa was committed to fighting "the barbarians," but it demanded that Venice prevent its markets from trading with the enemy. As Genoa had called a halt to trade relations with the Mongols, it was asking Venice to follow suit. The events taking shape mirrored those of the 1340s, when the war with Jani Beg had forced the two cities to form a united front. To compensate for the potential damage from the interruption in Veneto-Mongol relations, Genoa guaranteed Venetian citizens maximum access to all its settlements on the Black Sea.[71] Furthermore, Genoa ordered its own authorities on the Black Sea to treat Venetians as allies.[72] In these weeks, Ludovico Contarini, Venetian

---

70. Giomo, *Libri commemoriali*, vol. 3, no. 260, p. 187.

71. Giomo, *Libri commemoriali*, vol. 3, no. 260, p. 187.

72. Giomo, *Libri commemoriali*, vol. 3, no. 264, p. 188.

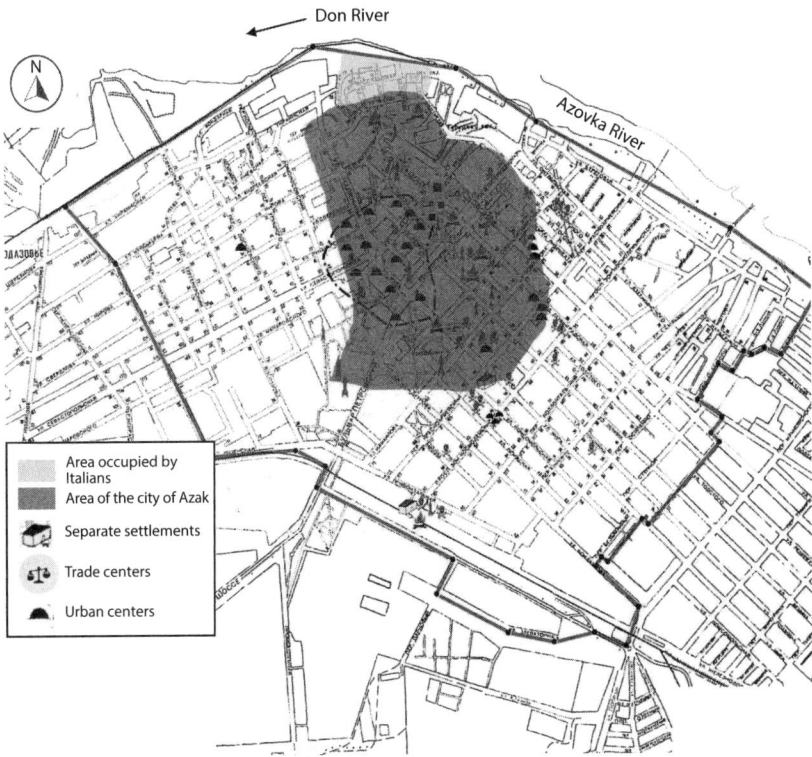

FIGURE 3. Topographic map of Tana in the 1390s. From the excavations of A. N. Maslovskij (based on Karpov, *Istorija Tany*).

consul in Tana and captain of the Romànian galleys, received an order from the motherland not to welcome aboard any *saracini e tarteri* (Saracens and Tatars).[73] Ultimately, Genoa managed to ward off the Mongol attack and guaranteed itself several years of peace before the arrival of Timur.[74]

The conflict between Tokhtamysh and Timur caused a slowdown in voyages made by Venetian galleys, though the Republic never entirely stopped sailing to the Sea of Azov. In the early summer of 1394, war was approaching the Latin settlements. In a resolution dated June 4, the Venetian senate permitted the captain of the galleys to travel as far as Tana only after evaluating whether circumstances were safe enough.[75] In case of danger, he had the option to stop in Caffa. On July 23, 1395, ships were explicitly told to enter the

73. Giomo, *Libri commemoriali*, vol. 3, no. 274, pp. 189–90.

74. Balard, *La Romanie génoise*, p. 93.

75. Thiriet, *Régestes des délibérations*, no. 853, p. 202.

port of Tana only after gathering information from the consul about the ongoing situation. Venetian fears came true a few months later: in the second half of the year, Timur attacked Tana. Perhaps this was part of a larger strategy in which Timur intended to destroy the trade centers that filled Jöchid treasure chests. Regardless of motive, Timur's attack caused substantial material damage and loss of human life for all of Tana's communities.

The blow was too harsh to absorb in the short term. Both Genoese and Venetians were forced to flee Tana, but this time they were not systematically expelled as they had been in 1308 and in 1343. Timur's destruction was short-lived and ended with the withdrawal of his troops. The consequences of his attack were mostly indirect. War in central Asia had made the routes to the north of the Caspian Sea, from Urgench to Astrakhan, unsafe, slowing down trade imports. Though Timur's quest for expansion did not cause a breakdown in communications, it certainly curtailed trade activities.[76]

When news of the attack reached Venice, reaction from the authorities was immediate. On February 22, 1396, the senate ordered the new consul of Tana, Blanco de Ripa, to go to Tokhtamysh and ask his permission to fortify the settlement, which had been seriously damaged by Timur.[77] Auctions for Romània–Black Sea galleys, held in the spring of 1396, were reduced to just slightly over 20 *lire di grossi* in comparison to the 100 of the year before. At the same time, bids for galleys bound for Alexandria and Beirut rose constantly, a clear sign of the gradual shift of Venice's commercial axis toward the Mediterranean.[78] In addition, a resolution dated July 13, 1396, warned the *patroni* of galleys bound for Tana to be cautious; they should inquire from the bailiff of Constantinople if conditions were safe before sailing beyond the straits. If the danger was too great, they were to head for Caffa and then on to Trebizond.[79] That same year, the ambassador of Trebizond Jacopo Gussoni—who was also the bailiff of the Venetian community—received from Byzantine Emperor Manuel III (1364–1417) the right to trade under the same conditions as those granted by the treaty signed with Alexios III: Venetians were allowed a church and a bank in the city, and could administer justice in the name and on the account of Venice for crimes committed by its citizens.[80]

76. On this position, see also Berindei and Veinstein, "La Tana-Azaq," pp. 124–26.

77. Thiriet, *Régestes des délibérations*, no. 898, p. 211.

78. Stöckly, *Le système de l'incanto*, pp. 378–86; Berindei and Veinstein, "La Tana-Azaq," p. 127.

79. Thiriet, *Régestes des délibérations*, no. 913, p. 214.

80. Giomo, *Libri commemoriali*, vol. 3, no. 54, pp. 244–45.

Despite the growing danger on Asian communication routes, the commercial outpost on the Sea of Azov was too important for Venice to give it up. The senate decided to send an ambassador to Tana in 1397, right after Timur's departure. Andrea Giustiniani was appointed and tasked with petitioning Tokhtamysh to renew the ongoing privileges, as all the documents had been destroyed during the sacking of the city.[81] He also requested further trade subsidies due to the heavy damage they had suffered, as well as permission to fortify the Venetian quarter.[82] Evidently, he was successful: as early as June 1397 the Romània–Black Sea galleys were auctioned off and voyages to Tana were explicitly mentioned.[83]

In the following years, trade with Tana resumed, slowly but surely. In January 1399, it was decided to send two cogs (ships suited to carrying heavy loads), which were allowed to dock for several weeks as long as they began their return journey by September 15. The vast capacity of these ships—over 500 barrels— suggests a substantial load. A new consul was sent to Tana at this time, Maffeo Barbarigo.[84] In June that year, the two Romània–Black Sea galleys that had been permitted were authorized to sail to Tana, and the auction prices rose, albeit slowly: one galley was assigned for 103 *lire* and 14 *soldi grossi*, and the other for 101 *lire* and 5 *soldi grossi*.[85]

Despite Timur's attack, in the late fourteenth century the Sea of Azov was still a popular destination. However, the main flow of trade with Asia had shifted southwards, and the Middle Eastern and north African ports were gradually replacing those of the Black Sea. Taking note of this new international picture, Venice adapted by intensifying its diplomatic and financial efforts in the Aegean and Egypt. Although Venice did not abandon the Black Sea, the prosperity it had promised in the previous century was now firmly in the past.

81. Thiriet, *Régestes des délibérations*, no. 927, p. 217.

82. Thiriet, *Régestes des délibérations*, no. 930, p. 217. Andrea Giustiniani had to request a reduction in the *commerchium* from 3 to 1.5 percent and earn the sympathy of the Mongol treasurer Mirsa, who, the document states, wielded great influence over Tokhtamysh.

83. Thiriet, *Régestes des délibérations*, no. 934, pp. 218–19.

84. Thiriet, *Régestes des délibérations*, no. 958, p. 222.

85. The five galleys of Beirut came to a total of 819 *lire di grossi*, the three of Alexandria to 647. Thiriet, *Régestes des délibérations*, no. 934, p. 219.

# 7

## After the Golden Horde

### VENICE AND THE MONGOLS UP
### TO THE OTTOMAN CONQUEST

### Tana's Reconstruction and Recovery after Timur

Timur's death in 1405 put an end to his foundering attempts to restore the
Mongol Empire, and triggered a prolonged war of succession that opened new
possibilities for the Latins entrenched on the Pontic coastline. The international picture evolved greatly due to the rise of Ottoman power and the complete political disintegration of the Mongol Empire in the West. Finally freed
of the "Tatar yoke," the grand duchies of Lithuania and Rus' began to exert
ever greater control over the territories of the Golden Horde and Crimea, as
well as over the trade routes that connected them to regional ports. In the first
half of the fifteenth century, new protagonists stepped onto the political stage,
in particular the grand duchy of Lithuania and the Ottoman Empire, who over-
lapped with local and regional potentates such as the khanate of Crimea, the
principality of Theodor, the empire of Trebizond, and the Byzantine Empire
itself. By then, the latter's sovereign power had been reduced to Constantinople. The Italian colonies, increasingly restricted both in their commercial
movements and their political sphere of action, struggled for survival amid
these turbulent currents. They were forced to juggle and redefine their strategies with each new situation, adjusting their priorities with the relative rise in
costs, risks, and uncertainties. Moreover, loss of access to Asian markets that
had once been guaranteed by the Mongols had narrowed a vast horizon that—
both from a practical and idealized trade perspective—had initially justified
the maintenance of a stable Black Sea presence. For the Venetians, whose logistical support was more fragile than that of the Genoese, adapting to new

needs meant making sacrifices. Above all, this affected the social composition of the Venetian population and the types of activities undertaken. However, what challenged the future of settlements on the Black Sea even more seriously than local hostilities and diminished profits was the change in direction of Venetian politics. On the one hand, Venice had chosen to expand into the Veneto and Lombard mainland, and on the other hand, it had redirected its trade with the East through Egyptian ports, where spices arrived via maritime routes from India and southeast Asia.

Despite the destruction wrought by Timur, Tana's Venetian community showed unfailing courage and resilience. At the dawn of the fifteenth century, the situation was overall positive. Trade quickly resumed both in Tana and in other Black Sea regions, including Trebizond, the other Venetian pole in Pontus. Nonetheless, dangers and uncertainties remained, causing progressive structural changes. As communities adapted to changing circumstances, we can identify two opposing trends. On the one hand, administrators and traders showed a dogged resilience in the face of change, using their considerable skill to reinvent their positions and goals. On the other hand, threats continued to grow—both near and far, symptomatic of a climate of uncertainty created by uncontrollable and unpredictable phenomena that the trader Giovanni Cornaro described as a series of "labyrinths."[1]

Such a climate of unease was not especially reassuring for the Venetian ships that continued to frequent the ports on the Black Sea. Still, the days of overland expeditions had come to an end; the central Asian and Iranian routes were firmly in the hands of Muslim merchants at the service of the Timurid government. Venetian and Genoese merchants were excluded—or rather, they had excluded themselves—due to the damage they had suffered at Timur's hands and the constant wars that rendered these routes impassable. Journeys to India and southeast Asia that were taken by Niccolò de' Conti, a native of Chioggia, are indicative of the maritime routes that had already replaced land routes, even though an Italian presence never fully materialized in these regions.[2]

---

1. Pienaru, "The Timurids and the Black Sea," p. 128.

2. Niccolò de' Conti's journey was included in the fourth book of the *Historiae de varietate fortunae* by Poggio Bracciolini in 1447. Many editions were published in the nineteenth century, the most notable being: Desimoni, "Pero Tafur"; Giardina, *I viaggi*; Bellemo, *La cosmografia e le scoperte geografiche*; Longhena, *Viaggi in Persia*; Poggio Bracciolini, *De l'Inde*.

In the early fifteenth century, the Grand Duke Vytautas of Lithuania (r. 1401–30), a steadfast ally of Tokhtamysh, wielded the most influence over Tatar politics. This was mired in conflicts between the Jöchid descendants and other political figures, such as Edigu Khan (1352–1419), against whom Vytautas had fought during the Timurid wars. In those years, a portion of the Tatar population had moved to Lithuania, and Vytautas continued to play a pivotal role in Crimean politics up to his death in 1430, seeking to take control of Caffa and Genoese possessions.[3] Tana remained untouched by Lithuanian expansion. Rather, the most pressing danger for this settlement was the belligerent activity of the Tatar warlords, who fought over what remained of the Mongol dominion, threatening the security of trade bases. Tatar leaders attacked Tana several times, forcing it to invest huge amounts of capital to reinforce its walls and fortifications, and to recruit a garrison from the motherland for its defense. In contrast, the Genoese continued to benefit from their dominant position as they remained entrenched in Caffa and in their other Crimean bases, as well as wielding control over the southern coast of the Black Sea. However much Caffa and the other colonies enjoyed independence from Genoa, which had alternately been dominated by the French and the Milanese, relations with the Venetians continued to be affected by tensions between the two republics.

A further cause for concern and instability was the rise of Ottoman power. Though this was only burgeoning in the early fifteenth century, it grew more intense after the ascension of Murad II (r. 1421–51) and up to the definitive collapse of what little remained of the Byzantine Empire. At the same time, Venetian foreign policy was focused on expanding and developing its mainland domains (*Stato de Tera*) in Veneto, Friuli, and Lombardy, as initiated by Doge Michele Steno (r. 1400–1413). Although Venice did not abandon its sea possessions, it gradually scaled back its interests in the Aegean, especially after the futile and costly defense of Thessaloniki and the failure of the "Crusade of Varna" against the Ottomans.

Trade and economic activities underwent further structural change, with Venice reducing its investments in long-distance quests that had previously embraced Asian markets. While the second half of the fourteenth century had seen merchants push as far as Sarai, the destruction of Tana had led to these spaces being reduced in favor of more local economies: the fish industry (especially dried fish and caviar), the slave trade, and transportation within the Black Sea. Breeding livestock was another vital economic activity of the

---

3. Kołodziejczyk, *The Crimean Khanate*, pp. 8–9; Khvalkov, "The Venetian Tana," p. 118.

Pontic steppe and was the source of commercial products such as leather and horses. Spices and raw silk continued to arrive via the central Asian markets under Timurid control, which Shah Rukh (r. 1405–47), son and successor of Timur, sought to keep open and active. Samarkand was the central hub of this trade, with routes to China.

## Venice between the Tatars, Genoese, and Ottomans

The war between Tokhtamysh and Timur had two significant impacts on the Black Sea's political stability. First, the catastrophic failure of Timur's plan to reunify the Mongol Empire based on the model of previous khans had, in fact, accelerated the dissolution of the Golden Horde. Second, the war had fostered the political fragmentation that had already been under way for some time (as outlined in the previous chapter), without producing a credible alternative. In the confusion that reigned in this first half of the fifteenth century, we can identify three main trends. The first of these was the ascent of local potentates, dominated by "khans" of rival Tatar aristocratic families and clans. These engaged in never-ending conflicts that reached their peak in 1446 with the creation of the khanate of Crimea by Haci I Giray (r. 1441–56).[4] The potentates were each relatively weak, and therefore sought alliances and agreements with other emerging powers. The most important among these were the grand duchy of Lithuania, the principality of Moscow, and the Ottoman Empire, which gave the potentates access to greater political and military interventions. The second trend was the consolidation of the Timurid dynasty in central Asia and Iran, based on the political and military structures created by Timur. This, too, was preceded by a period of infighting and could not revitalize the effective communication and commercial osmosis between the Asian routes and the Mediterranean trade that had once been under Mongol control. Lastly, long-distance trade shifted to the maritime routes of the Indian Ocean, which depended on Alexandria and other Egyptian ports.

In such times of constant—and at times sudden—change, Italian outposts on the Black Sea lacked military strength to intervene in local wars, and were thus forced to rely on diplomatic operations and defensive interventions.

---

4. Born in 1397 and a Chinggisid (a descendant of Toqa Timür), Haci I Giray imposed himself as the khan of Crimea thanks in part to the support of the Grand Duchy of Lithuania. On this subject, see Ágoston and Masters, *Encyclopedia of the Ottoman Empire*, pp. 155–56; Kołodziejczyk, *The Crimean Khanate*, in particular pp. 32–41.

While Caffa and the Genoese possessions in the southern Black Sea were safer, thanks to their geographical location and considerable fortifications, Tana was much more exposed. As we saw in chapter 6, in the aftermath of the city's destruction in 1396, Consul Blanco de Ripa went to see "Tokhan" (Tokhtamysh) to seek permission to fortify the Venetian quarter.[5] This defensive autonomy for Tana's inhabitants became a priority for many years, as their only means of escape and survival was to seek shelter in Caffa. Diplomacy and payment of trade duties were clearly not enough to guarantee their safety if rival armies aimed to seize these sources of income—or destroy them completely—if they could benefit the enemy.

The settlement was aware of its vulnerability and sought a difficult political balance, taking risks that often cost the lives of its citizens and government representatives. In fact, Tana was still a prosperous city in a relatively poor economic context, and became a magnet for various khans vying for power over trade and tax revenues, or who simply wanted to plunder the city and steal from its inhabitants, as in 1410, when the city was attacked by Pulag Beg Khan. Tana renewed its defensive efforts right after another Tatar attack in 1418, at the hands of the Mongol Kerimberi Khan.[6] According to Marin Sanudo, the sack of the city resulted in the deaths of 640 merchants, but led to massive investments: 1,000–3,000 ducats a year were spent on constructing additional walls, stone towers, and drawbridges. These building works continued into the 1420s, and it was thanks to their completion in 1429 that Tana was able to withstand the 1431 siege by Ulugh Berdi.[7]

These were complicated years for the politics of the Golden Horde. In 1431, Ulugh Mehmed Khan went to war with Baraq and Devlet Berdi.[8] The previous year, among other events, Haci I Giray had seized power over what would become the khanate of Crimea (the exact date of its foundation is disputed).[9] Venice asked Genoa for help—a move of great significance that cannot be understated, as Genoa had threatened Tana by sea with artillery, while the Tatars had attacked it from the mainland.[10] During this period, Genoa and

---

5. Thiriet, *Régestes des délibérations*, no. 898, p. 211; Doumerc, "Les Vénitiens à La Tana," p. 7.

6. Doumerc, "Les Vénitiens à La Tana," p. 7; Doumerc, "La Tana au XVe siècle," pp. 261–63; Pubblici, "Venezia e il Mar d'Azov," p. 479.

7. Dupuigrenet Desroussilles, "Vénitiens et Génois," p. 115.

8. Dupuigrenet Desroussilles, "Vénitiens et Génois," p. 116.

9. Kołodziejczyk, *The Crimean Khanate*, pp. 7–9.

10. Doumerc, "Les Vénitiens à La Tana," p. 8.

Venice were still in conflict on the Black Sea; hence, these hostilities may make it seem paradoxical for Venice to request help from Genoa in attacking the Tatars from the sea.[11] However, the outcome of this "assistance" is unclear; it seems Genoa took advantage of it to further weaken Venice's defenses.[12]

In October 1431, a fleet of five Venetian galleys commanded by Andrea Loredan sailed toward Caffa in a show of force after what they deemed to be Genoa's betrayal of the anti-Tatar pact. Unfortunately, two galleys were wrecked right before the port of Caffa, and the Venetians—including Loredan—were captured and imprisoned. Although there were no direct clashes between the two fleets, the climate remained hostile (and the Venetians in prison) until the Peace of Ferrara in 1433.[13] The new consul, Sinerio Querini, was given a substantial sum of money (2,000 ducats) to mitigate the crisis, further aggravated by the outbreak of the plague, which caused many deaths. Further fortifications were completed in 1437, but the Tatars attacked once again, burning down the Venetian district in 1442; led by Consul Marco Duodo, the Venetian community managed to escape unscathed.[14]

Although conflicts between Tatar clans threatened Tana's existence, undoubtedly the main danger to the Venetian presence on the Black Sea was the rise of the Ottoman Empire. At the start of the fifteenth century, the empire was first weakened by defeats inflicted by Timur on Bayezid I (r. 1389–1402), and then by internal conflicts for succession among Sultan Mehmed I's children, which ended with the ascension of Murad II. During this period of political instability, Venice sought to protect its trade routes and bases in the Aegean, which allowed for passage through the straits and trade with the Black Sea. To this end, the Venetian government spared no diplomatic or military effort to reach an agreement with the sultan, wielding its naval power when necessary. The first clashes between the Ottoman and Venetian fleets (commanded by Pietro Loredan) took place off the coast of Gallipoli on May 29, 1416. Venice emerged victorious.

In 1419, a treaty was finalized between Doge Tommaso Mocenigo (r. 1414–23) and Sultan Mehmed I, in which the sultan recognized Venice's sovereignty

11. Dupuigrenet Deroussilles, "Vénitiens et Génois," p. 116.

12. According to Marino da Mosto, the armed galley requested from Tana to Caffa to repel the Tatars would actually have been used against the Venetians themselves. Dupuigrenet Desroussilles, "Vénitiens et Génois," pp. 116–17.

13. Khvalkov, "The Venetian Tana."

14. Skržinskaja, "Storia della Tana," p. 9.

over thirty-eight cities and islands in Romània. Nevertheless, the Republic's position in the region remained far from secure.[15] Despite ongoing efforts to maintain diplomatic relations with the Ottomans—interspersed with shows of strength and naval blockades—Venetian–Ottoman ties grew increasingly strained following the ascent of the young Murad II to the throne in 1421.

The 1420s proved particularly challenging for Venice, which was forced to expend vast sums of money and military resources on occupying and defending Thessaloniki. The city had fallen to the Byzantine Emperor, whose reign was increasingly vulnerable to the advancing Ottomans, making him more dependent on external support. During this period, Venice's diplomatic and military strategy operated on several fronts: halting Turkish advances, holding its ground in the Aegean, and simultaneously fending off Genoese competition. Furthermore, the Republic had to carefully navigate its delicate relationships with Milan and the other European powers. While access to the Black Sea remained critical for trade, Venice's means of maintaining its own positions steadily lost their effectiveness. The balance of power depended on Venice's ability to maintain a precarious equidistance between the Byzantines and the Turks amid a growing climate of instability. The defeat suffered in Thessaloniki—captured and pillaged by the Turks in 1430, with thousands of inhabitants enslaved—curtailed Venice's ability to maneuver. Moreover, the Republic was forced to retreat from seemingly secure and long-established positions, whose defense had come at great financial and military cost.

These developments inevitably had repercussions on the entire Venetian trade network in the Levant, especially as it became increasingly evident that the Byzantine Empire's days were numbered. The Crusade of Varna, which effectively marked Christianity's final campaign against an Islamic power, was based on unstable alliances between powers with divergent and often conflicting interests. The papacy sought to force the Orthodox churches into union with the Catholic Church, while the Hungarians and Poles aimed to reclaim the Balkans and halt further Ottoman advances. The Venetians, for their part, were focused on maintaining their privileges in Constantinople and ensuring trade routes to the Black Sea remained open. Negotiations were complex, particularly over financing, and dissent was difficult to quell. Though the crusade had two initial victories that forced the Ottomans to request a truce, this was likely a strategic move. At that point, divisions within the Christian army were deepened, with some in favor of an agreement, and others—in particular the

---

15. Nicol, *Byzantium and Venice*, p. 358.

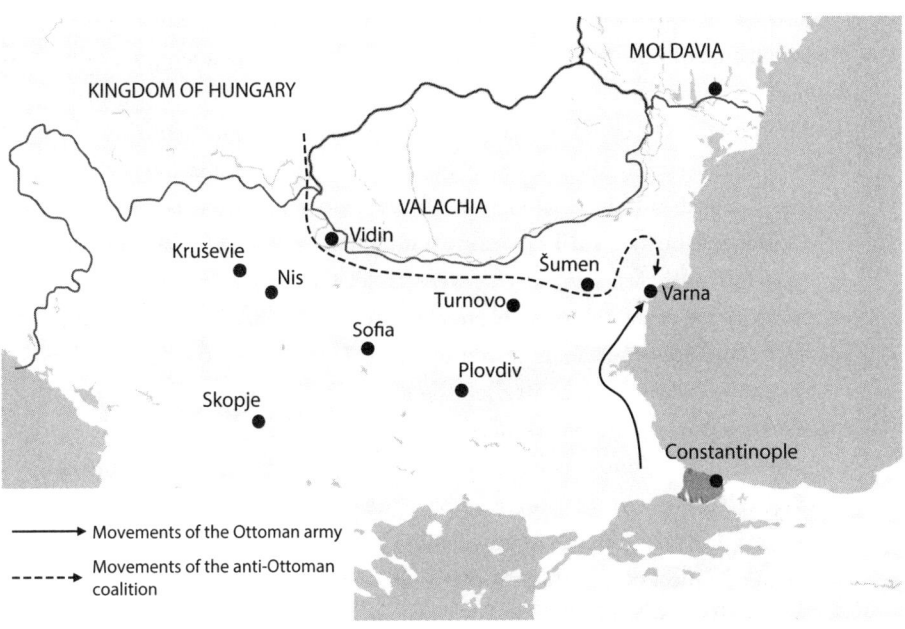

MAP 16. The Varna Crusade (1444)

pope—strongly opposed to it, unwilling to see the crusade (organized with some difficulty) end prematurely. However, the continued campaign quickly saw a crushing defeat at the Battle of Varna in 1444, in present-day Bulgaria. This failure was largely due to a lack of coordination among the crusader forces, compounded by their inferior size and tactical difficulties after they became trapped between Lake Varna and the Black Sea coast. The Ottomans later triumphed once again in the 1448 Battle of Kosovo. By this point, it was clear that Turkish control over the Black Sea route was inevitable, and the defense of Constantinople would soon become impossible.

It was obvious that the Turks could easily block access to the city, thereby severing the vital link that still connected the Italian colonies to their motherland. Once again, the structural differences between Genoa and Venice shaped their relations with the Ottoman Empire. While Venice relied on state diplomacy, which typically ensured relatively stable conditions, Genoa preferred to negotiate locally, independent of support from its government, which was unstable during this period. Genoa also held a stronger position than Venice on the Black Sea, with its military and commercial strength, along with the protection offered by the imposing fortifications around its settlements. This transformed its network of colonies into significant political entities. Despite the imbalance of power, Venice and Genoa faced similar challenges, finding themselves in increasingly precarious positions. However, even in the face of shared danger, they could not come to an agreement. Venice continued to support, albeit secretly, the principality of Theodor against Caffa and the other Genoese bases in Gothia, located in southwest Crimea. The port cities of Yamboli, Yalta, and Lusta (Alushta), along with a narrow strip of coast land (referred to as Parathalassia in Greek), were under Genoese rule, known as the captainship of Gothia; this control effectively deprived the Theodorites of sea access.[16] The Genoese had acquired these ports through a treaty signed in 1380 with the Tatars, who controlled the region at the time, and established that these regions would be exempt from customs duties.[17]

After the fall of Constantinople in 1453, Venetian diplomacy swiftly moved to revive relations with the Sublime Porte (the central government of the Ottoman Empire), aiming to keep the Straits open for its ships. Although the Ottoman conquest of Constantinople dealt a serious blow to Venetian interests on the Black Sea, it did not immediately sever ties. A treaty between Venice and Mehmed II in 1454 ensured the safety of all Venetians in the former Byzantine capital, secured the passage of their ships, and the safety of trade.[18] However, this delicate balance between cooperation and obstruction was not destined to last.

The empire of Trebizond was conquered by the Ottomans in 1461. Although Timur had revived trade across Tabriz, the failure of the Timurid attempt to restore the Mongol Empire led to a decline in Persian trade, which fell under the control of rival Turkoman tribes (the Qara Qoyunlu and Aq Qoyunlu). Despite this, Trebizond maintained its independence for a time and remained a crucial hub for regional trade, serving more as a terminal than a mere stopover for goods heading inland. Both the Genoese and Venetians sourced products from the surrounding regions, particularly metals from Anatolian mines, with key exports including alum, copper, iron, and silver.[19]

For the Venetians, Trebizond constituted the third point of a crucial triangle that connected Tana on the Black Sea, Trebizond to the south, and Constantinople. In the fifteenth century, these three hubs still marked the strongholds

16. Gorovei, "The Principality of Theodoro," pp. 154–55.

17. Canestrini, "Il Mar Nero e le colonie degli italiani," pp. 11–12.

18. *Diplomatarium veneto-levantinum*, vol. 2, pp. 382–84.

19. Karpov, *L'impero di Trebisonda*, p. 39.

of Venetian trade, but this structure was soon to unravel. The fall of Trebizond signaled another step toward Ottoman dominance of the Black Sea, which was increasingly turning into a *mare nostrum* under Turkish control. As the political balance in the region shifted decisively from the north (ruled by the khans of the Golden Horde, remnants of the Mongol Empire) to the south under the Ottoman sultans, the fate of the Italian colonies was sealed.

During this period, there was a widespread belief throughout Italy in the inevitability of a domino effect following the fall of Constantinople. It was feared that all Italian possessions in the Black Sea and Aegean regions would soon topple, opening the door to further Ottoman advance beyond the Balkans. In response to this conviction, two opposing visions emerged: one advocated for European unity to resist Ottoman expansion through a new crusade, while the other proposed that each state mobilize independently to defend against direct attacks. In reality, forming an anti-Turkish coalition proved impossible, despite complaints from many quarters, particularly within the Church. Powers most directly affected by Ottoman expansion, such as Venice, relied primarily on their own diplomatic efforts to salvage what could still be saved and, above all, to keep trade routes open. However, diplomacy alone was not enough to prevent conflict. In 1463, hostilities with Mehmed II erupted. The war ended in 1479, but by 1475 the Ottomans had already captured Tana, marking the end of Venice's presence on the Black Sea.

To complete this tale, we should highlight the relations between Venice and the Mamluk Sultanate, which played a pivotal role in the broader reorganization of trade with the East during the fifteenth century. Despite Venice's significant involvement in the anti-Mamluk crusade of 1365, led by Peter I of Lusignan, king of Cyprus, this did not seem to negatively affect subsequent relations between the Serenissima and the sultanate. In fact, it was the Genoese, who had also participated in the crusade with a smaller army, who suffered the consequences. Venice's favorable standing with the sultan's court can likely be attributed to its far-sighted diplomacy and the ability of its merchants to position themselves as key partners to the sultan, thus promoting beneficial trade policies.

The main reason for the rapprochement between Venice and the Mamluk Sultanate, particularly after the Peace of Turin in 1381, was Venice's desire to establish direct relations with Mamluk Egypt, bypassing the Cypriot mediation that had previously been necessary. Genoa had an important base in Famagusta, which served as a bridge for trade with the Egyptian coasts. However, by the early fifteenth century, raids and piracy had intensified along the coasts of Egypt and Syria, led by Genoese, Catalans, and Cypriots evading their governments' control. In contrast, Venice had tighter control over its citizens, and therefore ensured that the agreements reached through diplomatic channels were honored, allowing it to maintain legal operations and expand trade volumes. Venice's reputation for reliability and the reach of its commercial networks into northern Europe guaranteed a consistent flow of trade for the Mamluks, especially for spices.

The state monopoly imposed by the sultan for spices in the first half of the fifteenth century required foreign merchants to purchase a set percentage of spices from the state before dealing with private suppliers. This system favored those, like Venice, who could buy in bulk and access both state and private markets. Among other things, the monopoly offered lower prices than the open market, meaning it did not necessarily disadvantage foreign merchants. Venetian merchants who invested in spices shifted their capital from the Black Sea to Alexandria, securing a privileged position compared to Genoa. The Genoese were relegated not only to a subordinate role but also faced increasing hostility. While they remained dominant in the Black Sea slave trade, which had been in their hands for some time, other opportunities were closing off to them. For Venice in this time, the Black Sea was no longer a gateway to the markets of the Far East, nor the primary source for spices. Thus, it had lost much of its allure, especially for long-term investors. While some trade continued, it increasingly focused on the local economy.

## The Economy of the Black Sea in the First Half of the Fifteenth Century

Timur's death not only halted the reconstitution of a vast post–Mongol Empire, but it also dealt a final blow to any lingering hopes Italian merchants had of securing direct access to Asian markets—a goal that, notably, was never actively supported by their respective governments. Central Asian merchants and agents dominated caravan routes, and much of the trade had already shifted toward the maritime routes of the Indian Ocean. The fifteenth century saw significant changes in Eurasian trade dynamics, driven by both immediate and distant factors. The collapse of the Mongol Empire in China led to a gradual closure of overland routes, which was counterbalanced in the early fifteenth century by renewed trade activities along maritime routes. However, China adopted an official policy of restricting trade, further limiting access. Key southern ports like Quanzhou and Guangzhou, which had for centuries hosted a thriving Muslim merchant community, were closed to long-distance trade due to hostility from the Chinese population, who resented the special privileges these foreign communities had enjoyed under Mongol rule.

The Ming emperors (1368–1644) adopted a xenophobic stance that shaped their restrictive policies on international trade. As early as 1371, a ban on private commerce was enacted and repeatedly reinforced, which accelerated the diaspora of merchant families. Expelled from Chinese ports, these merchants dispersed across southeast Asia: the Philippines, Malaysia, Indonesia, and east India. Though this exodus of strongly rooted communities did not lead to a fracture in trade between China and the Indian Ocean, it did cause a significant restructuring. Admiral Zheng He's expeditions between 1405 and 1433, though impressive in scale, did not set out to or succeed in establishing a new commercial order between China and the West. Instead, they served to promote diplomatic relations grounded in a tributary system, whereby China expected other states to accept a position of political subordination in exchange for privileges, including access to trade. Under the Ming dynasty, international relations were governed primarily by political concerns, with trade becoming secondary. Although foreign delegations continued to visit Beijing, these came later and were largely part of a "tribute presentation" to the Chinese emperor by states that identified as tributary nations. In practice, only by accepting political subordination could foreign states access trade, significantly limiting the scope of commercial exchange between China and other countries.

Ming China certainly no longer offered Islamic and western merchants the privileged status, logistical and financial support, or the freedom of movement that had been granted under Mongol rule. Most crucially, long-established markets on the southern coasts were abandoned, fostering the development of alternative trading networks and diasporic communities in southeast Asia. These new forms of exchange, while more flexible, were also less secure and less permanent. In essence, this marked a reversal of the trend seen in the thirteenth century. Under the Mongols, the Black Sea had become a global crossroads for trade, but by the fifteenth century, it had reverted to a more regional role, increasingly overshadowed by the maritime routes that connected east Asia via India to Egypt. During this period, the Indian Ocean trade route, stretching from the coasts of western India to Sumatra, was explored and documented by Chioggia-born Niccolò de' Conti. While his account represents the experience of an individual traveler, it still documents the vitality of sea-based commerce. Moreover, his report, written shortly after his return, made this new geographical reality immediately known and appreciated in Italy.[20]

As for the Black Sea, it must be noted that the shifting trade routes did not immediately spell the end for the Venetian and Genoese colonies. Trade remained active, justifying the continued defense and maintenance of the Tana community. While the political pressures of the time could have easily led to the swift dissolution of this community, we must consider how and why they obstinately resisted despite facing high risks—not only from the hostility of the Tatars and Ottomans but also from recurring famines and plague outbreaks. In the case of Tana, which was more vulnerable to raids compared to the Genoese possessions in Crimea, two main reasons can be identified. First, the profitability of industries established decades earlier, particularly in fishing and maritime transport, incentivized their continued presence. Second, the colony's ongoing integration with the economy of the former Golden Horde fostered a mutual dependency. This relationship made the colony's economy more reliant on the production activities of the mainland and the Pontic steppe, while simultaneously allowing profitable trade to continue.

To better understand this situation, we can examine the cargo of some Venetian cogs in Tana in 1402. An analysis of the goods reveals a clear dominance of local products: leather (18 percent), fish (17), caviar (34), slaves (8), with smaller quantities of wax (4), cured meats, walnuts, and metals. Imports from distant regions, such as central Asia and China, consisted of spices (11 percent), silk (5), and Oriental fabrics (1).[21] This bill of lading offers valuable insight into the Venetians' continued economic involvement, which can be summarized in two primary activities: direct production and imports from the Golden Horde. Direct production, managed locally by Venetian companies, centered on the fisheries industry, particularly the production of caviar, which was especially abundant in the Sea of Azov. Meanwhile, the economy of the Golden Horde, which had grown substantially in the fourteenth century, supplied various goods from distinct sectors. Agriculture provided wheat and millet, while the nomadic pastoral economy contributed hides, horses, cattle, tallow wax, and cured meat. Additionally, the region boasted a thriving hunting and gathering economy, which provided furs, game, beeswax, dried fruit— and slaves, captured by nomads and sold to foreign traders.

20. See note 2 above.
21. Karpov, "Kak feniks iz pepla."

Grains, especially wheat, millet, and barley, as previously mentioned, were among the most in-demand products in Europe. However, in the fifteenth century, grain imports declined, especially for Genoa, which had been more active in the sector, but also for Venice. This decline was partly due to a general shortage of wheat, as production in the Danube and Ukrainian regions experienced a slowdown in the early fifteenth century due to climatic factors.[22] Caffa, for instance, repeatedly faced wheat shortages and was forced to rely on imports.[23] At the same time, Venice became less dependent on Eastern imports, thanks to the expansion of its mainland territories (the *Stato de Tera*) in Veneto, Lombardy, and Romagna during the first half of the fifteenth century.

The Golden Horde was also abundant in fruits and vegetables, with melons and watermelons being particularly popular. Due to the region's extensive pastures, livestock breeding and sheep farming were central to its economy, with hides and horses being significant exports. Venetian politician and trader Giosafat Barbaro (1413–94) noted that a particular breed of oxen was transported from Crimea through Poland and Transylvania, reaching as far as Germany.[24] Furthermore, the nomads of the Golden Horde were skilled hunters. Leather and fur, sourced from animals such as ermine, sable, fox, beaver, and squirrel, formed an essential part of the Horde's exports, regardless of quality.[25]

Lastly, the slave trade remained an active part of the economy. Venetians arrived in Tana in increasing numbers, and many of these were celibate males; those who could afford to bought female slaves as concubines or domestic help. When Ambassador Pietro Loredan arrived in Tana in 1416, he engaged a merchant to purchase five slaves at an average price of 220 bezants. Similarly, in 1439, Alessandro Zeno and Jacomo Badoer purchased 150 slaves for Sicily at an average price of 107 *hyperpyrons*.[26] Some of these relationships became *more uxorio* (as man and wife) and were recognized as such in wills. As in the previous century, most of the slaves were from Tatar and Circassian communities, often young individuals who had been abducted or sold by their parents during times of famine. While these transactions occurred locally, it remains

22. The first decades of the fifteenth century in the Novgorod region were characterized by extreme temperatures, both hot and cold. There were famines in 1420–23. Huhtamaa, "Climatic Anomalies."

23. Karpov, "The Grain Trade."

24. Barbaro and Contarini, *Travels to Tana and Persia*, p. 20.

25. Barbaro and Contarini, *Travels to Tana and Persia*, p. 34

26. Doumerc, "Les Vénitiens à la Tana," p. 11.

unclear how many slaves were actually transported to Venice or other parts of Europe. Some Venetians returned home with slaves they had bought in Tana, but it is difficult to confirm whether this was the main channel for importing slaves. Evidence suggests that the prices for slaves declined in this period, possibly indicating a drop in demand (see chapter 11).[27]

Among the local industries, the fishing sector was the most developed, encompassing the catching, preservation, and export of fish, particularly sturgeons, which thrived in the Sea of Azov due to the salty waters at the estuary of the Don. Coastal fishing zones, or fish farms, were dominated by Venetians, whose companies had been active for generations. One prominent example is the Civran family, represented by several members (Luca, Niccolò, Daniele) who resided in Tana.[28]

The greater concentration of commercial activities did not necessarily result in a drastic decline in profits or the closure of trade between the Black Sea and Europe. Instead, it reflected a narrowing of the operational scope of the merchants, who nonetheless remained vulnerable to the volatility of the political landscape. The risks they faced grew proportionally to the diminishing security and production guarantees previously provided by Mongol rulers. Fish farms were often managed in partnership with non-Venetians, such as Greek or even Genoese partners. In fact, sources reveal a diverse range of activities where Venetians worked alongside other Italians and locals, maintaining the region's long-standing cosmopolitan character, despite periodic ethnic and political tensions.

The archives of Niccolò de Varsis and Benedetto de Smeritis, notaries in Tana from 1430 to 1440, give us some idea of how the commercial landscape had narrowed.[29] Cities like Astrakhan, Urgench, and Samarkand had at one time been present in the notary records, only to now disappear—but this did not necessarily mean that the goods were no longer arriving from those markets. Rather, it suggests that trade with regions east of the Volga was now being conducted via intermediaries, largely controlled by Turkish, Persian, and central Asian merchants. Goods from the East, such as spices and silk, continued to arrive, though in smaller quantities, with most arriving in Trebizond via Tabriz. In 1404, when the Tabriz route was still open, Venice imported 31 tons of silk, 20 of pepper, 20 of indigo, 7 of cinnamon, 4 of ginger, 41 of leather, and an unspecified number of pearls. Although these quantities were smaller than

27. Doumerc, "Les Vénitiens à la Tana," p. 11.
28. Doumerc, "Les Vénitiens à la Tana," p. 10.
29. Khvalkov, "The Society of the Venetian Colony of Tana."

the imports from Beirut and Alexandria, they were still significant enough to justify Venice's continued presence in the region.[30] Long-distance trade persisted, though it was considerably diminished. Between 1405 and 1450, auctions for galleys to the Black Sea accounted for a quarter of all Levantine auctions and, in particularly favorable periods (phases of peace or with no obstacles), they rose to as much as 38 percent.[31]

Lastly, it is important to note that while exports from Europe to the East existed, they were relatively limited compared to the vast volume and value of imports. Wool and linen fabrics of exceptional quality, produced in various parts of Europe, held a dominant and central position among the exports.[32] Less significant, though still present, were items of European craftsmanship, especially glass, weapons, and jewelry. However, these exports did not compensate for the value of imports. We can hypothesize that the trade deficit was covered by the export of precious metals as a means of payment (see chapter 10). Additionally, transportation services provided by Venetian and Genoese ships contributed to the local economy and should be considered part of the overall exports.

## Government and Society in Fifteenth-Century Tana

In general, the Venetian community in Tana experienced a demographic decline during the first half of the century, but the composition of the population also changed. After the devastation wrought by Timur, which severely impacted the Venetians in Tana, the city was partially rebuilt by locals who continued their businesses, as well as by new immigrants, including craftsmen and traders. These newcomers did not necessarily have prior business or family ties to Tana.

Various people traveled to Caffa and Tana in hopes of improving their economic situation, often arriving with debts or insufficient capital to invest.[33] The consul, who held the highest authority, was always appointed by the senate and supported by a council of twelve merchants.[34] However, the post had gradually lost its appeal. In the past, it had been a lucrative role, as the consul not only received a salary, but could also invest in local trade. During this

30. Pienaru, "The Timurids and the Black Sea," p. 134.
31. Khvalkov, "The Commercial Significance," pp. 137–38.
32. Khvalkov, "A Regionalisation or Long-Distance Trade?"
33. Karpov, "New Documents," p. 34.
34. Doumerc, "Les Vénitiens à la Tana," p. 12.

period, however, rising risks, fewer investment opportunities, and increasing expenses made the position less desirable. When the senate could not meet the city's financial needs, it was the consul who had to raise funds locally, sometimes imposing special taxes on merchants.

One of the local government's greatest concerns was the defense of the city, leading to a major rise in public spending. This was not only for the construction of fortifications, completed in 1429, but also for the maintenance of a permanent garrison. The garrison consisted of twenty-five to thirty professional crossbow-men, each paid 4 ducats a month.[35] In the 1430s, the failure to consistently pay the soldiers resulted in their abandonment of the garrison. Men sent to Tana were unwilling to remain in such a remote and isolated location without receiving their promised wages. It is curious that the Venetians did not attempt to resolve the defense issues by recruiting local troops. However, it seems they believed foreign mercenaries were unreliable and would desert in times of crisis, or perhaps there was a lack of trained residents to form a civic militia.

The financial difficulties Tana faced in 1429–30 strained its relations with Tatar authorities, who continued to demand payment of the *terraticum* (land tax) that had already been paid to the khan of the Golden Horde. Unsurprisingly, this created tensions with the local aristocracy, who often directed their frustrations at the merchants. There are numerous accounts of Venetians being forced to return home empty-handed after being robbed by Tatars and Circassians.[36] Essentially, individual merchants were not only threatened by a general state of lawlessness and the absence of protection and reimbursement guarantees that had existed under the Mongol Empire, but also by failures in payment and potential diplomatic breakdowns with local rulers. Ulugh Berdi's attack on Tana in 1431 was a manifestation of a latent threat that, while infrequent, remained ever-present; constant diplomatic efforts were required to resolve conflicts.[37]

Health and welfare services were available to the city's residents. A physician was sent to Tana at the request of the senate and paid an annual salary of 40 *sommi*. One such physician was Giacomo di Milano, who offered health care to the residents in 1411–17. His name appears in various wills as someone present at the time of death. Aid for the poor and the sick was given by the confraternity of the Scuola di Santa Maria and Sant'Antonio, as well as the churches and convents of San Francesco and San Domenico, which had been established by missionary orders in the previous century.[38]

Otherwise, life in Tana remained that of a frontier, characterized by various forms of cooperation with the local population. Aside from the incident of 1431, relations between the Venetians and Genoese did not escalate into crises and open conflicts that had made coexistence so difficult in the fourteenth century. Trade between Venice and the Black Sea continued, though subject to ups and downs driven by political uncertainties. On the whole, it remained a significant source of Venetian imports. The economy of the Golden Horde continued to supply grain, slaves, and other products in demand by European markets. Moreover, the Venetians themselves became producers and contributed to the service economy. Both Tana and Trebizond still offered opportunities, though less frequent, to acquire silk and spices, which were always in high demand in Europe. This trade, while increasingly insecure and exposed to the risk of looting, still attracted young adventurers eager to sail to the Black Sea in pursuit of business, like Giosafat Barbaro.

The Venetian population began to decline, and the number of mixed marriages grew, fostering greater integration between the local population, especially Greeks, Russians, and Italians. Political uncertainties reduced the volume of commercial capital, which was increasingly diverted to North African ports. Merchants were subject to extraordinary taxes and levies for the defense of Tana and municipal expenses. Chronic financial difficulties plagued local authorities during this period, driven by three main factors: insufficient support from the motherland, a sharp rise in military and fiscal expenses (including taxes payable to the various Tatar khans who dominated the political scene), and finally, the reduced liquidity of Tana's residents. The latter was exacerbated by the changing social fabric of the Venetian community, which saw a diminishing presence of noble families.

## Epilogue

By the mid-fifteenth century, particularly after the Ottoman conquest of Constantinople, the Venetian presence on the Black Sea and the Aegean seemed on the brink of vanishing. Despite diplomatic efforts and military resistance, there was a widespread awareness that their days were numbered. Those with property and invested capital sought to sell what they could and return home

38. Pucci Donati, "Accoglienza e assistenza," p. 559.

with whatever they managed to salvage. This marked the final chapter in a story that should not be considered a capitulation, but rather the inevitable result of political developments far beyond Venice's ability to control. While the Mongol conquest had opened the doors to the Black Sea, the Ottoman conquest had firmly closed them.

The final phase in the history of Venetian Romània was neither marked by a sudden decline in trade following the collapse of the Mongol Empire, nor by the destruction wrought by Timur. Instead, these events initiated a long process of adaptation and re-establishment of commerce on new foundations, just as the political conditions Venetians had to navigate also changed. As this process unfolded, carefully monitored by the Venetian state and its representatives, other developments emerged that would eventually marginalize the Black Sea and diminish its importance in Venice's overall economy.

Two particularly important trends emerged in this period: first, Venice's expansion into the mainland, and second, the Mamluks' embrace of international trade through north African ports, following the lifting of the papal ban on trade with the sultans. These strategic and geopolitical shifts offered new opportunities for investment and profit that the Black Sea could no longer guarantee. Throughout the first half of the fifteenth century, periods of crisis alternated with times of growth and prosperity, reflecting the Venetians' determination to maintain their presence in markets and regions that they had frequented for over a century and had become deeply integrated with. Nonetheless, it is clear that the opportunities created by the Mongol conquest had ceased to exist.

The twilit and nostalgic tone of the writings by Giosafat Barbaro, the adventurous Venetian diplomat who first went to Tana in 1436 and who returned to Tartary several times until 1452, evoke a sense of an era coming to a close. Recalling a conversation with a Tatar while standing before the walls of Tana, Barbaro remembered his companion's words: "Those who are afraid build towers."[39] The vast expanses of Asia had grown smaller, and the Venetians now found themselves entrenched behind fortified walls, looking out over what resembled the "desert of the Tartars"—once an open, relatively safe space for exploration and dreams of wealth, but now inaccessible. It was the end of one era, but a new one was on the horizon, also defined by navigation and trade. Venice would not take part in this new phase of world history, yet its experience on the Black Sea, like that of Genoa, served as both a prologue and historical precursor.

39. Barbaro and Contarini, *Travels to Tana and Persia*, p. 18.

# PART II

# People, Instruments, and Goods

# 8

# Marco Polo

## Understanding His Legacy

Imagine a world made up of maritime stretches, crossed by ships of relatively low tonnage (such as large trade and slender war galleys), relying solely on portolan charts, coastal navigation by sight without the aid of a magnetic compass, with enemy ships lurking behind promontories and in bays, and the steadfast defenses of commercial hubs, crucial for Venice's wealth yet also its very survival. This was the world of Mediterranean Venetian commerce in the Levant in the early thirteenth century, spanning from the Adriatic Sea to Constantinople. None yet had an inkling of the geopolitical changes in the coming years, which would force Venetian merchants to venture beyond the familiar Mediterranean ports and their hinterland. Fourteenth-century Europe underwent vast transformations in geographical, political, and human knowledge; these changes are akin to those sparked by the oceanic navigation and colonization of America in the sixteenth century. Yet, unlike this more modern European expansion to the New World, the opening of the Mediterranean world to Asia depended on non-European events and agents—in particular the Mongols and their conquests in eastern Europe, the Middle East, and Asia. In fact, the Mongol discovery of Europe sparked an early globalization that united three continents.

Examining the second half of the thirteenth century, before these new horizons were laid bare, reveals the incredible story of the Polo family: both protagonists and beneficiaries of these new spaces, of new connections, and all the potential therein. Alongside the travels of Odoric of Pordenone, the memoirs of Hayton of Corycus, and the tales of Mandeville, *The Travels of Marco Polo* (*Il Milione* in Italian) bore precious knowledge back to Europe, the reception and dissemination of which helped shape the natural and human geography of the East, turning it from a realm of myth and legend to something more concrete. How concrete his reports were is a question much more accurately answered by readers of today than those of his time.

The relationship between the events of Marco's life (and those of the Polo family in general) and Venice's interest in the Mongol world cannot be interpreted based on a linear rationale of cause and effect, as if it were Marco's tales in the *Milione* that opened Venetians' eyes to the riches of Asia, triggering its commercial initiatives. This is certainly not the case, as neither Marco nor his family forged long-lasting relations with the East after their return from China. In fact, Marco was not especially esteemed by his fellow citizens. For a long time, readers doubted whether his adventures were true. Nor can the rise of Italian merchants traveling to China be ascribed to the popularity of his book. Nonetheless, albeit indirectly, Marco's experiences mark a cardinal moment in our understanding of the motivations and means of Venetian merchants, the spheres they moved in, the instruments and knowledge required for trade with the East, and, lastly, the cultural horizons that gradually expanded due to contact with a civilization as diverse as China of the Yuan dynasty.

Although we cannot evaluate how readers of the *Milione* used Marco's knowledge, everything we do know tells us that the importance of the book as a guide to Asian markets—if this was even the case—was decidedly modest. The *Milione* did not have the same function or reach as the *Pratica della mercatura* or the *Codex Cumanicus*, as it was never adopted as a *vade mecum* or guide to trade with the East, despite being the first source of precise and detailed information on Mongol Asia's economic and commercial geography. Firstly, though the *Milione* is written from a commercial perspective, it is not expressly addressed to the mercantile classes, nor did they use it as a guide for commerce, as the Polos' experiences in China remained relatively isolated and mostly fortuitous. Secondly, Marco had aspirations that went beyond a mercantile utility, evidenced by the fact that he turned to Rustichello da Pisa to bestow literary legitimacy upon his memoirs. Clearly, from the very start, his collection of tales were conceived to be more than a mere "manual." Whether this was a conscious choice or the fruit of circumstance, we cannot say for sure. Yet one thing is certain: for the rest of his life, Marco Polo made every effort to expand the book's renown and to gain recognition for himself. A peculiarity of the *Milione* is that it addresses an audience that did not fully exist at the time of its publication, which was a point of frustration for Marco Polo. Nevertheless, Marco paved the way for other stories about and representations of Asia. Though these stories were a combination of legend and reality, they made the continent seem closer and more visible to European readers. Thus, the Mongols moved firmly into the heart of this new geographical and human universe.

Marco Polo's book is essential reading if we are to understand the first steps in the relationship between Venice and the Mongols. Though the *Milione* had a lesser impact on defining policies or stimulating contacts, it offers a sketch of the mentality of a Venetian merchant faced with the extraordinary new world of Asia. The book captures the shared cultural and cognitive background of Marco Polo and his contemporaries, in terms of education, social class, and economic interests. The market knowledge it describes is material and practical, though no less complex. After all, this was a world where nothing was standardized; means of exchange, costs, prices, products, and quality all varied from port to port, from market to market. Profit margins were slim, and risks were high. Hence, a merchant's experience was worth its weight in gold, particularly where it concerned international trade. Marco was immersed in a world of trade from a young age, and quickly acquired basic skills in reading, writing, arithmetic, and navigation. He gained linguistic, financial, and monetary knowledge on his travels with his father and uncle, both of whom were seasoned merchants. In fact, they were among the first to travel to China in the 1260s.

The pages of the *Milione* reveal the Polos' desire to explore far-flung places—not as representatives of the expanding state of Venice, but rather as enterprising merchants in search of business, who found themselves dragged into a wholly unexpected adventure by pure chance. The key to this independence of individual merchants was exclusively due to the privileges and protection afforded them by the Mongol rulers. The Polos, and the many merchants who followed, benefited not only from free movement in the Mongol territories, but were also guaranteed insurance and compensation to encourage trade. This reduction—or even the complete removal—of risks offered protection so great that foreign traders pledged their services to the Mongol lords in return. The Polos were the precursors of this practice. An impartial reading of the *Milione* shows how all the opportunities enjoyed during the many travels were subject to permission granted by the Mongol rulers.

Descriptions of the relationship between Marco, the khan, and the court no doubt reflect the conventions and norms throughout the Mongol Empire. It was not solely a relationship founded on money, as those forged by ambassadors and missionaries who traveled to the Mongol court with specific instructions from their leaders. Marco Polo was *directly* in the service of the Mongols. This position granted him certain privileges, as he became part of a hierarchical structure that put him in direct and exclusive contact with the khan and the aristocracy. One such privilege is that he could afford to lack any interest in learning the Chinese language; some modern commentators believe this to have been impossible, citing it as evidence of the *Milione*'s overall lack of credibility. However, Polo would have had little to no contact with the general Chinese population, as in the days of Kublai Khan they had scant political presence and were of low social status. Moreover, in contrast to the other great communicator of the Chinese civilization to the West, the Jesuit priest Matteo Ricci (1552–1610), who lived three centuries later, Marco Polo was not interested in, nor was he prepared for a religious or intellectual encounter with Chinese culture. These factors always remained alien to him. Chinese was also not the lingua franca of the spheres he moved in; instead, these were dominated by Turkic and Persian, in addition to Mongolian. Place names and other foreign terms mentioned in the *Milione* show his greater proximity to these languages, rather than to Chinese. Thus, it is the two focal characteristics of the *Milione*—his attention to trade and his personal relationship with the Mongols—that form the key to framing Marco Polo in the history of Venetian expansion in the Mongol Empire.

## The Polos in China

As we have already seen, by about 1260 in Europe, the apocalyptic terror sparked by the first Mongol invasions had since given way to curiosity and increased exploration, encouraged by the Mongols themselves. Taking an anti-Islamic stance, European sovereigns actively forged diplomatic relations with Mongol rulers. It was in this climate of cautious openness that Matteo and Niccolò Polo, most likely in late 1260, embarked on a journey to the Mongol territories beyond the Black Sea. The men were as yet unaware of the hardships the Mongol dominions were facing, with fratricidal wars fracturing their dominions in Russia and Persia, as well as in Mongolia and China. Indeed, it was the civil war between Berke Khan, ruler of the Golden Horde, and Hülegü Khan, conqueror of the caliphate, which prevented the Polos from returning to their base on the Black Sea. This political turmoil sparked the series of events—as extraordinary as they were fortuitous—that flung the Polo brothers far beyond their initial intentions.

When the brothers reached Berke's court in Bolghar, not far from Sarai in the Lower Volga, the khan welcomed the Polos with the same generosity he had bestowed upon other merchants. Due to the ongoing hostilities, the brothers were unable to return to Sudak, from whence they had come. Instead, they decided to continue eastward and venture into central Asia. For three long years they remained in the flourishing trade hub of Bukhara (present-day Uzbekistan), waiting to return to where they had set out originally. We imagine that Bukhara, the heart of the Mongol Empire, offered them the chance to acquire precious information—not just on trade, but also on the shifting political situation. Between 1263 and 1264, they met with a Mongol nobleman, sent by Hülegü to the court of his brother Kublai, who had now become the grand khan. The Polos seized the opportunity with a nose for business as well as adventure. They joined the nobleman, and the following year (probably 1265) they arrived at Kublai's court. Most likely the Polos' meeting with the Mongol sovereign took place in a city in what is currently Inner Mongolia, built by Kublai between 1256 and 1264, and renamed Shangdu (the "upper capital," also referred to as Xanadu in literature). Marco Polo himself would visit this famed city in 1275. Shangdu was the political center from which Kublai controlled both northern China and the rest of Mongolia. Here, the khan extended his generous hospitality to the Polos, and, as was his custom, questioned them about their rulers, governments, laws, military strategies, the Pope, the Roman Catholic Church, and the customs of the Latins. They conversed in Turkic and Tatar (i.e., Mongolian), without the need for interpreters, as it seems the Polos had learned these languages during the years spent living in Bukhara. This is a significant detail, considering the extent to which language barriers had proven challenging in previous communication attempts between Christian missionaries and Mongol rulers. It offers a glimpse of a new European mindset, made up of extensive firsthand experiences and a preference for direct communication, though the use of interpreters (dragomans or truchmans) became more widespread later on.

Kublai and the Polos established a relationship of mutual understanding. This was unsurprising, given the typical attitude of the Mongols, who were curious about foreign people, yet were rarely successful in their attempts at diplomatic relations. The khan entrusted the Polos with a message (in Turkic) for the Pope, and had them accompanied by an envoy, who was charged with bringing back the Pope's reply. In his letter, Kublai requested that one hundred wise men be sent to his court, educated in the Christian religion and in various Western arts, and that they should clearly demonstrate how the Christian religion was superior to his local religions. This is of particular interest, as it implies that the Mongols were wary of previous religious missions, which had floundered due to language barriers. At the court of Möngke Khan, William of Rubruck had stumbled into a dispute with representatives of other religions, and by his own admission, his attempts to explain the Christian religion had failed. To the Mongols, his attempt must have been extremely disappointing, and Kublai was thus offering the Christians a second chance to explain the basis of their beliefs. The khan also requested an ampoule of oil from the lamp of the Holy Sepulcher in Jerusalem. The request for such a "tribute" reveals that Kublai perceived the Roman Church to be a spiritual and intellectual power, rather than a secular one, and therefore intended to establish initial contact on a religious and philosophical level.

On the return journey, the Mongol nobleman fell ill, and the Polos were forced to continue alone, albeit under the protection guaranteed by the imperial safe-conducts. After traveling for three years, the two brothers finally reached Yumurtalik. From there, in April 1269, they headed to Acre, the Christian bastion in Palestine, where they learned that Pope Clement IV had died a few months earlier, in November 1268. From Acre they returned to Venice to await the election of the new pope. In 1271, in a subsequent visit to Acre, the Polos met the papal legate Teobaldo Visconti, who would shortly thereafter ascend the papal throne as Gregory X. Only then did the Polos finally get an answer that they could take back to Kublai Khan. However, this reply was considerably inferior to what the Mongol ruler was expecting: the Pope gave them some letters, an ampoule containing the oil from the lamp of the Holy Sepulcher, and only two monks. The latter returned soon after they had left, consumed by the hardships of traveling. Niccolò and Matteo Polo's second journey brought them to China, where they would remain for seventeen years. Since their last meeting, Kublai had completed his conquest of the Song dynasty and founded the Yuan rule. It was on this journey that young Marco (1254–1324), aged seventeen, accompanied his father, Niccolò, and his uncle, Matteo. He would later recount this journey, concisely and directly, in his introduction to the *Milione*.

If the Polos are to be recognized as the precursors of Venice's expansion in the East, it is worth exploring the exact nature of their business in Crimea, and the reasons for their journey into Mongol territory. They departed from Sudak, a city that just a few decades later would become one of the main hubs of Italian trade on the Black Sea. There are speculations that when Matteo and Niccolò left Venice and headed to Constantinople and then Sudak, they had no bases in either city.[1] However, there is little evidence for this view. The outbreak of war between Berke and Hülegü had interfered with the Polos' return to Constantinople, and if they had had a base on the Black Sea, then surely this is where they would have gone. Marco tells us that the Polo brothers were stranded in Bolghar, one of Berke's residences on the Lower Volga, and due to his defeat, the road to the Black Sea was unsafe. To reach Sudak, they would have had to cross war zones in the Caucasus or in the Lower Volga. In other words, the same war that blocked their return to Constantinople also blocked their passage to Sudak. In light of all this, it is apparent that the Polos' failure to return to Crimea is irrelevant to the question of whether any family member—particularly Marco "the elder" (Marco Polo's great-uncle)—owned a *fondaco* in Sudak before 1260, when the Treaty of Nymphaeum closed off Venetian access to the straits.

Records show that Marco "the elder" lived in Sudak for some time, probably until 1280. Later, after his return to Venice, his business and his property were managed by his son Niccolò (the younger). It is uncertain whether these affairs were part of the family enterprise that united the Polos' investments in Asia, but it is likely that these contacts with Crimean trade encouraged Matteo and Niccolò (the elder, cousin of Niccolò the younger) to embark on their journey to the East. It appears this was an exploratory journey to meet Berke Khan, and to curry his favor by bringing him gifts of precious gemstones from Constantinople, all in an effort to expand their business in the territories of the Horde. In the absence of direct relations or trade treaties with the Venetian state, the merchants' strategy was to open a space for themselves via private investments and by obtaining the protection of local rulers. Detailed studies of the notarial deeds and wills left by various Polos suggest that it was Marco "the elder" and his son, Niccoló (the younger) who had the least economic success. This can be ascribed to their withdrawal of investments in Crimea around 1280. After the fall of Acre, competition for control over Black Sea routes intensified. Despite a truce between Genoa and Venice in 1270, tensions simmered until the conflict came to a head in 1291 with skirmishes that later erupted into the Second Venetian–Genoese War (1294–98). After 1280, the Genoese presence in Caffa, which had been active in previous years, grew ever more intense.[2] Undoubtedly, these were troubling years for the Venetians,

---

1. Jacoby, "Marco Polo."
2. Balard, "Gênes et la mer Noire"; Balard, "Les Génois en Crimée."

filled with uncertainty and risk, particularly financial in relation to their investments in Crimea.

In contrast, the Polo brothers who went to Asia, Niccolò the elder and Matteo the elder, amassed wealth both in tangible and intangible assets. It was Marco "the voyager" who benefited most from the family business, both as the heir to substantial portions of the family estate, and as a shrewd and cautious—and perhaps tight-fisted—private investor. His will and inventory of his assets reveal a considerable amount of cash, real estate, and valuables.[3] Marco Polo traveled for business even after he returned to Venice, but not for long. After 1300, although he continued to invest in various enterprises, it appears that Marco stayed in Venice. Perhaps this was due to his advancing age (he turned fifty in 1304), although his energy was most likely taken up by overseeing his interests and local investments, and above all in publicity for his book. He commissioned numerous copies to be distributed to powerful and influential people.

With their complex business affairs both in and outside the family, the Polos are a prime model of a merchant-class dynasty. Their economic foundations were trade and investments, all managed by this bona fide intergenerational family business. This type of financial organization allowed for a concentration of capital to be invested in costly yet potentially lucrative trips. Nonetheless, the risks were high. On their way back from China, the Polos were robbed of a substantial amount of money in Trebizond, which was then controlled by the Genoese. The loss led them to ask the Venetian government for compensation, and this could have been fulfilled based on the wealth that the state had confiscated from the Genoese during battles and raids. Unfortunately for the Polos, they were only able to recover a fraction of the money lost, and only after many years had passed.

There is no doubt that the Polos were forerunners of the expansion of Latin trade in the East. It is in some ways surprising, therefore, that they did not capitalize on their geographical, mercantile, and linguistic knowledge with investments in the territory of the Golden Horde, particularly when Venetian trade was on the rise in Tana and other Pontic settlements. In part, we can attribute this to the fact that the generation of Marco "the voyager," his younger brother Matteo, and their cousins, had little interest when it came to investing in those relationships with the Mongols of which Marco himself and his father had been protagonists. Another factor was Marco's character. Many

3. Jacoby, "Marco Polo."

found him to be cantankerous, a man set on his own interests and determined to find fame. This may have contributed to fading impulses for commercial adventures, along with a breakdown of the family's unity. Another reason for the curbing of new investment in those lands may have been the withdrawal from business on the Black Sea by Niccolò the younger (son of Marco "the elder," and cousin once removed of Marco "the voyager").

Of these hypotheses, we believe the first to be the most likely: the dissolution of the family business that was formed by the generation of Marco's father. The Polos seemed more interested in acquiring property in Venice, moving from the area of San Severo, in the *sestiere* of Castello, to that of San Giovanni Grisostomo near Rialto. This intriguing switch between journeys across vast expanses and moves from one *sestiere* to another, where one's social class was based on how prestigious your quarter was and the type of home you lived in, reminds us of the supreme importance of the local interests that tied Venetians to their city. Not even Marco Polo, the greatest example of medieval exploration, is an exception to this rule.

## Marco Polo and the Grand Khan

Marco Polo enjoyed a position of considerable privilege in his relationship with the khan. Not only did he have unlimited access to the court, which is in itself extraordinary, but he could also travel the country far and wide under imperial protection, and claimed to be charged with important duties of a sensitive nature for which he was presumably well paid. Marco came into Kublai's good graces not as a representative of a state, but due to his personal merits. Notably, during his time at court, he learned the customs of the Mongols, as well as their language and writing system (he claimed to know various writing systems). Alongside his adept skills at archery that astonished the court, Marco gained a reputation for being likable, prudent, and wise.

Thanks to these qualities, Kublai selected Marco for a special mission to the far-flung province of Caragian, from the Mongol Karajang, which was part of what is present-day Yunnan province in southwest China. Expecting Kublai to be interested in the local customs and traditions, Marco wrote up a report for the khan. This report can be read in the *Milione,* in a section dedicated to the Caragian region.[4] It describes Marco Polo's first mission on behalf of the

---

4. See the various editions of Marco Polo's work listed in the bibliography.

khan, and is filled with fascinating economic details that we will return to later in this chapter.

Upon his return from this mission, Marco was officially hired to serve the emperor. For the next seventeen years, Kublai continued to assign Marco various missions across the empire. At times, Marco traveled for his own personal affairs, but always with the blessing and permission of the khan.[5] Throughout his travels, he continued gathering information, and "took pains to know about and understand everything that could have pleased the Khan."[6] Kublai greatly appreciated this and thus kept Marco in a privileged position as part of his inner circle, despite this intimacy causing envy and disapproval among the aristocracy. We can surmise that the wealth of knowledge Marco had gathered was the result of research conducted on behalf of the khan, eager to be informed on all the aspects of his vast empire. To that end, Marco obtained special favors and the freedom of movement he needed to fully explore the most far-flung territories. With this in mind, it is not so far-fetched to believe that the *Milione* is—at least in part—a collection of reports addressed to Kublai Khan.

However, Marco had great difficulty leaving the empire. The Polos required the khan's consent not only to be given official leave, but above all to have adequate protection. As Marco recounts, despite the riches they had accumulated, they were not free to leave. By then, the khan had also grown old, and they were concerned that he might die, leaving their fate in the hands of his successor, who may not have granted the necessary permits. Marco's account reveals that the three Polos had a subservient relationship with the khan, as they were in the khan's service and depended on him. He continually rejected their pleas to return to Venice, as he "loved them too much" and could not accept the idea that they should leave him.

It was only the good fortune of an "arranged" marriage according to Mongol customs that allowed the Polos to finally return home. Around 1291, three Mongol noblemen arrived at Kublai's court to ask the khan on behalf of their lord, the Ilkhanate emperor Arghun, for a new bride as their queen had recently passed away. Unbeknownst to the messengers, Arghun himself had passed away during their journey. Kublai granted Arghun to take the Princess Kokejin (the name can be translated as "Celestine"[7]) as his consort, but the

---

5. Polo, *The Description of the World*, vol. 1, pp. 16–17.

6. Polo, *The Description of the World*, vol. 1, p. 17.

7. Although Francis Cleaves acknowledges that the name Celestine is derived from the Mongolian *köke*, which, according to its most common definition, means blue, blue-green, or light

return journey proved impossible due to a new war that blocked the overland passage. The Ilkhanate ambassadors decided to return to Persia by sea, and the Mongol noblemen insisted that the Polos should accompany them, so they might rely on Marco's nautical and geographical knowledge, gleaned from his recent return from India. It was this triple coincidence—the arrival of the Mongol delegation, the blocked land route, and the decision to travel by sea—that finally allowed the Polos to leave Kublai. However, it should be noted that their departure was still linked to a service performed for their khan. In practice, their subservience to their Mongol lord was never called into question, nor did the Polos succeed in disentangling themselves from the relationship. It was ironic, then, that the rendering of service is what this break required.

This type of bond is no doubt representative of a more general conception of the relationship established between the Latins and the Mongols throughout the various territories of the empire. Those who entered the service of Mongol aristocrats did so with the knowledge that they could not leave without a special and unilateral concession. For instance, much has been written about two Italians, the Genoese Buscarello de' Ghizolfi and the Sienese Tommaso Ugi, contemporaries of Marco Polo, who held the posts of *qurci* (bearer of the bow) and *ilduci* (bearer of the sword), respectively, at the court of the Ilkhanids.[8] These two posts involved great responsibility, which tells us that the two men were very high within the ranks of the imperial "bodyguard," who not only performed military but also administrative duties. We cannot rule out the hypothesis that Marco Polo was also a part of the Mongolian imperial guard (*keshigten*), evidenced by his skill at archery, which suggests military training.[9]

The Mongols often used Latins in their expeditions, but regardless of Buscarello's mercantile origins (in Tabriz) and probably of the Sienese as well, the conferment of Mongol titles and their role within the Ilkhanid diplomacy and administration made them to all effects servants of the khan—no more nor less than Marco.[10] We have no records of the exact terms of their relationship with Arghun and Oljeitu, but it is unlikely that they could enter and leave

blue (still present in the toponyms Kokonor and Huhhot), he chooses the translation "dark" (and thus "dark-skinned woman") even though this meaning is rarely attested to. "Celestial" blue was a sacred color for the Mongols, and it had divine and spiritual associations that could, in turn, be associated with a personal name. Cleaves, "A Chinese Source."

8. Lockhart, "The Relations"; Richard, "Buscarello de Ghizolfi."

9. Regarding the hypothesis that Marco may have been an imperial bodyguard, see Haw, *Marco Polo's China*, pp. 165–68.

10. Jackson, "World Conquest and Local Accommodation."

Mongol service as they wished. A notary act tells us that Buscarello left two slaves in the service of his wife Grimaldina, but this is a modest bequest for someone who served as ambassador, and it raises doubts about the circumstances of his service.[11] Another Italian ambassador in the service of Ghazan was "Isolo" il Pisano, known as Ciolus or Zolus Bofeti di Anastasio. He served the Ilkhanids as ambassador and probably also as governor and commissioner in the Levant; however, it is likely he was also a clever braggart.[12] All these various figures appear and disappear throughout diplomatic and notarial records without leaving personal testimonies. Marco Polo's destiny would likely have been just as obscure, entrusted solely to testamentary notes and legal documents, if not for his fortunate decision to record his memoirs.

Some historians hypothesize that Marco served Kublai as *ortaq*, a Turkic–Mongol term for a merchant (of either western or Middle Eastern descent) at the service of Mongol aristocrats in China, and as such endowed with government licenses and permits.[13] The term signifies "partner," thus indicating a form of partnership, and was a system formalized by Kublai in 1268.[14] In fact, it is possible that all the Polos, including Matteo and Niccolò, held such a position. However, it is difficult to imagine that there were strict separations between the various roles within the imperial entourage. Marco was a trusted person of the court and could have traveled as an imperial envoy or ambassador, secretary, merchant, supervisor, or officer, depending on his mission and rank.

Lastly, let us turn to the vexing question of Marco Polo's presumed "governorship" in Yangzhou.[15] Scholars have carried out exhaustive research on the matter, and the consensus is that Marco Polo lived in this important city for three years, probably from 1282 to 1284, but certainly not as a governor, one of the highest positions with great responsibility. Unsurprisingly, Marco was occasionally employed in the administration of the empire as an officer. Interpretive challenges have mostly arisen due to conflicting readings of the different manuscript traditions. What we can safely say is that, at the age of twenty-eight, Marco was entrusted with tasks that allowed him to directly deal with various offices for fiscal and commercial matters, lending his descriptions their precision.

11. Balard, "Gênes et la Mer Noire," pp. 379–80.
12. Richard, "Isol le Pisan."
13. Vogel, *Marco Polo Was in China*, pp. 75–76.
14. Endicott-West, "Merchant Associations in Yüan China," p. 133.
15. Vogel, *Marco Polo Was in China*, pp. 348–64.

Ultimately, all hypotheses on Marco Polo's position in relation to the khan are plausible due to contemporary sources that prove the range of possibilities offered to Latins in the Mongol courts. It is therefore essential that we do not confuse the extraordinary nature of Marco's literary legacy with the alleged extraordinary nature of his position in China. Marco and the Polo family shared the destiny of other Latins who came into the good graces of Mongol lords, not as representatives of their states but as individuals, and they carried out government tasks thanks to their knowledge and (we presume) their valued skills in commercial, diplomatic, or military fields. No doubt their loyalty to the khan must have been absolute and exclusive, yet we have no way of knowing whether they had the freedom to leave their service and return to their homeland with accumulated possessions and knowledge. Marco's account, if it does accurately portray the relationships between the Mongol khans and their western servants, leads us to imagine that these were difficult relationships to break. It is this very difficulty that perhaps explains the lack of personal information about other men who held such positions of power, yet who did not have the chance to record and transmit their own experiences. If the *Milione* is truly a unique work, it is so in the sense that the circumstances of its creation were entirely singular and fortuitous—and not in the sense of Marco's experience itself.

## Marco Polo's Commercial Geography

In the China described by Marco Polo, distant provinces were connected in an organic network of trade: rivers and canals connected cities via their shores, while fleets transported all kinds of goods. This was the lifeblood of the empire. It is no surprise that it was a Venetian who described this symbiosis of trade and navigation in such a precise, detailed, and meticulous way. For Marco Polo, it was a familiar environment, which gave him a natural inlet to delving deep into the subject matter, without the need for mental effort or complex translation that would have been nigh on impossible for those unfamiliar with this line of work. Recent studies show that information on coins, taxes, and commercial data is difficult to interpret for anyone without a mercantile background. In fact, it was precisely this gap in historical knowledge that fueled the controversy (now resolved) regarding Marco's presence in China. For this, we are grateful to Hans Ulrich Vogel, who accurately reconstructed the mercantile knowledge presented in the *Milione*, particularly details on coins, salt, and taxes. It is only thanks to the expertise of a historian specializing in China's economy and the medieval world that we can now truly understand and appreciate Marco's knowledge. Thus, the concept of "mercantile geography" provides us with two categories of interpretation (geography and trade), which allow us to connect—albeit imperfectly—with the perspective of a young Venetian in the mid-thirteenth century, a man who absorbed and memorized what he saw through the lens of his own period and culture.

While it is true that Marco's intention was not to write a handbook about trade,[16] but rather to describe the "marvels" he encountered, it is also true that his cultural background was that of a merchant who interpreted reality through codes from which he could not escape, regardless of his own literary ambitions and self-aggrandizing intentions. Finally, of particular note is just how anxious Marco was for western readers to believe him. He went to great lengths to underscore the truth of his accounts, and this commitment to building "credibility" may explain the plain and detached nature of the descriptions, some of which were embellished by Rustichello to better suit the style that was in vogue at the time. However, his accounts of countries and their customs read as if they are reported by a documentary almanac. Of course, as previously mentioned, this may have been the case, being a collection of Marco's travel diaries and reports to the khan, perhaps written in one of the various languages he knew. Ramusio's edition refers to the *memoriali* (memoirs) that Marco Polo is said to have compiled during his travels.[17] This is an apocryphal insertion, not corroborated by the manuscript tradition, but nevertheless it presents an interesting perspective. In contrast to thirteenth-century Europe, where it was rare for merchants or travelers to carry notebooks in which they could keep a diary or take notes of their journeys, this was a common practice among the literati in thirteenth-century China. Anyone who knew how to write could find a pen, ink, and brush to record travel notes. Diaries and *biji* (notebooks filled with notes and memories) were already widespread during the Song dynasty (960–1279). Ramusio's additions tie into a fascinating hypothesis that Marco did save his *memoriali*, and that these might have been the source of the facts and numbers in his book. Although this is just speculation, it would mean that the *Milione* is a combination of writing and memory, and Marco's original notes recorded the more technical and complex aspects he learned: distances, numbers, currency exchange rates, and meteorological matters. In order to succinctly but not superficially analyze the wealth and precision of the

16. Jackson, "Marco Polo and His 'Travels.'"
17. Polo, *The Description of the World*, vol. 1, p. 73.

information presented by the *Milione*, we will delve into three representative passages to explore the knowledge Marco Polo conveys to us—particularly about trade.

## The City of "Cambaluc" and Paper Money

Marco Polo's Cambaluc (or Khanbaliq) was the capital of Kublai Khan's China, which is present-day Beijing (then called Dadu in Chinese). More than ever, Marco was impressed by the bustling traffic of people and goods from distant countries and from every province of "Cathay." These goods were first and foremost meant for the sovereign and the court, but were also for all the noble residents and soldiers stationed around the city. Each day, almost a thousand carts of silk entered the city, including the gold-spun cloth that was so highly prized by the Mongols, who greatly increased its production. At the time, silk was even more common than hemp or cotton.

Cambaluc was the home of the imperial mint and was also where paper money was produced. With some irony, Marco compared the emperor to an alchemist who invented a kind of philosopher's stone, a process that could transform something of little value—such as the bark of a mulberry tree—into gold and pearls. The secret was, in fact, paper produced from the pulp within the bark. The sheets were cut into various sizes, then printed with the emperor's red seal, making every banknote legal tender that the khan could then exchange for gold, silver, or any precious stones. These banknotes could have different face values, and were equivalent to the Venetian *mezzo grosso d'argento*, the *grosso*, or even two *grossi*. Producing this form of money was cheap, and it allowed the khan to buy whatever he wanted, as it was mandatory to accept it as payment.

Marco Polo is the medieval author to provide us with such a complete picture of the manufacture and circulation of paper money, and its Venetian equivalent. In 1260, once Kublai Khan had risen to the imperial throne, he initiated a vast monetary reform for his entire empire, which included northern China and Mongolia. This switch to the use of paper money was mainly due to the scarcity of silver or other suitable materials that could satisfy the huge expenses, especially military, of an expanding empire. Marco Polo either chooses not to say this, or perhaps he is unaware of it. Nevertheless, his description of the system is accurate, and offers approximate equivalents between the various types and values of the banknotes in the Mongol empire and the coins in circulation in the West, such as the Venetian silver *grosso*, the silver *dernier tournoir* (*tornesel*), and the gold bezant. Even a citizen of one of Europe's richest cities could not fail to be dazzled by the grand khan's endless wealth and his ingenious mechanism that allowed for its accumulation.

Marco sang the praises of this system, which allowed one to travel without being weighed down by money; indeed, one banknote worth ten bezants hardly weighed as much as one bezant (a gold bezant weighed 4.5 grams). Foreign merchants—Indians foremost among them—were forced to sell their valuables (gold, silver, gemstones, and pearls) to the emperor. He would have them evaluated by experts, then would compensate the merchants with a generous banknote of the same value, which was immediately accepted because it was greater than what they would have received on the open market. They could then purchase anything they wanted and take it back to their respective countries. Periodically, the khan would announce that anyone who owned precious objects could take them to the mint and receive a favorable exchange. In this way, the khan was able to amass fabulous treasures. Furthermore, if a banknote was spoiled, it could be taken to the mint and exchanged for a new one for a fee of 3 percent of its face value. Lastly, aristocrats who needed precious objects for personal use could draw up a list, go to the mint where such objects were stored, and use banknotes to buy them. However much the Song (960–1279) and Jin (1115–1234) dynasties had previously used paper money as a substitute for metallic coins, the Mongols were the ones to turn this form of currency into the principal means of exchange. The system was imposed on the entire empire, even though—as we shall see—other forms of payment prevailed in certain southern provinces.

So, how did this system work? If trade was the driver for the circulation of money, the khan himself was the pivot and anchor of the monetary system, insofar as it was his laws that enforced the strict punishment for forgery or the refusal to accept banknotes. The law and order that prevailed in the Mongol regimes—albeit imposed by a sword's edge—were essential to the maintenance of a financial, commercial, and fiscal order based on a purely symbolic tool. Its value was solely guaranteed by the existence of a state capable of imposing its use, and maintaining the infrastructure necessary for the production and circulation of banknotes, including the preparation of the paper, its printing, control, and accounting.

Marco's book gives us a clear idea of how these banknotes worked: not just the exchange of precious goods (acquired by the state) for paper money, but also the issuance of new banknotes and their exchange for non-precious goods, such as silk and cotton. Just as the issuance of banknotes was the prerogative and monopoly of the state, so was the collection and safeguarding of precious objects, which both foreign merchants and private citizens purchased with this paper money. Such items were kept in "stabilization storehouses." Much has been written about the "compulsory legal tender" of paper money in the Yuan era, but when Marco Polo wrote that people could go to the storehouses and purchase precious objects with banknotes he did not exclude some form of convertibility, albeit in limited quantities. The only fact that cannot be verified is the presence of twelve experts who were tasked with estimating the currency exchange value of the goods presented at the storehouses.[18] The state had access to gold, silver, and other precious goods, obtained in exchange for paper, at practically no cost. However, it is also true that the state was forced to pay in silver or gold for imports from abroad, as this was the obligatory tender in international transactions. Furthermore, the khan and his government officials used precious goods to reward or pay aristocrats, high officers, military figures, and probably foreign ambassadors. All this is exhaustively confirmed by Chinese sources, while among those of Marco Polo's contemporaries who also mention paper money, we find neither the expertise nor the accuracy of the information in the *Milione*. Ultimately, as Vogel states: "The comparison with Chinese sources demonstrates that Marco Paolo's description of the production, distribution, and functions of Yuan paper notes are in almost all cases perfectly congruent with the information provided by the historiographical records or historical remains."[19]

## The Province of Caragian (Yunnan, Dali)

One of the few areas where paper money did not circulate was southwest China. Present-day Yunnan Province, which in the *Milione* is referred to as Caragian, was the scene of Marco's first mission on behalf of Kublai. It is described after Sichuan (the city of Chengdu, Caindu) not in chronological order of his journey but rather based on geography: going from west to east, from the Black Sea to central Asia, to Mongolia, and, lastly, to the imperial capital. Finally, in his descriptions of China, from the western to the eastern provinces, he ends in India and southeast Asia. As previously mentioned, it is likely that this chapter is a form of the report originally presented to Kublai. As with his narratives of other places, Marco dwells on the economic aspects

18. Vogel, *Marco Polo Was in China*, pp. 167–68 and 213.
19. Vogel, *Marco Polo Was in China*, pp. 243–48.

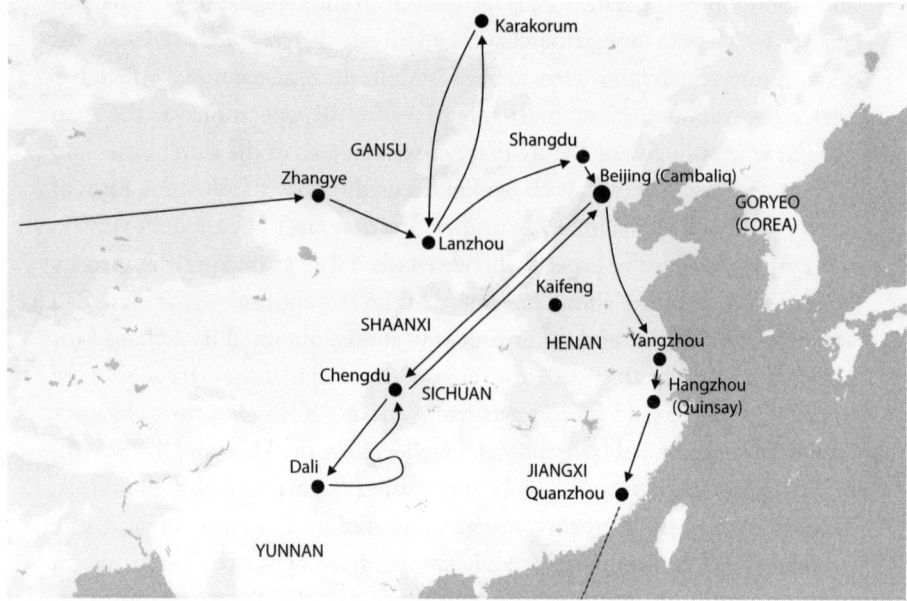

MAP 17. Marco Polo's China

that he felt were particularly noteworthy. In this chapter, he offers readers a precise and complete description of the use, circulation, and value of cowrie shells.

From a monetary perspective, the provinces of Caragian and Zardandan in Yunnan were not integrated with the rest of the empire (Cathay and Manzi, that is, north and south China). Instead of paper money, cowrie shells were used for small everyday transactions, while gold was used for higher values. However anomalous this may have been in contrast to the legal monetary regime in the rest of the empire, the use of shells was equally state-controlled to prevent violations connected to the illegal import of the currency. Financially, Yunnan was much more integrated with southeast Asia, and especially India, where the shells came from. In this system, the basic unit of measure was a string of eighty shells, equal to a unit of silver, that is, a *saggio*. This exchange value helps us establish that an ounce of Chinese silver (*liang*) was equal to 726 shells. Chinese sources, however, cite higher exchange rates, which indicates considerable currency fluctuations, ranging from 960 to over 2,000 shells for an ounce of silver. On the other hand, silver had a particularly high value in the region because of its alleged scarcity, while gold had a relatively low value, given the abundance of gold straw and nuggets in the region's rivers. While the abundance of gold in Yunnan is widely confirmed by Chinese sources,[20] the scarcity of silver in "Zardandan" (western Yunnan) is harder to believe, given that the silver exported to India from the late thirteenth to the late sixteenth century came from Yunnan. According to Vogel, most silver mines in Yunnan were in the eastern part of the province, which means that this supposed scarcity can be explained by the exports themselves, as silver was traded for gold at a very favorable exchange rate abroad.[21]

There are many similarities between Marco's tale and Chinese sources. He clearly singled out the origin of the cowrie shells (Bengala), the countable measure of eighty shells, and the absence of paper money, the only exception in the whole empire. Furthermore, he also names the regions where an imperial edict in 1301 prohibited the illegal import of shells, which are confirmed by Chinese records. Historical sources and archeological finds confirm this same "economic geography," proving that Marco's journey to Caragian involved a reconnaissance mission upon the khan's request.[22] Marco's particular cultural background and the technical tools at his disposal allowed him to focus on issues of an economic, monetary, and commercial nature, thus unraveling complex aspects of the local economy and trade.

## The City of Quinsai (Hangzhou)

The chapter on the city of Quinsai (or Kinsay) in Marco Polo's book is especially important in that it provides yet another detailed example of his knowledge of finances.[23] He vividly depicts a city filled with exuberant productivity and economic well-being, citing the abundance of silk, for instance. Yet, Marco also alludes to the heavy military presence that held the local population in check. Each of the city's 12,000 bridges (and he is precise on their number) was watched over by guards who monitored citizens' movements and enforced the evening curfew. The khan's reasons for this strict control were twofold. First, Hangzhou was the capital of southern China (Manzi), which had

---

20. Vogel, *Marco Polo Was in China*, p. 49; Polo, *The Travels of Marco Polo*, vol. 2, pp. 85ff.

21. For more on cowrie shells as a form of payment in various parts of the ancient world, and particularly their use in Yunnan in Marco Polo's time, refer to Yang, *Cowrie Shells*, pp. 94–123.

22. Vogel, *Marco Polo Was in China*, pp. 364–98.

23. For more on Quinsai, refer to Vogel, *Marco Polo Was in China*, pp. 365–98 and Polo, *The Travels of Marco Polo*, vol. 2, pp. 185–218.

recently been "pacified." And second, the city was a key center where the khan could collect tax revenues generated by commercial taxes.

Hangzhou was also the heart of the production and sale of salt, and revenues were calculated based on an equivalence between the *toman* (*tümen* in Mongolian means 10,000) and the golden *saggio*. Depending on the version of the *Milione*, the value of a *toman* is either 70,000 or 80,000 *saggi*. Thus, salt revenues amounted to 5,600,000 or 6,640,000 *saggi*. These were nominal values in gold, but payments were made in paper currency. Aside from salt, Hangzhou's treasury generated many other tax revenues, such as silk produced by family manufacturers, wheat, alcohol, and vinegar. Mining of minerals such as copper, iron, aluminum, lead, gold, and silver was also subject to taxation, as was the cutting of bamboo and timber. Marco explains that the revenue corresponded to 210 *toman*, which equaled 14,700,000 golden *saggi*: a vast amount. It was this, like many other apparently exaggerated assertions, that earned Marco's book the nickname *Milione*. Yet, if we compare these numbers with Chinese sources, and by reducing both to the same unit of measurement (keeping in mind that exchange rates fluctuated), the results are perfectly compatible: the Chinese sources cite a range of 469,799 to 906,040 ounces of silver, while Marco Polo states 554,210 to 818,362.[24] No other source that cites the taxes—and we have only found mention in the works of Persian historian Wassaf (d. ca. 1328) and in the travel account of Odoric of Pordenone—is as accurate as Marco Polo's. This confirms that Marco had direct experience in Hangzhou's tax revenue offices (the Commission on the Distribution of Salt was created by the Mongolian government in 1277–78), probably as a supervisor appointed by the khan himself.

## Venice in China: A Missed Opportunity?

Today we know that Marco Polo's memoirs are more accurate in their descriptions of material life and economic and financial conditions than in his descriptions of political, social, and cultural information. We can therefore surmise that the *Milione* is the fruit of his extensive experiences with mainly economic tasks. As we have already hypothesized, Marco most likely embarked on trade activities either for himself and his family, or as *ortaq* for the khan and Mongol aristocracy. The *Milione*'s framework is founded in his knowledge of

24. Vogel, *Marco Polo Was in China*, p. 375.

trade, which was the norm for any young Venetian raised in a family devoted to commerce, and his personal aptitude, which featured an especial curiosity about and attention to financial mechanisms. Marco's book was conceived to describe a new world, and it recounts experiences shared by other Latins of the time and the services rendered to the Mongol governors who ruled Asia. At times, these services were diplomatic, at others administrative or of a military nature. What is clear in the *Milione* is one Mediterranean merchant's commitment to identifying and defining the markets and mechanisms the Mongols had granted him access to. The Polos were united with their contemporaries in the overlapping roles they played, alternating between being merchants, ambassadors, and officers at the service of the khan. Marco's accounts offer a glimpse into this significant aspect of the Venetian—and the greater Latin— presence among the Mongols: that of the private enterprise made up of personal initiatives and paths dictated by often fortuitous circumstances.

The following chapters discuss the tools that allowed Venetians to penetrate Mongol-controlled markets. Primarily, these were tools involved in an enormous effort to make different commercial cultures compatible. Of course, these efforts were not the domain of a single sphere of knowledge; rather, they were part of a collective that included many elements: the estimation of goods and markets, knowledge of geography and routes, convertibility of currency, weights, and measures, as well as calculation of risks and dangers. Over time, gathered experiences were transformed into an ability to expand Venetian activities. Trade was no longer limited to individuals and families, but became the collective effort of a state that reached beyond its Mediterranean borders, establishing a direct relationship with the very nerve centers of the Mongol Empire.

Considering Marco Polo and his book, we become aware of one significant fact: however much *Il Milione* represents a major contribution to a knowledge of Asia, its influence on the general context of relations between Venice and the Mongols was close to non-existent. The Polos were private citizens who played no official role in Venetian expansion in Asia. If Venice, as a Mediterranean power, had a presence on the Black Sea, the same cannot be said for China, which remained outside the range, action, or interests of the Venetian government. Venice never sent official delegations to try to lay the groundwork for an organized presence such as the one that existed in the Black Sea. Nor did the Venetian state establish diplomatic relations with the Mongol khans apart from those of the Golden Horde or the Ilkhanate: rulers of those places where Venice had established a substantial presence. Nor can we accuse the Mongols of having closed off the road to Cathay that had been opened by the Polos. In fact, they had always been welcoming, actively encouraging diplomatic initiatives. If we consider the extraordinary adventure of the Polos as a positive episode in the greater context of relations between Europe and China, it is solely for coincidental reasons—but mainly because it was the Mongols themselves that paved the way for communication with Asia.

# 9

# An Interconnected Continent

## Venetian Merchants and New Horizons of Trade

During Venice's period of expansion into the Mongol Empire, the role of merchants underwent significant changes. Expanding markets and the need to operate far from one's homeland unquestionably contributed to this transition from traveling merchant—someone who journeyed, bought and sold goods, and assumed all the risks of the trade—to that of the sedentary entrepreneur of the fourteenth century. These entrepreneurs now led companies with agents scattered across major markets in Europe and the Levant, managing operations from a distance.[1]

Many of the evolutionary processes in mercantile practices, which had developed throughout previous decades, reached their full maturity during the thirteenth century. In this time, Venice had made great strides in building an "Aegean system" that ensured the continuous flow of goods and people from the Adriatic to the Black seas. By the late thirteenth century, the growing presence of Venetians in Mongol-ruled territories had opened new markets and simultaneously required state involvement in trade expansion. The vast distances, the high risks, and the lengthy travel times called for large, long-term investments. Consequently, the primary financial resources came from the upper classes and affluent sectors of Venetian society. This led to a more integrated relationship between merchants and the state in regions east of Constantinople. Romània–Black Sea galleys often carried members of the Venetian aristocracy, destined for Tana, Tabriz, and all other Black Sea markets. These individuals engaged in both commercial ventures and government roles, with little distinction between the two.

1. Kedar, *Mercanti in crisi*, pp. 47–48.

Venice thrived on trade, and it was through trade that it amassed its fortune. Beginning in the early thirteenth century, its expansion into the eastern Mediterranean and beyond the Dardanelles established the city as a central hub for Eurasian commerce. Venice became the main entry point for goods arriving from the East, which were then distributed across European markets, transforming it into Europe's great emporium. Although this system generated substantial wealth for its citizens, not all Venetians benefited equally. Participation in mercantile activities was largely determined by an individual's social status within Venice's rigidly stratified society.

In thirteenth-century Venice, anyone who wished to engage in trade had to belong to a specific social category: the *cittadini* (citizens), which comprised the middle-to-upper classes, representing no more than 5 percent of the population.[2] These citizens included members of prominent Venetian families of ancient lineage (*originarii*), as well as those who had migrated to Venice, established permanent residency, and paid taxes (*de intus et de extra* or *de fora*).[3] The state provided legal protection to its merchants, both at home and abroad, and intervened in disputes between merchants and producers, merchants and buyers, and other buyers. This intervention was crucial in ensuring the smooth functioning of Venice's commercial systems.

While production and trade were clearly distinct, the collaboration between the producers (often a *popolano*, man of the people) and merchants was remarkably close. Merchants bore the costs of various artisan trades, either by paying for rental expenses or directly supplying raw materials. For example, furs imported from Rus' were processed in Venice before being sold throughout Europe, and cotton from Syria and Egypt followed a similar pattern.[4] In other words, although merchants were not directly involved in the production of consumer goods, the expansion of their operations, with a resulting increase in raw materials and finished products, was an essential factor for the growth of productive activities in Venice and beyond. Furthermore, Venetian trade with Constantinople, Egypt, Syria, and the broader Middle East stimulated the development of regional markets. These markets were integrated into commercial arteries that branched beyond the Mediterranean basin, serving as

2. Romano, *Patricians and Popolani*, p. 29; Hocquet, "I meccanismi dei traffici," p. 534.
3. Caravale, "Le istituzioni della Repubblica," p. 305.
4. Sapori, "I beni del commercio internazionale," pp. 17–18.

vital terminals for Asian trade routes that stretched as far as India and China.[5]

The Mongol conquests had significantly expanded opportunities for commercial exchanges, not only by improving market access but above all through the relatively "liberal" *ante litteram* (policies) of Mongol governments. The khanates formed a coherent political system, though not yet unified administratively, which allowed the Venetian and the Mediterranean commercial systems to connect with territories and economies that had previously been inaccessible or only reachable via intermediaries. This coincided with an acceleration of a trend from the previous century, toward the integration of regional economies into the greater framework of international trade.[6] In other words, the Mongol conquests created greater freedom for merchants and facilitated their activities by standardizing commercial tariffs and reducing—if not eliminating—the risks of robbery. For example, sources confirm the relative safety of the "Tana route" during the first half of the fourteenth century.[7] By the second half of the thirteenth century, merchants could already accurately estimate the costs of transportation, taxes, and the risks involved in long-distance trade, allowing them to make informed calculations regarding their investments and profit margins.

To support and sustain the presence and activities of Venetian merchants in newly expanding commercial areas, several advancements were made in the second half of the thirteenth century. Shipbuilding skills were honed, navigation techniques were improved, and the frequency and regularity of voyages increased, along with greater understanding of these new territories. Public investments also saw a notable rise during this period. In this chapter, we will focus particularly on trade routes, innovations in shipbuilding, and the legal tools that encouraged investments through the formation of various trade associations.

Regarding logistical support for overland journeys, the spread of mendicant orders—Franciscan and Dominican—in Asia, made possible also by the

---

5. Hocquet, "I meccanismi dei traffici," p. 530.

6. From around the mid-twelfth century, the markets in central Asia and India oriented to western demand. Products from the Far East arrived in Adjab in the Red Sea, and continued overland toward the Nile delta, and from there to Alexandria and Damietta. This was another reason why, in the first half of the thirteenth century following the Fourth Crusade, Venice did not invest in resources to cross the straits and settle on the Black Sea.

7. Pegolotti, *La pratica della mercatura*, p. 22.

Mongols' religious tolerance, contributed to the creation of shelters that merchants could use as well. One example is the *fondaco* of the Franciscans in Zaitun (Quanzhou, in southern China). In every Venetian settlement far from the homeland, churches, confraternities, schools, vegetable gardens, and artisanal workshops emerged, all managed by these mendicant orders. Venetian merchants in Tana opened taverns, bought mills, and managed bakeries. From a broader perspective, the Black Sea became a vibrant crossroads for the interaction of daily life and religions, connecting the Latin West to the Mongol East and the Islamic world.

Navigating beyond the European cultural sphere, dominated by Latin and Greek, also meant finding a new common language and alternative communication tools. Among these, Persian and Turkic stood out as widespread lingua francas in the East, especially useful for western merchants on long journeys. However, merchants were advised to employ intermediaries and interpreters, even though these were not always reliable. Within the Mongol Empire, Venetian merchants—like others traveling along these routes—communicated in at least four languages: their vernacular as well as Latin, Persian, and Turkic. The Black Sea was not only multiethnic but also multilingual.

We must also consider that in the fourteenth century, travel from Tana to Cathay took 284 days—about nine and a half months—depending on variable climate conditions, natural obstacles such as deserts and mountain ranges, and the risk of encountering war zones. Among the many dangers were the chance of being attacked and robbed along the way. In other words, such a journey required enduring hardships and sacrifices, as well as a bold spirit of adventure and the necessary knowledge to navigate these challenges.

In official communications and private Venetian writings, Latin remained the primary language. However, in the fourteenth century, the vernacular began to gain prominence, gradually complementing Latin in bureaucratic matters and, in private trade-related communications, even replacing it. This shift extended, albeit less frequently, to official treaties. As we explored in the last chapter with Marco Polo, beyond transportation and linguistic adaptation, engaging with new commercial worlds also required navigating commensurability and equivalences in exchange systems, from currency to weights and measures. Ensuring the mutual understanding of these essential trade tools was a concern well documented in merchant handbooks. In the following chapters, we will explore these aspects of maritime trade, which are inherently linked to broader issues of cultural exchange and interaction between Europe and the Mongol Empire.

Finally, we must mention the financial tools required to facilitate the circulation of money and to protect investments. Innovations in banking and commerce, such as letters of exchange and insurance policies, while less widespread in Venice compared to other Italian cities, were likely driven by the growing need to access increasingly distant markets and to manage greater risks. Commercial investments relied on an integrated system involving the government, merchants, investors, and creditors in Venice, all of whom were in sync with the timing of the *mude* (*mudas*, or ship convoys) sailing to the Black Sea. In Crimea, Tana, or Trebizond local "banks" operated to support these ventures. To attract investments when the state-regulated *mudas* were about to set sail, the cost was lower in Venice compared to more distant locations. Companies and banks, especially Florentine ones, along with private investors, flocked to Venice in the weeks preceding the departure of the *galee da mercato* (market galleys) to offer their credit services. Merchants and shipowners in need of capital could borrow on credit from banking companies, repaying with interest upon their return. These credit agencies profited not only from the interest but also from the exchange rate fluctuations between different currencies.[8]

To finance longer journeys, merchants often brought valuable, easily transportable goods, particularly precious items. This explains why, in 1250, when Niccolò and Matteo Polo set sail from Constantinople to cross the Black Sea, they had to purchase many pieces of jewelry to bring with them as offerings to gain access to the court of Berke Khan of the Golden Horde.[9] Upon returning, the profits from their voyages were in the form of various currencies, requiring a complex financial system, as detailed in merchant handbooks like the one written by Pegolotti.

The defense of settlements and the reduction of risks were crucial factors in enabling trade activities. The Venetian emporia on the Black Sea, particularly those in Mongol territories, were far from the motherland, and their protection relied on the modest forces of local garrisons. In contrast, Genoa built more effective defensive structures in Caffa and other colonies, leaving Venetian settlements considerably more vulnerable. Venetian records provide detailed information on the defensive measures in Tana and the costs incurred to maintain a regular supply of arms and men. However, it was especially after

8. Tognetti, "Le compagnie mercantili-bancarie," pp. 705–6; Mueller, *Money and Banking*, vol. 2, pp. 288–355.

9. Polo, *Il Milione*, ed. Bertolucci Pizzorusso, p. 2.

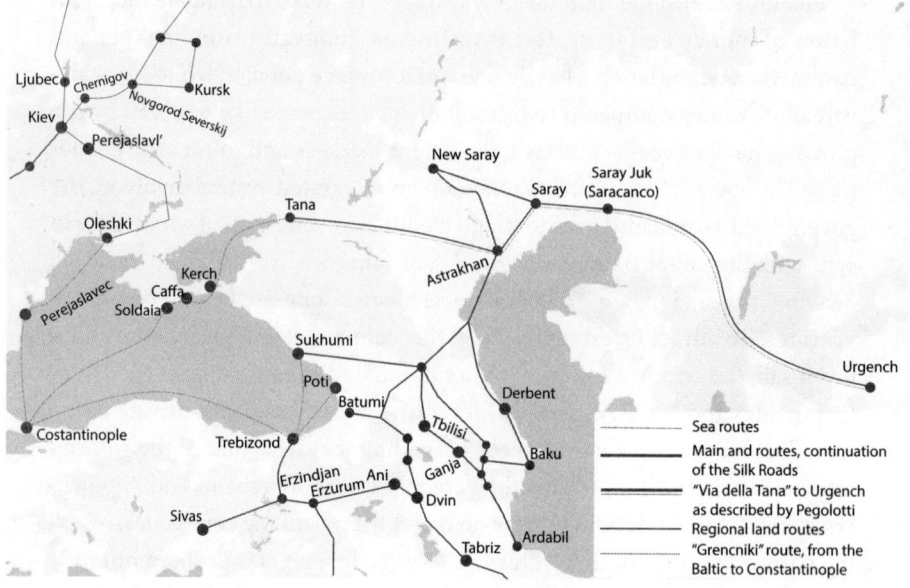

Ljubec Chernigov Kursk
Novgorod Severskij
Kiev
Perejaslavl'
Oleshki
Tana
New Saray
Saray
Saray Juk
(Saracanco)
Astrakhan
Kerch
Perejaslavec
Caffa
Soldaia
Sukhumi
Urgench
Poti
Derbent
Batumi
Costantinople
Tbilisi
Trebizond
Baku
Erzindjan Ani
Erzurum Ganja
Sivas Dvin
Ardabil
Tabriz

Sea routes
Main and routes, continuation
of the Silk Roads
"Via della Tana" to Urgench
as described by Pegolotti
Regional land routes
"Grencniki" route, from the
Baltic to Constantinople

MAP 18. Major trade routes in the northern sector, Black Sea–Caspian
Sea–central Asia

Timur's sack of the settlement in 1395 that Venice made significant investments
to construct new fortifications and to maintain a permanent garrison. Despite
these efforts, Venice primarily relied on maritime defenses and diplomacy,
which were less costly but carried greater risks. These measures often proved
inadequate to protect Venetian citizens from external threats, be they Mongol
or Genoese. The legal aspect of protection was more important than a strictly
defensive or military aspect, as it allowed Venice (like Genoa) to appeal to
Mongol authorities to safeguard its citizens' interests and safety. On the trade
routes, the *pax mongolica* established a set of norms, detailed in treaties and
agreements between states, that regulated the relationship between the Mongols and merchants, offering protection, reducing risks, and enabling merchants to make realistic profit projections.

## Eurasian Trade Routes

Whether traveling by sea or land, navigating the entire communication network known as the "Silk Roads" required significant time and expense. Traders
would arrive on merchant galleys in Trebizond or Tana and then continue
their journey overland toward Asia. Latin trading posts in north Pontus were
connected to the north with the southern Russian steppe, and to the east with

central and east Asia.[10] This transit system, established between the mid-thirteenth and the early fourteenth centuries, operated through a chain of stops that unfurled along routes determined not only by geography but also by the new geopolitical and commercial framework created by the Mongols. The system was essentially divided between two main routes: southern and northern, with a third less-traveled central route.

The nerve center of the southern route was in Tabriz, the hub for trade with Mongol-controlled territories in the Middle East since Ilkhan Abaqa made the city his residence. Travelers could reach Tabriz from Ayas Trebizond, or sometimes overland from Samsun. The journey from Tabriz to Trebizond took twelve to thirteen days on horseback without wagons, or "30–32 days of caravan travel."[11] This was likely the most commonly used route until the 1340s, as it is the only one described in great detail—station by station—by a seasoned trade expert like Pegolotti,[12] and earlier by the author of the *Nottario*,[13] and by Marco Polo. However, this route is completely absent from the Venetian *Tarifa*, which was written a few decades later (though not before 1345).[14] This route was used in the opposite direction, from east to west, by the Nestorian monk of Chinese origin, Rabban Sauma, when he traveled from Baghdad to Rome to meet the pope in 1287.[15] The Franciscan friar Odorico da Pordenone (d. 1331) also traveled this path in 1318.[16] Trebizond and Tabriz were still connected to Sivas (Sebaste, in present-day Turkey),[17] which had played an important role in commercial transits from the early thirteenth century. This is evidenced by the construction of travel shelters, commissioned by Seljuk Sultan

10. The bibliography on this topic is vast. See Lopez, *Studi sull'economia genovese*; Lopez, *Nuove luci sugli italiani*, pp. 83–145; Allsen, *Commodity and Exchange*.

11. Pegolotti, *La pratica della mercatura*, p. 29.

12. Pegolotti, *La pratica della mercatura*, pp. 28–29 and comment pp. 389–91; Paviot, "Les marchands italiens," p. 73.

13. This concerns a merchant handbook written by an anonymous author, most likely a Florentine, a few years before Pegolotti's *Pratica*. The manuscript was rediscovered in the Biblioteca Marucelliana in Florence by Bautier. Bautier did not assign the handbook a title, using the first lines of the manuscript to identify it: *Nottario de più chose*. The French historian published extracts of the document in proceedings of the international conference on medieval commerce held in Beirut in 1966 (Bautier, *Les relations économiques*, pp. 263–332).

14. *Tarifa*, pp. 4–6.

15. Borbone, *Storia di Mar Yahballaha*.

16. Odorico da Pordenone, *Relatio de mirabilibus*.

17. Bautier, *Les relations économiques*, pp. 282–83. The anonymous author of the *Nottario* provides a list of the goods that could be found in Trebizond after arriving overland by caravan from Tabriz.

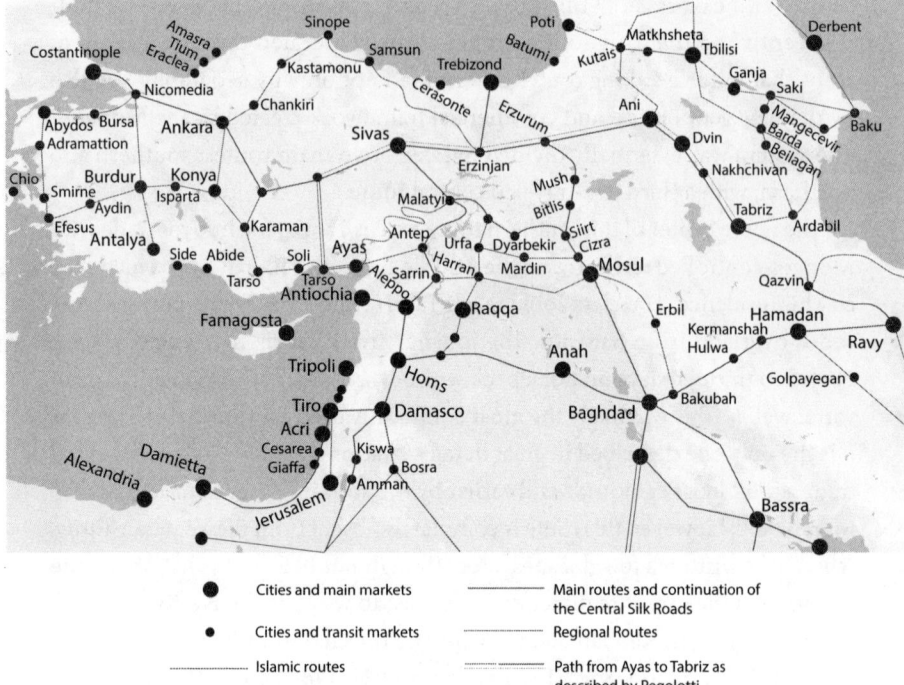

MAP 19. The main transit routes of the Ilkhanate and surrounding regions in the first half of the fourteenth century

Kaykavus (or Kay Khusraw II, r. 1237–46) and the Persian vizir Muzafer in 1271–72.[18]

Since Egyptian ports, particularly Alexandria, were closed to western merchants, those heading toward the Persian Gulf would first set off for Tabriz and then continue on through Savah, Avah, Kasan, Yazd, Kirman, and finally Hormuz (Marco Polo's *Cormos/Cremosu*), which was the principal port for voyages to the Far East.[19] From Hormuz, navigation proceeded across the Indian Ocean to Baruch and Cambay, with overland travel continuing as far as China. This journey took at least two years and was therefore very expensive. It was from Hormuz that Odorico da Pordenone set sail for China in 1322.[20] By 1325, he found many Venetian merchants in Zaitun (Quanzhou), a flourishing port on the southern coast of modern Fujian and a significant commercial stopover

18. Peacock, *Islam, Literature and Society*, pp. 119 and 122 and p. 119, n. 12.

19. Bautier, *Les relations économiques*, p. 284.

20. Odorico da Pordenone, *Relatio de mirabilibus*.

in southeast Asia.[21] A shorter but more challenging route to China from Tabriz ran overland, passing through Mashad, Merv, Samarkand, Kashgar, and Yarkand. This was the road used by Mongol officials traveling between China and Iran.[22] Lastly, from Ayas one could reach Baghdad via Tabriz, thereby avoiding Mamluk-controlled Syria.

The northern land route was safer but longer. From Tana, travelers would head to Astrakhan, north of the Caspian Sea, and continue through the cities of central Asia to Almaligh, passing through the oases of Kashgar and Yarkand; after crossing the Gobi Desert, the route curved southeast toward present-day Beijing.[23] In the 1330s, the journey from Tana to Astrakhan took twenty-five days by ox-drawn cart, while using horses reduced the travel time to ten–twelve days. The road was considered safe because, as Pegolotti noted, *si trovano moccoli assai, cioè gente d'arme* (there are many Mongols, that is, military people), referring to Mongol soldiers who ensured the safety of travelers and escorted caravans. However, after the death of Berdi Beg in 1359, travel became riskier due to conflicts within the Golden Horde.[24]

From Astrakhan, travelers had to cross the Volga River, often requiring one day of navigation to reach the next stop, Sarai. From Sarai, they could proceed to Saraichik,[25] where they had the option of sailing down the river (a relatively short eight-day trip with lower taxes on goods) or continuing overland, which took longer and was more expensive. From Saraichik, merchants entered Turkestan and continued to Urgench, a bustling city with a rich market that offered ample opportunities for profit. The journey to Urgench in central Asia was long: twenty days on a camel-drawn cart. From there, travelers proceeded to Otrar, a journey of thirty-five to forty days journey by *cammello con carro* (camel with wagon). If merchants carried fewer goods, it was advisable to travel

21. Lopez, *Nuove luci sugli italiani*, p. 50.

22. Paviot, "Les marchands italiens," p. 83.

23. Lopez, *Nuove luci sugli Italiani*, pp. 92–93; also Skržinskaja, "Storia della Tana," p. 33. Pegolotti, *La pratica della mercatura*, p. 21; Bautier, *Les relations économiques*, p. 286.

24. In 1360, Venetian merchant Giovanni Barozzi entrusted the Saracen banker Coza Azi Aza with a large load of merchandise, including silk and precious goods, for an overall value of 50 *sommi*, to be sold in Sarai. On September 24, the two went to see a notary in Tana to stipulate an agreement of indemnity as Coza declared he had been robbed of all the goods during his journey. Archivio di Stato di Venezia (hereafter ASV), Cancelleria Inferiore (hereafter CI), Notai, reg. 1, fasc. 7, busta 19, reg. 1, fol. 40r.

25. Pegolotti's "Saracanco" is a complicated toponym, but almost certainly comes from today's Saray-Jük, a city on the Ural River. See Jackson, *The Mongols and the West*, p. 296.

directly from Sarai to Otrar, bypassing Urgench. This trip took around fifty days. From Otrar, the route led to Almaligh, which required another forty-five days, usually with a pack mule. From Almaligh (present-day Xinjiang), the journey continued southeast to "Camesu" (modern Zhangye) in the Gansu corridor,[26] a trip that took another seventy days. At this point, travelers reached Cathay,[27] where *sommi d'argento* could be exchanged for banknotes because it was *terra di mercantia* (a land of trade). After a further thirty days of travel, they finally reached the last stop, the capital, Khanbaliq, that is, near modern Beijing. Pegolotti described this as *la mastra città del paese del Gattaio* (the major city in the country of Cathay) and the seat of the imperial mint.[28]

Preparations for long journeys involved securing essential provisions such as food, clothing, and even altering one's appearance to suit the cultural norms of the regions being traversed. For example, travelers departing from Tana were advised to bring flour and salted fish, as other necessities could be purchased along the route. To blend in with the local population, growing a beard was recommended, while communication was facilitated by hiring skilled interpreters. The travel party was typically limited to a few servants, and it was discouraged to bring women on such expeditions. Along the way, travelers could rest at postal stations or villages, where they could exchange their horses or purchase supplies. One of the key logistical innovations of the Mongol Empire was the *yam*, a sophisticated postal system that guaranteed rapid communication over long distances. Maintained in every corner of the empire, this system allowed couriers to change their horses frequently and thus cover great distances at remarkable speed.

The very fact that Pegolotti's account is so specific about goods, weights, measures, and transit routes confirms that there was a steady and organized flow of Latin merchants to the East. Typically, these merchants began their journey from Venice, aiming to stop at a settlement governed by Venetian authorities, such as Trebizond, Tana, or Tabriz, which were relatively close by. Once they reached their initial destination, further travel was often necessary to acquire goods from the trade hubs of central Asia, many of which were

---

26. Formerly Kanchow: Pegolotti, *La pratica della mercatura*, pp. 21 and 23.

27. Pegolotti's "Cassai" (Pegolotti, *La pratica della mercatura*, p. 21) cannot be Marco Polo's "Quinsai," the metropolis of Cina Song (Moule, "Marco Polo's Description"), because "Quinsai" corresponds to today's Hangzhou, a city near China's eastern coast, far from the route described by Pegolotti. It is likely that Pegolotti's "Cassai" is a corruption of Cathay, that is, the khanate of the Yuan in general, which was accessed by passing through Kanchow/Zhangye.

28. Polo, *Il Milione*, ed. Bertolucci Pizzorusso, pp. 126–28; Vogel, *Marco Polo Was in China*, p. 106.

linked to Sarai. It was less common for traders to embark on long journeys deep into Asia from the outset.

A well-known and well-documented case is that of the Loredan brothers. In 1338, Giovanni and Paolo Loredan aimed to reach Delhi, and formed a company that included Andrea Loredan—perhaps a cousin—along with Marco Soranzo, Marino Contarini, and Baldovino Querini.[29] Giovanni, having previously traveled to China, was experienced in long-distance trade. Following the advice of merchant handbooks, Giovanni carried textiles for trade en route, as well as cash and precious stones. The merchants departed from Venice, heading first to Constantinople, and then set sail for Tana. From there, they followed the northern route, which Pegolotti had described as safe day and night. Their journey took them through Astrakhan, Sarai, and Urgench. In Astrakhan, they crossed the Volga, where boats were used in the summer and sleds in winter, and most travelers avoided the transitional seasons. The Venetians spent around fifty days in Astrakhan, likely having arrived in the fall, too soon to cross the river. Giovanni had secured funds for the journey in July, and the expedition had set off shortly thereafter.[30]

After crossing the Volga, they faced the most difficult leg of the journey— the deserts of central Asia and the trans-Himalayan passes that would take them to India. Sadly, Giovanni never reached his destination: he fell ill and died in Ghazna. The rest of the company eventually arrived in Delhi, where they presented their precious gifts to Sultan Muhammad ibn Toghluk (r. 1325–51), who rewarded them with the enormous sum of 200,000 bezants.[31] A portion of this sum was used to cover taxes, repay the loans taken out during the journey, and other essential expenses. The remainder—over 100,000 bezants—was invested in pearls, which were easy to transport and held great value. Pearls and gemstones were especially advantageous in the Mongol Empire, where precious goods were not taxed. On their return journey, the group once again stopped in Urgench, where they disbanded (Baldovino Querini had also passed away by this point). Although details of the later stages of their journey are scarce, we do know that the survivors headed toward Persia, avoiding Tana—likely due to the crisis that had already begun by late 1343. In the end, the profits probably did not justify the high risks, the lengthy journey, and, above all, the loss of lives.[32]

29. Lopez, "Da Venezia a Delhi nel Trecento."
30. Lopez, "Venezia e le grandi linee."
31. Lopez, *Nuove luci sugli italiani*, p. 58; Hocquet, "I meccanismi dei traffici," pp. 538–39.
32. Lopez, *Nuove luci sugli italiani*, pp. 60–61.

While we cannot be certain how representative the experience of the Loredan brothers was in terms of costs and risks merchants were willing to take,
it does illustrate the strong allure of the East, which often raised hopes for
substantial profits. As mentioned earlier, expeditions of this kind were relatively rare. The limited documentation suggests that it was more typical—and
profitable—for merchants to pursue trade in stages, with stops in Astrakhan,
Urgench, or Sarai. In these cities, European products were exchanged for Asian
products, which were then shipped from Tana back to Europe.

In the fourteenth century, there was another path to China, known as the
central route, which was the shortest option. Starting from the port of Trebizond, travelers continued overland to Tabriz, then passed through the cities
of Erzerum, Erzindjan, Ani, and Dvin. After reaching the capital of the Ilkhanate, the journey would proceed to Mashad in northeastern Iran, then on to
Merv, and finally Samarkand. From there, travelers would cross the Pamir
mountain passes and traverse the Gobi Desert before arriving in China. However, this route was fraught with dangers due to the difficult terrain and the
political instability of central Asia.

Over time, the northern route became the most popular choice, due to the
papal ban on entering Egypt, which complicated the use of the southern
routes. Additionally, ongoing conflicts—such as the wars between the Mamluks and the Ilkhanate, and between the Ilkhanate and the Golden Horde—
further restricted southern access. The decline of the Ilkhanate led merchants
to withdraw from Tabriz after 1340. As a result, Tana gradually gained strategic
importance, becoming the most advanced and enduring emporium within the
Venetian commercial network in the East.[33] While long-distance journeys
were less common due to logistical challenges, reaching Tana, Trebizond, or
even Constantinople was relatively straightforward, thanks to maritime transport. Indeed, navigation was one of the most innovative sectors in Venice in
the thirteenth and fourteenth centuries, both legally and technologically.

## Ships and Navigation

While Venetian sailors were undoubtedly experts at navigating the Aegean
Sea, entering the Black Sea posed greater challenges. Since ancient times, the
Mediterranean was considered relatively safe, while the Black Sea, a closed
basin, was known for its difficult environmental conditions, particularly its

33. Berindei and Veinstein, "La Tana-Azaq," p. 116.

winds and currents. Major rivers of eastern Europe, such as the Don, the Dnieper, and the Danube, flow into the Black Sea, reducing its saltiness. The differences in water density and temperature create surface currents that move from northeast to southeast—opposing the sailing routes from Constantinople to the Crimean ports. Moreover, the Black Sea's susceptibility to cyclones has led to numerous shipwrecks caused by violent storms since ancient times. The contrasting climates between the eastern and the western regions, divided by the Crimean Peninsula, also resulted in intense storms. This unique combination of climatic and oceanographic factors forced sailors to follow the Anatolian or Romànian coastlines, rather than attempting a direct crossing between Constantinople and Crimea. Ships bound for Tana had to travel along the eastern coast of the Black Sea before reaching Crimea, where they contended with adverse currents to pass through the Kerch Strait and to enter the Sea of Azov. The seasonal regularity of the winds dictated the rhythm of voyages back and forth.

The thirteenth century saw the introduction of the compass, making it possible to calculate routes without relying on the stars, thus enabling navigation during the winter months. However, maritime traffic still diminished significantly from November to February due to harsh weather conditions and strong northeasterly and southwesterly winds. Entering the Sea of Azov was even more difficult in colder months, as coastal waters could freeze. Despite these navigation difficulties, as well as specific trade and military challenges, advancements in shipbuilding helped overcome many of these obstacles.

## Venetian Shipbuilding between the Thirteenth and Fourteenth Centuries

In 1224, Venetian authorities ordered the seizure of several houses near the arsenal and initiated the construction of new docks.[34] During these same years, the demand for timber steadily rose as it was needed for both construction and shipbuilding.[35] The state recognized that the shipbuilding industry was central to the city's power, with its success depending on innovation, efficiency, and the expansion of production. To preserve naval resources, laws were enacted to

---

34. Stöckly, Le système de l'incanto, p. 43; Luzzatto, Storia economica di Venezia, p. 41.
35. Stöckly, Le système de l'incanto, p. 43; Luzzatto, Storia economica di Venezia, p. 41.

prohibit private individuals from selling vessels to anyone other than Venetian citizens, except for ships that were old or inefficient.[36]

Timber for shipbuilding was purchased directly by the state and came from the alpine forests of Cadore, the Apennines, and the Dalmatian hinterland.[37] Hemp and pitch also became essential materials, with demand for these increasing throughout the thirteenth century. City authorities imposed equally strict regulations on their trade. In the early 1200s, most shipyards were private—only one belonged to the state—but from the second half of the century, the state took over the naval industry. Private individuals would then buy or charter ships constructed in state-owned shipyards.

In the first half of the fourteenth century, the system of *incanti* (auctions) was introduced, allowing state galleys to be leased to private patrons through competitive tenders. Between 1310 and 1324, the naval arsenal was expanded and modernized. From 1321, the great council introduced a mixed management system in which ships were constructed in state shipyards with private capital.[38] By 1333, the state had gained the ability to independently manage its navy by leasing its galleys to private entrepreneurs. The price of leasing each ship was proportional to market demand, which was calculated based on the anticipated profits from the markets the ships were destined for.[39] The integration of public and private systems yielded economic benefits for both the state and individual entrepreneurs. Private individuals thus formed consortia that covered all financial costs of ship construction and goods acquisitions, while from 1318 onward, the state ensured the supply of public ships and auctioned them to these private consortia.

## The Ships

The maritime powers of Venice and Genoa were measured by the quality and quantity of ships they were able to launch.[40] In general, Venice remained faithful to Mediterranean tradition, with most naval innovations driven by internal needs rather than external influences.[41] Throughout the thirteenth

---

36. Lane, *Venice: A Maritime Republic*, p. 45.

37. Dorigo, "Le espressioni d'arte," p. 849.

38. Stöckly, *Le système de l'incanto*, pp. 105–6.

39. Concina, *L'arsenale della Repubblica di Venezia*, p. 26; Dumerc, "Gli armamenti marittimi," pp. 626–27.

40. Melis, "I trasporti e le comunicazioni nel medioevo," p. 7.

41. Tucci, "L'impresa marittima."

century, ships of various types were primarily small, with limited tonnage. This was largely due to the high costs of outfitting, the shorter range of commercial transportation, and the limited number of ports that could accommodate large-draft ships.

Latin ships—both commercial and military—were essentially of two types: galleys and round ships. Merchants sailed on "round ships," which were sail-powered vessels without oars. These ships were equipped with two side rudders, up to twenty anchors, two to three masts, and featured both a forecastle and an aftcastle. During the thirteenth century, the tonnage of these ships increased. In 1268, when King Louis IX of France was organizing a crusade, he sought modern and efficient ships from the Italian maritime cities for "overseas voyages" (*pro passagio transmarino*). Venice provided the king with fifteen ships, including its largest vessel, the *Roccaforte*, capable of carrying up to 500 tons of goods.

In the thirteenth century, Venetian shipbuilding focused heavily on the galley, a vessel powered by both oars and sails. Galleys were agile, fast, and easy to maneuver, making them particularly effective for military purposes.[42] There were two main types: slim (light) and wide (heavy) galleys. Slim galleys, also known as *fuste, galeotte,* or *brigantini,* were initially designed for warfare but were then adapted for commercial use during the thirteenth century, then known as market galleys. With a ratio of width to length being one to eight, these vessels were mainly used to transport light, less bulky goods, such as jewelry, perfumes, and spices. The beam-to-lenght ratio was one to eight.

The larger galleys, equipped with twenty-five to thirty benches on each side and typically manned by two or three oarsmen per bench, emerged in Venice at the end of the thirteenth century and were favored for voyages on the Black Sea.[43] Oars were essential for entering and exiting harbors and navigating during unfavorable winds. However, in open waters, when the wind was favorable, Latin sails—two or more per mast—were hoisted. The oarsmen were free and salaried men, skilled in both maritime and military arts, as they were expected to take up arms when necessary.

Since 1303, sailing on the Black Sea was done with a large galley "the size of Romània" (*mensuris Romaniae*) with a capacity of approximately 80 tons.[44]

---

42. Karpov, *La navigazione veneziana*, p. 22; Lane, *Navires et constructeurs*, p. 14.

43. Lane, *Venetian Ships*, p. 9.

44. According to an anonymous fourteenth-century chronicle, the state sent the large galleys to Romània for the first time in 1290; however, it is likely that this is an anachronism. Lane, *Le navi di Venezia*, p. 158; Stöckly, *Le système de l'incanto*, p. 105.

This modified large galley was a Venetian invention, showcasing the city's maritime skill and shipbuilding technology. It combined the maneuverability of galleys with the power and cargo capacity of round ships. Throughout the fourteenth century, efforts were made to increase its speed, often by adding more oarsmen per bench,[45] with crew sizes ranging from a minimum of 60 to a maximum of 250 men.[46] Over time, the tonnage of these Romània–Black Sea galleys rose to 140 tons in the hold. It is possible that the Venetian state started to send large galleys to Romània in 1290.[47]

An important innovation for Black Sea navigation in the fourteenth century was the "cog" (*cocca*), which replaced the traditional round ship for voyages to the west. The name "cog" likely originated from the *kogge* ships used in Baltic trade as early as the twelfth century.[48] The cog was hailed as a revolutionary development in Mediterranean navigation.[49] The Florentine chronicler Giovanni Villani noted that by 1303, Genoese, Venetians, and Catalans had started using cogs because they were safer and more economical, marking a "great change in navigation in our seas."[50] The cog was better suited to voyages that faced challenging maritime conditions and became a regular cargo ship for Black Sea routes, although the large galley remained the primary means of transportation for trading with the Levant. Nevertheless, the first recorded mention of a cog in Venice dates back to 1310.[51]

Cogs had a large tonnage capacity, ranging from 300 to over 500 tons, and featured a single rudder positioned at the center of the stern. They had one to three decks and typically sported a single mast with a square sail, though some cogs were equipped with three to four masts and two to three forecastles, which could reach as high as 23 feet.[52] The design of the cog allowed it to turn with the wind and better withstand rough weather compared to galleys and round ships, while requiring a relatively small crew of just thirty to forty men. Cogs were well suited for long-distance journeys, making them reliable and

45. Lane, *Venetian Ships*, p. 32.

46. Karpov, "Drevnejšie postanovlenija senata," p. 26; Lane, *Venetian Maritime Law*, p. 30.

47. Lane, *Le navi di Venezia*, p. 158; Stöckly, *Le système de l'incanto*, p. 105.

48. Unger, *The Ships in the Medieval Economy*, pp. 178–80.

49. Lane, *Venetian Ships*, p. 38.

50. Villani, *Nuova Cronica*, pp. 148–49; Hocquet, *La sel et la fortune de Venise*, vol. 2, p. 104.

51. Tucci, "L'impresa marittima," pp. 646–47.

52. Hocquet, *La sel et la fortune de Venise*, vol. 2, p. 108; Karpov, "Drevnejšie postanovlenija senata," p. 28.

economically viable vessels.[53] However, their slow maneuverability and small crew made them difficult to defend, leaving them vulnerable to pirate attacks. As a result, large galleys were preferable to many, as they combined the cargo capacity of round ships with the speed and maneuverability of galleys.

In addition to ships destined for long-distance travel, there were other types of vessels active on the Black Sea, the most common of which was the *tauride* or *tarretta*. This ship featured a single deck, one or two masts with a Latin sail, and two side rudders. It was a mixed sail and oar vessel capable of carrying up to 200 tons of cargo but was primarily used for transporting people.[54] During the Crusades, for example, *taurides* were employed to transport pilgrims. By the mid-fourteenth century, a number of merchants in Tana owned at least one *tauride*.

### The Pattern of Black Sea Voyages: The Mude

In Venice, the state not only controlled shipbuilding but also regulated navigation and the organization of commercial convoys, which were often escorted by armed galleys.[55] The term *muda* in Venice referred both to the convoy of ships (which never traveled alone but always in groups) and to the pattern of voyages, defining the specific periods during which authorities permitted navigation.[56] Only the most valuable, small, and lightweight goods (*havere subtile*)—such as spices, precious items, and silk—fell under the strict regulations of the *mude*, and were thus subject to strict public oversight. In contrast, heavy goods—such as timber, salt, wheat, oil, and wine—though still under state control, were exempt from the scheduled voyages regulated by the state.[57]

The Romània–Black Sea maritime route was officially inaugurated by Venice at the beginning of the fourteenth century.[58] Although Venetian ships passed through the Bosphorus earlier, these were not regular voyages systematically organized under state control. In fact, they were "not galleys of

53. Lane, *Venetian Ships*, p. 38. On August 15, 1360, in Tana, Ser Barnaba Gerardo appears as the patron of a cog docked in the port: ASV, CI, Notai, busta 19, reg. 7, fasc. 1, fol. 33v.

54. Tucci, "L'impresa marittima," pp. 637–38.

55. Luzzatto, *Storia economica di Venezia*, p. 42.

56. Hocquet, "I meccanismi dei traffici," pp. 587–88. In the fourteenth century, the term is used in some documents in a military context (Stöckly, *Le système de l'incanto*, p. 27).

57. Stöckly, *Le système de l'incanto*, pp. 25–26.

58. Stöckly, *Le système de l'incanto*, p. 101.

Romània, but galleys headed to Romània."[59] From 1301 onward, the Black Sea route became a regular and meticulously organized operation, with more ports emerging over time, making navigation easier and offering crews more support and greater security. During periods when Venice had secure control over Levantine routes, the convoys would stop at Ragusa, Durrës, Corfù, Glarentza (Dyma in Morea), Coron, Modon, Crete, and Negropont before reaching Constantinople, where they stopped for a few days. From there, they crossed the straits to the Anatolian coast, continuing to Trebizond and then northward to Tana. From 1330, convoys arriving in Constantinople would split into two groups: one stopped at Trebizond, and the other continued on to Crimea and Tana. The two *mude* would then reunite in Constantinople before returning together to Venice. Between 1320 and 1350, Venice organized thirty voyages to the Black Sea. Twelve times the convoys split in Constantinople into two groups of ships, separately heading to Trebizond and Tana. Thirteen times the ships only went to Trebizond, and five times only to Tana.[60]

Unlike other trade routes where private initiative played a key role, voyages to the Black Sea remained under strict state control. A special commission of five "wise men" (*extraordinarii*), appointed by the senate from 1321 to 1329, was responsible for overseeing these voyages. They collected freight charges from the patrons of the galleys, allowing the state to maintain direct oversight of Levantine trade activities. However, this system also proved costly for the treasury, prompting a shift toward partial privatization of the voyages. As mentioned earlier, the state introduced the auction system to encourage private involvement in long-distance navigation while keeping a degree of control. Often, especially during times of international political crises and heightened danger, the state directly committed itself to arming the Black Sea galleys.

Generally, the state-armed galleys sent to the Black Sea departed once or twice a year. Records show that in 1324, 1330, and 1339, two voyages were organized, but it is likely that biannual *muda* were more frequent.[61] These voyages typically set sail in July. Based on the regularity of these trips, we can

---

59. Stöckly, *Le système de l'incanto*, p. 105.

60. Stöckly, *Le système de l'incanto*, p. 108, no. 56.

61. Authorities attempted to organize journeys in the spring and fall, but the project was unsuccessful as a March departure prevented the return of the galleys to Venice before those of Flanders had left, and they had been synchronized with these. The September departure did not allow the galleys to return before winter. In any case, the customary rhythm of navigation was altered at that time due to conflicts with Genoa. Karpov, *La navigazione veneziana*, p. 64. See also Dini, "I viaggi dei mercanti"; Stöckly, *Le système de l'incanto*, pp. 26–27.

divide the voyages to Romània and the Black Sea into three historical intervals. From 1301 to 1350, convoys departed between June and July, consisting of two to ten galleys, with up to four reaching Tana, where they remained for five to eight days. After a four-year hiatus due to the conflict with Genoa (1351–54), the voyages resumed in 1355, with departures moved forward by a month. During this period, ships departed between July 15 and August 15, staying in Tana for from eight to fourteen days. Another interruption occurred during the War of Chioggia (1377–81). Navigation resumed in 1382, following the same pattern, with departures between July 18–20 and August 15, and an average of two galleys reaching Tana, where they would stay for eight to fourteen days.[62] However, after 1382, Venetian galleys would only stop in Tana once, in 1393.

## Legal and Associational Instruments

### Statutes and Pacts

In Venice, productive and commercial activities—including navigation—were regulated by ordinary and extraordinary contracts known as statutes, as in the rest of communal Italy.[63] The first Venetian statutes were drafted between the late twelfth and early thirteenth century. These statutes codified customary law, creating an increasingly complex legal framework. Trade played a significant role in the early statutory rule book created during the reign of Doge Enrico Dandolo (r. 1192–1205). Out of seventy-four chapters, thirteen were devoted to trade, addressing a range of topics from contract types to ship regulations. As Venetian commerce and society evolved, so did the statutes, being continuously amended to address cases not covered by existing laws. This ongoing development culminated in a major legal project under Doge Jacopo Tiepolo in 1242, who organized Venetian law into a code of five books. This code, with numerous later additions, remained the legal foundation until the eighteenth century. One of the most notable additions to Tiepolo's code is the *Liber Sextus* of 1346, a collection of maritime laws that had been developed over time.[64]

Although detailed, constantly revised, and expanded, Venice's written legislation was not always sufficient to regulate every aspect of the city's complex

62. Stöckly, *Le système de l'incanto*, p. 103.

63. For a picture of the legal system protecting the Venetian merchants, see Pansolli, *La gerarchia delle fonti*.

64. Crescenzi, "Il diritto civile," pp. 409–10. Rösch, "Il gran guadagno," pp. 240–41.

administrative machine between the thirteenth and fifteenth centuries. When written rules did not cover certain matters, customary law—or usage—played a significant role as a primary source of normative authority in medieval western societies. Maritime statutes primarily focused on technical aspects such as tonnage or ship dimensions rather than the intricate regulations governing activities like trade or transportation.[65] Trade with the East fell under the rules concerning *extra culfum* ships—those navigating seas beyond the Adriatic, farther from the homeland. By the time Venice had established settlements on the shores of the Black Sea, the body of written laws was generally sufficient to handle most cases. However, when an event occurred that was not covered by existing regulations and customary law (*consuetudo*) could not resolve the issue, recourse was made to *arbitrium*, or arbitration. Although this practice was in decline by the early fourteenth century, it often led to cases being brought before the great council, whose rulings carried the force of law.

The close identification of the merchant class with the city's nobility prevented Venice from developing a merchant guild comparable to those in other Italian mercantile cities. In maritime cities, particularly Venice, merchants saw themselves aligned with the commune and, through it, exercised control over commercial activities, influencing both domestic and foreign policies. This does not mean, however, that intermediate legal entities—characteristic of medieval political systems—were absent in Venice. These entities, such as families, schools, brotherhoods, and craft guilds, were fundamental grassroots organizations that played a crucial role in the functioning of medieval Venetian society.[66] Such groups were also important as "producers" of the *consuetudo* (customary law), serving as vital sources of law alongside the public authorities.[67]

The establishment of emporia on the Black Sea and Venetian penetration into the Mongol Empire marked a significant expansion of Venice's commercial—and consequently, legal—sphere, necessitating state

---

65. Rösch, "Il gran guadagno," pp. 240–41.

66. Crouzet-Pavan, *Venice Triumphant,* pp. 259–65; Caravale, "Le istituzioni della Repubblica," pp. 303–4.

67. This is a rather complex topic that rests on the history of medieval law. In the thirteenth- and fourteenth-century cities of northern Italy (and beyond), customary law originated from the needs of the citizens who had produced it, and was therefore dominated by a fundamental respect for the hierarchy of law. This does not mean it was not important in Venice as well, which already had many of the requisites of a modern state. However, the "myth" of the centralized state was revised by more recent historiographies. For more detail on this debate, see Caravale, "Le istituzioni della Repubblica," p. 304.

intervention to regulate these activities. Venetian authorities took great care in developing rules that would be recognized by the sovereigns of the regions in which they operated, aiming to protect their interests and prevent conflicts. Agreements made with the Mongols were, with few exceptions, *pacta*—the most binding legal instrument that Venice had issued since the early Middle Ages. A key element of the *pactum* was reciprocity, which required mutual recognition of the clauses detailed in the agreement. One of the hallmarks of Venetian diplomacy was the detailed instructions given to ambassadors to anticipate any eventuality during negotiations. Delegations sent to the khans of the Golden Horde or the Ilkhanate adhered to this practice. While ambassadors often succeeded in securing their demands, the *pactum* was always the result of long and laborious negotiations, made more complex by communication barriers and cultural differences. Despite the Venetians' diplomatic acumen, it was the openness of the Mongols and their interest in maintaining trade relations that led to a common ground, with shared economic interests providing the foundation for mutual understanding.

The Mongols were unwilling to compromise on their sovereign prerogatives. Thus, from their perspective, the *pacta* were always framed as imperial concessions, issued in the form of edicts from the khan. These agreements also defined the terms for the settlement and operations of the Venetians within Mongol territory. For instance, they outlined the extent of the lands allocated to the Venetians and the methods for constructing their quarters, which included storehouses, homes, streets, and other necessary structures, such as baths, ovens, and mills. Additionally, the *pacta* laid down legal rules to be observed by Venetians in Mongol territory and clarified the role of the consul, who represented the Republic. In practice, the *pacta* established the relationship between the judicial authority of the Venetian consul and the local Mongol authorities, defining their respective jurisdictions in cases of disputes or crimes. The agreements also specified the tax regime for individuals operating in Mongol territory, covering taxes, deductions, and exemptions on traded goods. Moreover, the *pacta* ensured the validity of wills drafted by Venetian citizens in Mongol territory. Given the high risk of death abroad and the potential size of a merchant's estate, state intervention was necessary to protect the interests of heirs, who were often investors themselves. As such, it was crucial to clearly regulate the management of assets left by a merchant who had died during a sojourn in Asia.

However detailed and specific the *pactum* was, its actual implementation was not always guaranteed in practice. Tensions persisted between the

Venetian and Genoese communities, as well as between Latin merchants and Mongol rulers, continuing to disrupt the lives and security of residents in Tana and other locations. These issues called for almost constant diplomatic interventions. While the combination of mature legal systems and experienced diplomacy helped create areas where Venetian merchants could operate, the existing frameworks were insufficient to support a truly international legal system—if such a system could even be said to exist at the time—that was universally recognized. These agreements were inherently fragile, offering limited guarantees and proving inadequate on more than one occasion. The fragility stemmed more from deep-seated conflict between Venetians and Genoese, or violations by Latin citizens, than from transgressions or noncompliance by Mongol authorities, though such incidents did occur.

## From the Commenda to the Compagnia

The two most common types of contracts in Venice from the second half of the thirteenth century were the *commenda* and the *compagnia*. The *commenda* contract, also known as *colleganza* (in Venice, the term *rogadia* was also used), was the most widespread form of economic and financial partnership for maritime trade. It helped mitigate the risks associated with sea voyages, making it well suited for merchant activities. The most popular form of *commenda* in Venice was the unilateral type. In this arrangement, a stable partner (*stans*) remained in the city, bearing no personal risk but providing the full capital for the commercial venture, typically in the form of goods or, less often, in cash. The traveling partner (*procertans*), who embarked on the voyage to destinations such as Tana or Tabriz, took on the material commitment and personal risks of the venture. Profits were usually distributed three-quarters to the stable partner and one-quarter to the traveling partner. There was also a less common bilateral *commenda* arrangement, where the stable partner contributed only three-quarters of the capital, and the profits were shared equally between both partners.

The *commenda* gained immediate success for two key reasons: first, it enabled the formation of enterprises where significant capital could be invested, offering the potential for equally high profits. Second, it allowed individuals who were excluded from the city's patrician class or the merchant profession—those who may have lacked the resources or expertise to establish an investment company—to participate in commercial ventures. Thanks to the *commenda* contract and the expanded operations of merchants in the second half

of the thirteenth century, much of Venetian society had the opportunity to
finance commercial activities—and many did. Family savings, whether modest or substantial, fueled the business ventures of Venetian merchant engaged
in trade with the East. For this system to function, it was essential to rely on
individuals with the knowledge and authority to draft legally binding documents. As a result, notaries were present in the port, drawing up *commenda*
contracts for anyone wishing to invest their capital in overseas trade.

In Tana and the Mongol Empire, *commenda* contracts were relatively rare
as the *compagnia* was preferred for reasons that will be explained later. However, there are some examples of *commenda* contracts related to transactions
involving widely traded goods in Eastern markets.[68] Analysis of these contracts shows that the capital invested by individuals was often modest, but this
type of agreement was not exclusive. The *commenda* merchant typically raised
capital by entering into multiple contracts before embarking on the journey.
This system of collective financing, conceptually similar to modern joint-stock
companies, allowed broader access to investments, including for sectors that
might otherwise have been excluded.[69]

At the beginning of this chapter, we described the evolving nature of the
merchant profession, and alongside it, the forms of association and methods
of capital investment also changed. The *commenda* proved, in some respects,
to be inadequate for long-distance trade. It placed the traveling partner in a
form of isolation, which, in distant lands, posed too many uncertainties and
did not guarantee the stable partner a reliable profit. Moreover, it was not
uncommon for the *procertans* (traveling partners) to embezzle a part of the
profits.[70]

From the early thirteenth century, alongside the *commenda*, the *compagnia*
emerged and eventually took precedence. Originally born as a family-based
association in the twelfth century, the *compagnia* evolved during the fourteenth
century into a more complex business entity, absorbing larger amounts of capital and involving not only family members but also external partners. Before

68. ASV, CI, Notai, busta 19, fasc. 7, reg. 1, fol. 7r; Pucci Donati, *Ai confini dell'Occidente*,
no. 48, p. 32.

69. In Venice more so than elsewhere, the *commenda* contract favored the creation of new
wealth, referred to in communal Italy as *homini novi*. However, long-distance journeys
(e.g. China) remained the prerogative of the aristocracy, the only class with the necessary
wealth. Kedar, *Mercanti in crisi*, pp. 71–73.

70. Kedar, *Mercanti in crisi*, pp. 51–52.

the fourteenth century, the *compagnia* faced resistance in maritime cities because its members were exposed to high risks due to the inherently perilous nature of long-distance sea voyages. However, this business model gradually gained traction for overland trade, which presented fewer risks.

When companies opened up to partners outside the family, and consequently to external capital,[71] they gradually became not only commercial entities but also financial ones, handling loans, exchanges, and international capital movements. Some also became industrial, directly linked to production activities. Despite this evolution, family ties remained a central characteristic of the *compagnia*, as seen in contracts concluded in Tana in the second half of the fourteenth century.[72] A significant portion of these agreements concerned commercial activities and *somministrazione* (supply).[73] It was not uncommon for Venetians to form companies with local merchants.[74] At times, the *compagnia* would dissolve before all the merchandise was sold, and in such cases, external professionals—often merchants themselves—were brought in to monetize the remaining goods. For example, in 1361, the merchant Giovanni Testa, active in Tana, held a batch of lacquer valued at 50 ducats that remained unsold after the expiration of his *compagnia* with Pietro Venier. He entrusted the sale to Michele Lizzi, a Florentine merchant, just as he had done with a stock of rabbit skins that, remaining unsold, he had entrusted to the merchant Giovanni da Verona.[75]

While the *commenda* was preferable for maritime travel, the *compagnia* became the most commonly used business structure by Venetians in the Golden Horde during the fourteenth century.[76] It was through *compagnia* contracts that the first long-term commercial relationships were forged between Venetian merchants and local producers, as well as merchants from central Asia,

71. ASV, CI, Notai, busta 19, reg. 7, fasc. 1, fols. 9r–11v.

72. ASV, CI, Notai, busta 19, reg. 7, fasc. 1, fol. 36r; ASV, CI, Notai, busta 117, fasc. Marco Marzella, n. 2, fol. 1v.

73. ASV, CI, Notai, busta 19, reg. 7, fasc. 1, fol. 11v; Pucci Donati, *Ai confini dell'Occidente*, no. 76, pp. 38–39; ASV, CI, Notai, busta 19, reg. 7, fasc. 1, fol. 17r; Pucci Donati, *Ai confini dell'Occidente*, no. 102, p. 46.

74. ASV, CI, Notai, busta 19, reg. 7, fasc. 1, fols. 9r and 10r; Pucci Donati, *Ai confini dell'Occidente*, no. 62, p. 35; no. 70, p. 37.

75. ASV, CI, Notai, busta 19, reg. 3, fols. 9r–11v. Pucci Donati, *Ai confini dell'Occidente*, no. 278, pp. 96–98.

76. ASV, CI, Notai, busta 19, reg. 4, fols. 15r and 21r; busta 117, fasc. Marco Marzella, no. 2, fol. 1r–v; busta 181, fasc. 5, fol. 67r; busta 130, fasc. 7/B, fols. 1r, 1v, 14v.

Arabia, Armenia, and the Jewish community. One notable example involves two Venetians, Marino del Rosso and Bartolomeo Bembo. In September 1360, they decided to open a tavern in the Armenian quarter of Tana (*contrata arminorum*). Marino provided the funds, while Bartolomeo paid for the goods arriving on the galleys in the following weeks, agreeing to share both costs and profits equally.[77] A few days later, the Muslim merchant (*saracenus*) Coza Azillyas rented land with a cellar (*fovea*) to the Venetian Niccolò Corner to open a catering business, again with an agreement to share costs and profits.[78] These examples illustrate how, in a *compagnia*, partners divided profits and losses based on their respective investments, and all were jointly responsible for third-party obligations. The partnership duration was also specified in the founding documents, and upon dissolution, the partners settled in a single account. These increasingly widespread, accessible, and sophisticated arrangements allowed Venetian merchants to secure the resources and means to expand their activities, even in previously unexplored regions.

77. ASV, CI, Notai, busta 19, reg. 1, fasc. 7, fol. 36r; Pucci Donati, *Ai confini dell'Occidente*, no. 216, p. 77.

78. ASV, CI, Notai, busta 19, reg. 1, fasc. 7, fols. 36f.; Pucci Donati, *Ai confini dell'Occidente*, no. 222, p. 79.

# 10

# The Means of Exchange

## Preliminary Considerations

A vast, interconnected trade system required exchange instruments that were universally recognized and accepted. However, the lack of a unified currency or broadly accepted standards across multiple commercial circuits—standards that would guarantee the convertibility between different monetary systems—proved to be a significant obstacle for the Mongol Empire. This was particularly challenging for an empire that relied heavily on commercial revenue to maintain its administrative and military solvency. Although this challenge was partially addressed by introducing new monetary regimes across the various khanates to facilitate international transactions, it fell short of a complete solution. In this regard, the Mongols were innovative—consider, for example, the spread of paper money in China, as discussed in chapter 8. Nevertheless, the creation of a single, unified monetary system that would both consolidate their empire and establish recognized standards never materialized.

In Europe, prior to the great commercial expansion of the twelfth and thirteenth centuries, the economy was characterized by a prevalence of virtual currencies, money of account, and a very limited circulation of physical money. Several factors contributed to this scarcity, including the difficulty in obtaining metals for minting coins, the high costs of minting, the widespread use of alternative payment methods (such as barter), and the monetary policies of Roman–Germanic Europe. From the eleventh century onward, the growth of the continental economy led to increased demand for money across Europe, even as its supply remained perpetually scarce.[1]

---

1. Buenger Robbert, "Il sistema monetario," pp. 410–11.

Although Venice was a multilingual and multicultural city, gaining access to the markets of the most remote parts of Asia and dealing with populations that had been largely excluded from European commerce before the rise of the Mongol Empire posed great communication challenges. These challenges affected both traders and the administration of Venetian communities on the Black Sea. The demand for translators and interpreters boomed, creating opportunities for new professions and communication specialists who could manage both oral interpretation and the written documentation exchanged between various chancelleries. For example, the linguistic structure of the treaties between the Golden Horde and Venice—available to us today mostly in Latin and, more rarely, in the vernacular—were originally drafted in Mongolian and later translated.

Another fundamental aspect of exchange was the equivalence between weights and measures across different systems. Today, if you tried to mentally convert the decimal metric system to the British imperial system, you might find it quite difficult. Now imagine a commercial world where merchants had to navigate multiple systems—not only within Italy but also across the Mediterranean, the Levant, the Mongol Empire, and in Chinese and Indian Asia. Italian merchants had to adapt to this complexity, in part by exporting their own measures, which had gained some standardization (such as the equivalence between the *libbra veneta* and the *libbra genovese*), and in part by adopting the local measures used at foreign trading posts. In this context, a merchant's flexibility and expertise were key to gradually reconciling the different measurement systems. Of great importance were the *pratiche di mercatura*, or merchant handbooks, which were essential guides for anyone in business. The Pegolotti merchant handbook, which has survived nearly intact, illustrates the crucial role of specialized merchant knowledge in conducting trade abroad. In contrast, the role of the Mongol Empire in fostering compatible and comparable systems was less visible, as it was a context less regulated than the financial sphere. This is perhaps unsurprising, given that the Mongol ruling class was more concerned with revenues and the circulation of money than with the technical intricacies of trade.

## The Mongols and Money

The many administrative systems and political divisions across the Mongol Empire made it impossible to establish a unified monetary system among the various regional economies. However, starting from the reign of Möngke Khan

(r. 1251–59), there was a tendency to standardize and unify the different forms of exchange and tax collection. The goal was to balance the need for centralized revenue with the pre-existing structures in the conquered territories. The first organized attempt at fiscal reform was implemented by Ögödei Khan in 1238, but it was during Möngke's rule that the most coherent regulations were introduced. These included a comprehensive census of the empire, and the establishment of stable forms of taxation, which replaced arbitrary levies and special taxes. While these reforms aimed to give the empire a more centralized administrative structure, they did not significantly alter the monetary systems in use within the individual khanates. Local mints continued to produce currency that circulated in the surrounding regions.

Mongol taxation was divided into four types. First, the *qubchur* was a form of tithe applied to nomads' livestock, from which only the descendants of Chinggis Khan and aristocrats were exempt. Second, a tax was imposed on conquered populations, which could take the form of local products, monetary contributions, valuables, or services and unpaid labor. Third, taxes on productive activities followed the practices of the conquered regions, with certain exemptions for religious institutions and specific social categories. Finally, by far the most lucrative tax for the Mongols was the *tamgha*, a tax on commerce tied to the movement of goods and people. Pegolotti often mentions this tax, using different terms for it (*tamunga, tamenga, camunoca*), and describes its application in relation to the goods being traded.

In terms of monetary circulation, the Mongol Empire relied on two key elements common across all khanates. First, as we have mentioned several times, commercial revenues played a central role in the fiscal system. The collection of taxes and duties from trade transactions and the transportation of goods naturally required a greater flow of money, driving the need for monetary instruments that could operate in various commercial contexts. This applied both locally, within each khanate, and, more importantly, between the khanates themselves and with foreign states. The pre-imperial systems, which relied on silk or uncoined metals for high-value transactions, were insufficient to meet the demands of the increasing volume of trade.

The second defining feature was the Mongol Empire's openness to foreign merchants, which was encouraged in each khanate, and thus fueled the growth of trade between commercial circuits that used different forms of coinage. This increased volume of commerce among the various circuits and fostered a real phenomenon of globalization, creating an international trade network that connected China, India, central Asia, Europe, and the Middle East. While within each khanate the Mongols could rely on pre-existing systems of exchange (such as barter or local currencies), their goal was to integrate these regional systems into a broader international dimension—a crucial task for the empire's survival. The financial and fiscal measures necessary to support this expansion laid the foundation for the monetary innovations and solutions that Mongol rulers and foreign merchants developed, albeit amidst enormous difficulties.

From a monetary perspective, Mongol rule was a period of constant experimentation. The Mongols led the process of trade internationalization, largely due to the empire's constant need for liquidity, much of which came from the substantial cash flow generated by commerce. Their attempt to create international commercial structures—through legal frameworks, political openness, and practical measures—was key to enabling currency convertibility and circulation across vastly different economic spheres. In many ways, the Mongol Empire was the precursor to the international monetary systems that European powers would only be able establish from the sixteenth century onward. The silver standard of the Spaniards in the sixteenth century and the international gold standard of the nineteenth century both followed in the footsteps of the Mongols.

The Mongols' initiative coincided with a period of significant innovation in Europe, spurred by what is often referred to as the "commercial revolution" of the late Middle Ages. This period introduced greater flexibility and multiplicity in the use of cash, which promoted currency convertibility. In the thirteenth century, both Europe and the Middle East relied on currencies made of precious metals—primarily gold and silver—which were well suited for international trade. In central and east Asia, silver was the dominant medium of exchange, while India had a higher demand for gold. Although both metals were known, partially monetized, and used for high-value transactions, establishing consistent equivalences between them proved challenging. Coins varied in weight and denomination, and their intrinsic value was influenced by their level of purity, which often differed depending on the mint or region in which they were produced. These variations had the side effect of driving metals toward particular markets, which in turn destabilized the broader circulation of money across regions.

In China, the Mongol government addressed the challenges of creating a unified currency standard for both the domestic market and foreign trade by issuing paper notes with equivalent values for silver and gold. As we have seen, foreign merchants could turn to government exchange offices to convert their own currency into the local one, which could then be reconverted into metal coins. Since the value of paper money was tied to silver, foreign merchants received their payments in the form of silver ingots, valued by weight.[2]

With silver being accepted throughout the Mongol Empire, as well as in Europe and Egypt, the silver ingot effectively became the standard monetary tool for international trade. In central Asia and Iran, the monetization system was closely tied to silver, with ingots known as *balish*[3] becoming a common form of payment, particularly in Turkestan from the later thirteenth century onward.[4] In China, a silver coin known as *dachao tongbao* was introduced in 1259. However, starting in the 1270s, under the Minister of Finance Ahmad Fanakati (d. 1282), the state made efforts to regulate the flow of silver by creating reserves and directly guaranteeing the solvency of the paper currency.[5]

According to recent studies, the rise of the silver ingot as a dominant form of currency can be attributed, in part, to the remittances of the Mongol aristocracy's appanages, spread across various khanates, particularly in China. This aristocracy required a reliable and universally accepted method for transferring funds. The revenues generated from their economic activities, which functioned much like modern companies with exclusive rights, needed to be

2. "Tutto l'argento che' mercatanti portano . . . il signore del Gattaio lo fa pigliare per sé e mettelo in suo tesoro, e' mercatanti che'l vi portano ne dà loro moneta di pappiero." (The Lord of Catai takes all the silver that merchants bring to China for the imperial treasury and gives them paper money in exchange.) Pegolotti, *La pratica della mercatura*, p. 23. Pegolotti's statement is confirmed by contracts found in central Asia, and referred to the Chagatai khanate (Kuroda, "The Eurasian Silver Century," p. 262). Ingots or *sommi* are discussed later in this chapter.

3. The term is of Persian origin and literally means pillow; in China, *balish* was the term that Italian merchants believed meant paper money: "moneta di pappiero, cioè di carta gialla coniata della bolla del detto signore [del Gattaio] la quale moneta s'appella balisci" (paper money, that is, yellow paper coined by mint of said man [from Catai] whose money is known as *balish*). Pegolotti, *La pratica della mercatura*, pp. 22–23.

4. In his accurate study, Kuroda suggests that the widespread dissemination of silver throughout Eurasia from the mid-thirteenth to the mid-fourteenth centuries was the result of an injection of "white" metal by the Mongols. Confirming this theory is the reversal of the trend in the early fourteenth century, when the circulation of silver decreased considerably almost everywhere, from China to the Black Sea. Furthermore, chemical analyses have revealed that the silver in circulation in central Asia, Crimea, Persia, and even in England during that period was most likely produced in China. Kuroda, "The Eurasian Silver Century," pp. 254–55.

5. Franke, "Aḥmad"; Atwood, *Encyclopedia*, p. 5.

quantified and transferred using a standard monetary unit; hence, the silver ingot prevailed.[6]

Efforts to introduce paper money into Ilkhanid Persia in the late thirteenth century ultimately failed, but it reflects the Mongols' ambition to establish a single, universally accepted form of payment and a unified system for converting metal currencies within the empire. It is reasonable to assume that if the monetary systems of Iran and China—the two major economic powers in Asia—had been unified, the Golden Horde and the Chagatai *ulus* would have likely adopted similar reforms. This could have led to a monetary revolution, foreshadowing modern currency systems by several centuries.

Known as *somo* in central Asia and *sommo* (pl. *sommi*) in Venice, the silver ingot weighed just over 200 grams of pure silver and became a universal means of payment in two forms: either as an ingot by weight or converted into local currency. Venetian merchants did not receive *sommi* from the Venetian state, but rather obtained them from private laboratories that melted down silver objects and coins, certifying both their weight and quality. Merchants would take these *sommi* to places like Tana or Tabriz, where they could be converted into local coins, most commonly aspers, with a seigniorage fee of around 6 percent. In the early fourteenth century, for every *sommo* converted into 202 aspers, the mint in Tana kept 12, leaving the merchant with 190. This process could be replicated in any city within the empire, regardless of the local currency, with costs varying slightly depending on the mint. In the thirteenth century, the exploitation of new silver mines in Bohemia created a surplus in Europe, particularly in Venice, which also sourced silver from the Tyrolean mines. This abundance not only fueled the production and circulation of *grossi* (see the section "Coinage in Venice" in this chapter), but it also provided the material conditions for Venice to enter the international silver system established by the Mongols.

For the Venetian merchants, liquid capital, the various goods—especially textiles—and valuable objects were the most common means of exchange in the markets of the Golden Horde and in international trade more broadly. In addition to the silver *sommi*, three other types of assets must be considered: the merchandise itself, precious objects like gemstones and pearls, and gold-based currency. Goods could be exchanged through barter, often for local products. Let us envision a trade culture where kegs of wine (exported to the Golden Horde) were exchanged for casks of caviar (imported into Europe),

6. Kuroda, "Why and How," pp. 29–30.

all without the direct use of money. Instead, accounts were settled with credit or through negotiation. However, precious items were not easily convertible into liquid assets, and while they could facilitate certain high-value transactions, we suspect they were used for another purpose. Although Mongolian commercial culture was open to foreign merchants it was not without restrictions. Access to markets, caravanserais, the protection of Mongol soldiers, and general passage rights were also tied to the relationships merchants formed with local governors and the khan himself. Therefore, valuable goods were primarily used as tribute or gifts necessary for conducting business with the Mongols and securing protection that only the local authorities could guarantee. A gift to a local lord was indispensable for gaining access and privileges, and sometimes the lord might reciprocate with a gift of greater value, resulting in a profitable exchange.

Venetians were accustomed to this system, where commercial opportunities opened only after appeasing political authorities. For example, in Trebizond, they managed to keep commercial tariffs low through substantial donations to the emperor. In reality, despite diplomatic treaties and negotiated concessions, merchants remained extremely vulnerable. Bringing valuable goods was essential for currying favor with Mongol aristocrats, safeguarding their investments, and navigating the unpredictable conditions faced in foreign lands. From the perspective of Mongol authorities, on the other hand, while foreigners enjoyed considerable privileges, they were nonetheless subject to their authority and were often required to join their service.

While *sommi*, merchandise, and precious goods formed the basis of international trade between the Venetians and the Mongols, gold was altogether another story. In the thirteenth century, gold played an important role in European monetization, particularly in Venice, where the introduction of the ducat in 1284 marked a peak. European gold coins, especially the florin and the ducat, quickly became the dominant means of exchange in international transactions across the Mediterranean and northern Europe. Although the Byzantine Empire had a long tradition of gold currency, *hyperpyron* coins had lost their credibility due to repeated devaluations, and were no longer accepted in international trade outside the Levantine and Pontic regions.

A gold coin was minted in the Ilkhanate, but this coin does not seem to have been in wide circulation, nor did it have the status of full-fledged "legal tender." These were sporadic issues based on the same dies (a type of stamp) as the silver *dirham*, making these coins the same weight. According to Pegolotti, in Tabriz, a merchant could convert his gold into coins. He refers to these as *casinini* (or *cassinini*), likely a coin minted under Ghazan. These coins were made of pure gold (23 carats and 1/8) and produced at the local mint in exchange for a seigniorage fee. The *cassinino* could be used in Tabriz, and it was worth 28 or 29 silver aspers of Tabriz. Pegolotti's observations about the circulation of silver coins suggests that silver was more widespread than gold. The *cassinino* was probably a gold *dinar*, similar to those issued by various Ilkhanid rulers, with a value ten times that of the silver *dinar*. In Persia, the exchange rate between gold and silver generally hovered around 1:10 (or sometimes less), remaining relatively stable throughout the Mongol period, as noted by Ibn Battuta.

In Venice, between 1285 and 1349, the gold-to-silver ratio favored gold, reaching a peak in 1328 when gold rose in value to 24 *grossi*, with a ratio of 1:14.2. As a result, bringing silver to Asia and exchanging it for gold benefited European merchants, who could capitalize on the exchange rate by purchasing gold in Asia and then converting it to silver in Rialto. After 1349, with the gradual devaluation of gold in Europe, the exchange rate settled around 1:10, increasing to 1:11 only toward the end of the century. A similar dynamic occurred between Persia and India, where differences in the value of gold and silver favored the export of gold from Persia (where it was cheaper) to India.

The circulation of money was heavily influenced by political decisions within each khanate, which likely represented the biggest obstacle to the systematization of international exchange mechanisms. Through monetary reforms, various states sought to adjust the value of silver and gold coins based on their needs—such as funding military expenses or reducing tax revenues due to declining production. To cover war expenditures, silver coins were often devalued, allowing the same amount of metal to mint more coins. This led to inflation across the economy, prompting the Ilkhanids to pass reforms and corrective measures.

In general, merchants had a vested interest in maintaining stable and commensurable values, which is why silver in its various forms remained the primary vehicle of exchange. The Mongols established this standard for not only commercial transactions within their empire but also for fiscal and tributary purposes (such as the aforementioned aristocratic remittances). This system intersected with Venetian monetization, where the *grosso* had already become a reference coin. From this encounter, the groundwork was laid for the simplification of exchanges, facilitated by the *sommi*—silver ingots measured by weight and coined as needed. The prevalence of bimetallism was supported by its usage in northern and western Europe, as well Egypt, Maghreb, and

India. An international commercial system could not function on a single standard alone; although it introduced certain imbalances and instabilities, it ultimately benefited Venice, the principal market for trading metals.

While the Islamic, Persian, and Chinese economies were largely monetized, unpaid labor, and other forms of exchange remained prevalent in the northern steppe and in the principalities of Rus' well into the late thirteenth century. Bartering was particularly common before the political stabilization following the conquests, as it had never entirely been abandoned.[7] In trade with foreign merchants, finished products like cloth (*tele* and *drappi*) might be used, but silver—whether in ingots or coins—was typically the standard medium of exchange. The mint in Sarai, for example, produced a silver coin called the *tamgha*, tied to the aforementioned withdrawal system, with one *sommo* equivalent to 120 *tamgha*.[8] For Venetian merchants, silver coins, textiles (*panni*), and precious goods were the most widespread and commonly accepted forms of payments in the markets of the Golden Horde. However, it is crucial to distinguish between the payment methods Venetians employed when dealing with European or Middle Eastern partners and those used in exchanges with the local population. Among Latin merchants, as well as Muslims, Armenians, Jews, and Greeks living in Crimea, coins were the primary form of payment. In contrast, when transacting with the Mongols, it was not uncommon for agreements to be settled by exchanging goods—especially *panni*—for other merchandise.[9]

In the Venetian settlements, gold ducats and silver *grossi* were in circulation, along with other coins such as *hyperpyrons*, florins, and *genovini*. However, according to Pegolotti, the most commonly used forms of currency in Tana were *sommi* and aspers, which, as previously mentioned, were best aligned with the silver standard used throughout the Mongol Empire. This observation by the Florentine merchant is corroborated by Venetian notarial acts. Besides aspers, small copper *folleri* were also in use, with an exchange rate of 1:16 to the asper. The *follero* was the coin typically used for small, everyday purchases, limited to items such as "herbs and minutiae required for the land" (*erbe e cose minute e bisognevoli per la terra*).[10]

---

7. Balard, *La Romanie génoise*, p. 645; Spuler, *Die Goldene Horde*, pp. 330–31.

8. Kuroda, "The Eurasian Silver Century," p. 261; *Tarifa*, p. 18. This text, probably written at the same time as Pegolotti's *Pratica*, provides facts from a few decades later and uses the dialect plural *tangi*.

9. Balard, *La Romanie génoise*, p. 645.

10. Pegolotti, *La pratica della mercatura*, p. 25.

Most of the coins in circulation were likely produced in Tana, where a mint was established. In the late thirteenth century, *aspri baricati*—named after Berke, the first khan of the Golden Horde—became widely used due to the ease of setting equivalences with other silver coins.[11] The internal economy of the Golden Horde, bolstered by the increase in international trade, saw consistent growth in the first half of the fourteenth century. However, as the asper devalued, likely due to wear and instability of the coinage,[12] a new, higher-value asper was introduced.[13] This new asper, along with other coins and *sommi*, remained the primary currency for transactions within Tana and the broader markets of northern Pontus. By the second half of the fourteenth century, this coin was primarily used for larger transactions, such as the purchase of slaves, buildings, and land. However, in exchanges involving goods, the formation of companies, loans, and inheritances, the silver *sommo* was preferred. While the *aspro baricato* continued to circulate, its use diminished over time and was mentioned less frequently in the records.[14]

## Coinage in Venice

The thirteenth century saw major changes in European and Mediterranean monetary policies, and Venice was no exception. During the twelfth and thirteenth centuries, Venice's commercial activities were concentrated between Fatimid Egypt and the Byzantine Empire. In these regions, Venetians used local currencies: Arab *dinars* and Byzantine *hyperpyrons*. The monetary landscape in the Byzantine Empire shifted notably with the First Crusade, which marked a turning point in its monetary system. Between the late eleventh and

---

11. This estimate is based on documents produced in Caffa by the Genoese notary Lamberto di Sambuceto, studied by G. I. Bratianu and M. Balard (Balard, *La Romanie génoise*, p. 659). In the mid-fourteenth century, the ratio between the *asper* and the *grosso* was almost 2 to 1 (1.66 aspers for one *grosso*). Lane and Mueller, *Money and Banking*, vol. 1, p. 300 and no. 44.

12. According to Balard, this was up to 40 percent; Balard, *La Romanie génoise*, p. 660.

13. In the 1340s, the exchange rate between the new *asper* and the *sommo* must have been around 1:55, that is, triple the *aspro baricato*. Balard, *La Romanie génoise*, p. 660; Balbi and Raiteri, *Notai genovesi in oltremare*, p. 141.

14. However difficult it may be to establish a fixed or official exchange rate, we can presume from notarial acts that, in Tana in 1359, the ratio of the *asper* to the *sommo* varied from 1:170 to 1:190, while an average ratio of 1:30 remained between the *asper* and the ducat, with some variations. In the 1360s, the new *asper* was devalued as well, for a ratio between the *asper* and the *sommo* of 1:200.

early twelfth centuries, Emperor Alexios I Komnenos initiated a comprehensive reform that included fiscal changes and the introduction of new coinage. The cornerstone of his reform was the creation of a stable currency system based around the new *hyperpyron* (*nomisma hyperpyron*) introduced in 1092. The *hyperpyron* was minted in 20½-carat gold, weighing 4.1 grams.[15] The aim of this reform was to address the empire's structural economic crisis, which was marked by rising public expenditures and persistent currency devaluation.[16] The introduction of these new coins brought stability to the currency system, with the value of the *hyperpyron* remaining relatively consistent for most of the twelfth century.[17] These coins were made of gold, like much of the currency circulating in the eastern and Islamic worlds at the time.[18]

Under the oversight of Doge Vitale Michiel (r. 1155–72), Venice resumed minting coins known as *albulus* or *blanchi*. These coins were distinctive in that they did not feature any iconographic references to the Germanic Emperor but instead bore the name of the doge, inscribed as "Michil Dux."[19] Although Michiel's experiment was short-lived,[20] it laid the groundwork for a new phase of financial expansion. The introduction of this stable currency provided immediate advantages to the local entrepreneurial class, offering them a reliable means of payment whose value was regulated by the state. This stability increased the acceptance of Venetian currency even beyond the city's borders.

The rise of Latin kingdoms in the East, the expansion of trade in the Levant, and the new transit routes opened by the Crusades facilitated a larger flow of

15. This was the same as Frederick II's augustal. Hendy, *Studies in the Byzantine Monetary Economy*, pp. 513–14. The first document to mention the *hyperpyron* dates back to 1093, in the will of S. Cristodulo di Patmos (Bertelè, "Moneta veneziana," p. 5 and n. 1).

16. Hendy, *Studies in the Byzantine Monetary Economy*, p. 516.

17. Hendy, *Studies in the Byzantine Monetary Economy*, p. 517.

18. Many studies on the availability and use of precious metals have demonstrated that, until the end of the eleventh century, it was almost exclusively gold coins that circulated throughout Asia and in the Byzantine Empire. Kuroda, "Why and How," pp. 23–25.

19. The money that featured Vitale Michiel's name—of which only a few examples have survived—is also known as *mezzo denaro*, although the weight and the purity (0.517 grams and 70/1000 of silver purity) bring it closer to the value of a third of a *denaro*, as determined by Buenger Robbert, "Il sistema monetario." See also Buenger Robbert, *The Venetian Money Market*, pp. 28–29 and Papadopoli, *Le monete di Venezia*, pp. 61–8.

20. As mentioned in chapter 1, the doge was assassinated upon his return to Constantinople after the ruinous expedition against Manuel Komnenos in 1171.

silver from Europe into eastern markets, where it held greater value.[21] From the second half of the twelfth century, this influx somewhat alleviated the silver shortage that had previously plagued the Asian regions, though it was not enough to reverse the persistent overvaluation of silver compared to gold.[22] During the rule of Doge Enrico Dandolo (r. 1192–1205),[23] at the turn of the twelfth and thirteenth centuries, Venice introduced the *grosso*, a silver coin of great purity,[24] specifically created to facilitate high-value transactions.[25] The Venetian *grosso* proved so successful that other Italian city-states like Genoa, Florence, Pisa, Siena, and Verona began minting their own silver *grossi* from the 1230s onward. However, Venice had a distinct advantage due to its greater access to silver, which it sourced from the Tyrolean mines. The import of silver into western Europe further increased from the mid-thirteenth century thanks to the opening of new mines in Bohemia and the Carpathians.[26]

The minting of the *grosso* boosted the expansion of Venetian merchants' operations in the East during the second half of the thirteenth century, later extending to Romània.[27] In these regions, the *grosso* was used alongside or as an alternative to the silver *hyperpyron* minted in the successor states of the Byzantine Empire after the Fourth Crusade, such as those issued by the mint of Nicaea. Meanwhile, Trebizond began minting its own silver coin—the asper—along with copper coins that imitated those used in Byzantium since the 1230s.[28]

21. Watson, "Back to Gold," p. 5. For the period under consideration, the author specifically discusses the "silver famine of the Muslim World." These events are confirmed in the more recent studies by Kuroda ("The Eurasian Silver Century," pp. 254–60 and "Why and How," pp. 25–26).

22. Watson, "Back to Gold," pp. 6–7.

23. Stahl, *Zecca*, p. 17.

24. 98.5 percent purity and 2.18 grams in weight. At the dawn of the thirteenth century, the Venetian *grosso* was exchanged for 26 *denari*, by that time referred to as *piccoli*; in 1350, one *grosso* was worth approximately 48 *denari piccoli*. Papadopoli, *Sul valore della moneta veneziana*, pp. 11–12; Bertelè, "Moneta veneziana," pp. 5–7.

25. Luzzatto, *Storia economica di Venezia*, p. 92.

26. Lane and Mueller, *Money and Banking*, vol. 1, pp. 168 and 287; Kuroda, "The Eurasian Silver Century," p. 251.

27. Bertelè, "Moneta veneziana," p. 6; Buenger Robbert, "Il sistema monetario," pp. 416–17. This was a coin with high intrinsic and stable value; hence, it was very much in demand by merchants who traded with Venetians.

28. Monetization in Trebizond is discussed later in more detail. Hendy, *Studies in Byzantine Monetary Economy*, pp. 522–24.

From 1250, various Italian and European cities initiated policies to support commercial expansion by minting new gold coins. In 1252, Genoa and Florence minted the *genovino* and the *fiorino*, respectively. This was followed by Lucca (1256) and Perugia (1259), then the English and French monarchies. However, none of these gold coins achieved immediate widespread success. Florence's florin (*fiorino*) only gained prominence at the end of the century when the pope designated it as the currency for the collection of the Holy See's revenues.[29] The florin served as the model for the Venetian great council when, in October 1284, by twenty-one votes to seven, it approved the minting of the ducat, a coin that surpassed the florin in value.[30] The ducat officially came into circulation in March 1285, introducing the first bimetallic system in Venice. These coins, primarily used in international transactions, were flanked by coins for low-value transactions such as *denari* (or *lira di piccoli*) and the *lira di grossi* (a *moneta di conto* or virtual currency), which were used mainly in financial transactions and tax matters.

In the Byzantine territories where Venetian and Genoese trade expanded, particularly beyond the Dardanelles, the empire attempted to maintain its prerogatives in coinage. Even when Genoa obtained the right to settle in Pera in 1304, one of the clauses explicitly prohibited the Genoese from minting their own coins.[31] Thus, a complex system of exchange rates and currencies emerged, which, on the one hand, supported the entry of Genoese and Venetian merchants into broader international trade and, on the other hand, further specialized the merchant profession in these regions. As trade shifted toward the Black Sea and the Asian routes, merchants had to adapt to the prevailing monetary regimes of the Golden Horde and the Ilkhanate. This adaptation materialized with the widespread use of the *sommo* as the main currency and exchange medium in Tana, as well as in Iranian and central Asian markets. Venice's first silver ingots, dating back to 1273, were modeled after the *grosso*, featuring the effigy of Christ on one side and St. Mark on the other.[32]

In the fourteenth century, the ratio between gold and silver fluctuated considerably in Venice, driven by a devaluation of the *grosso* in the first quarter

29. Stahl, *Zecca*, p. 212.

30. "Tam bona et fina per aurum, vel melior ut est florenu." Stahl, *Zecca*, p. 31.

31. Balard, *La Romanie génoise*, p. 644.

32. Lane and Mueller, *Money and Banking*, vol. 1, p. 162.

of the century, followed by the rapid devaluation of gold in subsequent decades. The higher relative value of silver compared to gold in Mongol territories and Asia encouraged the practice of speculating on the movement of metals between different markets. The lower cost of gold relative to silver across the markets of the Black Sea, Iran, and central Asia led to a significant outflow of silver from west to east. Pegolotti's account is very valuable here, as he provides an exchange rate for the *sommo* that effectively connects the entire economy of the Black Sea: "One *sommo* of silver from Tana is valued in Pera at nine *hyperpyrons*, with the *sommo* weighing seven and a half ounces and consisting of an alloy of eleven ounces and seventeen *denari* of pure silver per pound."[33]

Alongside the *sommo*, Venetians in the East primarily used the *grosso*,[34] as evidenced in notarial records from Crimea and the Sea of Azov. Additionally, the *lira di grossi* served as a nominal reference currency, particularly useful for overcoming challenges in exchanging physically circulating *grossi* with local coinages.[35] In practice, a system was established where *sommi*, silver *grossi*, and *lire di grossi* were the preferred currencies. Initially, the silver ingots were minted with high-quality silver close to the *grosso* (that is, 96.5% purity as compared to 98.5% of the *grosso*), but over time, less pure ingots (0.925 purity) were minted, known as *sterlini*.[36] Just like the coins, silver ingots experienced devaluation over the years.[37] Moreover, as mentioned earlier, Venetian authorities granted private workshops the permission to produce small silver ingots, the *sommi*, weighing around 200/400 grams, specifically for the markets of the Golden Horde.[38]

---

33. Pegolotti, *La pratica della mercatura*, p. 53.

34. Day, "Banca e moneta a Venezia," p. 740.

35. Soon after the *grosso* was minted, after 1250, the value of the *lira* was set at 1:240 silver *grosso*. See also Papadopoli, "Il bimetallismo a Venezia," pp. 201–2.

36. Pegolotti mentions both (*sterlini* and *verghe della bolla di Vinegia*), p. 61. The last mint to receive *sterlini* was that in Yumurtalik, which in 1347 ended up in the hands of the Mamluks. Lane and Mueller, *Money and Banking*, vol. 1, p. 163.

37. Lane and Mueller calculate that the purity of Venetian ingots fell from 0.965 purity in 1273 to 0.949 in 1422 (*Money and Banking*, vol. 1, p. 164 and nos. 8 and 9).

38. These ingots were *piccoli come un dito di dama* (as small as a lady's finger) and were produced by private laboratories and not the state mint. They were called "verghe d'argento di sommo" (*verge d'arzento de sumo*: Lane and Mueller, *Money and Banking*, vol. 2, p. 164 and no. 10).

## Communication: Translators and Interpreters

Since its foundation, Venice had been a multilingual and multicultural city. During the Middle Ages, Venetians were accustomed to cultural diversity, and merchants who spent extended periods abroad were often well prepared to communicate in diverse linguistic contexts. The Mongol Empire was no exception, opening up new spaces, although news about Mongol society and customs had been trickling into Europe since the 1240s. The plethora of languages and dialects encountered in Levantine and Asian bazaars called for sophisticated linguistic knowledge. By the second half of the thirteenth century, interpreters and translators—often the same individuals—became fully-fledged professionals. These *turcimanni* (interpreters) or *dragomanni* (dragomans), as they were known, based on the Arabic term *targiumān* for interpreter, were essential not only for oral communication but also for translating official documents, agreements, commercial accords, and contracts in chancelleries. Their services added to the expenses of embassies, consulates, and commercial transactions.[39]

The Mongolian language was used in various areas of the court to draft official documents, but there was no lingua franca for communication across the empire. The local bureaucracies of the different khanates were dominated by the written languages of the conquered peoples, who had more extensive administrative skills. Mongolian, written in Uyghur,[40] remained largely confined to the aristocracy, which, in the generations following the conquest, became increasingly multilingual and cosmopolitan. Ata Malik Juvaini (1226–84), a historian and Persian minister serving the Mongol khans,[41] attributed the rise of the Mongolian language during his time as governor of Baghdad to the

---

39. Sinor, "'Pray to God on my behalf,'" p. 178.

40. Juvaini, *The History of the World-Conqueror*, vol. 2, p. 523.

41. According to Juvaini, Chinggis Khan only knew Mongolian (*The History of the World-Conqueror*, vol. 1, p. 225). Born in 1226 in Khorasan, Juvaini came from a family of court bureaucrats, first at the service of the Seljuks and then at the service of the Khwarazmian sultan. His younger brother Šams-al-Din Moḥammad married the daughter of Arghūn Āqā, governor of Khorasan and close adviser to the ilkhan Hülegü, who nominated him ṣāḥeb(-e) divān (minister of finance). Ata Malik was an influential figure at the Ilkhanid court, the personal adviser of the emir Arghūn Āqā. In 1259, Hülegü nominated him governor of Baghdad. He is the author of one of the most detailed histories of the Mongols, *Tarīkh-i Jahān-gushā* (*The History of the World-Conqueror*), who recorded as far as 1260, more than twenty years before his death in 1284.

cultural decline of the Arab–Persian world.[42] Despite this, certain languages gained prominence and facilitated communication. For demographic and cultural reasons, Persian and Turkic spread throughout various levels of civil and political society in west and central Asia, eventually becoming dominant. In China, too, if we believe Marco Polo's accounts, these languages were commonly used in Mongol courts and administration, before the reassertion of Chinese as the official language.

In western settlements along the Black Sea, the coexistence of diverse communities fostered close proximity between customs, traditions, cultures, and languages. Tana was no exception, and due to its central role as a hub of commercial exchange, it became a melting pot of different populations. Each community likely communicated internally in its own vernacular. Venetians used both the vernacular for informal communication and Latin for most official documents, though wills from the mid-fourteenth century onward were often drafted in the vernacular before being translated into Latin. In interactions with the local population, the most common language in Tana—and throughout the northern Black Sea region—was Turkic-Cuman, widely spoken in the north Caucasus and the western steppe. The *Codex Cumanicus*, a trilingual glossary (Latin, Persian, and Cuman), with several parts and later additions,[43] dated to the early fourteenth century, serves as tangible evidence of the linguistic adaptability required of Italian merchants. Historian Juvaini writes that after several months of service the governor of Khwarazm Chin Tëmur, the secretary of state, Sharaf ad-Dīn (d. 1245), had mastered Turkic and "no longer needed interpreters" to facilitate his travels.[44]

42. Juvaini, *The History of the World-Conqueror*, vol. 1, pp. 7 and 98; vol. 2, p. 523. The last passage in particular reveals Juvaini's ironic tone when he states that the son of the emir Khoja Fakhr-ad-Din Bihishti was the youngest because "he knew how to write the Mongolian language in Uyghur," a sign that it was a recent acquisition at the start of the Ilkhanate of Arghun in 1258, "and this is, in our day and age, the essence of knowledge and skill."

43. The document was produced to be used by merchants frequenting the ports and the settlements in Crimea. It is currently held at the Biblioteca Nazionale Marciana in Venice (Cod. Mar. Lat. 549). Its date is uncertain. The first paper of the manuscript in our possession was drafted in July 1303 (fol. 1r), but some parts of the text seem older, while others are the result of later juxtapositions and revisions. In addition to the document, see Schmieder and Schreiner, *Il codice cumanico e il suo mondo*. There is a more recent edition of the *Codex* in Turkic, curated by Güner, *Kuman bilmeceleri*.

44. Juvaini, *The History of the World-Conqueror*, vol. 2, p. 523.

Cuman was also used in the official documents of Venetian–Mongol diplomacy. When Venice and Uzbek Khan in 1333 formalized the agreement that allowed the Venetians to form a settlement in Tana, diplomats drafted the document in Cuman. The Polish Dominican Dominic translated it into Latin.[45] Similarly, the Franciscan friar and interpreter Benedict, also Polish, accompanied John of Plano Carpini during his mission *ad Tartaros* in 1245, reaching as far as Karakorum. However, for the remainder of the journey, the Franciscan friar had to hire two additional interpreters, Temur and Shonakuur, both of whom were Turks.[46] Turkic was therefore indispensable for navigating the Mongol Empire's northern routes. According to available sources, this linguistic situation persisted from the time of Plano Carpini's journey in 1245 until the 1330s or 1340s, when Pegolotti compiled his merchant handbook.[47]

Pegolotti states that "Turcimanno in più linguaggi, e calamanci in *tarteresco* [cioè, mongolo, da kelemenči], sono gente che temperano e dànno a intendere linguaggi da uno linguaggio a un altro che non si intendessoro insieme." (Turciman in several languages, and Calamanci in Tatar [that is, Mongolian, from *kelemenči*], are those who interpret and help people understand from one language to another when they cannot understand each other.)[48] He advised merchants embarking on the *viaggio del gattaio* (journey to Cathay)[49] to bring with them an interpreter who was proficient in the Cuman language. As a merchant himself, Pegolotti recognized the necessity of a universally comprehensible system of measurements. Whenever he listed weights, measures, or product names, he wrote them *in più lingue* or *in più linguaggi* (in several tongues or in several languages). In another passage, Pegolotti emphasizes the importance of hiring a good Turcoman interpreter, saying that one should not be frugal when it comes to hiring quality because *il buono non costa quello d'ingordo che l'uomo non s'ene megliori via più.*[50]

45. *Diplomatarium veneto-levantinum*, vol. 1, pp. 243–44.

46. Whom Friar John called *tartari*: "nobis dati fuerunt et tres tartari, due qui erant decani et alius rat homo Bati." Pian del Carpine, *Historia Mongalorum*, pp. 308–9. Sinor, "'Pray to God on my behalf,'" p. 179.

47. On the date of Pegolotti's *Pratica*, see Sinclair, *Eastern Trade and the Mediterranean*, pp. 4ff.

48. Pegolotti, *La pratica della mercatura*, p. 19.

49. Named after the Kitan regime, which had dominated part of north China as the Liao dynasty from the tenth to the twelfth centuries.

50. The phrase, however difficult it may be to translate literally, indicates that the more you spend the less you spend, because a bad interpreter would prove to be a terrible investment

The consul of Tana employed an interpreter who held a permanent position within the Venetian consulate, but not always to satisfactory results.[51] In August 1370, the consul complained to the senate about the interpreter's poor performance.[52] The authorities suggested that he assess whether the interpreter could be motivated to improve; otherwise, they advised he should be dismissed and replaced with a more efficient individual. The importance of the role is evidenced by the senate's allocation of 30 *sommi* per year for the consul to hire an interpreter and translator. However, interpreters were not always locals. In Tana, a certain Niccolò Darcerono (*nostrum venetum*) was highly regarded, to the point that the senate authorized the consul to raise his salary to 36 *sommi* to ensure his continued service.[53]

In addition to Turkic, another widely spoken tongue was Persian, the cultured language of much of central Asia. The letters that Güyük gave to the Franciscan delegation led by John of Plano Carpini, intended for Pope Innocent IV, were written in Mongolian, and it was through Cuman interpreters that the Franciscan was able to translate them into Latin. Besides the Latin translation, a Persian version was also required.[54] When, in 1247, another delegation of missionaries sent by Pope Innocent IV, led by the Dominican Ascelin of Cremona, reached the Mongol commander Baiju *noyon* in the Caucasus, two letters from the pope had to be translated from Latin into Mongolian. To accomplish this, Ascelin was assisted by interpreters who translated from Latin to Persian and from Persian to Mongolian.[55] The Franciscan William of Rubruck, during his trip to Karakorum in 1253, hired an interpreter, whom he referred to as *homo dei* (man of God). Unfortunately, this interpreter turned

---

(*ingordo*), while a good one, however costly, would offer advantages greater than the money spent (*non s'ene migliori via più*). See also Lopez et al., *Medieval Trade in the Mediterranean World*, p. 356, n. 54.

51. In 1359, the consul Pietro Caravaello's interpreter was Guglielmo Bon, a Venetian. Archivio di Stato di Venezia (hereafter ASV), Cancelleria Inferiore (hereafter CI), Notai, busta 19, reg. 7, fasc. 1, fol. 13v; Pucci Donati, *Ai confini dell'Occidente*, no. 85, p. 41. In 1383, it was Pietro detto Gata. ASV, CI, Notai, busta 130, fasc. 7/B, fol. 13v.

52. "Non attendit ad curiam cosulis et ad negotia que sibi committuntur": Venezia–Senato, *Deliberazioni miste*, vol. 20, p. 248.

53. It is worth noting that the senate recommended that the consul of Tana exert great care and respect for the law—*cum maxima sufficientia et legalitate*—should he decide to fire the interpreter and hire a new one. Venezia–Senato, *Deliberazioni miste*, vol. 20, p. 248.

54. Pian del Carpine, *Historia Mongalorum*, pp. 308–9; Sinor, "'Pray to God on my behalf,'" p. 180.

55. Sinor, "'Pray to God on my behalf,'" p. 180: Roux, *Les explorateurs au Moyen Age*.

out to be unreliable, as "he was not very intelligent" and, more problematically, consumed large amounts of alcohol. When Rubruck found himself before Möngke Khan in need of an interpreter, *homo dei* was too drunk to communicate even a single word of what the khan had said.[56] It is not surprising, therefore, that in his *Itinerarium*, Rubruck frequently recommended hiring a good interpreter, regardless of the cost.

Latin remained the official language in use by Venetian authorities for legal texts, as it continued to be the formal language of western bureaucracies. However, the vernacular was also widespread in Venice, and many wills drafted in Tana by Venetian citizens were written using a mix of languages: protocols and eschatocols were in Latin and the body in the vernacular. Typically, the notary would ask the individual whose will was being drafted if they preferred to proceed in Latin or in the vernacular. Diplomatic documents were occasionally composed in the vernacular, and there are instances of letters from Mongol khans or Egyptian sultans being translated into Venetian instead of Latin, or alongside it. The Latins were not the only ones learning foreign languages. According to Rashid ad-Din,[57] Ghazan was fluent in Latin, in addition to Chinese, Arabic, Persian, and other languages. At the Ilkhanid court, the use of Latin was not uncommon,[58] likely due to the considerable presence of westerners in Tabriz and other cities within the Ilkhanate.

In conclusion, while the available sources are insufficient to fully capture the range of solutions and experiences related to multilingual communication, both written and especially oral, it is clear that great efforts were made on both sides to bridge linguistic gaps. Both cultures developed tools and strategies to navigate a world that was even more linguistically and culturally diverse than the Mediterranean.

## Weights and Measures

Venetians living and working on the Black Sea, in Tana, and Tabriz had to manage a complex and diverse system of measurement that, as with coins and foreign exchange, required specialized skills. That said, some consistency can

56. Sinor, "'Pray to God on my behalf,'" p. 180. Jackson and Morgan, *The Mission of Friar William of Rubruck*, p. 134.

57. *Rashiduddin Fazlullah's Jami'ü't-Tawarikh—Compendium of Chronicles*, p. 465.

58. Hope, *Power, Politics, and Tradition*, p. 179; Meyvaert, "An Unknown Letter of Hulagu," pp. 250–51.

be seen in the fact that, not only on the Black Sea, but also in Iran and central Asia, Genoese units of measurement (or at least measurements borrowed from Genoese ones) were prevalent. This was not only due to Genoa's dominant position, but especially to the Venetians' later arrival on the Black Sea. Since the second half of the thirteenth century, from 1261 onward, the Genoese had set the standards—first in Pera and then in Caffa. Venice had to adjust its own gauge to the routes and rules already established by Genoese expansion in Gazaria, Persia, and beyond. In addition to Genoese measures, the units used in Tana were likely based on local customs or standards introduced by the Mongols (though the sources are not explicit on the matter) before being converted into measures commonly used by Venetian merchants.

Pegolotti clearly outlines the measurement units used in Tana, specifically the *cascito*, the *libbra* of Tana, and the *tocchetto*. The *cascito* corresponded to slightly more than five Venetian *staia* and was primarily used for weighing dry goods, mainly grains.[59] Alongside the *cascito*, the *cantaro* and the *libbra* of Tana were commonly used as units of weight.[60] Heavier goods were weighed in *libbre* of Tana, such as wax,[61] *ladano* (*cistus villosus*, a rockrose resin with a vanilla scent used in food), pepper, ginger, and "all the large spices," meaning coarser varieties. The *libbre grosse* was used to weigh metals like iron, copper, and tin, as well as cotton, and *robbia* (madder, a plant in high demand for dyeing fabrics), hides, parchments, tallow for candles, cheese, linen, oil, and fruit. On the other hand, the *libbre sottili* was used for lighter and more valuable items such as silk, saffron, and amber, which Pegolotti notes was bought *lavorata a modo di paternostri*, meaning in bead-like grains.

Furs and hides, which were very common in the markets of the Golden Horde, were typically traded based on quantity. For instance, ermine and *vai* (squirrel) furs were bought in bulk, with Pegolotti stating that *dàssene 1020 per uno migliaio* (1,020 furs were counted as 1,000). Their cost was high due to the

---

59. According to Pegolotti one cascito of *biado* in Tana corresponded to 5 Venetian *staia*. If the Venetian *staio* measured 83.31 liters, one *cascito* was 416.55 liters, which the Venetians then converted to bushels, where one bushel of Venice was equivalent to 4 *staia* for a total of 333.24 liters. Pegolotti, *La pratica della mercatura*, p. 25; ASV, CI, Notai, busta 19, reg. 7, fasc. 1, fols. 19r and 19r; Notai, busta 130, fasc. 7/B, fol. 16r.

60. Notaries used the *cantaro* as a measure of weight for any merchandise. One *cantar* corresponded to 100 rolls, 5 *mene*, or 150 Genoese pounds. ASV, CI, Notai, busta 19, reg. 7, fasc. 1, fols. 12v, 17v e 22r; Pucci Donati, *Ai confini dell'Occidente*, nos. 80, 104 and 128, pp. 40, 47 and 54.

61. For example, 26 *cantari* of wax were calculated *ad pondum Tane*, or in pounds of Tana. ASV, CI, Notai, busta 130, fasc. 7/B, fol. 16r.

labor involved in producing them, and in Tana, they were readily available, having been transported from the north via trade routes that, since the early Middle Ages, connected the Baltic with the Byzantine Empire.[62] Other furs sold included fox, sable, stone marten, and wolf. Additionally, the proximity to the nomadic tribes of the northern Black Sea ensured that cowhide (*coia di bue*, according to Pegolotti[63]) and horsehide were also available, often recorded in sales contracts drawn up by notaries.[64]

The fishing industry was highly active in Tana, especially in the fishing and breeding of sturgeon. Sturgeons were sold dried, usually in bundles of twenty, and are often mentioned in Venetian notarial acts as collateral for cash loans.[65] Goat hides were also sold in bundles, while cowhide was typically traded in *noveri* of 100 pieces each. Caviar, which was highly prized and expensive, was sold in *fuschi*.[66] The term *fusco*, meaning "filled with fish eggs," is somewhat ambiguous, and according to Pegolotti, it referred to the lower half of the fish, "from halfway down toward the tail." This likely indicates a unit of measure used specifically for caviar, varying on the fish's size. Caviar arrived in Tana from the coastal ports of the Sea of Azov, and was shipped throughout Romània, reaching as far as Constantinople.[67] In Tana, the *tocchetto* was also in use, a unit of weight equal to approximately 800 grams, mainly for goods sold in small quantities.[68] Wine was sold in kegs, and while Pegolotti did not provide specifics regarding their volume, he did note that "all Latin wines are sold in kegs as they are."[69] Fine wines like malvasia, as well as other wines from the Aegean Islands, were sold in *mitri* (meters), with one *mitro* being just over ten liters.[70]

Genoese measures were also prevalent in Tabriz. Heavier spices were sold in hundreds of *mene* (or *mine*).[71] The *mina* was a unit of measurement used for

---

62. ASV, CI, Notai, busta 19, reg. 7, fasc. 1, fol. 43r.

63. Pegolotti, *La pratica della mercatura*, p. 24.

64. ASV, CI, Notai, busta 19, reg. 7, fasc. 1, fol. 33r.

65. ASV, CI, Notai, busta 19, reg. 7, fasc. 1, fol. 32r; busta 130, fasc. 7/B, fol. 17v; Pucci Donati, *Ai confini dell'Occidente*, no. 188, p. 70.

66. ASV, CI, Notai, busta 130, fasc. 7/B, fols. 1v, 14v.

67. ASV, CI, Notai, busta 130, fasc. 7/B, fols. 14v, 17v.

68. "Ad esempio la cera." ASV, CI, busta 19, reg. 3, fols. 25r–26r; Pegolotti, *La pratica della mercatura*, p. 24.

69. Pegolotti, *La pratica della mercatura*, p. 24.

70. Pegolotti, *La pratica della mercatura*, pp. 24, 25, and 53; *Tarifa*, p. 47. Numerous documents mention wine in *mitri*. See ASV, CI, Notai, busta 19, reg. 7, fasc. 3, fols. 3r–v, 12r–13r, 20r–23r.

71. On the *mina* and its use in the fourteenth century, see Giagnacovo, *Appunti di metrologia mercantile*, pp. 121–22.

dry goods, especially salt, in both Genoa and Florence, where it equaled half a *staio*.[72] In the Mongol Empire, the value of the *mina* varied in different markets.[73] It was also used to weigh silk, linen, coral, amber, silver, cinnabar, and tin. Finer spices, on the other hand, that were *sottili*, were sold in fractions, such as "tenths of a *mina*." Woolen cloth was sold by the *pezza*, with one *pezza* amounting to around 25 meters of fabric, or 2 ⅓ *picchi*, where one *picco* measured 61 cm. The same applied to *cammellotti* (*ciambellotti*), a rough-textured fabric made with camel hair or goat's wool. Pegolotti uses the term *garbellare* to describe the inspection of cloth and spices, which was usually the seller's responsibility, except for lacquer, where both buyer and seller shared the task.[74] Unlike woolen cloth, canvases were measured by a shorter *picco*, 40 cm instead of 61 cm. Silk bolts were sold by the *pezze*, while canvas was measured "by the picco." The "*picco di Gazeria*" was a unit of length equivalent to about 60 cm. A fabric known as organza, imported from Urgench and named after the city, was regularly sold in public bazaars.[75] Gemstones, gold, and pearls were sold in *saggi*, while silver was sold in *carats*.[76]

## Levies and Taxes

Merchants were subject to a tax known as the *tamunga*,[77] which in Tabriz amounted to 5 bezants minus half an asper for every 100 bezants of the total value of transported goods. Certain products sold by Venetians, such as wool, canvas, furs, and tin, were taxed at a lower rate—4 bezants minus one third of an asper for every 100. Precious goods, on the other hand, were considered *merce franca* and exempt from taxation. Additionally, a service fee of half an asper for every 100 was charged for *senseraggio* (brokerage). Pegolotti notes that merchants would also customarily offer a gratuity to the broker, writing *quello che ti piace di fare cortesia al sensale* (whatever you feel is appropriate to give the broker).[78]

---

72. Neverthelss, in the Mongol Empire salt was weighed in *moggi* (ASV, CI, Notai, busta 30, fasc. 7/B, fol. 14v), and the same was true in Constantinople and Pera (Pegolotti, *La pratica della mercatura*, p. 39).

73. Pegolotti, *La pratica della mercatura*, p. 147.

74. Pegolotti, *La pratica della mercatura*, p. 27: "one half belongs to the seller, the other to the buyer."

75. ASV, CI, Notai, busta 19, reg. 7, fasc. 1, fol. 37v.

76. According to Pegolotti, a *saggio* weighed 4.38 grams. Pegolotti, *La pratica della mercatura*, pp. 25–26.

77. See the section "The Mongols and Money" above.

78. Pegolotti, *La pratica della mercatura*, p. 28.

Since the market in Tabriz was directly connected to the ports of Ayas and Trebizond, Pegolotti writes that *il peso e la misura di Torisi è tutt'uno con quello di Trebisonda* (the weights and measures of Tabriz are the same as those of Trebizond).[79] Venetian merchants unloaded their galleys at these two ports and then transported goods via caravan to the capital of the Ilkhanate. Goods purchased in Tabriz were then shipped back toward Venice. During Pegolotti's time, neither the Genoese nor the Venetians paid taxes in Ayas whether for imports or exports. However, Pisan merchants, by then struggling to manage trade with eastern Mediterranean markets, were subject to a 2-percent tax on the total value of goods transported, both incoming and outgoing.[80]

In Trebizond, merchants were exempt from taxes on goods entering or exiting, though a 3-percent sales tax was imposed on all merchants except for the Genoese.[81] For goods unloaded at the port of Trebizond and destined for the Tabriz market, a fixed tax of 28 aspers of Trebizond per *soma* (cargo) had to be paid to the central treasury, along with an additional asper per *soma* to the city administration. For goods traveling in the opposite direction, from Tabriz to Trebizond, the tax was 14 aspers per *soma* to the treasury, plus the standard asper to the city. According to Pegolotti, the import duty in Tana was 4 percent of the value of goods sold by Genoese merchants to Venetians, while all other merchants paid 5 percent. Exported goods were not subject to customs tariffs, and gold, silver, and precious stones were also tax-exempt; however, silk was taxed 15 aspers per *libbra*.[82]

79. Pegolotti, *La pratica della mercatura*, p. 29.
80. Pegolotti, *La pratica della mercatura*, p. 60.
81. Pegolotti, *La pratica della mercatura*, p. 31.
82. Pegolotti, *La pratica della mercatura*, p. 25.

# 11

# Goods, Merchandise, and Slaves

## Goods

Fernand Braudel once compared trade circuits to electric circuits: they only work in a closed system.[1] This analogy holds true for trade between Venice and the Levant, where the flow of goods heading East was matched by a return flow of goods to the West, though not always of equal value. Despite the difficulties faced by both Europe and Asia in the fourteenth century, particularly in the latter half, the volume of goods from the East arriving in Venice did not diminish. In fact, it grew and diversified. Spice imports increased, with Romània–Black Sea galleys arriving to Rialto with goods like Indian pepper, Middle Eastern ginger, and cloves and cinnamon from the Indian subcontinent. While these "light" goods guaranteed high profits, it was the heavier goods—referred to as *grosse*—such as wheat, salt, oil, and silk from the Pontic region that dominated western markets during this period. Later, from the mid-fourteenth century onward, there was a marked increase in the number of slaves purchased in Tana and other cities within the Golden Horde, who were subsequently sold in nearby markets or transported to Venice.

Until the Treaty of Nymphaeum, Italian merchants sourced exotic goods such as spices, cotton, sugar, linen, silk, rose water, and pearls from three major eastern Mediterranean markets: Acre, Alexandria, and Ayas. In return, they exported products like Apulian olive oil, Sicilian wheat, Calabrian wine,[2]

---

1. Braudel, *Afterthoughts on Material Civilization and Capitalism*, p. 127; quoted in Dini, "I circuiti del commercio internazionale," p. 635.

2. Made in Crotone and much sought after in the Levant, even a century later; cf. Archivio di Stato di Venezia (hereafter ASV), Cancelleria Inferiore (hereafter CI), Notai, busta 19, reg. 1, fasc. 3, fols. 15v–16r.

Neapolitan walnuts, soap bars from Marseilles, and Sicilian wines from Messina and Scalea.[3] From the Fourth Crusade onward, and especially after 1261 when the Black Sea trade routes opened up, these merchants benefited from secure bases and transport routes that allowed for regular trade flows in both directions. To the traditional markets of north Africa, Constantinople, and Palestine were added the Anatolian coast markets like Trebizond and Smisso, along with Crimean ports from which wheat was imported. The Sea of Azov further contributed fish, wax, fur, dried fruit, wine, slaves, and grains. Finally, central and east Asia supplied various grades of silk, shipped to Venice, further diversifying the trade network.[4]

Sources indicate a shift in the types of goods traded in Crimea, particularly in Tana, from the early fourteenth century onward. By the end of the thirteenth century, the bulk of merchandise traded by Latin merchants in the region was local produce. However, two decades later, there was a noticeable increase in goods of Asian origin. The opening of the Mongolian route through central Asia, with its western terminus in Tana, boosted the flow of goods produced in China, central Asia, and the Baltic.[5] Trade between Venice and the Mongol Empire, especially with Tana, was largely seasonal, tied to the synchronization between the voyages of regularly scheduled galleys (*galee di linea*) departing from Venice and the caravans arriving from Asia at the Black Sea.

The Mongols established business and partnership arrangements between the aristocracy and merchants, which fit seamlessly into the broader context of international cooperation between Latin and eastern merchants. These partnerships were supported by legal and administrative frameworks that facilitated their operations. While commercial activities generated high profits for the state, the imperial officers of the Golden Horde ensured favorable conditions for merchants operating within their territories, including fiscal privileges outlined in treaties with Genoa and Venice. The emporia in Mongol territories also benefited from their proximity to east Asian markets. The Mongols profited not only from the flow of goods entering and leaving their

---

3. Da Canal, *Zibaldone da Canal*, pp. 42–52.

4. Dini, "I circuiti del commercio internazionale," p. 638.

5. See, for instance, the acts of Lamberto di Sambuceto, which he drafted in Caffa in 1290. In the many documents examined by G. I. Bratianu and later M. Balard, fish and furs make up the majority of goods purchased by the Genoese merchants in Tana. For a more recent summary, see Karpov, *Istorija Tany*, p. 247.

domains but also from transaction fees and revenues. By fostering and supporting international trade, they gained direct access to valuable merchandise.

Venice not only profited from buying and selling goods or what it charged for
maritime transport; it also benefited financially from capital that was brought
back by returning merchants. Venetian merchants, upon concluding their activities abroad and deciding to return home, were required to pay a tax, which, in
the second half of the fourteenth century, amounted to 1 percent of the total
value of the wealth they brought with them. In 1371, for instance, Corradino de
Vecchi, a Venetian merchant from Verona, informed the Venetian authorities of
his desire to return after spending three years in Tana. He declared that he had
left in 1367 with almost nothing (*quasi nichil secum portavit*), seeking income to
support his wife and three children who had remained in Venice. During his
three years at the Don delta, with the support of the Venetian authorities in the
region (*suffragio nobilium vestrorum quibus adhesit in dictis partibus*), he established a thriving trade between Tana and Sarai, eventually amassing a modest
fortune of 1,500 gold ducats.[6] However, not every merchant was as skilled or
fortunate. While many Venetian citizens became wealthy in Tana,[7] others returned home after years abroad with less to their name than when they had left.

## Imports

The goods traded by Venetian merchants between Venice and Tana, as well as
between Venice and Trebizond, can be broadly categorized into luxury goods
and precious metals, raw materials, and staple foodstuffs. Some of these items
were available in Europe, but domestic production often failed to meet demand. For instance, by the thirteenth century, the consumption of salt had
surpassed what could be supplied by the salt pans of Chioggia and southern
Italy, where Venice traditionally sourced it. As a result, Venetian merchants
in Tana began purchasing salt extracted from the salt pans near Kerch in
Crimea.[8] Similarly, in the latter half of the thirteenth century, the demand for
cotton increased, as it began to spread as an alternative to wool. Fustian, a fabric made from a blend of wool and cotton, gradually became a key export from
Europe to the East. Alum, a mineral essentially for the dyeing industry as a
mordant, was also in high demand. Grains, never sufficient in local supply,

6. Venezia–Senato, *Deliberazioni miste*, vol. 30, pp. 489–90.
7. See, for instance, Venezia–Senato, *Deliberazioni miste*, vol. 33, pp. 193–94.
8. ASV, CI, Notai, busta 19, reg. 7, fasc. 1, fol. 43r; busta 130, fasc. 7/B, fol. 14v.

were imported from Crimea: ports such as Caffa, Tana, Porto Pisano, Cembalo, and others became increasingly important throughout the fourteenth century for the provision of wheat and less refined grains and seeds.

Wheat and other grains from the Black Sea region were crucial to the Venetian economy. Typically, these goods were transported on private ships, which often sourced their supplies from the smaller ports of the Sea of Azov, closer to the production areas.[9] Although private navigation is largely absent from public records, it frequently appears in notarial documents related to the wheat trade in Tana. For example, on April 28, 1360, the shipowner Grava del fu Giorgio di Stanzi from Smisso leased his ship, anchored in Tana along with its crew of twenty-one sailors, to the Venetian Giovanni Bembo, who agreed to load 460 *moggi (bushel)* of wheat for transport to Pera. As part of the agreement, Bembo and the crew could keep up to 40 *moggi* for themselves.[10] On May 22, 1360, the Genoese shipowner Giovanni della Maddalena similarly leased his ship to Bembo, who loaded it with 500 *moggi* of wheat for transport to Venice.[11] The importance of wheat is further underscored by the Venetian *Tarifa,* which explicitly stated that wheat could not be exported without authorization (*senza grazia*).[12] At times, wheat was even used as collateral for transporting precious metals. For example, in May 1360, the Venetian merchant Michele Signolo entrusted a shipment of raw silver valued at 250 *hyperpyrons* to Gaspare Soranzo di Corone, a shipowner docked in Tana. In exchange for transport, the shipowner gave Signolo 120 *moggi* of wheat as collateral.[13]

Another iconic product of international trade arriving from the East was silk. The development of Italy's silk industry in the thirteenth century increased the demand for raw silk, and local and Mediterranean production could not

---

9. Karpov, *Istorija Tany,* p. 253.

10. ASV, CI, Notai, busta 19, reg. 7, fasc. 1, fol. 18r; Pucci Donati, *Ai confini dell'Occidente,* no. 109, pp. 48–49. A great many cases like this are mentioned in the records (ASV, CI, Notai, busta 19, fols. 18v, 19r, 39f.; Pucci Donati, *Ai confini dell'Occidente,* nos. 113, 114, 115, 245, pp. 49–51 and 84).

11. ASV, CI, Notai, busta 19, fol. 19r; Pucci Donati, *Ai confini dell'Occidente,* no. 116, p. 51. The document specifies that *moggi* are to be considered according to the weight of Constantinople, and the cost of leasing is established as a ducat and 18 *grossi* per *moggio.* Wheat was loaded onto the ship of Giovanni della Maddalena and the price was raised to 3.25 per *moggio,* to be repaid within one month of the ship's arrival in Venice.

12. *Tarifa,* p. 21.

13. ASV, CI, Notai, busta 19, reg. 7, fasc. 1, fol. 18v; Pucci Donati, *Ai confini dell'Occidente,* no. 113, pp. 49–50.

meet this demand. This shortfall opened the door for imports, particularly from the Caspian Sea region and China. Interestingly, Italian records do not mention Chinese silk until 1257, when the term *seta captuia* (with variations such as *catuxta* and *catuya*) appeared for the first time in Genoese notarial minutes.[14] By the second half of the century, Chinese raw silk began to appear in Lucca, the heart of Italy's silk industry, mainly imported by Genoese merchants.

From the late thirteenth century, silk made its way from the Far East to the Caspian Sea region, then traveled to Constantinople via two primary routes: Tana in the north and Tabriz in the south. By the fourteenth century, silk had become one of the most widely traded products, with an expanding knowledge of various types of silk, many of which were named after their places of origin. Pegolotti identifies fifteen types of silk. For example, *mercadasia* (or *merdacascia*) silk was high-quality fabric produced in Merv,[15] while *cannaruia* silk came from Karabakh in the southern Caucasus. Many transactions also mention *seta ghella*, likely produced in Gilan, Persia, on the southern coast of the Caspian Sea.[16] In general, Chinese silk was considered inferior in quality compared to that produced in central Asia. Traders often opted to buy raw or semifinished silk, which was more cost-effective, to minimize potential losses from the long journey and exposure to the elements. During the peak of silk traffic, particularly between the second half of the thirteenth century and the 1340s, profits were mainly driven by quantity over quality.[17]

From the second half of the thirteenth century, Venetians bought fish in the Black Sea, especially sturgeon,[18] which had been fished in Tana for quite some time. When William of Rubruck arrived in Sudak in 1253, he observed that "to the east of that province . . . there is a city called Matrica [now Matrega, south of the Kerch Strait] where the Tanai River [the Don] enters the

14. Lopez, "China Silk in Europe," p. 73.

15. Pegolotti, *La pratica della mercatura*, p. 300; Balard, *La Romanie génoise*, p. 726.

16. Pegolotti, *La pratica della mercatura*, pp. 208 and 301; Balard, *La Romanie génoise*, p. 726.

17. Balard, *La Romanie génoise*, p. 730. Lopez did some calculations and concluded that, on the one hand, Chinese silk did cost less (around 30 percent) than the kind produced in Merv or in Gilan. However, due to the product's low quality, Chinese silk was rarely mentioned in the documents, which cite general types of silk rather than *catuya* silk, etc., which was preferred. See Lopez, "China Silk in Europe," p. 75 and ASV, CI, busta 19, reg. 3, fols. 9r–11v where, in September 1361, the Venetian merchant and native of Pistoia, Giovanni Testa, stated that he owned *panni di seta* (silk cloth) worth 40 ducats, which were destined for the Flanders market.

18. Pegolotti, *La pratica della mercatura*, p. 24; Bautier, *Les relations économiques*, p. 314.

sea of Pontus through a delta some twelve miles across," and "the merchants coming from Constantinople who reach the previously mentioned city of Matrica send their boats as far as the Tanai River to buy dry fish, especially sturgeon."[19]

Even when the Mongolian routes in central Asia were open and bustling with traders, local production remained central to Tana's exchange economy, alongside goods from distant markets like China and India.[20] By the first half of the fourteenth century, given the profitability of the fish trade,[21] Venetians and Genoese began producing fish locally.[22] The Genoese were particularly active in the sturgeon trade,[23] and by the fourteenth century, they were joined by the Venetians who purchased sturgeon in the ports of the Sea of Azov (Vosporo and Porto Pisano), as well as in Sarai.[24] The fish did not always reach Venice, as supplies were often resold in the Black Sea ports, such as Caffa, Trebizond, Smisso, and Constantinople, or even in the Aegean islands.

Other local agricultural products could be found in Tana, such as hazelnuts and apples.[25] Products from the Russian and Baltic economies, including

19. Rubruck, *Itinerarium,* in *Sinica Franciscana,* vol. 1, pp. 5–6. Rubruck, *Viaggio in Mongolia,* pp. 9–10.

20. For instance, on December 1, 1386, Vittore Gioioso, a Venetian, received from Giovanni di Arezzo, the consul's *sescalco* (senechal), 4 *sommi* for two barrels of sturgeon he would receive in April 1387. Vittore offered his thirteen-year-old slave named Amore as collateral. ASV, CI, Notai, busta 130, fasc. 7/B, fol. 17v; Pucci Donati, *Ai confine dell'Occidente,* no. 587, p. 202.

21. ASV, CI, Notai, busta 130, fasc. 7/B, f. 15v.

22. ASV, CI, Notai, busta 19, reg. 2, fasc. 7, fol. 16r; busta 130, fasc. 7/B, fol. 15v; Pucci Donati, *Ai confini dell'Occidente,* no. 95, pp. 44–45.

23. Balletto, "Il commercio del pesce"; Balard, *La Romanie génoise,* pp. 706–7. The notarial documents of the Genoese notary Lamberto di Sambuceto, written up in Caffa between 1289 and 1290, include eight *patti di nolo* (hire agreements) to go to La Copa to load fish. See Bratianu, *Actes des notaires génois,* pp. 262–91. ASV, CI, Notai, busta 19, reg. 7, fasc. 1, fol. 28r; Pucci Donati, *Ai confini dell'Occidente,* no. 161, p. 63.

24. Bautier, *Les relations économiques,* p. 316. These regions, mentioned in detail by the merchant manual discovered and published in part by Bautier in 1970, are absent from Pegolotti's text. This is notable, as both works are of Florentine origin, though Pegolotti's is likely from a slightly later period. It remains unclear whether, during the years when the merchant serving the bank was writing, Venetians were permitted to trade in the peripheral ports of the Sea of Azov.

25. ASV, CI, Notai, busta 19, reg. 7, fasc. 3, fol. 3r–v; Pucci Donati, *Ai confini dell'Occidente,* no. 272, p. 92.

hides, furs, wax,[26] lacquer,[27] and meat preserved with honey, were also imported.[28] Items from the pastoral and hunting economies often appeared in contracts and wills. For example, in July 1360, three hundred salted hides owned
by the Greek merchant Giovanni Fachiamola were transported on a ship sailing
from Tana to Pera.[29] On August 26, 1360, the "Saracen" merchant Coza Man-
suth sold Pietro Penzi 870 salted hides and 348 cowhides for a total of 220
*sommi*.[30] In the will drafted on September 18, 1361 by Giovanni Testa, a Venetian merchant from Pistoia, rabbit skins valued at 56 *grossi*, destined for Flemish
markets, were listed among the other goods.[31] Another key imported product
was wax, which was in high demand in Europe for candle-making. Tallow was
used in its two forms, the first derived from animals, the second from beeswax.
The latter was cleaner and more fragrant, and was imported from the East,
considered a luxury product. In contrast, sources show that tallow in bars
(*pani*) was more common but still an essential material for candle-making.[32]

26. ASV, CI, Notai, busta 19, reg. 7, fasc. 3, fols. 9r–11v; Pucci Donati, *Ai confini dell'Occidente*, no. 278, pp. 96–98; ASV, CI, Notai, busta 130, fasc. 7/B, fol. 1v.

27. ASV, CI, Notai, busta 19, reg. 7, fasc. 3, fols. 9r–11v; Pucci Donati, *Ai confini dell'Occidente*, no. 278, pp. 96–98.

28. ASV, CI, Notai, busta 189, no. 5, doc. of April 24, 1380, notary Vittore Scalipiero; Pucci Donati, *Ai confine dell'Occidente*, no. 486, p. 176.

29. ASV, CI, Notai, busta 19, reg. 7, fasc. 1, fol. 28r; Pucci Donati, *Ai confini dell'Occidente*, no. 161, p. 63.

30. ASV, CI, Notai, busta 19, reg. 7, fasc. 1, fol. 34r; Pucci Donati, *Ai confini dell'Occidente*, no. 200, p. 73.

31. ASV, CI, Notai, busta 19, reg. 7, fasc. 3, fols. 9r–11v; Pucci Donati, *Ai confini dell'Occidente*, no. 278, pp. 96–98.

32. ASV, CI, Notai, busta 19, reg. 7, fasc. 1, fol. 15r; busta 130, fasc. 7/B, fol. 16r; Pucci Donati, *Ai confini dell'Occidente*, no. 90, p. 43; Bautier, *Les relations économiques*, p. 314; Pegolotti, *La pratica della mercatura*, p. 24. On April 11, 1360, Rizzardo and Antonino di Riva, two Genoese brothers, sold Giacomo Giuntini and Giuliano di Grazia wax for a total value of 30 *sommi* at the price of 2 *sommi* and 14 *saggi* per *cantaro* (ASV, CI, Notai, busta 19, reg. 7, fasc. 1, fol. 17v; Pucci Donati, *Ai confini dell'Occidente*, no. 104, p. 47). In the will drawn up in Tana on May 14, 1384, the Venetian merchant Primasio di Ragusa determined that the wax and fish he owned should be sold in accordance with his trustees' wishes (ASV, CI, Notai, busta 130, fasc. 7/B, fol. 19v; Pucci Donati, *Ai confini dell'Occidente*, no. 488, p. 179). On July 2, 1385, Dalmazio Bocca, a Geno-ese merchant, sold the Venetian Ettore Bembo 26 *cantari* of wax *secondo il peso di Tana* (accord-ing to the weight of Tana) at the price of 47 bezants per *cantaro*. Bembo guaranteed the sale with 50 *moggia* of *biada* that he kept in a warehouse (*fovea*) in Tana's Venetian quarter (ASV, CI, Notai, busta 130, fasc. 7/B, fol. 16r; Pucci Donati, *Ai confini dell'Occidente*, no. 557, p. 196).

Spices were among the most traded products from the East.[33] The Mongol Empire played a crucial role in facilitating their trade, but the bulk of spices originated from India, passing through Persia and Tabriz via the Hormuz Strait. The most in-demand spices were pepper and ginger, which Italian merchants bought from Muslim traders whose commercial networks stretched as far as south China.[34] From Tabriz, spices reached Europe through what we have described as the southern route, with their first stop being the port of Ayas. From there, they were transported overland to Trebizond and then shipped to Mediterranean ports. This lucrative trade flow remained stable until the 1340s, when the political instability and collapse of the Ilkhanate forced western merchants to abandon Tabriz and Persia.

The volume of spices traded in Tana was smaller. The anonymous author of the trade manual known as *Nottario*, likely compiled between 1310 and 1320, explicitly mentions that *spezierie d'ogni ragione, ma poche* (spices of all kinds, albeit few) were acquired in Tana.[35] Both Pegolotti and the Venetian *Tarifa* gave less attention to spices, focusing more on weights, measures, and prices in Tana. Moreover, the trade was not one-sided, as Venetian merchants also exported saffron to the Golden Horde, which was produced not only in Italy but also in the Middle East, Syria, and Egypt.[36]

Pearls and precious stones were both highly important and extremely profitable. The author of the *Nottario* writes that *trasi dalla Tana per portare verso ponente ... perle d'oriente d'ogni ragione* (from Tana pearls of every value are brought to the West), with most pearls originating from India and Tibet.[37] Additionally, precious stones arrived in Tana from China via central Asia. As mentioned earlier, these items were essential for anyone traveling within the confines of the Mongol Empire due to their light weight and high value.

33. Freedman, *Out of the East*.

34. In particular, see chapter 4 of Chaffee, *The Muslim Merchants*.

35. Bautier, *Les relations économiques*, p. 314.

36. Ashtor, *Levant Trade*, pp. 162–63; Pegolotti, *La pratica della mercatura*, p. 24; Bautier, *Les relations économiques*, p. 314.

37. Bautier, *Les relations économiques*, p. 314.

## Exports

The goods that Italians exported to eastern markets primarily consisted of textile products and metals. The Venetians exported linen cloth, French wool textiles (*panni*), and cotton throughout the Mongol Empire.[38] The cotton, often sourced from the Middle East—with the finest coming from Acre and the kingdom of Lesser Armenia—was then exported to regions such as Tana, Urgench, Almaligh and Sarai. The cotton was ginned (*maputo*),[39] likely referring to the fiber being cleaned of the rest of the plant.

While it is true that silver mainly flowed from Europe to the East, Venetian merchants frequently imported silver from Tana and transported it back to Venice,[40] or reinvested it in regional markets.[41] Regardless, the quantity of metals exported to the East was considerable. These were metals of all kinds: iron, tin, and copper, mainly used for weapon manufacturing. Tin, sourced from the mines of Devon and Cornwall in southwest England, was loaded onto Venetian galleys of Flanders in English ports and shipped to Venice and onward to the Levant.[42] From the early 1300s, Venetian merchants also purchased German and Bohemian tin.[43] Occasionally, brass is also mentioned in the records. For example, on September 22, 1360, *ser* Marco di Filippo Venier went to the notary Benedetto Bianco in Tana to appoint Antonio Ariano as his

38. ASV, CI, busta 19, reg. 3, fols. 5v–6v, 9r–11v, 23v–24r; Pucci Donati, *Ai confini dell'Occidente*, no. 275, p. 94; no. 278, pp. 96–98, and *inventario dei beni del fu Andalò Basso*, pp. 105–6.

39. Pegolotti often mentions this being preferred for trade due to clean cotton's higher value and lesser volume it took up on the galley. Pegolotti, *La pratica della mercatura*, p. 24, 63, 77; Bautier, *Les relations économiques*, p. 314.

40. ASV, CI, Notai, busta 19, fols. 20r, 28r; Pucci Donati, *Ai confini dell'Occidente*, nos. 119, 160, 161, pp. 52, 63.

41. On May 21, 1360, the Venetian merchant Antonio Venier sold to the company of Giovanni Grifoni a stock of silver for a total of 377 *hyperpyrons* (ASV, CI, Notai, busta 19, fol. 19r; Pucci Donati, *Ai confini dell'Occidente*, no. 114, p. 50). On November 23, 1362, the Genoese merchant Andalò Basso, a resident of Tana, listed in his will fifty silver *verghe* (ASV, CI, busta 19, reg. 3, fols. 20r–23r). In September 1363, the Venetian merchant *ser* Marco Rosso received from *ser* Matteo de Prato, who was also a Venetian from the Giudecca, both of them residents in Tana, silver for a value of 250 ducats, to be paid off when the galleys of Romània, currently *ad flumine Tane*, had returned to Venice (ASV, CI, busta 19, reg. 3, fols. 20r–23r).

42. Ashtor, *Levant Trade*, pp. 159–60; Blanchard, *Mining*, pp. 667–68; see also Hatcher, *English Tin Production*.

43. See, for instance, Lupprian, *Il Fondaco dei Tedeschi*.

proxy to collect what Zanachi Barbafella (another Venetian) owed him (Venier) for a consignment of brass wire.[44] Even more significant was the copper trade, as this metal was alloyed to make bronze for minting coins, furnishings, and many other objects. Much of the copper came from German mines and was traded in Venice through Saxon and Bohemian merchants at the Fondaco dei Tedeschi. Slovakian copper production also expanded notably during the fourteenth century. Additionally, iron and lead were exported. Sources reveal that more merchants were involved in the iron trade in Tana at this time.[45]

In addition to *panni* and metals, wine was among the most important products exported.[46] Venetian merchants exported Greek wine,[47] produced in the Aegean islands, as well as Italian wine from the Mezzogiorno.[48] Wine was also exported beyond Tana, as evidenced by the will of the Genoese merchant Manuele Guarnieri, who, in partnership with Zilio Dentado, sold wine in Cabardi and Porto Pisano.[49] Greek wine, purchased in the Aegean and sold in Tana, could fetch up to 4 *sommi* per cask,[50] while local wine from Solgat typically cost 2.25 *sommi* per cask.[51] Numerous examples of the wine trade can be found in documents, particularly in trade records and wills that passed

---

44. ASV, CI, Notai, busta 19, fol. 39r; Pucci Donati, *Ai confini dell'Occidente*, no. 239, p. 83.

45. The deed cited above states that Zanachi Barbafella had purchased some iron clubs from Filippo Venier, in addition to the brass wire. ASV, CI, Notai, busta 19, fol. 8v; Pucci Donati, *Ai confini dell'Occidente*, no. 59, p. 34.

46. ASV, CI, Notai, busta 19, fasc. 1, fols. 39f.; Pucci Donati, *Ai confini dell'Occidente*, no. 245, p. 84.

47. ASV, CI, Notai, busta 19, reg. 2, fols. 17v, 23r; reg. 3, fols. 2r–v, 3r–v, 5v–6v, 12r–13r, 20r–23r; loose parchments, doc. of September 23, 1263; busta 130, fasc. 7/B, fol. 14v; Pucci Donati, *Ai confini dell'Occidente*, no. 106, p. 48.

48. Between 1359 and 1360, the wine from Tropea that Venetian merchants exported to the Black Sea was sold for an average of 1.6 *sommi* per cask, while two years later Greek wine was sold for 5 *sommi* per cask (ASV, CI, Notai, busta 19, reg. 7, fasc. 3, fols. 12r–13r, and 20r–23r; Pucci Donati, *Ai confini dell'Occidente*, no. 272, pp. 98–99 and no. 285, pp. 102–5). Wine could also be purchased in Trebizond; in 1362, it was sold in Tana for 14 *aspri* per *mitro* (ASV, CI, Notai, busta 19, reg. 7, fasc. 3, fols. 18r–19r; Pucci Donati, *Ai confini dell'Occidente*, no. 284, p. 102).

49. ASV, CI, Notai, busta 19, reg. 7, fasc. 3, fols. 15v–16r; Pucci Donati, *Ai confini dell'Occidente*, no. 282, pp. 100–101.

50. ASV, CI, Notai, busta 19, reg. 7, fasc. 1, fols. 25v–26r, 12r–13r; Pucci Donati, *Ai confini dell'Occidente*, nos. 152 and 153, p. 61.

51. ASV, CI, Notai, busta 19, reg. 7, fasc. 1, fols. 2r, 9r, 13v, 14r, 15r, 17v, 23r–v; Pucci Donati, *Ai confini dell'Occidente*, nos. 7, 64, 83, 84, 86, 91, 106, 136, 139.

through notary offices, offering a detailed perspective of these transactions. For example, on September 4, 1359, the Venetian merchant Francesco di Segna, residing in Tana, sought a notary to collect 7.5 silver *sommi* from Nicoletto de Toris for four casks of wine from Tropea.[52] On December 14, that same year, another Venetian merchant living in Tana, Pietro Gatto, lent *ser* Bortolano Cattelan de Bassi 3.5 silver *sommi* to buy two casks of Tropea wine.[53] That same day, Gatto lent two silver *sommi* to Vittorio Fioravanti, another Venetian merchant, to purchase a cask of Tropea wine.[54] In August 1362, in Tana, Bernardo Bonvesin dictated his will to the notary Benedetto Bianco, including two casks of Tropea wine worth 5 silver *sommi* among his possessions. He also included a debt of 12 *aspri baricati* owed to the Genoese merchant Ottobono Piccamiglio for Greek wine. On October 18, 1362, the Genoese merchant Andreolo di Murta drafted his will in Tana, which referenced a business partnership with his brother Leone for the sale of wine from Corona in Tana and Porto Pisano.[55]

The will of the Genoese merchant Andalò Basso, a resident in Tana, vividly illustrates the wealth one could accumulate through the wine trade. His estate included a warehouse where his partner, Niccolò Spinola, resided, along with 15 casks of Greek wine stored on the premises. Among his outstanding debts were 5 silver *sommi* owed by the Venetian Tommaso di Bora for the purchase of Greek wine. Additional credits tied to the wine trade included a debt from Carlotta di Albenga for malvasia, 500 *aspri baricati* owed by the tavern keeper Ianixio, and a sum of money from Filippa, the widow of Giorgio Stornello, also for malvasia.[56] In January 1360, the Venetian Pietro de Ognibene, a resident of Tana, borrowed 4.5 *sommi* from the merchant Coza Machomuth di Solgat to buy two casks of local wine (*mostus de Solcati*).[57]

52. ASV, CI, Notai, busta 19, reg. 7, fasc. 1, fol. 2r; Pucci Donati, *Ai confini dell'Occidente*, no. 7, p. 22; Pegolotti, *La pratica della mercatura*, p. 39, 136, and 189.

53. ASV, CI, Notai, busta 19, reg. 7, fasc. 1, fol. 13r; Pucci Donati, *Ai confini dell'Occidente*, no. 82, pp. 40–41.

54. ASV, CI, Notai, busta 19, reg. 7, fasc. 1, fol. 13v; Pucci Donati, *Ai confini dell'Occidente*, no. 84, p. 41.

55. ASV, CI, Notai, busta 19, reg. 7, fasc. 3, fols. 16v–17v; Pucci Donati, *Ai confini dell'Occidente*, no. 283, pp. 101–2.

56. The documentation offers many more such cases. ASV, CI, Notai, busta 19, reg. 7, fasc. 1, fol. 16r; Pucci Donati, *Ai confini dell'Occidente*, nos. 96–98, p. 45.

57. ASV, CI, Notai, busta 19, reg. 7, fasc. 1, fol. 14v; Pucci Donati, *Ai confini dell'Occidente*, no. 91, p. 43.

## The Slave Trade

During the second half of the fourteenth century, much of the merchandise in demand in Europe—ranging from foodstuffs and manufactured goods to raw materials from the East—passed through Venice and other Italian cities. Despite political upheavals within the Mongol khanates, which disrupted the flow of people and goods, and despite intermittent conflicts with Genoa, Venice retained its position as a central hub in the commercial network linking the Mediterranean to Europe. The voyages of the state-owned market galleys continued without interruptions, except during times of war. Even in the most challenging periods, Venetian merchants persisted in conducting business on the Black Sea, always returning after temporary withdrawals due to political crises. One of the most consistent aspects of this trade was the slave market, which rarely faltered throughout the fourteenth century. In fact, the slave trade served as a crucial indicator of the economic and financial health of the trade relations between the Mongol markets and the foreign merchants who frequented them.

Notwithstanding the many challenges faced by the Venetian settlement in Tana over its nearly two centuries of existence, the slave trade remained one of its most profitable enterprises. The merchants involved in this trade were not always exclusively focused on the buying and selling of slaves. Some dealt solely in slaves, while others purchased them together with other goods. There were also merchants who had no involvement in the slave trade at all.

Human trafficking from East to West began to flourish in the tenth century, driven by merchants from Rus' who expanded their reach from central eastern Europe to the Byzantine Empire. Venetian merchants entered this trade in the twelfth century, acquiring slaves from the Middle East, the Balkans, Istria, and Dalmatia, then selling them across the Mediterranean. Mongol invasions directly influenced the slave supply, as conflicts and raids swelled the ranks of captives who were enslaved. The loss of personal freedom turned these individuals into commodities, making them subject to purchase and sale like any other goods.

As the number of available slaves grew, from the second half of the thirteenth century through the first half of the fifteenth century, despite periods of stops, declines, and recoveries, Italian merchants also acquired more slaves. Initially, from the early fourteenth century, the slaves were mostly Greek, captured during wars in the Aegean islands, or children from impoverished families. By the late thirteenth century, the Mongol Empire had become the primary source of slaves, especially the eastern zone of the Golden Horde, which was populated by nomads and easily accessible to Venetian merchants stationed in Tana. The Ilkhanate, however, remained largely excluded from these major slave trade flows, partly due to limited access to captives and abductees, but mainly because the Mongol Persian state fell into crisis and collapsed in the mid-fourteenth century, just as the slave trade was intensifying.

The Mamluk Sultanate required male slaves to serve in its army;[58] in Italy, households of the entrepreneurial class needed domestic servants, artisans sought young male apprentices, and rural estates required laborers for the harvest. In addition, the major cities of the Golden Horde also demanded enslaved workers. However, the number of slaves reaching Italy was relatively small compared to the overall traffic. Voyages of galleys from Tana to Venice were long and fraught with dangers. Transporting a ship full of slaves posed many risks, from the spread of disease during the journey to fatalities, pirate attacks, and shipwrecks. Consequently, the slaves who actually reached Venice were a minority compared to those sold in intermediate markets along the way.[59]

The fourteenth century witnessed an unprecedented surge in the slave trade from Mongol markets to Europe. Several factors contributed to this increase, including regional conflicts, the rising demand for labor due to the demographic decline in Europe, which had begun at the start of the century, and the catastrophic loss of lives caused by the plague in 1348. We can therefore assume that the convergence of greater slave availability in Mongol-ruled regions and the widespread need to replace the diminished workforce, especially unskilled labor, fueled the expansion of this market.[60] In the Golden Horde, much of the population consisted of nomadic Turkish shepherds and peasants enslaved by the Mongol government or the nobility of Rus'. Their impoverished conditions and lack of political or legal protection made these communities prime targets for slave traders—not only Italians but also Armenian, Arab,

---

58. In a treaty with three signatories from 1263, Michael VIII Palaiologos had given the Mamluk sultan Baybars, with the consent of Berke Khan of the Golden Horde, permission for ships transporting slaves from the Black Sea to Egypt to pass through the straits. Barker, *Egyptian and Italian Merchants*, pp. 166–67; Karpov, *Istorija Tany*, p. 252.

59. Among these, one of the most active throughout the fourteenth century, was Crete. See Quirini Popławska, "The Venetian Involvement," p. 276 and no. 78.

60. Balard indicated that in the two years after the devastating plague, there was a temporary rise in the number of male slaves sent from Crimea to Genoa. Balard, "Slavery in the Latin Mediterranean," p. 242; Barker, *That Most Precious Merchandise*, in particular chapter 3.

and Turkic traders, as evidenced by the purchase and sales contracts recorded by Venetian notaries operating in Tana. The trade spanned from the Black Sea coasts to the major cities in the Golden Horde, such as Sarai and Astrakhan.

Those who did not directly engage in the slave trade were members of the Mongol ruling class, who instead focused on regulating it. The nobles at the head of the various *tümen*[61] functioned as the administrative and legal authorities overseeing the activities of foreign merchants, including the buying and selling of slaves. However, by the second half of the fourteenth century, records show the presence of Tatar merchants, often as vendors in the slave trade. Many slaves were sourced from the local population, who, driven by poverty or necessity, sold family members.[62] Children or grandchildren were frequently sold due to the lack of means for survival.[63] Sometimes entire families ended up on the slave market, especially during times of conflict or

---

61. The *tümen* was a unit of ten thousand soldiers that also served as an administrative and territorial division under the jurisdiction of Mongol rulers. This unit was further divided into smaller units called thousands and hundreds, adhering to the decimal system used in the Mongol army. Historical documents reveal local vendors and buyers originating from the centenary of Thazich (ASV, CI, Notai, busta 19, reg. 7, fasc. 1, fol. 17r; Pucci Donati, *Ai confini dell'Occidente*, no. 103, p. 47). Or a Circassian female slave originally from the *milliario Achboga* (ASV, CI, Notai, busta 19, reg. 7, fasc. 1, fol. 22v; Pucci Donati, *Ai confini dell'Occidente*, no. 131, p. 55). Or a Mongol female from the *milliario Melichbey* (ASV, CI, Notai, busta 19, reg. 7, fasc. 1, fol. 25r; Pucci Donati, *Ai confini dell'Occidente*, no. 147, p. 59). The decimal districts appearing in the notarial sources seem to bear the name of the Mongol *noyon* who headed them.

62. For those of us in the third millennium, poverty seems the most apparent and understandable reason for a family to part with a child. However, the historical sources provide little insight into the lived reality of enslavement from the perspective of the enslaved. While the merchants' role in the transaction is well documented, the experience of those being traded remains obscure. The available documents, which are numerous and detailed, focus on contracts for sales and wills. The sales contracts typically list the slave's age, sex, price, and health status, while the wills reflect the owner's generosity as they approached death, often choosing to free their slaves in their final moments.

63. ASV, CI, Notai, busta 19, fasc. 7, reg. 2, fols. 12v, 17r, 23r, 23v and reg. 4, fol. 36r; Pucci Donati, *Ai confini dell'Occidente*, nos. 79, 103, 135, 138, pp. 39–40, 47, and 56. The documents often speak of the need for Russian or Mongolian families to sell their children. In this case as well, the majority were women who had ended up widowed and forced to turn to notaries. One such case was Donna Ocholinato, widow of Dmitrij, who sold her 15-year-old daughter to the Venetian merchant Bertolino Magnamosto (ASV, CI, Notai, busta 19, fasc. 7, reg. 1, fol. 21v; Pucci Donati, *Ai confini dell'Occidente*, no. 125, pp. 53–54). The previously mentioned document (fol. 23r) interestingly notes the fact that the Mongol Apanas was present and consenting to the deed being signed when he sold his 13-year-old sister to the Venetian merchant Marco Contarini.

widespread destitution. These families were often sold at lower prices[64] due to the higher cost of maintaining them and the reduced life expectancy of older family members. Among the slaves destined for foreign markets, the majority were young men, many of whom were recruited into the Mamluk army or assigned to labor-intensive tasks.

Another common situation involved families handing over their children to merchants for training purposes, allowing the children to learn the trade. This arrangement was not considered slavery but rather an apprenticeship or form of mid- to long-term training. In exchange, the children received a small wage, along with room and board, clothing, and shoes.[65] This practice was particularly common among Venetian or Italian families who entrusted their children to merchants for the purpose of learning the trade, though some local families also used this system of "transitory servitude."[66] In certain cases, children were even given to Venetian merchants as collateral for loans until the debt was repaid.[67]

Slaves were a particularly diversified "commodity," with prices fluctuating based on factors such as age, sex, health, and other individual traits. Physical health was typically noted by the notary at the signing of the contract with the phrase *sana omnibus menbris et ad morbo chaduco*, indicating that the individual was healthy and free from epilepsy. The peak market value for both male and female slaves was typically reached between the ages of sixteen and twenty. Generally, slave prices steadily increased throughout the thirteenth and fourteenth centuries, with a considerable decline around 1363, only to rise again a few years later. The reasons for this fluctuation are not entirely clear. While the conflicts within the Golden Horde and the expansion of Lithuania

64. ASV, CI, Notai, busta 19, reg. 4, fol. 4v; Pucci Donati, *Ai confini dell'Occidente*, no. 309, p. 114. This was an entire family, consisting of a father, mother, and 6-year-old boy, sold for a total of 115 aspers. At the time, a slave could cost up to 700 aspers.

65. If the family could afford it, it chose the length of the service and paid a pre-agreed amount to the merchant for every year that their son spent in the workshop. ASV, CI, Notai, busta 130, fasc. 7/B, fols. 15r, 15v; Pucci Donati, *Ai confini dell'Occidente*, no. 528, pp. 189–90 and no. 543, p. 193.

66. Such as in the case of the Mongol Cozichar and his brother Ianbas, who ceded to Giovanni Besagna one of their relatives as an errand boy for seven years in exchange for 10 *sommi d'argento* (ASV, CI, Notai, busta 130, fasc. 7/B, fol. 15v; Pucci Donati, *Ai confini dell'Occidente*, no. 546, p. 193).

67. ASV, CI, Notai, busta 19, reg. 4, fol. 23v; Pucci Donati, *Ai confini dell'Occidente*, no. 141, pp. 57–58.

into territories of Rus' led to a larger supply of potential slaves, the severe outbreak of plague in 1363 within the Golden Horde, which caused thousands of deaths, likely contributed to the temporary drop in prices.[68]

Children and young adults were also trafficked; up to the age of twelve, they were less expensive, while adolescents could fetch twice as much.[69] By the second half of the fourteenth century, the number of local merchants involved in the slave trade surpassed that of the Venetians, likely due to the increased risks for those who ventured out to Sarai or Astrakhan during a period of political instability and rising conflicts. This heightened danger is evidenced by the surge of property sales in Tana around the same time, as recorded by the Venetian notary Nascimbene Scarena.[70] From the 1380s onward, the rise of Tokhtamysh and subsequent political stabilization seemed to improve the situation, given that both local and longer-distance trade became active again, along with rising slave prices.[71] Despite various fluctuations, the average price of slaves remained consistently high throughout the fourteenth century.

The most extensive series of documents at our disposal pertains to Venetian notarial acts drafted in Tana during the second half of the fourteenth century. A close examination of these records reveals that the majority of slaves during this period was female, constituting 74.78 percent of the total. From 1359 to

68. Alexander, *Bubonic Plague*, p. 15. See also Shamiloglu, "The Impact of the Black Death."

69. ASV, CI, Notai, busta 19, reg. 7, fasc. 4, fols. 4v, 6r and 6v; Pucci Donati, *Ai confini dell'Occidente*, nos. 308, 314 and 316, pp. 113, 115, and 116.

70. ASV, CI, Notai, busta 181, fasc. 5, fols. 67r–v, 67v, 68v, 69r; Pucci Donati, *Ai confini dell'Occidente*, no. 456, pp. 161–62, no. 457, p. 162, no. 465, p. 164 and no. 471, p. 165. The information concerning merchants active in Sarai from 1371 is considered reliable. At the time, Corradino de' Vecchi, who worked between Tana, Urgench, and Sarai, was authorized to bring back to Venice all his belongings for a value of 1,500 ducats (Venezia–Senato, *Deliberazioni miste*, vol. 30, pp. 489–90). In 1378, a dispute arose between Niccolò Arpino and Marco Nani over an unpaid batch of honey; this was heard before the consul of Tana, Donato Moro, in April 1380. The two merchants stated they had reached an agreement in Sarai in January 1378 (ASV, CI, Notai, busta 189, n. 5; Pucci Donati, *Ai confini dell'Occidente*, no. 486, p. 176, doc. dated April 24, 1380, notary Vittore Scalipiero).

71. The caravan route to Astrakhan was open when the merchant Primasio of Ragusa dictated his will to the notary Niccolò Natale in Tana and asked his partners to bring a load of carobs to be sold in "Aziterchan." The will also mentions Solgat, where Primasio declared he had a credit of 15 bezants: ASV, CI, Notai, busta 130, fasc. 7/B, fol. 1v; Pucci Donati, *Ai confini dell'Occidente*, no. 488, pp. 179–80. In March 1384, the Venetian merchant Giovanni Servodio was *habitator in Aziterchan*: ASV, CI, Notai, busta 130, fasc. 7/B, fol. 13v; Pucci Donati, *Ai confini dell'Occidente*, no. 505, pp. 184–85.

1362, the proportion of female slaves was even more pronounced, averaging over 86 percent. However, in 1363, a year for which the data is particularly comprehensive, the female-to-male ratio shifted, with the percentage of male slaves rising to 30 percent. This shift might be attributed to the political upheavals of that year (see chapter 6), as well as the labor shortages caused by the devastating plague that struck the Golden Horde.

The predominance of female slaves during times of political stability and in the absence of major disruptions can be attributed to the fact that these slaves, whether in Italy or locally, were mostly destined for domestic work, unlike in the Mamluk Sultanate, where many were employed for military purposes. It was not uncommon for merchants to purchase female slaves to serve as household servants in Tana and later take them back to Italy.[72] Some of these women also became concubines[73] to merchants living in Tana, and many bore children from these unions. In some cases, these relationships led to the emancipation of the slave, followed by marriage to their former owner.[74] Both male and female slaves could also be "leased" for a specific period, with terms determined by the merchants and officials residing in Tana.[75]

The female-to-male ratio shifted toward the end of the century, and between 1381 and 1383, males accounted for 57 percent of the total slave population. Given the smaller amount of data available for this period compared to previous years, this trend reversal can be explained by the developing conflict

72. ASV, Notarile, Testamenti 361, reg. 1, fol. 129r; reg. 3, fol. 2r–v; Pucci Donati, *Ai confini dell'Occidente*, no. 1, pp. 19–20. In his will, stipulated at the mouth of the Don on August 7, 1359, Brandaia di Simone of Florence freed three slaves, a female and two males, who lived with him in Tana, while another slave named Elena was sent to Venice with his children.

73. The topic was studied in depth by Origo, "The Domestic Enemy"; see also Phillips, *Slavery from Roman Times*, pp. 105–7.

74. ASV, CI, Notai, busta 19, reg. 7, fasc. 3, fols. 6v–7v, 12r–13r; Pucci Donati, *Ai confini dell'Occidente*, no. 276, pp. 94–95 and no. 279, pp. 98–99; ASV, CI, Notai, busta 130, fasc. 7/B, fol. 17v; Pucci Donati, *Ai confini dell'Occidente*, no. 581, p. 201. It was often the owner himself who wished to marry his slave. In this case as well, he had to go before a notary and officially register the slave's liberation, which is what Francesco Bragadin, consul of Tana in 1385, did with his slave Antonina: ASV, CI, Notai, busta 130, fasc. 7/B, fol. 18r; Pucci Donati, *Ai confini dell'Occidente*, no. 589, p. 203.

75. ASV, CI, Notai, busta 19, fasc. 7, reg. 1, fol. 12r; Pucci Donati, *Ai confini dell'Occidente*, no. 78, p. 39. In October 1359, Giovanni Bembo, councilor to the Venetian consul in Tana, received rental payments from two Alan merchants for a young girl (for whom the notary indicates neither age nor provenance) for one year at the price of 300 aspers, almost half the average sales price.

in the northwestern region of Rus'. This conflict both increased the availability of male captives and made it more profitable to sell them for military purposes. Although the overall volume of slaves exchanged declined in the fifteenth century, women remained the majority, representing 74 percent of the total.

The average age of the slaves was higher for females, at 14.87 years, compared to 12.8 for males. Additionally, there was a higher number of young female slaves, between 14 and 18 years of age. The ethnic background of the slaves varied, but the majority were recorded in the documents as "Tatar." Between 1359 and 1366, out of 249 contracts examined, more than 76 percent referred to individuals of *genere Tatarorum*. The remaining slaves were divided between Circassians (23), Mongols (21), Alans (5), and a single Greek slave.[76] By the early fifteenth century, as Timurid forces advanced, the recruitment of Tatar slaves declined considerably, both in Genoa and in Venice. A similar trend was observed in Tana.

In fourteenth-century Europe, Christians—those who had been baptized— could not legally be enslaved, meaning that the trade of slaves was restricted to "pagans." In the contracts drawn up by notaries in Tana, slaves were often baptized immediately after purchase, signifying that the individual could no longer be resold. Of the total number of slaves involved in buying and selling transactions, 115 were baptized (49.14 percent). In Tana, much like in Caffa, slaves typically stayed for a short time, passing through on their way to other markets unless they were intended to work in local households.[77]

Both in Tana and Venice, an enslaved person could work to purchase their own freedom or be freed upon their owner's death.[78] However, the bond of slavery did not always end with their masters' lives. In their wills, owners could

76. ASV, CI, Notai, busta 19, reg. 7, fasc. 1, fol. 5v; Pucci Donati, *Ai confini dell'Occidente*, no. 39, p. 30.

77. Balard, *La Romanie génoise*, p. 292; Bratianu, *Recherches sur le commerce génois*, p. 229. Bratianu refers to the situation at the end of the thirteenth century, but this trend can be generalized to the following century, keeping in mind that in the second half of the fourteenth century the slave trade in the Levant reached its peak; Verlinden, *L'esclavage dans l'Europe médiévale*, vol. 2.

78. In most cases, those writing their wills did not limit themselves to just freeing their slaves; they also left them small sums of money so that they could build an independent future. ASV, CI, Notai, busta 19, reg. 7, fasc. 3, fols. 2r–v, 6v–7v, 7v–8v, 18r–19r, 25r–26r; ASV, CI, Notai, busta 19, reg. 7, fasc. 7, pergamene sciolte, doc., September 23, 1361 (Pucci Donati, *Ai confini dell'Occidente*, no. 413, pp. 140–41); ASV, CI, Notai, busta 20, carta 361; ASV, Notarile Testamenti, 924, doc., November 29, 1364; ASV, CI, Notai, busta 130, fasc. 7/B, fol. 1v; Pucci Donati, *Ai confini dell'Occidente*, no. 488, pp. 179–81.

stipulate that their slaves remain in service to their heirs for a specified period after their death.[79] There were instances in which owners chose to free their female slave without providing a reason, as in the case of the former consul of Tana, Francesco Bragadin, who decided to take the young Antonina with him to Venice, thereby freeing her from bondage.[80]

Throughout the fourteenth century, slaves formed a significant, though not dominant, portion of the population in many central northern Italian cities. Tatar slaves constituted the majority in local transactions and at the ports of arrival, a fact noted by Petrarch.[81] By the late fourteenth century, around 10 percent of the total population in Venice and Genoa were enslaved individuals. In Florence in 1372, out of 357 recorded slaves, 274 were Tatars, making up 77 percent of the enslaved population.[82] Records from the 1360s also indicate that numerous Venetian families owned Tatar slaves.[83]

79. ASV, CI, Notai, busta 130, fasc. 7/B, fol. 13v; Pucci Donati, *Ai confini dell'Occidente*, no. 509, p. 185. This document is particularly interesting because the person writing his will had established that when he died, his slave, a young "Saracen," should remain in service to his widowed wife for three years. However, the girl expressly asked to be freed upon payment of 400 *aspers*. The Venetian merchant Benedetto di Romagna dictated his own will to the notary Benedetto Bianco and ordered that his slave remain with his wife for six years after his death, and that she then be freed and that she marry. In addition to her freedom, Benedetto left a dowry of 1,000 silver *aspers* for his slave: ASV, CI, Notai, busta 19, reg. 7, fasc. 3, fols. 25r–26r (Pucci Donati, *Ai confini dell'Occidente*, no. 286, pp. 106–7).

80. Notarial act dated July 3, 1386, ASV, CI, Notai, Busta 130, fasc. 7/B, fol. 18r; Pucci Donati, *Ai confini dell'Occidente*, no. 590, p. 203.

81. Karpov, *Istorija Tany*, p. 252 and n. 49.

82. Among others, there were 30 Greeks, 13 Russians, 8 Turks, and 4 Circassians (Origo, "The Domestic Enemy," p. 336; Gioffrè, *Il mercato degli schiavi*, p. 14). It is no coincidence that it was a Florentine, Domenico di Benci, who was the most active slave trader in Tana between 1359 and 1362. In Genoa, the majority of slaves imported in the fourteenth century were also made up of Tatars (Balard, *La Romanie génoise*, pp. 794 and 799). Balard calculated that 64 percent of slaves in Genoa were *genere Tatarorum*; after Tatars, the ethnicity most represented were Circassians at just 7.1 percent.

83. For Venice, there is no systematic study of the documentation in comparison to the fourteenth and fifteenth centuries in addition to the one undertaken by Lazzari (*Del traffico e delle condizioni*). Of considerable importance is the section by Verlinden devoted to the topic (*L'esclavage dans l'Europe médiévale*, vol. 2, pp. 550–710). For Genoa, aside from Gioffrè, *Il mercato degli schiavi*, see, concerning the fourteenth century, Balard, *La Romanie génoise*, pp. 785–833. A more recent article is by Quirini Popławska, "The Venetian Involvement"; see also Barker, *That Most Precious Merchandise*, in particular chapter 5; ASV, Procuratori di S. Marco, Misti, commissarie, busta 123, 128, 144, 147, 150, and 166.

The slave trade persisted into the first half of the fifteenth century,[84] although the ethnic composition and origin of the slaves changed. By the early fifteenth century, the recruitment of Tatar slaves had diminished considerably in Tana,[85] Genoa,[86] and Venice.[87] While the incidence of buying and selling remained high, it declined compared to the period from 1359 to 1370, confirming a trend that had started in the late fourteenth century. During this time, the number of Rus' (*Rutheni*) and Circassian slaves in Venice rose due to internal conflicts in the Golden Horde, the Timurid wars, and frequent Mongol raids on Russian–Lithuanian territories.[88] In 1359–85, Tatars accounted for over 90 percent of slaves traded, but by 1404–8, their share dropped to 36.8 percent. Conversely, Rus' slaves rose from 1.2 to 5.7 percent, and Circassian slaves increased to 47.3 percent. Between 1413 and 1415, Tatar slaves fell further to 5.5 percent, while Rutheni surged to 72.2 and Circassians to 27.7 percent. The fluctuating prices of slaves mirrored their availability. According to the Massaria di Caffa register, the *introitu Sancti Antonimi* still being paid in 1410.[89] On August 10, 1427, as a ship approached from Tana with over 400 male and female slaves (*ultra numeros quadringentorum inter sclavos et sclavas*), the Venetian senate, anticipating worsening sea conditions, authorized the captain to dock in Istria, where the slaves could stay until late December.[90]

During this period, the typical slave merchant was usually a recently settled Venetian in Tana, though there were also instances of Muslim traders, likely originating from central Asia.[91] The merchants of Sarai were gradually replaced by those from Persia and Transoxiana (Urghench, Merv, Samarkand), a shift that was probably encouraged years earlier by the advance of Timur.

84. Verlinden, *L'esclavage dans l'Europe médiévale*, vol. 2, pp. 955–63 and Barker, *That Most Precious Merchandise*, chapter 5.

85. Prokof'eva, "Akty"; De Colli, *Moretto Bon*; ASV, Procuratori di S. Marco, Misti, commissarie, buste 11, 64, 79, 94, and 147/a.

86. Gioffrè, *Il mercato degli schiavi*, pp. 15 and 58; while in 1400–24 in Genoa there were about 105 Tatar slaves (41.5 percent), from 1425–49 that number fell to 57 (slightly more than 19 percent). The *Rutheni* grew from 51 (20 percent) to 123 (41.6 percent).

87. Verlinden, "Le recrutement des esclaves," p. 126.

88. Quirini Popławska, "The Venetian Involvement," pp. 284–85.

89. Verlinden, *L'esclavage dans l'Europe médiévale*, vol. 2, p. 953.

90. "Que dictos sclavos et sclavas conduci facient Venetias usque per totum mensem decembris Proximus": ASV, Senato Misti, LVI, fol. 120.

91. De Colli, *Moretto Bon*, nos. 25, 31, and 32; Prokof'eva, "Akty," no. 69, p. 85.

In conclusion, the supply of slaves was driven by poverty and war, and it was the Genoese and Venetians who produced the demand. Factors such as the establishment of the Mamluk state, the increasing wealth of Italian families, and recurring plagues heightened the demand for slaves, which coincided with their ample supply in Asia. Throughout the fourteenth century, despite fluctuations—often caused by conflicts between the Italian republics and the Mongols—Genoese and Venetian slave merchants prospered in human trafficking, especially in Tana. Although there was a temporary decline due to the Timurid attacks, the slave trade persisted, never truly ceasing. Over time, the source of slaves shifted; a once predominant Tatar presence was replaced by slaves from Rus', and a largely female demographic began to balance out between sexes. Nevertheless, the slave trade within the Mongol Empire—or rather, its remnants—endured until 1475, when the Ottomans put an end to the Venetian presence in these eastern territories.

# Conclusion

AT THE beginning of the fourteenth century, works such as the *Codex Cumanicus*, Francesco Balduccio Pegolotti's *La Pratica della Mercatura*, and Marco Polo's *Il Milione* reflect a sophisticated and well-developed literary tradition. This body of literature, comprising travel guides, merchants' manuals, and personal memoirs, circulated among Italian traders, documenting their exploration of regions unknown or inaccessible to previous generations. The East, once veiled in myth and apocalyptic imagery, had become more tangible and comprehensible than ever before. Notarial acts and wills provide a wealth of names and brief yet telling accounts of individuals who opened both maritime and overland routes from Venice. These documents describe the various stages of travel, stopovers in key cities, business transactions, and the agreements signed along the way. Although the exact fortunes made in these distant lands remain unclear, what is certain is that for nearly two centuries, Venice fiercely defended its citizens' access to the markets of the Mongol Empire. The Mongols were not seen as enemies; rather, the true commercial rivalry was with Genoa. In this unexpected intersection of Asian opportunities and European ambition, one of the most pivotal episodes in the thirteenth and fourteenth centuries unfolded: the creation of a global commercial network built on Mongol political power and the trading prowess of Mediterranean maritime republics.

Throughout this book, we have outlined the various stages of a process that historical literature has sometimes referred to as the "expansion" of medieval Europe.[1] Viewed from a wider perspective, the broadening of Europe's horizons and the growth of its commercial networks resulted from the integration of diverse regional systems in the aftermath of the political upheaval

---

1. Phillips, *The Medieval Expansion*.

caused by Mongol conquests.[2] Although it is undeniable that the Mongol Empire facilitated trade, communication, and opened doors to foreign merchants, its key role has only recently been fully appreciated, thanks to studies highlighting the active involvement of Mongol rulers, merchants, and intermediaries in fostering trade.[3] Mongol commercial culture—with its partner institutions, logistical support, compensation guarantees, merchant-friendly tariffs, and legal frameworks for individuals of all backgrounds and religions—was the main catalyst that enabled many cultures within the empire to interact and blend. It was in this context that Latin merchants found reliable and interested counterparts in the very "Tatars" whose conquests had once spread panic across Europe just a few decades earlier.

The system that emerged was neither entirely stable nor devoid of conflicts, and it might even seem short-lived. However, to dwell on its duration or judge its effectiveness based on imperfect mechanisms would be reductive and anachronistic. Beyond the many new insights gained, the integration of multiple commercial networks played a pivotal role in fostering the growth of productive structures, investments, forms of exchange, and communication channels. The importance of the Genoese and Venetian bases in the Black Sea as key junctions between previously loosely connected economic areas has long been recognized: linking the northern Mediterranean, which extended to the Flanders markets; the southern Mediterranean, stretching from north Africa to India and the Persian Gulf; and the eastern routes into central Asia and China. This form of globalization was unprecedented, and the opportunities it offered unfurled before Europeans in an almost unexpected way. Venice, always eager to expand its horizons, was quick to embrace the challenge.

It is important to remember that this vision of an integrated, secure commercial world, stretching from China through Persia to Europe—defined by the free circulation of goods and people—was, first and foremost, a Mongol ambition. This dream was eagerly adopted by the Mediterranean powers that had long relied on trade as the cornerstone of their existence and success. The most fascinating aspect of this period lies not only in what was achieved, but also in the anticipation of what still seemed possible. Individuals and states alike made remarkable efforts to establish new forms of exchange and communication. The greatest obstacle to these ambitions was the internal fragmentation of Latin Europe, which frequently hindered the creation of cohesive and

2. Abu-Lughod, *Before European Hegemony.*
3. Allsen, *Commodity and Exchange.*

functioning spaces for cooperation and coexistence. Additionally, Mongol political instability, beginning with the collapse of the Ilkhanate, significantly diminished the chances of long-term success.

Venice was at the forefront of forging new connections and routes, but it approached these challenges differently from its primary rival, Genoa. Venice's distinctiveness lay in its state-controlled systems, which included careful oversight of consular representations, a preference for resolving disputes through diplomacy rather than military engagement, and exceptional negotiating skills. The rigidity of the Venetian system left little room for the development of local autonomy, ensuring that a rotating consular presence was consistently maintained in key locations such as Tana, even in times of crisis. The motherland's involvement was constant, offering Venetians the assurance of state protection, especially during difficult periods, like those following Timur's destruction of the settlement. However, this security applied mainly to Black Sea trading posts. Individuals venturing beyond into more distant regions did so with considerably less protection.

While the Mongol Empire "functioned" until the second half of the fourteenth century, treaties guaranteed the compensation for lost goods wherever Mongol authority was recognized. This authority primarily refers to the khans of the Golden Horde, with whom Venice maintained fairly continuous diplomatic relations, and secondarily the Ilkhanate, which also granted protections to Latin merchants. However, no direct diplomatic relations existed between Venice and the Mongol emperors of China or with the rulers of the Chagatai khanate. While Kublai Khan and his successors invited western representatives on several occasions—the Polos, for example, acting as envoys for the pope at the khan's request—Venice never extended its efforts beyond securing access to the Black Sea as a key point of contact between Asian and Mediterranean trade networks.

Within the regions stretching from the Aegean to Tana, Venice's interests as a state and those of individual Venetian merchants were closely aligned, with both depending on one another. However, when merchants ventured deeper into Mongol territories, the protections offered by treaties decreased the farther they moved from consular seats. In these remote areas, merchants had to rely on personal relationships with the Mongols to secure safety and logistical support. The influx of western goods and money into Asian markets was as desirable to the Mongols as finding buyers for their own products. This mutual interest allowed merchants and Mongols to bridge cultural, linguistic, and religious divides.

In this regard, the Mongols were no less innovative than Italian merchants. The functioning of their empire depended not only on maintaining safe roads, but also on developing standardized means of organizing trade through various fiscal and monetary systems. The introduction of paper currency and universal calculation methods in China, for example, was one of the most coherent efforts to build a unified exchange system, though divisions between the various khanates and local resistance prevented its wider adoption. Nevertheless, the mere attempt to create a standardized system was enough to attract merchants. Despite the numerous challenges, access to local markets and the circulation of information through commercial treaties allowed merchants to move and operate within territories where they enjoyed protection.

As many scholars have pointed out, the political instability within the Tatar world, beginning in the 1360s, disrupted the flow of trade along major intercontinental arteries. However, as we have sought to demonstrate, the end of the *pax mongolica* should not be interpreted as an inevitable and gradual decline in the Venetian presence within the "farthest Mediterranean" of the Black Sea. Instead, we put forward a different theory: the key to understanding this period lies in Venice's adaptability to a constantly shifting landscape. This adaptability was shaped not only by power struggles within Christendom but also by complex international developments. It was this capacity to adjust that allowed Venetians to continue engaging in Black Sea trade with the "Tatars" and other central Asian merchants long after the Mongol Empire had dissolved.

The presence of Venetian individuals on routes to China or India, while symbolically significant, was relatively minor in the broader scheme of the Republic's strategic objectives. As we have emphasized, Venice never sought official diplomatic relations with distant courts. The merchants' ability to access far-flung markets was driven by individual initiative and the protection they were able to secure from local rulers. The balance between risk and reward on long-distance ventures was left to the discretion of private investors. The Venetian state, for its part, concentrated on securing free access, favorable tariffs, and diplomatic protection in regions where it could establish and sustain an official presence. In this effort, Venice spared neither resources nor manpower.

Genoa, in comparison to Venice, enjoyed two distinct advantages. First, it held a dominant position in the Black Sea, excelling in trade volume, demographic presence, military fortifications, and control over lucrative commercial sectors, such as the slave trade. Second, the Genoese settlers in the Pontic colonies, such as the Caffiotes, were politically and economically more independent of their homeland than their Venetian counterparts. As a result, they formed a local, and at times semi-autonomous, power. The internal strife and foreign pressure that characterized Genoa's medieval history contributed to these overseas settlements evolving into self-governing communities, closely tied to Caffa's economy and local administration. These colonies maintained a broad network throughout the Black Sea, bolstered by the large Genoese community in Pera. Though ties with the motherland were never completely severed, the trend consistently moved toward greater independence.

Neither the Genoese nor the Venetians operated in a cultural or political vacuum. Both had to navigate a complex landscape of ethnic and religious diversity, interacting with various communities—Greek, Tatar, Armenian, Jewish, Islamic, and others—well established in the regions they entered, initially as traders and travelers, and later as residents and investors integrated into the local socioeconomic fabric. The expansion of Italian communities as political and military powers often strained relations with local populations and rulers. These tensions were further aggravated by the pre-existing rivalry between Genoa and Venice, which not only persisted in these isolated territories but intensified, transferring their ongoing conflicts to the Black Sea arena. Their interactions with Mongol authorities became yet another front in their competition, each city striving to assert dominance. Genoa's supremacy in the region was eventually undermined by Venice, which skillfully used diplomacy to secure privileges from the khan of the Golden Horde. A key concession was the acquisition of land in Tana, which became crucial not only for access to the Black Sea but also for establishing a direct and stable relationship with the khan. This legal, commercial, and territorial arrangement allowed Venice to capitalize on its position, expanding its interests both locally and internationally.

The legal protection Venice had carved out under the khan's authority was the passport it needed to access markets—a central pillar of the Republic's strategy, which always rested on cultivating state relationships. However, the challenges were enormous. Communication, for instance, posed a significant problem. Interpreters and translators, essential for avoiding misunderstandings with unpredictable consequences, commanded exorbitant fees due to their critical role. Moreover, Mongol authorities were uncompromising in their governance, often enacting collective punishments for transgressions, whether real or perceived. This created a precarious situation for Venetians, as the Mongols did not distinguish between the different Latin, Frankish, or Christian groups. As a result, Venetians constantly faced the risk of being penalized for the actions of others within the wider "Latin" community. One notable instance of this collective vulnerability was the slave trade, in which many Christians were regrettably involved. Toqta Khan's strong opposition to the buying and selling of Mongols led to repercussions for all Latins. Yet, despite these tensions, the trade continued largely unchecked.

It is ironic that the greatest crisis the Venetians faced within the Golden Horde stemmed from the actions of a single individual. The person's criminal actions plunged the entire Latin community into panic, caused an enormous amount of material damage, and triggered a protracted war—one that likely, as an unexpected and indirect consequence, contributed to the outbreak of plague in Europe starting in 1348. Reflecting on the tension between collective and individual interests, it is puzzling that the Venetian community chose to prioritize individual protection over the collective good. Their decisions to shield one of their own from Mongol justice, risking the loss of all their merchants' assets, contradicts the usual conduct of Venetian authorities, who frequently sought Mongols' protection, especially against the Genoese. This incident highlight's Venice's difficulty in fully integrating into the Mongol legal system. It also suggests that, in isolated outposts like Tana, governmental oversight was weak, allowing Venetian nobles to evade justice with the help of support networks. The Venetian senate's response—banning the culprit from the Black Sea for the rest of his life—was far from proportional to the devastation caused, the loss of human lives, and the prolonged interruption of commerce. This episode demonstrates the limitations of the Venetian state's power in Tana, despite the presence of consuls, councils, administrators, and a local militia. Their authority was restricted to serving the needs of the community, such as recovering lost goods or negotiating trade tariffs, rather than maintaining law and order.

These limitations became even more evident during Timur's rise to power and the subsequent period. The internal conflicts within the Golden Horde severely weakened its institutions and political structures, and Venice, which had depended on the stability of those institutions for its defense and protection, found itself similarly weakened. From the 1380s onward, the trajectories of Genoa and Venice in Gazaria began to diverge sharply. Genoa, despite the weakening of its government at home, experienced a surge of autonomy in its Pontic colonies. In contrast, Venice—while demonstrating strength through its expansionist polices on the mainland and in the Mediterranean—followed a path of fortification and gradual reduction of its activities and investments in Tana. For Venice, the Pontus was just one aspect of its broader political and commercial strategy. Initially, from the Treaty of Nymphaeum (1261) until the death of Berdi Beg (1359), the Black Sea had been a priority. However, its importance waned in the following decades due to a combination of factors: the rise of the Ottomans, increasing hostility from the Tatars, and renewed diplomatic ties with the Mamluks, which reopened access to lucrative Egyptian markets. As a result, funding for Tana's defense dwindled. Apart from a few companies firmly established in the region, the Venetian community suffered a demographic decline, shrinking business volumes, and decreased investments. The population became more transient, and commercial activities increasingly relied on local agents rather than Venetian merchants.

The Italian presence in the Mongol Empire was far more diverse and complex than it is often portrayed. This diversity stemmed from the unique nature of the merchant diaspora, the varying quality of relationships with the homeland, and the merchants' ability to navigate interactions with local authorities and populations. The differences between Genoa and Venice, frequently highlighted by scholars, had significant consequences for the dynamics between merchants and the state, as well as between the state and its colonies, especially as the Mongol Empire entered into decline. The diminishing influence of Venice in Romània, particularly during the fifteenth century, should not be interpreted as a failure of its commercial system, nor solely as the consequence of the collapse of the *pax mongolica*. Similarly, the strength of Genoa's foothold in Gazaria did not ultimately shield the city from its gradual decline. These contrasting trajectories reflect deeper complexities in how each city managed its overseas presence and responded to external challenges, revealing that the nature of the Italian presence in the Mongol world was anything but homogeneous.

The creation of the Mongol Empire created immense opportunities for the most advanced sectors of the thirteenth-century European mercantile economy. These were "equal opportunities" in that the Mongols did not discriminate between their subjects based on ethnicity, religion, or origin—be they Latins, Saracens, Christians, or Muslims, for example. This lack of discrimination was likely due to their limited understanding of the complex political dynamics of Europe and the Middle East. However, this should not be mistaken for negligence or ignorance. The Mongols were remarkably consistent in their efforts to organize a vast transcontinental trade network, effectively linking Asia and Europe into a unified, interconnected system despite their internal divisions.

The attempt was exceptionally ambitious, one that would only be fully realized centuries later with the discovery of maritime routes linking the world's oceans. Venice positioned itself at the heart of this grand endeavor, driven by its strengths, objectives, and commercial interests. Those who embraced its risks saw their aspirations partly fulfilled and partly thwarted, yet they knew they were part of a global and cosmopolitan venture. This experience led them to forge connections with people of every race, to learn new languages, appreciate foreign customs, and even re-examine their own ways of life. During his time in Tana, the Venetian nobleman Giosafat Barbaro hosted a "Tatar" ambassador returning from Cathay in 1436, hoping to purchase jewelry from him. In their conversation, Barbaro was surprised to learn that the "Lord of China" had knowledge of the Franks. This encounter revealed to him that not only did the Chinese and Tatars dominate the trade routes and markets, but they also possessed vast knowledge about distant cultures.

At the twilight of their adventures in the outermost frontiers of Europe, the Venetians were left with little more than the walls and towers they retreated behind, while the Mongol Empire had already become a fading memory. The next chapter in the history of globalization would be written by new empires, but it would be built upon the knowledge, values, and experiences that had once connected the fortunes of the Venetians and other Italian merchants to the Mongols, world's conquerors.

# APPENDIX A

# Navigation

TABLE 1. Galleys of Romània awarded and amount paid, for the period 1332–1349 (in lire di grossi)

| Year | Number of galleys awarded | Average cost per auction | Total charters paid |
|------|---------------------------|--------------------------|---------------------|
| 1332–33 | 20 | 77.10 | 1542.50 |
| 1336–39 | 27 | 76.70 | 2072.40 |
| 1340–44 | 14 | 74.67 | 1175.50 |
| 1345–49 | 15 | 77.40 | 1161.50 |

Source: Stöckly, *Le système de l'incanto*, p. 371.

TABLE 2. Galleys of Romània awarded and amount paid, for the period 1350–69 (in lire di grossi)

| Year | Number of galleys awarded | Average cost per auction | Total charters paid |
|------|---------------------------|--------------------------|---------------------|
| 1350 | 5 | 61.70 | 308.50 |
| 1351–54 | War of the Straits, navigation is interrupted | | |
| 1355–59 | 14 | 110.70 | 1549.20 |
| 1360–64 | 21 | 52.30 | 1098.20 |
| 1365–69 | 22 | 48.50 | 1067.30 |

Source: Stöckly, *Le système de l'incanto*, p. 372.

TABLE 3. Galleys of Romània awarded and amount paid, for the period 1370–89 (in lire di grossi)

| Year | Number of galleys awarded | Average cost per auction | Total charters paid |
|------|---------------------------|--------------------------|---------------------|
| 1370–74 | 17 | 33.50 | 570 |
| 1375–77 | 7 | 27.50 | 138 |
| 1378–81 | War of Chioggia, navigation is interrupted | | |
| 1383–86 | 13 | 149.30 | 746.70 |
| 1387–89 | 4 | 80.30 | 321.20 |

Source: Stöckly, *Le système de l'incanto*, p. 373.

TABLE 4. Galleys of Romània awarded and amount paid, for the period 1390–1409 (in lire di grossi)

| Year | Number of galleys awarded | Average cost per auction | Total charters paid |
|------|---------------------------|--------------------------|---------------------|
| 1390–94 | 15 | 296.40 | 1482.20 |
| 1395–99 | 9 | 149.96 | 749.80 |
| 1403–07 | 10 | 183.80 | 918.90 |
| 1407–09 | 4 | 41.70 | 208.23 |

Source: Stöckly, *Le système de l'incanto*, p. 374.

TABLE 5. Galleys of Romània awarded and amount paid, for the period 1410–29 (in lire di grossi)

| Year | Number of galleys awarded | Average cost per auction | Total charters paid |
|------|---------------------------|--------------------------|---------------------|
| 1410–14 | 12 | 230.60 | 1152.80 |
| 1415–19 | 12 | 39.20 | 469.90 |
| 1420–24 | 15 | 79.80 | 1196.25 |
| 1425–29 | 15 | 30.50 | 458.20 |

Source: Stöckly, *Le système de l'incanto*, p. 374.

TABLE 6. Galleys of Romània awarded and amount paid, for the period 1430–52 (in lire di grossi)

| Year | Number of galleys awarded | Average cost per auction | Total charters paid |
|------|---------------------------|--------------------------|---------------------|
| 1430–34 | 18 | 49.60 | 893 |
| 1435–39 | 18 | 101.50 | 1826.10 |
| 1440–44 | 15 | 134.80 | 2021.50 |
| 1445–49 | 12 | 228.40 | 2741 |
| 1450–52 | 9 | 171.40 | 1542.60 |

Source: Stöckly, *Le système de l'incanto*, p. 374.

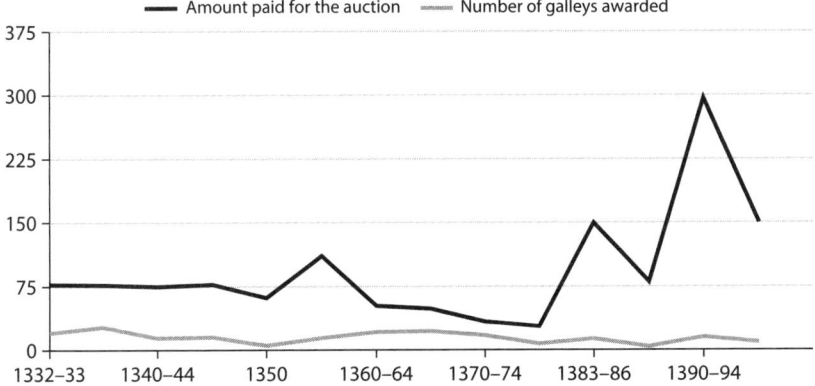

GRAPH 1. Comparison between the curve for the average auctions and the number of galleys of Romània awarded in the fourteenth century

GRAPH 2. Comparison between the curve for the average auctions and the number of galleys of Romània awarded in the fifteenth century

# Money

TABLE 7. Ratio between the Byzantine hyperpyron and Venetian soldi in the thirteenth century

| Year | Place of issue | Hyperpyrons | Venetian soldi |
|------|----------------|-------------|----------------|
| 1226 | Constantinople | 1 | 34 and 8 dinars |
| 1228 | Rialto | 1 | 38 |
| 1228 | Modon/Coron | 1 | 35 |
| 1274 | Modon/Coron | 1 | 26 |

TABLE 8. Weight of Venetian grosso in grams: 1211–1311

| Period (Doge) | Weight |
|---------------|--------|
| 1192–1205, Enrico Dandolo | 2.18 |
| 1205–1229, Pietro Ziani | 2.22 |
| 1229–1249, Jacopo Tiepolo | 2.16 |
| 1249–1253, Marino Morosini | 2.13 |
| 1253–1268, Ranieri Zeno | 2.14 |
| 1268–1275, Lorenzo Tiepolo | 2.11 |
| | 2.16 |
| | 2.01 |
| 1275–1280, Iacopo Contarini | 2.14 |
| 1280–1289, Giovanni Dandolo | 2.04 |
| | 2.18 |
| 1289–1311, Pietro Gradenigo | 2.14 |

Source: Vogel, *Marco Polo Was in China*, p. 472.

TABLE 9. Ratio between gold and silver in Venice from the late thirteenth to the mid-fourteenth centuries

| Years | Quantity of silver per unit of gold |
|---|---|
| 1284 | 10.6–11.3 |
| 1285 | 10.9–11.1 |
| 1286 | 12.9 |
| 1296 | 13.1 |
| 1297 | 13.4 |
| 1301 | 13 |
| 1303–5 | 14.2 |
| 1308 | 14.2 |
| 1318 | 13.9 |
| 1328 | 14.1 |
| 1342 | 15.2 |

TABLE 10. Trend in the value of the asper compared to the sommo in the second half of the fourteenth century

| Year | Ratio sommo : asper | Weight of the asper in silver grams |
|---|---|---|
| 1374–75 | 1:139.25 | 1.57 |
| 1381–82 | 1:142 | 1.54 |
| 1391 | 1:150 | 1.46 |
| 1399 | 1:193 | 1.13 |
| 1409 | 1:200 | 1.09 |

TABLE 11. Variations in weight of the silver dirham in the Ilkhanate after the Ghazan reforms

| Period | Weight in grams | Variation in negative | Standard |
|---|---|---|---|
| Ghazan–Oljeitu T/ B:(1295–1313) | 2.16 | — | — |
| Oljeitu (1313–16) | 1.99 | 0.17 | 7.8 |
| Abu Said (1316–29) | 1.85 | 0.14 | 7.4 |
| Abu Said (1329–32) | 1.62 | 0.23 | 12.4 |
| Abu Said (1332–35) | 1.44 | 0.18 | 11.1 |

Source: Smith, *The Silver Currency*, p. 18.

TABLE 12. Equivalency between the silver sommo and the aspro baricato of Gazaria

| Year | Number of aspri baricati per sommo |
|------|------------------------------------|
| 1290 | 120 |
| 1333 | 150 |
| ca. 1340 | 190 |

Source: Balard, *La Romanie génoise*, p. 660.

TABLE 13. Equivalency between the silver sommo and the new asper of Gazaria

| Year | Number of aspri baricati per silver sommo |
|------|-------------------------------------------|
| 1344 | 50 |
| 1374–75 | 139 |
| 1381–82 | 142 |
| 1386–87 | 145* |
| 1391 | 150 |
| 1399 | 193 |
| 1409 | 200** |

*Up to a maximum of 172
**Up to a maximum of 237
Source: Balard, *La Romanie génoise*, pp. 660–61.

# APPENDIX C

# Weights, Measures, and Taxation of Goods in the Mongol Empire

TABLE 14. General equivalencies of weights and measures in Tana, according to Pegolotti

| Units of measurement | Equivalency |
|---|---|
| 1 cantaro | 100 rotoli; 5 mene; 150 libbre grosse genovesi |
| 1 libbra grossa genovese | 20 rotoli; 12 tocchetti (i.e., 26.47 grams per tocchetto) |
| 1 libbra sottile genovese | 12 once |
| 1 sommo | 45 saggi |

TABLE 15. General equivalencies in Tabriz, according to Pegolotti

| Units of measurement | Equivalency in Venice |
|---|---|
| 100 mene | 300 libbre sottili (1 libbra sottile was equal to 0.3012 kg) |
| 1 mena of silk | 6.25 libbre sottili (1.88 kg) |
| Indaco | 125 libbre sottili |
| 100 braccia of linen | 110 picchi |

TABLE 16. Correspondence of units of measure between Tana and Venice

| Units of measurement | In Venice | In Tana | Type of merchandise |
|---|---|---|---|
| Picco | 125 braccia | 100 braccia | Textiles |
| Mena | 6 libbre, 2 once | 6 libbre | Silk |
| Mena | 1 = 8 libbre sottili | 1 = 156 libbre sottili | Spices (pepper, ginger, lacquer), coral |
| Mazzo | 5 libbre sottili | 10 | Spun gold (thread) |
| Botte | 3 bigonce | 1 | Wine |

TABLE 17. Correspondence of units of measure between Sarai, Astrakhan, and Venice

| Units of measurement | In Sarai and Astrakhan | In Venice | Type of merchandise |
|---|---|---|---|
| Picco | 100 | 118 braccia | Textiles |
| Mina | 1 | 6 libbre, 2 once | Silk |
| Mina | 20 (1 cantaro) | 1 = 8 librre sottile | Spices (pepper, ginger, lacquer), coral |
| Mazzo | 1 | 1.2 libbra sottile | Spun gold (thread) |
| Botte | 1 | 1 | Wine |
| Risma | 1 | 1 | Paper |
| Libbra grossa | | 1 = 5 libree | Metal (iron, tin, copper, cinnabar), honey |

TABLE 18. Equivalencies between a mina and libbre genovesi, according to Pegolotti

| | |
|---|---|
| Sarai | 6 libbre, 2 once |
| Urgench | 3 libbre, 9 once |
| Utrar | 3 libbre, 9 once |
| Almaligh | 2 libbre, 8 once |
| Ganzhou | 2 libbre |

# The Tana Slave Trade between the Fourteenth and Fifteenth Centuries (Out of a Total of 293 Documents Analyzed, Including Sales Contracts and Wills)

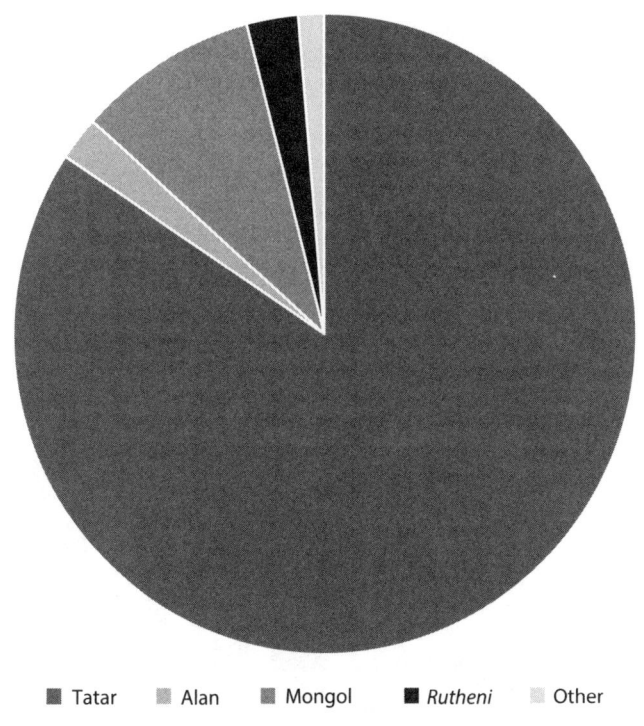

■ Tatar    ▨ Alan    ▨ Mongol    ■ *Rutheni*    ▨ Other

GRAPH 3. Provenance of slaves traded in the fourteenth century (1359–85)

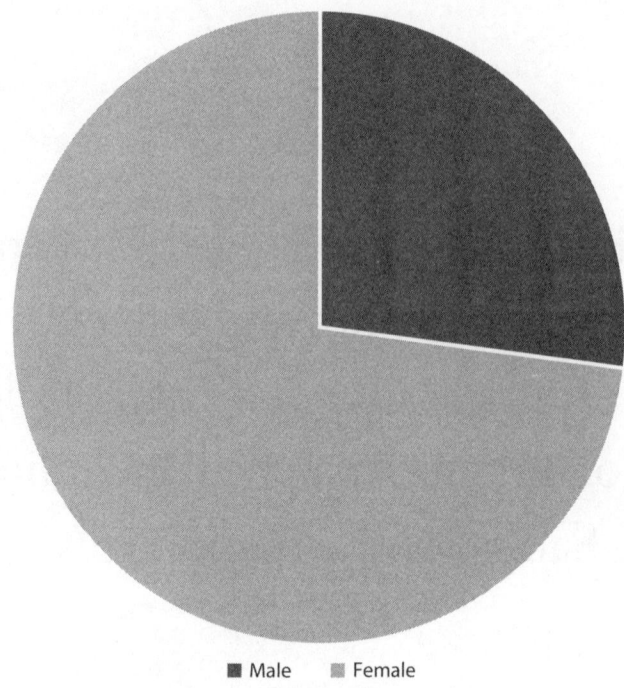

■ Male   ■ Female

GRAPH 4. Division by sex of slaves traded in Tana in the fourteenth century: total (1359–85)

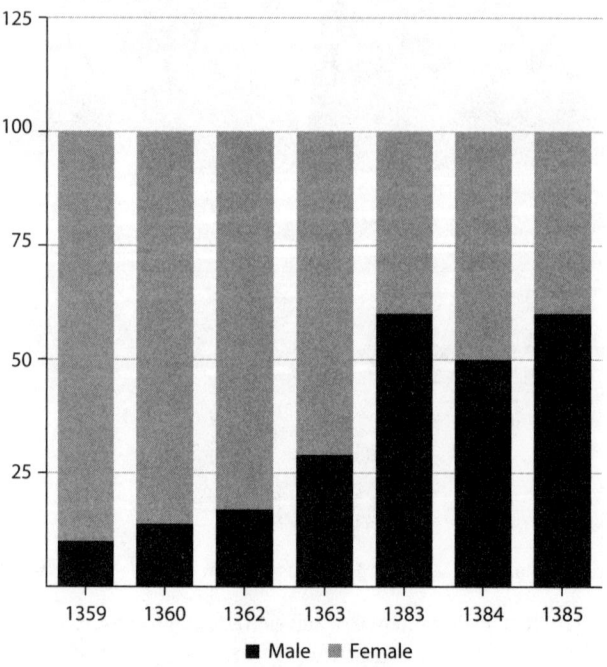

■ Male   ■ Female

GRAPH 5. Division by sex of slaves traded in Tana in the fourteenth century (in percent)

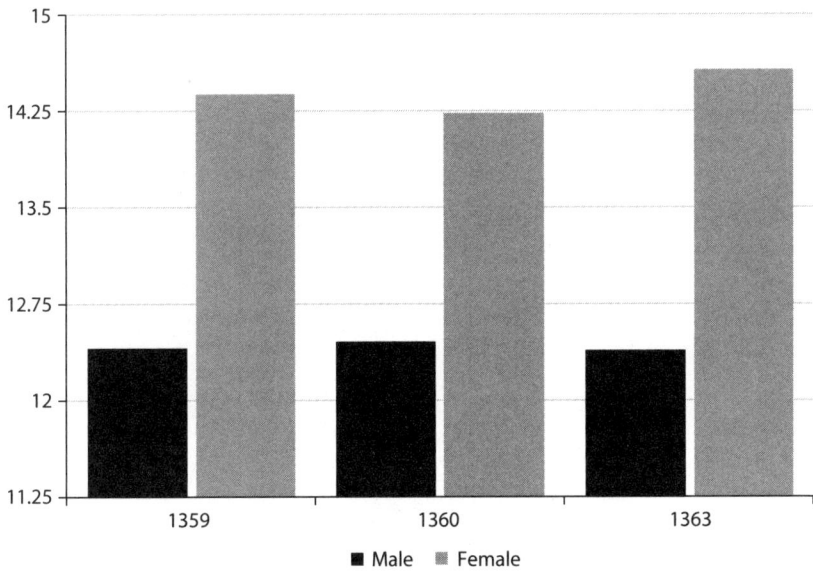

GRAPH 6. Average age of slaves divided by sex in the period 1359–63

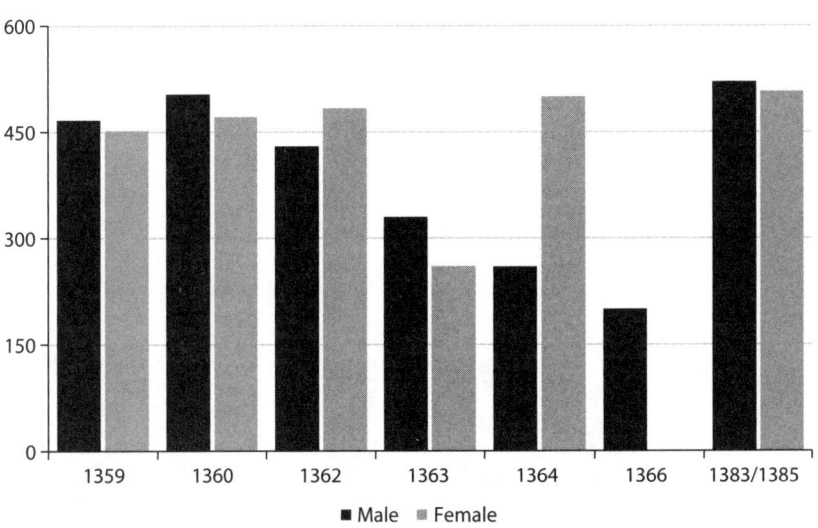

GRAPH 7. Average price of slaves in the fourteenth century (in aspers)

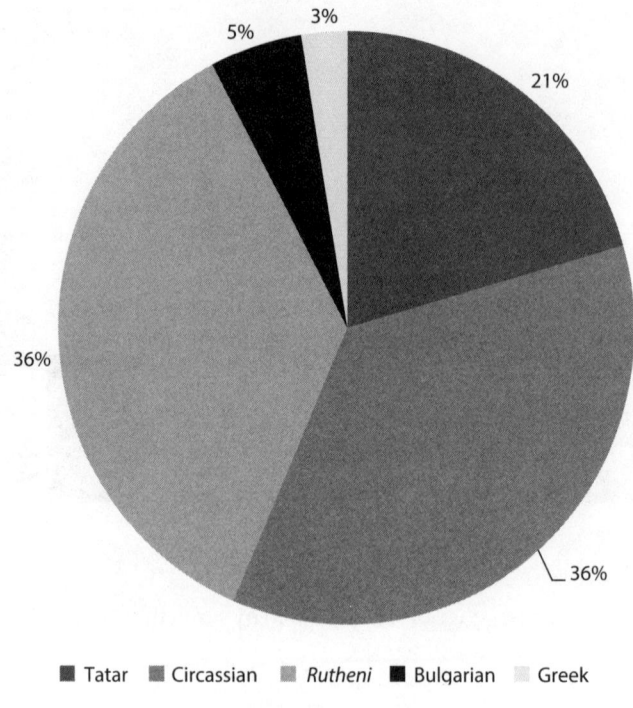

GRAPH 8. Provenance of slaves in the period 1404–15

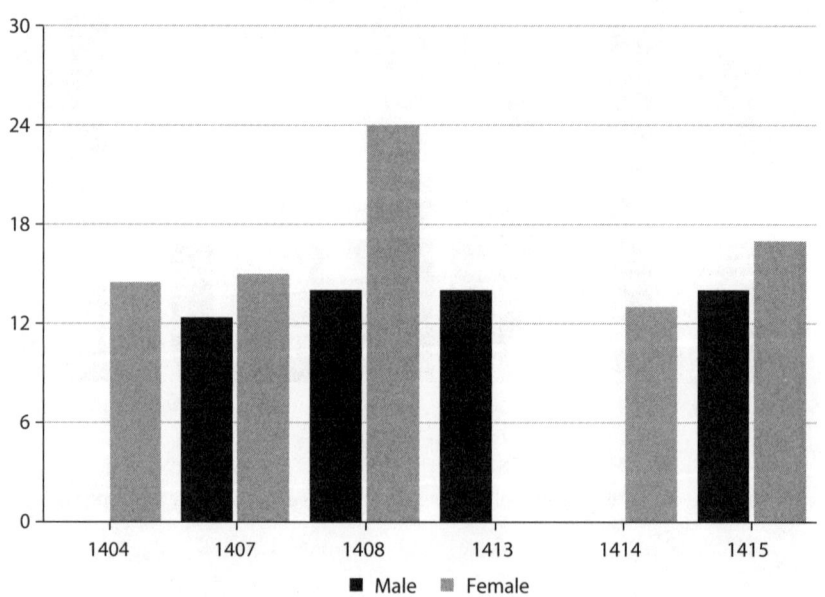

GRAPH 9. Average age of slaves divided by sex in the period 1404–15

# BIBLIOGRAPHY

Abu-Lughod, Janet L., *Before European Hegemony: The World System AD 1250–1350*, Oxford, Oxford University Press, 1989.

Ágoston, Gábor, and Bruce Masters, *Encyclopedia of the Ottoman Empire*, New York, Facts On File, 2008.

Aigle, Denise, "From 'Non-Negotiation' to an Abortive Alliance. Thoughts on the Diplomatic Exchanges between the Mongols and the Latin West," in *The Mongol Empire between Myth and Reality: Studies in Anthropological History*, Leiden, Brill, 2014, pp. 157–98.

———. "The Letters of Eljigidei, Hülegü, and Abaqa: Mongol Overtures or Christian Ventriloquism?," in *Inner Asia*, 7.2 (2005), pp. 143–62.

———. *The Mongol Empire between Myth and Reality: Studies in Anthropological History*, Leiden, Brill, 2014.

Akropolites, George, *The History*, ed. and trans. Ruth Macrides, Oxford, Oxford University Press, 2007.

Al-Dīn, Rashīd, *The Successors of Genghis Khan*, trans. John A. Boyle, New York, Columbia University Press, 1971.

Alexander, John T., *Bubonic Plague in Early Modern Russia: Public Health and Urban Disaster*, Oxford, Oxford University Press, 2003.

Alfani, Guido, Luca Mocarelli, and Donatella Strangio, "Italian Famines: An Overview (ca. 1250–1810)," Dondena Working Papers, 84 (2015).

Alishan, Ghewond M., *L'Armeno-Veneto: compendio storico e documenti delle relazioni degli Armeni coi Veneziani: primo periodo, secoli XIII-XIV*, 2 vols., Venice, Stab. Tip. Armeno, S. Lazzaro, 1893, vol. 1.

Allsen, Thomas T., *Commodity and Exchange in the Mongol Empire: A Cultural History of Islamic Textiles*, Cambridge, Cambridge University Press, 1997.

———. "The Cultural Worlds of Marco Polo," in *The Journal of Interdisciplinary History*, 31 (2001), pp. 375–83.

———. *Culture and Conquest in Mongol Eurasia*, Cambridge, Cambridge University Press, 2001.

———. "Mongolian Princes and Their Merchant Partners, 1200–1260," in *Asia Major*, 2 (1989), pp. 83–126.

———. "Prelude to the Western Campaigns: Mongol Military Operations in the Volga-Ural Region, 1217–1237," in *Archivum Eurasie Medii Aevi*, 3 (1983), pp. 5–24.

———. "The Rise of the Mongolian Empire and Mongolian Rule in North China," in *The Cambridge History of China*, vol. 6: *Alien Regimes and Border States, 907–1368*, eds. Herbert Franke and Denis C. Twitchett, Cambridge, Cambridge University Press, 1994, pp. 321–413.

———. "Sharing out the Empire: Apportioned Lands under the Mongols," in *Nomads in the Sedentary World*, eds. Anatoly M. Khazanov and André Wink, London, Routledge, 2012.

Amitai, Reuven, "Between the Slave Trade and Diplomacy: Some Aspects of Early Mamluk Policy in the Eastern Mediterranean and the Black Sea," in *Slavery and the Slave Trade in the*

*Eastern Mediterranean (c. 1000–1500 CE)*, eds. Reuven Amitai and Christoph Cluse, Turnhout, Brepols, 2017, pp. 401–22.

———. "Diplomacy and the Slave Trade in the Eastern Mediterranean: A Re-Examination of the Mamluk-Byzantine-Genoese Triangle in the Late Thirteenth Century in Light of the Existing Early Correspondence," in *Oriente Moderno*, 88 (2008), pp. 349–68.

———. "Northern Syria between the Mongols and Mamluks: Political Boundary, Military Frontier, and Ethnic Affinities," in *The Mongols in the Islamic Lands: Studies in the History of the Ilkhanate*, Aldershot, Ashgate Variorum, 2007.

———. "The Resolution of the Mongol-Mamluk War," in *Mongols, Turks, and Others*, eds. Reuven Amitai and Michal Biran, Leiden and Boston, Brill, 2005, pp. 359–90.

Amitai-Preiss, Reuven, *Mongols and Mamluks: The Mongol-Ilkhanid War, 1260–1281*, Cambridge, Cambridge University Press, 2009.

Angold, Michael J., "The Byzantine Empire, 1025–1118," in *The New Cambridge Medieval History*, vol. 4, eds. David Luscombe and Jonathan Riley Smith, Cambridge, Cambridge University Press, 2004, pp. 217–53.

———. *The Fourth Crusade: Event and Context*, Abington and New York, Routledge, 2015.

Appuhn Karl, *A Forest on the Sea: Environmental Expertise in Renaissance Venice*, Baltimore, MD, Johns Hopkins University Press, 2009.

Ashtor, Eliyahu, *Levant Trade in the Later Middle Ages*, Princeton, NJ, Princeton University Press, 1983.

———. *A Social and Economic History of the Near East in the Middle Ages*, London, Variorum, 1978.

———. *Storia economica e sociale del Vicino Oriente nel Medioevo*, trans. Sergio Antonucci, Turin, Einaudi, 1982.

Atwood, Christopher P., "The Date of the 'Secret History of the Mongols' Reconsidered," in *Journal of Song-Yuan Studies*, 37 (2007), pp. 1–48.

———. *Encyclopedia of Mongolia and the Mongol Empire*, New York, Facts on File, 2004.

Ayalon, David, *The Mamlūk Military Society*, London, Variorum, 1979.

Balard, Michel, "1261. Genova nel mondo: il trattato di Ninfeo," in *Gênes et la mer / Genova e il mare*, Genoa, Società Ligure di Storia Patria, 2017, pp. 529–50.

———. "A propos de la bataille du Bosphore: L'expédition génoise de Paganino Doria à Constantinople (1351–1352)," in *Travaux et Mémoires du Centre de Recherche d'Histoire et Civilisation de Byzance*, 4 (1970), pp. 431–69.

———. "Colonisation and Population Movements in the Mediterranean in the Middle Ages," in *Byzantium and the West: Perception and Reality (11th–15th C.)*, eds. Nikolaos G. Chrissis, Athina Kolia-Dermitzaki, and Angeliki Papageorgiou, London, Routledge, 2019, pp. 25–37.

———. "Gênes et la mer Noire (XIIIe–XVe siècles)," in *Revue Historique*, 270 (1983), pp. 31–54.

———. *Gênes et l'outre-mer*, 2 vols., Paris, Mouton, 1973.

———. "Les Génois en Crimée aux XIIIe–XVe siècles," in *Archeion Ponton*, 35 (1979), pp. 201–17.

———. "La lotta contro Genova," in *Storia di Venezia. Dalle origini alla caduta della Serenissima*, vol. 3, Rome, Istituto dell'Enciclopedia Italiana, 1997, pp. 87–126.

———. *La Mer Noire et la Romaine génoise, XIIIe–XVe siècles*, London, Variorum, 1989.

———. "L'Occident, Byzance et la mer Noire vers 1200," in *Itinerari medievali e identità europea*, ed. Roberto Greci, Bologna, Clueb, 1999, pp. 49–59.

———. *La Romanie génoise (XIIe-début du XVe siécle)*, 2 vols., Rome: Ecole Française de Rome; Genoa: Società Ligure di Storia Patria, 1978.

————. "Slavery in the Latin Mediterranean (Thirteenth to Fifteenth Centuries): The Case of Genoa," in *Slavery and the Slave Trade in the Eastern Mediterranean (c. 1000–1500 CE)*, eds. Reuven Amitai and Christoph Cluse, Turnhout, Brepols, 2017, pp. 235–54.

————. "Le transport des esclaves dans le monde méditerranéen médiéval," in *Slavery and the Slave Trade in the Eastern Mediterranean (c. 1000–1500 CE)*, eds. Reuven Amitai and Christoph Cluse, Turnhout, Brepols, 2017, pp. 352–74.

Balbi, Giovanna and Silvana Raiteri, *Notai genovesi in oltremare: atti rogati a Caffa e a Licostomo*, Genoa, Istituto internazionale di studi liguri, 1973.

Balletto Laura, "Il commercio del pesce nel Mar Nero sulla fine del Duecento," in *Critica Storica*, 13.3 (1976), pp. 390–407.

Barbaro, Josafa, and Ambrogio Contarini, *I viaggi in Persia degli ambasciatori veneti Barbaro e Contarini*, eds. L. Lockhart, R. Morozzo della Rocca, and M. F. Tiepolo, Rome, Poligrafico 1973.

————. *Travels to Tana and Persia: A Narrative of Italian Travels in Persia in the 15th and 16th Centuries*, New York, Franklin, 1963.

Barbon, Ferdy H., "I segni dei mercanti a Venezia nel Fondaco dei Tedeschi," in *Atti e memorie dell'Ateneo di Treviso*, 23 (2005–6), pp. 103–22.

Barker, Hannah, *Egyptian and Italian Merchants in the Black Sea Slave Trade, 1260–1500*, New York, Columbia University, 2014.

————. *That Most Precious Merchandise: The Mediterranean Trade in Black Sea Slaves, 1260–1500*, Philadelphia, PA, University of Pennsylvania Press, 2019.

Bartusis, Mark C., *The Late Byzantine Army: Arms and Society 1204–1453*, Philadelphia, PA, University of Pennsylvania Press, 1997.

Bauden, Frédéric, "Mamluk Diplomatics: The Present State of Research," in *Mamluk Cairo, A Crossroads for Embassies: Studies on Diplomacy and Diplomatics*, ed. Malidka Dekkiche, Leiden, Brill, 2019, pp. 1–104.

Bautier, Robert H., *Les relations économiques des Occidentaux avec les pays d'Orient au Moyen Age : Points de vue et documents*, Parigi, S.E.V.P.E.N., 1970.

Bellemo, Vincenzo, *La cosmografia e le scoperte geografiche nel secolo XV e i viaggi di Nicolo De' Conti*, Padua, Tipografia del Seminario, 1908.

Benedictow, Ole J., *The Black Death: 1346–1353. The Complete History*, Woodbridge, Boydell & Brewer, 2004.

Benigno, Francesco, and Giuseppe Giarrizzo, *Storia della Sicilia*, vol. 3, Rome–Bari, Laterza, 1999.

Berindei, Mihnea, and Gilles Veinstein, "La Tana-Azaq de la présence italienne à l'emprise ottomane (fin XIIIe-milieu XVI siècle)," in *Turcica*, 8.2 (1976), pp. 110–201.

Berindei, Mihnea, and Giustiniana Migliardi O'Riordan, "Venise et la Horde d'Or fin XIIIe— Début XIVe siècle: A propos d'un document inédit de 1324," in *Cahiers du Monde russe et soviétique*, (1988), pp. 243–56.

Bernardini, Michele, *Tamerlano. Il conquistatore delle steppe che assoggettò l'Asia dando vita a una nuova civiltà*. Rome, Salerno, 2022.

Bernardini, Michele, and Donatella Guida, *I Mongoli. Espansione, imperi, eredità*. Turin, Einaudi, 2012.

Bertelè, Tommaso, "Moneta veneziana e moneta bizantina," in *Venezia e il Levante fino al secolo XV. Atti del I convegno Internazionale di storia della Civiltà Veneziana (Venezia 1–5 giugno 1968)*, ed. Agostino Pertusi, 2 vols., Florence, Olschki, 1973–74, vol. 1, pp. 3–146.

Bertolotto, Gerolamo and Angelo Sanguineti, *Nuova serie di documenti sulle relazioni di Genova con l'imperatore bizantino*, Genoa, Sordo muti, 1898.

Bigalli, Davide, *I Tartari e l'Apocalisse*, Florence, La nuova Italia, 1971.

Biran, Michal, "Diplomacy and Chancellery Practices in the Chagataid Khanate: Some Preliminary Remarks," in *Oriente Moderno*, 88.2 (2008), pp. 369–93.

———. *The Empire of the Qara Khitai in Eurasian History: Between China and the Islamic World*, Cambridge, Cambridge University Press, 2005.

———. *Qaidu and the Rise of the Independent Mongol State in Central Asia*, London, Routledge, 2013.

Blanchard, Ian, *Mining, Metallurgy, and Minting in the Middle Ages*, vol. 3, *Continuing Afro-European Supremacy, 1250–1450*, Stuttgart, Franz Steiner Verlag, 2001.

Borbone, Pier Giorgio, *Storia di Mar Yahballaha e di Rabban Sauma: Un orientale in Occidente ai tempi di Marco Polo*, Turin, Zamorani, 2000.

Borsari, Silvano, "Il commercio veneziano nell'impero bizantino nel XII secolo," in *Rivista Storica Italiana*, 76 (1964), pp. 982–1011.

———. *Il dominio veneziano a Creta nel XII secolo*, Naples, Fiorentino, 1963.

———. *Studi sulle colonie veneziane in Romania nel XIII secolo*, Naples, Tip. La buona stampa, 1966.

Bratianu, George I., *Actes des notaires génois de Péra et de Caffa de la fin du treizième siècle: 1281–1290*, Bucharest, Académie roumaine, 1927.

———. "Les origines de la guerre de Curzola (1294–1299) entre Gênes et Venise," in *Mélanges d'Histoire Générale*, ed. Marinescu, Cluj, Institut d'Histoire Générale, 1927, pp. 87–100.

———. *Recherches sur le commerce génois dans la mer Noire au XIIIe siècle*, Paris, Geuthner, 1929.

Braudel, Fernand, *Civiltà materiale, economia e capitalismo: Le strutture del quotidiano (secoli XV–XVIII)*, vol. 2, Turin, Einaudi, 1981.

Brett, Michael, *The Fatimid Empire*, Edinburgh, Edinburgh University Press, 2017.

Bridbury, Anthony R., "Thirteenth-Century Prices and the Money Supply," in *The Agricultural History Review*, 33.1 (1985), pp. 1–21.

Broadbridge, Anne F., *Women and the Making of the Mongol Empire*, Cambridge, Cambridge University Press, 2018.

Bryer, Anthony, and Michael Ursinus, eds., *Manzikert to Lepanto: the Byzantine world and the Turks, 1071–1571. Papers Given at the Nineteenth Spring Symposium of Byzantine Studies*, Amsterdam, Hakket, 1991.

Buenger Robbert, Louise, "Il sistema monetario," in *Storia di Venezia. Dalle origini alla caduta della Serenissima*, vol. 2, eds. Gherardo Ortalli and Giorgio Cracco, Rome, Treccani, 1995, pp. 409–36.

———. *The Venetian Money Market, 1150–1229*, Florence, Olschki, 1971.

Büntgen, Ulf, and Nicola Di Cosmo, "Climatic and Environmental Aspects of the Mongol Withdrawal from Hungary in 1242 CE," in *Scientific Reports*, 6.1 (2016), pp. 1–9.

Cahen, Claude, "La campagne de Mantzikert d'après les sources musulmanes," in *Byzantion*, 9 (1934), pp. 613–42.

———. *Pre-Ottoman Turkey: A General Survey of the Material and Spiritual Culture and History, c. 1071–1330*, New York, Taplinger, 1968.

Canale, Michele Giuseppe, *Della Crimea del suo commercio e dei suoi dominatori*, 3 vols., vol. 2, Genoa, Sordo muti, 1855.

Canestrini, Giuseppe, *Documenti spettanti al commercio dei veneziani con l'Armenia e Trebisonda, Ragusa e Negroponte (1201–1321)*, Florence, Cellini, 1854.

———. "Il Mar Nero e le colonie degli italiani nel Medio Evo," in *Archivio Storico Italiano*, 5.1 (1857), pp. 3–28.

Cantor, Norman F., *In the Wake of the Plague: The Black Death and the World It Made*, London, Pocket, 2001.

Caravale, Mario, "Le istituzioni della Repubblica," in *Storia di Venezia. Dalle origini alla caduta della Serenissima*, vol. 3, Rome, Istituto dell'Enciclopedia Italiana, 1997, pp. 299–364.

Ceccarelli Lemut, Maria Luisa, "Pisa nel Mediterraneo durante il XIII secolo," in *Bollettino storico pisano*, 75 (2006), pp. 1–20.

Cecchetti, Bartolomeo, "Testamento di Pietro Vioni veneziano fatto a Tauris (Persia) MCCLXIV, X dicembre," in *Archivio Veneto*, 26 (1883), pp. 161–65.

Cessi, Roberto, "La tregua fra Venezia e Genova nella seconda metà del sec. XIII," in *Archivio veneto-tridentino*, 4 (1923), pp. 1–55.

Chaffee, John W., *The Muslim Merchants of Premodern China: The History of a Maritime Asian Trade Diaspora, 750–1400*, Cambridge, Cambridge University Press, 2018.

Chajdarov, Timir F., "Épidemija čumy v XIII-XIV vekaxh i eë posledstvija," in *Épidemii i prorodnye kataklizmy v Zolotoj Orde i na sopredel'nych territorijach (XIII-XVI vv.). Sbornik Naučnych Statej*, ed. Il'nur M. Mirgaleev, Kazan, 2018, pp. 47–62.

Cherubini, Giovanni, *Agricoltura e società rurale nel medioevo*, Florence, Sansoni, 1972.

———. "La 'Crisi del trecento.' Bilancio e prospettive di ricerca," in *Studi storici*, 15.3 (1974), pp. 660–70.

Cheynet, Jean-Claude, "Mantzikert: un désastre militaire?," in *Byzantion*, 50.2 (1980), pp. 410–38.

Chinazzo, Daniele, *Cronica de la guerra da Veniciani a Zenovesi*, ed. Vittorio Lazzarini, Venice, Deputazione di Storia Patria per le Venezie, 1958.

Chrissis, Nikolaos G., *Crusading in Frankish Greece: A Study of Byzantine-Western Relations and Attitudes, 1204–1282*, Turnhout, Brepols, 2013.

Ciocîltan, Virgil, *The Mongols and the Black Sea Trade in the Thirteenth and Fourteenth Centuries*, Leiden and Boston, Brill, 2012.

Cleaves, Francis Woodman, "A Chinese Source Bearing on Marco Polo's Departure from China and a Persian Source on his Arrival in Persia," in *Harvard Journal of Asiatic Studies*, 36 (1976), pp. 181–203.

Cohn, Samuel K., *The Black Death Transformed: Disease and Culture in Early Renaissance Europe*, London, Arnold, 2002.

Concina, Ennio, *L'arsenale della Repubblica di Venezia*, Milan, Electa, 2006.

Costa, Maria M., "Sulla battaglia del Bosforo: 1352," in *Studi Veneziani*, 14 (1972), pp. 197–210.

Crescenzi, Victor, "Il diritto civile," in *Storia di Venezia. Dalle origini alla caduta della Serenissima*, vol. 3, Rome, Istituto dell'Enciclopedia Italiana, 1997, pp. 409–74.

*Cronaca senese di autore anonimo del sec. XIV*, eds. Alessandro Lisini and Fabio Iacometti, orig. in *Rerum Italicarum Scriptores*, ed. Ludovico Antonio Muratori, vol. 15, Milan: Societatis Palatinae, 1729.

Crouzet-Pavan, Elisabeth, *Venezia trionfante. Gli orizzonti di un mito*, Turin, Einaudi, 2001.

———. *Venice Triumphant: The Horizons of a Myth*, Baltimore, MD, Johns Hopkins University Press, 2005.

Curta, Florin, "A Note on Trade and Trade Centers in the Eastern and Northern Adriatic Region between the Eighth and the Ninth Century," in *Hortus Artium Medievalium*, 16 (2010), pp. 267–76.

———. *Southeastern Europe in the Middle Ages, 500–1250*, Cambridge, Cambridge University Press, 2006.

Da Canal, Martin, "La Chronique des Véniciens de Maistre Martin da Canal: Première Partie," in *Archivio Storico Italiano*, 8 (1845), pp. 268–447.

———. *Les estoires de Venise: cronaca veneziana in lingua francese dalle origini al 1275*, ed. Alberto Limentani, Florence, Olschki 1972.

Da Canal, Nicolò, *Zibaldone da Canal. Manoscritto mercantile del sec. XIV*, ed. Alfredo Stussi, Venice, Comitato per la pubblicazione delle fonti relative alla storia di Venezia, 1967.

Dashdondog, Bayarsaikhan, *The Mongols and the Armenians (1220–1335)*, Leiden, Brill, 2010.

Dawson, Christopher, *Mission to Asia*, Toronto, University of Toronto Press and Medieval Academy of America, 2008.

———. *The Mongol Mission: Narratives and Letters of the Franciscan Missionaries in Mongolia and China in the Thirteenth and Fourteenth Centuries*, London, Sheed and Ward, 1955.

Day, John, "Banca e moneta a Venezia fra medioevo e rinascimento," in *Studi Storici*, 27.3 (1986), pp. 737–42.

De Clavijo, Ruy González, *Viaggio a Samarcanda: 1403–1406: un ambasciatore spagnolo alla corte di Tamerlano*, ed. Paola Boccardi Storoni, Rome, Viella, 1999.

De Colli, Sandro, *Moretto Bon: notaio in Venezia, Trebisonda e Tana (1403–1408)*, Venice, Comitato per la pubblicazione delle fonti relative alla storia di Venezia, 1963.

De' Conti Nicolo, *Le voyage aux Indes de Nicolo De' Conti*, eds. Geneviève Bouchon, Diane Ménard, and Anne-Laure Amilhat-Szary, Paris, Chandeigne, 2004.

De Mussi, Gabriele, "Historia de morbo sive mortalitate quae fuit anno Domini MCCCXLVII, red. H. Haeser," in *Archiv für die gesammte Medicin*, 2 (1841), pp. 25–59.

De Rachewiltz, Igor, "Marco Polo Went to China," in *Zentralasiatische Studien*, 27 (1997), pp. 34–92.

———. *Papal Envoys to the Great Khans*, London, Faber & Faber, 1971.

De Rachewiltz, Igor and May Wang, eds., *In the Service of the Khan. Eminent Personalities of the Early Mongol-Yuan Period (1200–1300)*, Wiesbaden, Harrassowitz, 1993.

*Deliberazioni del Maggior Consiglio di Venezia*, ed. Roberto Cessi, 3 vols., Bologna, Zanichelli, 1931–50.

Desimoni, Cornelio, "Pero Tafur, i suoi viaggi e il suo incontro col venez. Niccolò de' Conti," in *Atti della Società ligure di storia patria*, 15 (1881), pp. 329–52.

Desmond, Martin H., "The Mongol Wars with Hsi Hsia (1205–27)," in *Journal of the Royal Asiatic Society*, 74.3–4 (1942), pp. 195–228.

———. *The Rise of Chingis Khan and his Conquest of North China*, New York, Octagon Books, 1981.

DeWeese, Devin A., *Islamization and Native Religion in the Golden Horde: Baba Tükles and Conversion to Islam in Historical and Epic Tradition*, Philadelphia, University Park, 1994.

———. "Toķtamish," in *Encyclopaedia of Islam. Second Edition Online*, eds. Peri J. Bearman, Thierry Bianquis, Clifford E. Bosworth, Emery van Donzel, and Wolfarth P. Heinrichs, Leiden, Brill, 2012, pp. 560–63.

Di Cosmo, Nicola, "Black Sea Emporia and the Mongol Empire: A Re-Assessment of the Pax Mongolica," in *Journal of the Economic and Social History of the Orient*, 53.1–2 (2010), pp. 83–108.

———. "Mongols and Merchants on the Black Sea Frontier," in *Mongols, Turks, and Others*, eds. Reuven Amitai and Michal Biran, Leiden and Boston, Brill, 2005, pp. 391–424.

———. "State Formation and Periodization in Inner Asian History," in *Journal of World History* 10 (1999), pp. 1–40.

*Die Chronik Johanns von Winterthur*, eds. Carl Brun and Friedrich Baethgen, in Monumenta Germanie Historica, *Scriptores Rerum Germanicarum*, Berlin, 1924, pp. 1–182.

Dini, Bruno, "I circuiti del commercio internazionale nel tardo Medioevo," in *Prodotti e tecniche d'Oltremare nelle economie europee. Secc. XIII-XVIII*, ed. Simonetta Cavaciocchi, Florence, Le Monnier, 1998 pp. 664–9.

———. "I viaggi dei mercanti e il commercio internazionale nel Medioevo," in *Viaggiare nel Medioevo*, ed. Sergio Gensini, Pacini, Prato, 2003, pp. 195–225.

*Diplomatarium veneto-levantinum. Sive acta et diplomata res venetas graecas atque levantis illustrantia 1300–1350*, ed. George Martin Thomas, Venice, Sumptibus, 1880.

*Diplomatarium veneto-levantinum. Sive acta et diplomata res venetas graecas atque levantis illustrantia 1351–1454*, ed. Riccardo Predelli, Venice, Sumptibus, 1889.

*Documenti del commercio veneziano nei secoli XI–XIII*, eds. Agostino Lombardo and Raimondo Morozzo della Rocca, Turin, Bottega D'Erasmo, 1971.

*Documenti relativi alla storia di Venezia anteriori al mille*, ed. Roberto Cessi, 2 vols., vol. 1, Padova, Gregoriana editrice, 1942.

Dorigo, Wladimiro, "Le espressioni d'arte: gli edifici," in *Storia di Venezia. Dalle origini alla caduta della Serenissima*, vol. 2, eds. Gherardo Ortalli and Giorgio Cracco, Rome, Treccani, 1995, pp. 803–62.

Dörrie, Heinrich, *Drei Texte zur Geschichte der Ungarn und Mongolen: Die Missionsreisen des Fr. Julianus O.P. ins Uralgebiet (1234/5) und nach Russland (1237) und der Bericht des Erzbischofs Peter über die Tartaren*, Göttingen, Vandenhoeck & Ruprecht, 1957.

Doumerc, Bernard, "Le dispositif portuaire vénitien (XIIe–XVe siècle)," in *Ports maritimes et ports fluviaux au Moyen Age. Actes des congrès de la Société des historiens médiévistes de l'enseignement supérieur public, 35ᵉ congrès*, La Rochelle, 2004, Paris, Éditions de la Sorbonne, 2005, pp. 99–116.

———. "Gli armamenti marittimi," in *Storia di Venezia. Dalle origini alla caduta della Serenissima*, vol. 3, Roma, Istituto dell'Enciclopedia Italiana, 1997, pp. 617–40.

———. "La Tana au XVe siècle: comptoir ou colonie?," in *État et colonisation au Moyen Âge et à la Renaissance. Actes du colloque international, Reims, 2–4 avril 1987*, ed. Michel Balard, Lion, L'histoire partagée, 1989, pp. 251–66.

———. "Les Vénitiens à La Tana (Azov) au XVe siècle," in *Cahiers du monde russe et soviétique*, 28.1 (1987), pp. 5–19.

Drimba, Vladimir, *Codex Comanicus: édition diplomatique avec fac-similés*, Bucharest, Editura Enciclopedica, 2000.

Dunnel, Ruth, "The Hsi Hsia," in *The Cambridge History of China*, vol. 6: *Alien Regimes and Border States, 907–1368*, eds. Herbert Franke and Denis C. Twitchett, Cambridge, Cambridge University Press, 1994, pp. 154–213.

Dupuigrenet Desroussilles, François, "Vénitiens et Génois à Constantinople et en mer Noire en 1431 d'après une lettre de Martino da Mosto, baile à Constantinople, au baile et aux conseillers de Nègropont," in *Cahiers du monde russe et soviétique*, 20 (1979), pp. 111–22.

*Encyclopaedia of Islam. Second Edition Online*, edited by Peri J. Bearman, Thierry Bianquis, Clifford E. Bosworth, Emery van Donzel, and Wolfarth P. Heinrichs, Brill, 2012. Online version: https://referenceworks.brillonline.com/browse/encyclopaedia-of-islam-2#.

Endicott-West, Elizabeth, "Merchant Associations in Yüan China: The 'Ortoy,'" in *Asia Major*, 2 (1989), pp. 127–54.

*Epistolae Merowingici et Karolini aevi*, eds. Ernst Dümmler, Wilhelm Gundlach, Walter W. Arndt, and Carl R. Rodenberg, Berlin, Weidmann, 1892.

Favereau, Marie, "The Golden Horde and the Mamluks," in *Zolotoordynskoe obozrenie*, 1 (2017), pp. 93–115.

———. *The Horde: How the Mongols Changed the World*, Cambridge, MA, Harvard University Press, 2021.

Favreau-Lilie [*sic*], Marie-Luise, "The Fall of Acre (1291): Considerations of Annalists in Genoa, Pisa, and Venice (13th/14th–16th Centuries)," in *Acre and its Falls: Studies in the History of a Crusader City*, ed. John France, Leiden, Brill, 2018, pp. 166–82.

Favereau, Marie, and Liesbeth Geevers, "The Golden Horde, the Spanish Habsburg Monarchy, and the Construction of Ruling Dynasties," in *Prince, Pen, and Sword: Eurasian Perspectives*, ed. Maaike van Berkel, Leiden, Brill, 2018, pp. 452–512.

Fennell, John L., *A History of the Russian Church*, London and New York, Routledge, 1995.

Fenster, Erwin, "Zur Fahrt der venezianischen Handelsgaleeren in das Schwarze Meer 1362," in *Byzantinoslavica*, 28 (1978), pp. 161–95.

Ferretto, Arturo, *Codice diplomatico delle relazioni fra la Liguria, la Toscana e la Lunigiana: ai tempi di Dante (1265–1321)*, Roma, Artigianelli, 1901.

Fletcher, Joseph, "Turco-Mongolian Monarchic Tradition in the Ottoman Empire," in *Harvard Ukrainian Studies*, 3 (1979), pp. 236–51.

Fomenko, Igor K., "Nomenklatura geografičeskich nazvanij prečernomor'ja po morskim kartami XIII-XVII vv.," in *Pričernomor'e v Srednie Veka*, 5 (2001), pp. 40–107.

Forbes Manz, Beatrice, *The Rise and Rule of Tamerlane*, Cambridge, Cambridge University Press, 1999.

Forchieri, Giovanni, *Navi e navigazione a Genova nel Trecento. Il Liber Gazarie*, Bordighera, Istituto internazionale di studi liguri, 1974.

Franke, Herbert, "Aḥmad," in *In the Service of the Khan. Eminent Personalities of the Early Mongol-Yuan Period (1200–1300)*, eds. Igor De Rachewiltz and May Wang, Wiesbaden, Harrassowitz, 1993, pp. 539–57.

———. "The Chin Dynasty," in *The Cambridge History of China*, vol. 6: *Alien Regimes and Border States, 907–1368*, eds. Herbert Franke and Denis C. Twitchett, Cambridge, Cambridge University Press, 1994, pp. 215–320.

Freedman, Paul, *Out of the East: Spices and the Medieval Imagination*, New Haven, Yale University Press, 2008.

Gallina, Mario, *Potere e società a Bisanzio: dalla fondazione di Costantinopoli al 1204*, Turin, Enaudi, 1995.

———. *Una società coloniale del Trecento: Creta fra Venezia e Bisanzio*, Venice, Deputazione, 1989.

Garzaniti, Marcello, "Le origini medievali dell'idea di 'santa Russia.' La commemorazione della battaglia di Kulikovo (1380) nella Narrazione del massacro di Mamaj," in *Reti Medievali Rivista*, 17.1 (2016), pp. 35–70.

Ghazarian, Jacob G., *The Armenian Kingdom in Cilicia during the Crusades: The Integration of Cilician Armenians with the Latins 1080–1393*, London, Routledge, 2020.

Giagnacovo, Maria, *Appunti di metrologia mercantile. Un contributo della documentazione aziendale Datini*, Florence, Firenze University Press, 2014.

Giardina, Francesco Saverio, *I viaggi di Nicolò de Conti: appunti su la relazione di essi*, Catania, Coco, 1899.

Giarenis, Ilias, "Nicaea and the West (1204–1261): Aspects of Reality and Rhetoric," in *Byzantium and the West. Perception and Reality (11th–15th C.)*, eds. Nikolaos G. Chrissis, Athina Kolia-Dermitzaki, and Angeliki Papageorgiou, London, Routledge, 2019, pp. 206–19.

Gibb Hamilton, A., *The Travels of Ibn Battuta AD 1325–1354*, Cambridge, Cambridge University Press, 1962.

Gilli-Elewy Hend, "Al-awādi al-ǧāmia: A Contemporary Account of the Mongol Conquest of Baghdad, 656/1258," in *Arabica*, 58.5 (2011), pp. 351–71.

Gioffrè, Domenico, *Il mercato degli schiavi a Genova nel secolo XV*, Genoa, Bozzi, 1971.

Giomo, Giuseppe, "Regesto dei Misti del Senato della Repubblica di Venezia," in *Archivio Veneto*, 17 (1879), pp. 126–40.

———. "Le rubriche dei libri Misti del Senato perduti," in *Archivio Veneto*, 17 (1879), pp. 251–73 and 18 (1879), pp. 40–69.

———. *Libri commemoriali della Repubblica di Venezia*, ed. Riccardo Predelli, 7 vols., Venice, 1876–1914.

Golden, Peter B., *An Introduction to the History of the Turkic Peoples: Ethnogenesis and State-Formation in Medieval and Early Modern Eurasia and the Middle East*, Wiesbaden, Harrassowitz, 1992.

Golden Peter B., Haggai Ben-Shammai, and András Róna-Tas, eds., *The World of the Khazars: New Perspectives. Selected Papers from the Jerusalem 1999 International Khazar Colloquium Hosted by the Ben Zvi Institute*, Leiden, Brill, 2007.

Golev, Konstantin, "The Cuman-Qïpchaqs and Crimea: The Role of the Peninsula in the Nomads' Relation with the Outside World," in *Archivum Eurasiae Medii Aevi*, 24 (2018), pp. 23–108.

Golubovich, Girolamo, *Biblioteca bio-bibliografica della Terra Santa e dell'Oriente Francescano*, vol. 3: *Dal 1300 al 1332*, Florence, Collegio di S. Bonaventura, 1919.

Gorovei, Ștefan S., "The Principality of Theodoro (Mangup) and Stephen the Great's Moldavia: Observations and Hypotheses," in *From Pax Mongolica to Pax Ottomanica*, eds. Ovidiu Cristea and Liviu Pilat, Leiden and Boston, Brill, 2020, pp. 146–68.

Green, Monica H., "Taking 'Pandemic' Seriously: Making the Black Death Global," in *The Medieval Globe*, 1.1 (2015), pp. 27–61.

———. "The Four Black Deaths," in *The American Historical Review*, 125.5 (2020), pp. 1601–31.

Grekov, Boris D., and Aleksandr Ju. Jakubovskij, *L'Orda d'Oro*, Rome, Editori riuniti, 1957.

Grigor'ev, A. P., "Zolotoordynskie chany 60-70-ch godov XIV v.: chronologija pravlenij," in *Istoriografija i istočnikovedenie stran Azii i Afriki: sbornik*, 7 (1983), pp. 9–54.

Grillo, Paolo, *L'aquila e il giglio: 1266, la battaglia di Benevento*, Rome, Salerno editrice, 2015.

Grousset, René, *The Empire of the Steppes: A History of Central Asia*, New Brunswick, NJ, Rutgers University Press, 1970.

Gumilev, Lev Nikolaevich, *Drevnjaja Rus' i Velikaja step'*, Moscow, Tovariščestvo Klyšnikov, Komarov i Ko, 1992.

Güner, Galip, *Kuman bilmeceleri üzerine notlar*, Istanbul, Kesit, 2005.

Guzman, Gregory G., "Simon of Saint-Quentin and the Dominican Mission to the Mongol Baiju: A Reappraisal," in *Speculum*, 46 (1971), pp. 232–49.

Haldon, John, *Warfare, State and Society in the Byzantine World 565–1204*, London, Routledge, 1999.

Halperin, Charles J., "The Battle of Kulikovo Field (1380) in History and Historical Memory," in *Kritika: Explorations in Russian and Eurasian History*, 14.4 (2013), pp. 853–64.

———. *Russia and the Golden Horde: The Mongol Impact on Medieval Russian History*, Bloomington, Indiana University Press, 2010.

———. "Russia in the Mongol Empire in Comparative Perspective," in *Harvard Journal of Asiatic Studies*, 43.1 (1983), pp. 239–61.

———. "The Russian Land and the Russian Tsar: The Emergence of Muscovite Ideology, 1380–1408," in *Forschungen zur osteuropäischen Geschichte*, 23 (1976), pp. 7–103.

———. "The Six-Hundredth Anniversary of the Battle of Kulikovo Field, 1380–1980, in Soviet Historiography," in *Canadian-American Slavic Studies*, 18.3 (1984), pp. 298–310.

———. "The Six-Hundredth Anniversary of the Battle of Kulikovo Field, 1380–1980, in Soviet Historiography," in *Russia and Mongols: Slavs and the Steppe in Medieval and Early Modern Russia*, eds. Victor Spinei and George Bilavschi, Bucharest, 2007, pp. 165–76.

———. "A Tatar Interpretation of the Battle of Kulikovo Field, 1380: Rustam Nabiev," in *Nationalities Papers*, 44.1 (2016), pp. 4–19.

Hatcher, John, *Plague, Population and the English Economy 1348–1530*, Oxford, Macmillan, 1977.

———. *English Tin Production and Trade before 1550*, New York, Oxford University Press, 1973.

Hautala, Roman, "Catholic Missions in the Golden Horde Territory," in *From Pax Mongolica to Pax Ottomanica*, eds. Ovidiu Cristea and Liviu Pilat, Leiden and Boston, Brill, 2020, pp. 39–65.

———. "Comparing Eastern and Missionary Sources on the Golden Horde's History," in *Zolotoordynskoe obozrenie*, 7.2 (2019), pp. 208–24.

———. "Early Hungarian Information of the Beginning of the Western Campaign of Batu (1235–1242)," in *Acta Orientalia Academiae Scientiarum Hungaricae*, 69.2 (2016), pp. 183–99.

———. "Jarlik xhana Uzbeka franciskancam Zolotoj Ordy 1314 goda: latinskij tekst, russkij perevod i commentarii," in *Zolotoordynskoe obozrenie*, 3 (2014), pp. 31–48.

———. "Latin Sources on the Religious Situation in the Golden Horde in the Early Reign of Uzbek Khan, in *Zolotoordynskoe obozrenie*, 4.2 (2016), pp. 336–46.

———. "Pis'ma franciskancev iz Zolotoj Ordy: svedenija latinskich istočnikov o religioznoj politike chana Uzbeka (1312/13–1341), in *Rossica Antiqua*, 1.9 (2014), pp. 63–103.

———. *V zemljach "severnoj Tartarii" svedenija latinskich istočnikov o Zolotoj Orde v pravlenie chana Uzbeka (1313–1341)*, Kazan, Mardžani, 2019.

Haw, Stephen G., *Marco Polo's China: A Venetian in the Rrealm of Khubilai Khan*, New York, Routledge, 2006.

Hendy, Michael F., *Studies in the Byzantine Monetary Economy c. 300–1450*, Cambridge and New York, Cambridge University Press, 1985.

Heyd, Wilhelm, *Le colonie commerciali degli italiani in Oriente nel Medio Evo*, ed. Giuseppe Müller, 2 vols., Venice, Antonelli, 1866–8.

———. *Storia del commercio del Levante nel medio evo*, Turin, UTET, 1913.

Hocquet, Jean Claude, "I meccanismi dei traffici," in *Storia di Venezia: Dalle origini alla caduta della Serenissima*, vol. 3, Roma, Istituto dell'Enciclopedia Italiana, 1997, pp. 529–616.

———. *La sel et la fortune de Venise*, 2 vols., Lille, Hocquet, 1979–82.

Holt, Peter M., *Early Mamluk Diplomacy, 1260–1269: Treaties of Barbars and Qalāwūn with Christian Rulers*, Leiden and New York, Brill, 1995.

———. "The Mamluk Institution," in *A Companion to the History of the Middle East*, ed. Youssef M. Choueiri, Malden, Blackwell Publishers, 2005, pp. 154–69.

Hope, Michael, *Power, Politics, and Tradition in the Mongol Empire and the Īlkhānate of Iran*, Oxford, Oxford University Press, 2016.

Huhtamaa, Heli, "Climatic Anomalies, Food Systems, and Subsistence Crises in Medieval Novgorod and Ladoga," in *Scandinavian Journal of History*, 40.4 (2015), pp. 562–90.

Hymes, Robert, "Epilogue: A Hypothesis on the East Asian Beginnings of the Yersinia Pestis Polytomy," in *The Medieval Globe*, 1.1 (2014), pp. 285–308.

*Il cantare di Igor'*, ed. Edgardo T. Saronne, Parma, Pratiche, 1988.

Ilieva, Aneta, *Frankish Morea, 1205–1262: Socio-Cultural Interaction between the Franks and the Local Population*, Athens, Basiopoulos, 1991.

Inalcik, Halil, *The Ottoman Empire: The Classical Age, 1300–1600*, trans. Norman Itzkowitz and Colin Imber, London, Weidenfeld and Nicolson, 1973.

———. *The Ottoman Empire: Conquest, Organization and Economy. Collected Studies*, London, Variorum, 1978.

Jackson, Peter, "The Crisis in the Holy Land in 1260," in *The English Historical Review*, 95.376 (1980), pp. 481–513.

———. *The Dissolution of the Mongol Empire*, Wiesbaden, Harrassowitz, 1978.

———. "Marco Polo and His 'Travels,'" in *Bulletin of the School of Oriental and African Studies*, 61.1 (1998), pp. 82–101.

———. *The Mongols and the West: 1221–1410*, London, Routledge, 2014.

———. "From Ulus to Khanate: The Making of the Mongol States, c. 1220–c. 1290," in *The Mongol Empire and its Legacy*, eds. Reuven Amitai and David O. Morgan, Leiden, Brill, pp. 12–38.

———. "William of Rubruck in The Mongol Empire: Perception and Prejudices," in Peter Jackson and David O. Morgan, *The Mission of Friar William of Rubruck: His Journey to the Court of the Great Khan Möngke, 1253–1255*, London; Routledge, 2017, pp. 54–71.

———. "World Conquest and Local Accommodation: Threat and Blandishment in Mongol Diplomacy," in *History and Historiography of Post-Mongol Central Asia and the Middle East: Studies in Honor of John E. Woods*, eds. Judith Pfeiffer, Sholeh Alysia Quinn, and Ernest Tucker, Wiesbaden, Harrassowitz, 2006, pp. 3–18.

Jackson, Peter, and David O. Morgan, *The Mission of Friar William of Rubruck: His Journey to the Court of the Great Khan Möngke, 1253–1255*, London, Routledge, 2017.

Jacoby, David, *The Encounter of Two Societies: Western Conquerors and Byzantines in the Peloponnesus after the Fourth Crusade*, Pittsburgh, American Historical Association, 1973.

———. "L'expansion occidentale dans le Levant: les Vénitiens à Acre dans la seconde moitié du treizième siècle," in *Journal of Medieval History*, 3.3 (1977), pp. 225–64.

———. Marco Polo, his Close Relatives, and his Travel Account: Some New Insights, in *Mediterranean Historical Review*, 21.2 (2006), pp. 193–218.

———. *Medieval Trade in the Eastern Mediterranean and Beyond*, London, Routledge, 2018.

———. "The Supply of War Materials to Egypt in the Crusader Period," in *Jerusalem Studies in Arabic and Islam*, 25 (2001), pp. 102–32.

———. "The Venetian Presence in the Latin Empire of Constantinople (1204–1261)," in *Byzantium, Latin Romania amd the Mediterranean*, London, Routledge, 2001, pp. 141–201.

———. "La Venezia d'Oltremare nel secondo Duecento," in *Storia di Venezia. Dalle origini alla caduta della Serenissima*, vol. 2, eds. Gherardo Ortalli and Giorgio Cracco, Rome, Treccani, 1995, pp. 263–99.

Jahn, Karl, "Paper Currency in Iran: A Contribution to the Cultural and Economic History of Iran in the Mongol Period," in *Journal of Asian History*, 4.2 (1970), pp. 101–35.

Jahnke, Carsten, "The Baltic Trade," in *A Companion to the Hanseatic League*, ed. Donald J. Harreld, Brill, 2015, pp. 194–240.

Juvaini, 'Ala-ad-Din 'Ata-Malik, *The History of the World-Conqueror*, 2 vols., ed. John A. Boyle, Cambridge, MA, Harvard University Press, 1958.

Kamalov, Il'jas, *Otnošenija Zolotoj Ordy c Chulaguidami*, Moscow, 2007.

Karpov, Sergej P., "The Beginning of the Time of Troubles in the Golden Horde and the Coup of Navruz Khan," in *Zolotoordynskoe Obozrenie*, 6.3 (2018), pp. 528–36.

———. "Black Sea and the Crisis of the Mid XIVth Century. An Underestimated Turning Point," in *Thesaurismata*, 27 (1997), pp. 65–77.

———. "The Black Sea Region before and after the Fourth Crusade," in *Urbs Capta: The Fourth Crusade and Its Consequences*, ed. Angeliki Laiou, Paris, Lethielleux, 2005.

———. "Drevnejšie postanovlenija senata venecianskoj respubliki o navigacii v Černoe more," *Pričernomor'e v srednie veka*, 4 (2000), pp. 11–18.

———. *The Empire of Trebizond and Venice in 1374–75: A Chrysobull Redated*, Birmingham, Centre for Byzantine Studies, 1978.

———. "Enforced Councilor: Franceschino Bon in Venetian Tana, 1342–1343," in *Quaestiones Medii Aevi Novae*, 16 (2011), pp. 265–9.

———. "Génois et Byzantins face à la crise de Tana de 1343 d'après les documents d'archives inédits," in *Byzantinische Forschungen*, 22 (1996), pp. 33–51.

———. "The Grain Trade in the Southern Black Sea Region: The Thirteenth to the Fifteenth Century," in *Mediterranean Historical Review*, 8.1 (1993), pp. 55–73.

———. *L'impero di Trebisonda: Venezia, Genova e Roma, 1204–1461: rapporti politici, diplomatici e commerciali*, Rome, Il Veltro, 1986.

———. *Istorija Tany (Azova). XIII-XVvv.*, St Petersburg, Aletejja, 2021.

———. "Kak feniks iz pepla: vozroždenie torgovli v Tane posle katastrofy 1395g.," in *Zolotoordynskoe Obozrenie*, 8.3 (2020), pp. 504–14.

———. "Krizis Tany 1343 g. v svete novykh istochnikov," *Vizantiyskiy Vremennik*, 55.1 (1994), pp. 121–26.

———. *Latinskaja Romanija*, St Petersburg, Aletejja, 2000.

———. "Il Mar Nero come carrefour di cultura nel Medio Evo," in *Teodorico e i Goti tra Oriente e Occidente*, ed. Antonio Carile, Ravenna, Longo, 1995, pp. 39–52.

———. "Načalo smuty v Zolotoj Orde i perevorot Navruza," *Zolotoordynskoe obozrenie* 6 (2018), pp. 528–36.

———. *La navigazione veneziana nel Mar Nero, XIII-XV secolo*, Ravenna, Girasole, 2000.

———. "New Documents on the Relations between the Latins and the Local Populations in the Black Sea Area (1392–1462)," in *Dumbarton Oaks Papers*, 49 (1995), pp. 33–41.

———. "On the Origin of Medieval Tana," in *Byzantinoslavica*, 56.1 (1995), pp. 227–35.

———. "Il problema delle tasse doganali nei rapporti tra Venezia e Trebisonda (XIV–prima metà del XV secolo)," in *Rivista di studi bizantini e slavi*, 3 (1983), pp. 161–71.

———. "Venecianskaja Tana po aktam kanclera Benedetto B'janko (1359–60gg)," in *Pričernomor'e v srednie veka*, 5 (2001), pp. 9–26.

———. "Veneciansko-trapezundskij konflikt 1374–1376 gg. ineizvestnyj mirnyj dogovor 1376 g.," in *Vizantijskij vremennik*, 39 (1978), pp. 102–9.

Kedar, Benjamin, *Mercanti in crisi a Genova e Venezia nel '300*, Rome, Jouvence, 1981.

———. "Segurano-Sakran Salvaygo: un mercante genovese al servizio dei sultani mamalucchi, c. 1303–1322," in *Fatti e idee di storia economica nei secoli XII-XX. Studi dedicati a Franco Borlandi*, eds. Bruno Dini, Vincenzo Giura, and Dente Zanetti, Bologna, Il Mulino, 1977, pp. 75–91.

Kehren, Lucien, *Tamerlan: l'empire du Seigneur de Fer*, Neuchatel, Baconniere, 1978.

Khvalkov, Evgeny A., "The Commercial Significance of the Venetian Tana in the 1430s," in *Eminak*, 4 (2019), pp. 131–40.

———. "A Regionalisation or Long-Distance Trade? Transformations and Shifts in the Role of Tana in the Black Sea Trade in the First Half of the Fifteenth Century," in *European Review of History/Revue européenne d'histoire*, 23.3 (2016), pp. 508–25.

———. "The Society of the Venetian Colony of Tana in the 1430s Based on the Notarial Deeds of Niccolò Di Varsis and Benedetto Di Smeritis," in *Studi Storici*, 57 (2016), pp. 93–110.

———. "The Venetian Tana in the System of International Relations in the Northern Black Sea Region in the 1430s," in *World of the Orient*, 4 (2019), pp. 113–29.

Kolia-Dermitzaki, Athina, "Byzantium and the Crusades in the Komnenian Era: Perception and Reality," in *Byzantium and the West: Perception and Reality (11th–15th C.)*, Nikolaos G. Chrissis, Athina Kolia-Dermitzaki, and Angeliki Papageorgiou, London, Routledge, 2019, pp. 59–83.

Kołodziejczyk, Dariusz, *The Crimean Khanate and Poland Lithuania: International Diplomacy on the European Periphery (15th–18th Century). A Study of Peace Treaties Followed by an Annotated Edition of Relevant Documents*, Leiden and Boston, Brill, 2011.

Korobeinikov, Dmitrij, *Byzantium and the Turks in the Thirteenth Century*, Oxford, Oxford University Press, 2014.

Kovács, Szilvia, "The Franciscans and Yaylaq Khatun," in *Acta Orientalia Vilnensia*, 13 (2016), pp. 45–59.

Kozin, Sergej, ed., *Storia segreta dei Mongoli*, Parma, Guanda, 2009.

Kozyr, I. A., "Syn'ovods' ka bytva 1362 roku u svitli arheologičnyh džerel," in *Zolotoordynskaja Civilizacija*, 7 (2014), pp. 189–98.

Kretschmer, Konrad, *Die Italienischen Portolane des Mittelalters: Ein Beitrag zur Geschichte der Kartographie und Nautik*, Berlin, Mittler und Sohn, 1909.

Krivošeev, Vladimirovic U., *Rus' i Mongoly: issledovanie po istorii severo-vostočnoj Rusi XII-XIV vv.*, St Petersburg, Akademia isseldovania kul'tury, 2003.

Kuroda, Akinobu, "The Eurasian Silver Century, 1276–1359: Commensurability and Multiplicity," in *Journal of Global History*, 4.2 (2009), pp. 245–69.

———. "Why and How Did Silver Dominate across Eurasia Late-13th through Mid-14th Century? Historical Backgrounds of the Silver Bars Unearthed from Orheiul Vechi," in *Tyragetia*, 11.1 (2017), pp. 23–34.

Kyrris, Costas, "John Cantacuzenus, the Genoese, the Venetians and the Gatalans (1348–1354)," in *Byzantina*, 4 (1972), pp. 331–56.

Laiou, Angeliki E. and Cécile Morrison, *The Byzantine Economy*, Cambridge, Cambridge University Press, 2007.

Lane, Frederic C., *Le navi di Venezia fra i secoli XIII e XVI*, Turin, Einaudi, 1983.

―――. *Navires et constructeurs à Venise pendant la Renaissance*, Paris, S.E.V.P.E.N., 1965.

―――. *Venetian Maritime Law and Administration (1250–1350)*, Milan, Giuffrè, 1962.

―――. *Venice: A Maritime Republic*, Baltimore, Johns Hopkins University Press, 1973.

―――. *Venetian Ships and Shipbuilders of the Renaissance*, Baltimore, Johns Hopkins University Press, 1992.

Lane, Frederic C., and Reinhold C. Mueller, *Money and Banking in Medieval and Renaissance Venice*. Vol. 1: *Coins and Moneys of Account*, Baltimore, Johns Hopkins University Press, 1985.

Lane, George, *The Early Mongol Rule in Thirteenth-Century Iran: A Persian Renaissance*, London, Routledge Courzon, 2003.

Langer, Lawrence N., "The Black Death in Russia: Its Effects Upon Urban Labor," in *Russian History* (1975), pp. 53–67.

Latimer, Paul, "The English Inflation of 1180–1220 Reconsidered," in *Past & Present*, 171 (2001), pp. 3–29.

Lazzari, Vincenzo, *Del traffico e delle condizioni degli schiavi in Venezia nei tempi di mezzo*, Turin, 1862.

*Letopisnyj sbornik, imenyemyj Patriaršeju ili Nikonovskoju letopis'ju (1177–1362 gg.)*, ed. Afanasij F. Byčkov, *Polnoe Sobranie Russikich Letopis'ej*, vol. 10, Moscow, Nauka, 1965 (original ed. Moscow, 1885).

Lev, Yaacov, *State and Society in Fatimid Egypt*, Leiden, Brill, 1991.

Lind, John, "Mongol Invasions of Russia," in *The Encyclopedia of War*, ed. Gordon Martel, Malden, Wiley-Blackwell, 2012.

Lock, Peter, *The Franks in the Aegean: 1204–1500*, London, Routledge, 2014.

Lockhart, Laurence, "The Relations between Edward I and Edward II of England and the Mongol Īl-Khāns of Persia," in *Iran*, 6.1 (1968), pp. 23–31.

Longhena, Mario, *Viaggi in Persia, India e Giava di Nicolò De Conti*, Milan, Alpes, 1929.

Lopez Robert S., "China Silk in Europe in the Yuan Period," in *Journal of the American Oriental Society*, 72.2 (1952), pp. 72–76.

―――. *The Commercial Revolution of the Middle Ages: 953–1350*, Cambridge, Cambridge University Press, 1976.

―――. "Da Venezia a Delhi nel Trecento," in *Su e giù per la storia di Genova*, Genoa, Edizioni dell'Università, 1975, pp. 137–59.

―――. "Nelle terre dell'Orda d'Oro: tre documenti genovesi inediti," in *Studia slavica mediaevalia et humanistica Riccardo Picchio dicata*, eds. Michele Collucci and Giuseppe dell'Agata, 2 vols. Rome, 1986, vol. 2, pp. 463–74.

―――. "Nouveaux documents sur les marchands italiens en Chine à l'époque mongole, communication du 11 février 1977," in *Comptes rendus des séances de l'Académie des Inscriptions et Belles-Lettres*, 121.2 (1977), pp. 445–58.

―――. *Nuove luci sugli italiani in Estremo Oriente prima di Colombo*, Genoa, Civico Istituto Colombiano, 1951.

―――. *Studi sull'economia genovese nel medio evo*, Turin, 1936.

―――. "Venezia e le grandi linee dell'espansione commerciale nel secolo XIII," in *Storia della civiltà veneziana*, ed. Vittore Branca, 3 vols., Florence, Sansoni, 1979, vol. 1, pp. 363–85.

Lopez, Robert S., Irving W. Raymond, and Olivia Constable Remie, trans. and eds., *Medieval Trade in the Mediterranean World: Illustrative Documents*, New York, Columbia University Press, 2001.

Lupprian, Karl Ernst, *Die Beziehungen der Päpste zu islamischen und mongolischen Herrschern im 13. Jahrhundert anhand ihres Briefwechsels*, Vatican, Biblioteca apostolica vaticana, 1981.

———. *Il Fondaco dei Tedeschi e la sua funzione di controllo del commercio tedesco a Venezia*, Venice, 1978.

Luzzatto, Gino, "La commenda nella vita economica dei secoli XIII e XIV con particolare riguardo a Venezia," in *Atti della Mostra bibliografica e Convegno internazionale di studi storici del diritto marittimo medioevale*, ed. Leone Adolfo Senigallia, Naples, Leone Adolfo, 1934, vol. 1, pp. 139–64.

———. *Storia economica di Venezia dall'XI al XVI secolo*, Venice, Marsilio, 1995.

Mackerras, Colin, *The Uighur Empire, According to the T'ang Dynastic Histories: A Study in Sino-Uighur Relations 744–840*, Canberra, Austalian National University Press, 1972.

Magdalino, Paul, "Between Romaniae: Thessaly and Epirus in the Later Middle Ages," in *Mediterranean Historical Review*, 4 (1989), pp. 87–110.

Malanima, Paolo, "Pisa and the Trade Routes to the Near East in the Late Middle Ages," in *Journal of European Economic History*, 16.2 (1987), pp. 335–56.

Manfroni, Camillo, "Relazioni di Genova con Venezia dal 1270 al 1290. Con documenti inediti tratti dall'Archivio di Stato di Venezia," in *Giornale storico e letterario della Liguria*, 2.1–2 (1901), pp. 361–401.

———. *Storia della marina italiana*, 3 vols., Rome, Forzani, 1897, repub. Milan, Res Gestae, 2015.

Markham, Clements R., ed., *Narrative of the Embassy of Ruy Gonzalez de Clavijo to the Court of Timour, at Samarcand, AD 1403–6*, Farnham, Ashgate, 2010.

Martin, Henry Desmond, *The Rise of Chingis Khan and His Conquest of North China*, Baltimore, Johns Hopkins University Press, 1977.

Martin, Janet, *Medieval Russia, 980–1584*, Cambridge, Cambridge University Press, 2007.

———. *Treasure of the Land of Darkness: The Fur Trade and its Significance for Medieval Russia*, Cambridge, Cambridge University Press, 1986.

Martini, Angelo, *Manuale di metrologia, ossia Misure, pesi e monete in uso attualmente e anticamente presso tutti i popoli*, Turin, Loescher, 1883.

Maslovskij A. N., "Podval kupečeskogo doma konca pervoj polovini XIV veka iz Azaka," in *Stepi Evropy v épochu Srednevekov'ja*, 6 (2008), pp. 93–124.

May, Timothy, "A Mongol-Ismâ'îlî Alliance?: Thoughts on the Mongols and Assassins," in *Journal of the Royal Asiatic Society*, 14.3 (2004), pp. 231–39.

———. *The Mongol Art of War*, Yardley, PA, Westholme, 2007.

McQueen, William B., "Relations between the Normans and Byzantium 1071–1112," in *Byzantion*, 56 (1986), pp. 427–76.

Medvedev, Igor P., "Dogovor Vizantii I Genui ot 6 maja 1352 g.," in *Vizantijskij Vremennik*, 38 (1977), pp. 161–72.

Melis, Federico, *I trasporti e le comunicazioni nel Medioevo*, ed. Frangioni Luciana, Florence, Le Monnier, 1985.

Mergiali-Sahas, Sophia, "In the Face of a Historical Puzzle: Western Adventures, Friars and Nobility in the Service of Michael VIII Palaiologos (1261–1282)," in *Byzantium and the West: Perception and Reality (11th–15th C.)*, eds. Nikolaos G. Chrissis, Athina Kolia-Dermitzaki, and Angeliki Papageorgiou, London, Routledge, 2019, pp. 275–85.

Meyvaert, Paul, "An Unknown Letter of Hulagu, Il-Khan of Persia, to King Louis IX of France," in *Viator*, 11 (1980), pp. 245–60.

Mirgaleev, Il'nur M., "The Golden Horde Policies Toward the Ilkhanate," in *The Golden Horde Review*, 2 (2013), pp. 217–27.

———. "The Golden Horde State in the System of International Relations," in *The Golden Horde Review*, 4 (2015), pp. 136–45.

Monaci, Lorenzo, *Laurentii de Monacis Veneti Cretae Cancellarii Chronicon De Rebus Venetis: Ab U.C. ad Annum MCCCLIV. Sive Ad Conjurationem [coniurationem] Ducis Faledro. Accedit ejusdem Laurentii Carmen [Seu Historia] de Carolo II. Rege Hungariae, &. Anonymi Sciptoris de causis belli exorti inter Venetos, & Ducem Ferrariensem*, Venice, Remondini, 1758.

Morgan, David, "The Decline and Fall of the Mongol Empire," in *Journal of the Royal Asiatic Society*, 19.4 (2009), pp. 427–37.

———. "The Mongols in Syria, 1260–1300", in *Crusade and Settlement: Papers Read at the First Conference of the Society for the Study of the Crusades and the Latin East and Presented to R. C. Smail*, Cardiff, Peter W. Edbury, 1985, pp. 231–35.

Morozzo della Rocca, Raimondo, *Fonti per la storia del commercio veneziano conservate presso l'archivio di stato*, Venice, Grazia, 1954.

———. "Notizie da Caffa," in *Studi in onore di Amintore Fanfani*, ed. Gino Barbieri, Milan, Giuffré, 1962, pp. 267–95.

———. "Sulle orme di Marco Polo," in *L'Italia che scrive*, 37 (1954), pp. 120–21.

*Moskovskij Letopis'nyj svod konca XV veka*, ed. Michajl N. Tichomirov, *Polnoe Sobranie Russikich Letopis'ej*, vol. 25, Moscow and Leningrad, Nauka, 1949.

Moule, Arthur C., "Marco Polo's Description of Quinsai," in *T'oung Pao*, 33.2 (1937), pp. 105–28.

Mueller, Reinhold C., *Money and Banking in Medieval and Renaissance Venice*. Vol. 2: *The Venetian Money Market: Banks, Panics and the Public Debt, 1200–1500*, Baltimore, Johns Hopkins University Press, 1997.

Müller, Giuseppe, *Documenti sulle relazioni delle città toscane coll'Oriente cristiano e coi Turchi fino all'anno MDXXXI*, Florence, Cellini e C., 1879.

Musarra, Antonio, *La guerra di San Saba*, Pisa, Pacini, 2009.

Mykhaylovskiy, Vitaliy, *European Expansion and the Contested Borderlands of Late Medieval Podillya, Ukraine*, Amsterdam, Amsterdam University Press, 2019.

Mys'kov, Evgenij P., *Politiceskaja istorija Zolotoj Ordy (1236–1313)*, Volgograd, VGU, 2003.

Necipoğlu, Nevra, "The Byzantine Economy and the Sea: The Maritime Trade of Byzantium, 10th–15th Centuries," in *The Sea in History: The Medieval World*, ed. Christian Buchet and Michel Balard, Woodbridge, Boydell & Brewer, 2017, pp. 437–48.

Nicol, Donald M., *Byzantium and Venice: A Study in Diplomatic and Cultural Relations*, Cambridge, Cambridge University Press, 1989.

———. *The Despotate of Epiros*, Oxford, Blackwell, 1957.

———. *The Last Centuries of Byzantium, 1261–1453*, Cambridge, Cambridge University Press, 1993.

Nicolle, David, *Manzikert 1071: The Breaking of Byzantium*, London, Bloomsbury, 2013.

*Nikanorovskaja letopis'. Sokrascenye letopisnye svody konca XV v.*, ed. A. N. Nasonov, Moscow and Leningrad, Nauka, 1962.

Nordenskiöld, Erik A., *Periplus: An Essay on the Early History of Charts and Sailing-Directions*, trans. Arthur F. Bather, Stockholm, Norsted & Söner, 1987.

Nystazopoulou, Maria, *Hē en tē Taurikē Chersonēsō polis Sougdaia : apo tou XIII mechri tou XV aiōnos*, Athens, Hyperesia, 1965.

Odorico da Pordenone, *Relatio de mirabilibus orientalium tatarorum*, ed. Annalia Marchisio, Florence, SISMEL, 2016.

Oikonomidès, Nicolas A., "The Medieval Via Egnatia," in *The Via Egnatia under Ottoman Rule (1380–1699)*, ed. Elizabeth A. Zachariadou, Rethymon, Crete University Press, 1996, pp. 9–16.

Origo, Iris, "The Domestic Enemy: The Eastern Slaves in Tuscany in the Fourteenth and Fifteenth Centuries," in *Speculum*, 30.3 (1955), pp. 321–66.

Origone, Sandra, "Genoa and Byzantium: Aspects of a Long Relationship," in *Byzantium and the West: Perception and Reality (11th–15th C.)*, eds. Nikolaos G. Chrissis, Athina Kolia-Dermitzaki, and Angeliki Papageorgiou, London, Routledge, 2019, pp. 38–55.

———. "Questioni tra Bisanzio e Genova intorno all'anno 1278," in *Chemins d'outre-mer. Études d'histoire sur la Méditerranée médiévale offertes à Michel Balard*, eds. Damien

Coulon, Catherine Otten-Froux, and Paule Pagès, Paris, Éditions de la Sorbonne, 2004, pp. 619–31.

Orlandini, Giuseppe, "Marco Polo e la sua famiglia," in *Archivio Veneto-Tridentino*, 9 (1926), pp. 1–68.

Ortalli, Gherardo, "Il ducato e la 'civitas Rivoalti.' Tra carolingi, bizantini e sassoni," in *Storia di Venezia. Dalle origini alla caduta della Serenissima*, vol. 1, Rome, Istituto dell'Enciclopedia Italiana, 1992, pp. 725–90.

———. "Venice and Papal Bans on Trade with the Levant: The Role of the Jurist," in *Mediterranean Historical Review*, 10.1–2 (1995), pp. 242–58.

Osswald, Brendan, "The Ethnic Composition of Medieval Epirus," in *Imagining Frontiers, Contesting Identities*, eds. Steven G. Ellis and Luďa Klusáková, Pisa, Plus, 2007, pp. 125–54.

Ostrogorsky, Georg, *Storia dell'impero bizantino*, Turin, Einaudi, 1968.

Pamuk, Şevket, "The Black Death and the Origins of the 'Great Divergence' across Europe, 1300–1600," in *European Review of Economic History*, 11.3 (2007), pp. 289–317.

Pansolli, Lamberto, *La gerarchia delle fonti di diritto nella legislazione medievale veneziana*, Milan, Giuffrè, 1970.

Papacostea, Şerban, "The Genoese in the Black Sea (1261–1453): Metamorphoses of a Hegemony," in *From Pax Mongolica to Pax Ottomanica*, eds. Ovidiu Cristea and Liviu Pilat, Leiden and Boston, Brill, 2020, pp. 13–38.

———"'Quod non iretur ad Tanam.' Un aspect fondamental de la politique Génoise dans la Mer Noire au XIVe siècle," in *Revue des études sud-est européennes*, 17.2 (1979), pp. 201–17.

———. Papadopoli, Nicolò, "Il bimetallismo a Venezia nel medioevo," in *Rivista di numismatica italiana*, 5 (1892), pp. 200–207.

———. *Le monete di Venezia*, Venice, Ongania, 1893.

———. *Sul valore della moneta veneziana*, Venice, Tip. Antonelli, 1895.

Paviot, Jacques, "Les marchands italiens dans l'Iran mongol," in *L'Iran face à la domination mongole: études*, ed. Denise Aigle, Tehran, Institut français de recherche en Iran, 1997.

Peacock, Andrew C. S., *Islam, Literature and Society in Mongol Anatolia*, Cambridge, Cambridge University Press, 2019.

Pegolotti, Francesco di Balduccio, *La pratica della mercatura*, ed. Allan Evans, Cambridge, MA, Medieval Academy of America, 1936.

Pelenski, Jaroslaw, *The Context for the Legacy of Kievan Rus'*, Boulder, CO, Columbia University Press, 1998.

Penna, Daphne, "Piracy and Reprisal in Byzantine Waters: Resolving a Maritime Conflict Between Byzantines and Genoese at the End of the Twelfth Century," in *Comparative Legal History*, 5 (2017), pp. 36–52.

Pertusi, Agostino, *Fine di Bisanzio e fine del mondo: significato e ruolo storico delle profezie sulla caduta di Costantinopoli in Oriente e in Occidente*, ed. Enrico Morini, Rome, Istituto Storico per il Medioevo, 1988.

——— "Venezia e Bisanzio: 1000–1204," in *Dumbarton Oaks Papers*, 33 (1979), pp. 1–22.

Petech, Luciano, "Les marchands italiens dans l'empire mongol," in *Journal Asiatique*, 250 (1962), pp. 549–74.

Petti Balbi, Giovanna, "Caffa e Pera a metà del Trecento," in *Revue des études sud-est européenes*, 16 (1978), pp. 217–28.

Phillips, J.R.S., *The Medieval Expansion of Europe*, Oxford, Oxford University Press, 1998.

Phillips, William D., *Slavery from Roman Times to the Early Transatlantic Trade*, Manchester, Manchester University Press, 1985.

Pian del Carpine, Giovanni di, *Historia Mongalorum. Viaggio di F. Giovanni da Pian del Carpine ai Tartari nel 1245–47*, ed. Giorgio Pullè, Florence, Carnesecchi, 1913.

————. *Storia dei Mongoli*, eds. Enrico Menestò, Maria Cristiana Lungarotti, Paolo Daffinà, Luciano Petech and Claudio Leonardie, Spoleto, CISAM, 1989.

————. *Viaggio a'Tartari di frate Giovanni da Pian del Carpine (Histroia Mongalorum)*, ed. Giorgio Pullè, Milano, Alpes, 1929.

Pienaru, Nagy, "The Timurids and the Black Sea," in *From Pax Mongolica to Pax Ottomanica*, eds. Ovidiu Cristea and Liviu Pilat, Leiden and Boston, Brill, 2020, pp. 113–45.

Počekaev, Roman Ju., *Tsari ordynskie: Biografii khanov i previtelej Zolotoj Ordy*, St Petersburg, 2010.

Poggio Bracciolini, *Historiae de varietate fortunae libri quatuor*, Bologna, Forni Ed., 1969.

————. *De l'Inde. Les voyages en Asie de Niccolò de' Conti. Texte établi et commenté par M. Guéret-Laferté*, Turnhout, Brepols, 2004.

Polo, Marco, *The Description of the World*, eds. Arthur C. Moule and Paul Pelliot, vol. 1, London, Routledge, 1938.

————. *Le Devisement dou monde*, eds. Mario Eusebi and Eugenio Burgio, Venice, Ca'Foscari, 2018.

————. *Il Milione*, ed. Valeria Bertolucci Pizzorusso, Milan, Adelphi, 1975.

————. *Milione. Le divisament dou monde: il Milione nelle redazioni toscana e franco-italiana*, eds. Gabriella Ronchi and Cesare Segre, Milan, Mondadori, 1982.

————. *The Travels of Marco Polo*, eds. Henry Yule and Henri Cordier, vol. 2, New York, Dover, 1993.

Polyak, A. N., "Novye arabskie materialy pozdnego srednevekov'ya o vostochnoy i tsentral'noy Evrope," in *Vostočnye istočniki po istorii narodov Jugo-Vostočnoj i Central'noj Evropy*, 3 vols., ed. Anna S. Tveritinova, Moscow, Nauka, 1969–74, pp. 29–66.

Pozza, Marco and Ravegnani, *I trattati con Bisanzio, 992–1198*, Venice, Il cardo, 1993.

Prawdin, Michael, *L'empire Mongol et Tamerlan*, Paris, Payot, 1937.

Preiser-Kapeller, Johannes, "Civitas Thauris. The Significance of Tabriz in the Spatial Frameworks of Christian Merchants and Ecclesiastics in the 13th and 14th Centuries," in *Politics, Patronage and the Transmission of Knowledge in 13th–15th Century Tabriz*, ed. Judith Pfeiffer, Leiden and Boston, Brill, 2014, pp. 251–99.

Pritsak, Omeljan, "Sougdaia," in *The Oxford Dictionary of Byzantium*, ed. Aleksandr P. Kazhdan, 3 vols., New York and Oxford, Oxford University Press, 1991, vol. 3, p. 1391.

Prochorov, Gelian M., "Etničeskaja integracija v Vostočnoj Evrope v XIV (ot isixhastvkich sporov do Kulikovskoj bitvy)," in *Rus'i Vizantija v epoche Kulikovskoj bitvy*, St. Petersburg, 2000, pp. 5–43.

Prokof'eva, N. D., "Akty venecianskogo notarija v Tane Donato a Mano (1413–1419)," *Pričernomor'e v srednie veka 4* (2000), p. 36–174.

Pubblici, Lorenzo, *Cumani. Migrazioni, strutture di potere e società nell'Eurasia dei nomadi (secoli X-XIII)*, Florence, Firenze University Press, 2021.

————. *Mongol Caucasia: Invasions, Conquest, and Government of a Frontier Region in Thirteenth-Century Eurasia (1204–1295)*, Leiden and Boston, Brill, 2022.

————. "Venezia e il Mar d'Azov: alcune considerazioni sulla Tana nel XIV secolo," in *Archivio Storico Italiano*, 163 (2005), pp. 435–83.

Pucci Donati, Francesca, "Accoglienza e assistenza negli insediamenti genovesi e veneziani di Caffa e Tana (secoli XIII-XV)," in *Alle origini del welfare*, ed. G. Piccinni, Rome, Viella, 2020, pp. 543–63.

————. *Ai confini dell'Occidente. Regesti degli atti dei notai veneziani a Tana nel Trecento. 1359–1388*, Udine, Forum, 2019.

Purcell, Maureen, *Papal Crusading Policy: The Chief Instruments of Papal Crusading Policy and the Crusade to the Holy Land from the Final Loss of Jerusalem to the Fall of Acre, 1244–1291*, Leiden, Brill, 1975.

Quirini Popławska, Danuta, "The Venetian Involvement in the Black Sea Slave Trade (Fourteenth to Fifteenth Centuries)," in *Slavery and the Slave Trade in the Eastern Mediterranean (c. 1000–1500 CE)*, eds. Reuven Amitai and Christoph Cluse, Turnhout, Brepols, 2017, pp. 255–98.

*Rashiduddin Fazlullah's Jami'ü't-Tawarikh—Compendium of Chronicles: A History of the Mongols*, ed. Wheeler M. Thackston, Cambridge, MA, Harvard University Press, 1998.

Ratchnevsky, Paul, *Genghis Khan: His Life and Legacy*, trans. and ed. Thomas Nivison Haining, Malden, Blackwell Publishing, 2006.

Ravegnani Giorgio, "La Romània veneziana," in *Storia di Venezia. Dalle origini alla caduta della Serenissima*, vol. 2, eds. Gherardo Ortalli and Giorgio Cracco, Rome, Treccani, 1995, pp. 183–232.

*Ravennatis anonymi cosmographia et Guidonis Geographica*, ed. Joseph Schnetz, Leipzig, Teubner, 1940.

Richard, Jean, "An Account of the Battle of Hattin Referring to the Frankish Mercenaries in Oriental Moslem States," in *Speculum* 27 (1952), pp. 168–77.

——. "Buscarello de Ghizolfi," in *Encyclopaedia Iranica*, ed. Ehsan Yar-shater, London, Routledge, 1990, vol. 4, p. 569.

——. "Isol le Pisan: un aventurier franc gouverneur d'une province mongole?," in *Central Asiatic Journal*, 14.1–3 (1970), pp. 186–94.

——. "La lettre de Hülegü à Saint Louis et l'entente avec les Mongols," in *Au-delà de la Perse et de l'Arménie. L'Orient latin et la découverte de l'Asie intérieure: Quelques textes inégalement connus aux origins de l'alliance entre Francs et Mongols (1145–1262)*, Turnhout, Brepols, 2005, pp. 174–93.

——. *La papauté et les missions d'Orient au moyen age (XIIIe-XVe siècles)*, Rome, Ecole Française de Rome, 2019.

Rogers, Greg S., "An Examination of Historians' Explanations for the Mongol Withdrawal from East Central Europe," in *East European Quarterly*, 30.1 (1996), pp. 3–26.

Romano, Dennis, *Patricians and Popolani: The Social Foundations of the Venetian Renaissance State*, Baltimore, John Hopkins University Press, 1987.

Romano, Ruggiero, "La storia economica. Dal secolo XIV al Settecento," in *Storia d'Italia. Dalla caduta dell'Impero romano al secolo XVIII. L'economia delle tre Italie*, eds. Philip James Jones, Ruggiero Romano, Jacques Le Goff, and Fernand Braudel, vol. 4, Turin, Einaudi, 2005, pp. 1813–1931.

Rösch, Gerhard, "Il gran guadagno," in *Storia di Venezia. Dalle origini alla caduta della Serenissima*, vol. 2, eds. Gherardo Ortalli and Giorgio Cracco, Rome, Treccani, 1995, pp. 233–62.

Rossabi, Morris, *Khubilai Khan*, Berkeley, University of California Press, 2009.

Roux, Jean Paul, *Les explorateurs au moyen age*. Paris, Hachette Littératures, 2006.

——. *Tamerlano*, Milan, Garzanti, 1995.

Rubruc, Guillelmus de, *Itinerarium*, in *Sinica Francescana*, vol. I, *Itinera et relationes fratrum minorum, seculi XIII et XIV*, ed. Anastasius Van De Wyngaert, Florence, Collegio di S. Bonaventura, 1929.

Rubruk, Guglielmo di, *Viaggio in Mongolia (Itinerarium)*, ed. Paolo Chiesa, Milan, Mondadori, 2011.

Runciman, Steven, *I Vespri Siciliani: storia del mondo mediterraneo alla fine del tredicesimo secolo*, Bari, Dedalo libri, 1971.

Sabitov, Žaksylyk M., "Emiry Uzbek-Chana i Džanibek-xana," in *Zolootordynskoe obozrenie*, 2.4 (2014), pp. 120–34.

——. "Voennoe protivostojanie Nogaja i chana Tokty," in *Voennoe delo Ulusa Džuči i ego naslednikov. Sbornik naučnych statej*, Astana, 2012, pp. 246–53.

Sanudo, Marin, *Vitae Ducum Venetorum ab anno CCCCXXI usque ad annum MCCCCXCIII*, in *Rerum Italicarum Scriptores*, vol. 22, Milan, Societatis Palatinae, 1733.

————. *Le vite dei dogi di Marin Sanudo*, ed. Giovanni Monticolo, in *Rerum Italicarum Scriptores*, vol. 22, Città di Castello, Lapi, 1900–11.

Sapori, Armando, "I beni del commercio internazionale del medioevo," in *Archivio Storico Italiano*, 113.1 (1955), pp. 3–44.

Sauli, Lodovico, "Imposicio Officii Gazarie," in *Historiae Patriae Monumenta*, Turin, 1838.

Saunders, J. J., *Muslims and Mongols: Essays on Medieval Asia*, ed. G. W. Rice, Christchurch, Canterbury University Press, 1977.

Schmieder, Felicitas, *Europa und die Fremden: Die Mongolen im Urteil des Abendlandes vom 13. bis in das 15. Jahrhundert*, Sigmaringen, Thorbecke, 1994.

Schmieder, Felicitas, and Peter Schreiner, *Il codice cumanico e il suo mondo: atti del colloquio internazionale, Venezia, 6–7 dicembre 2002*, Rome, Ed. di Storia e Letteratura, 2005.

*The Secret History of the Mongols: A Mongolian Epic Chronicle of the Thirteenth Century*, ed. Igor de Rachewiltz, Leiden, Brill, 2004.

Seyfeddini, Ahmed Mohammed, *Monetnoe delo i denežnoe obraščenie v Azerbajdžane XII-XV vv*, 2 vols., Baku, Elm, 1978–81.

Shamiloglu, Uli, "The Impact of the Black Death on the Golden Horde: Politics, Economy, Society, Civilization," *Zolootordynskoe obozrenie*, 5.2 (2017), pp. 325–43.

————. "Preliminary Remarks on the Role of Disease in the History of the Golden Horde," in *Central Asian Survey*, 12.4 (1993), pp. 447–57.

Shawcross, Clare T. M., *The Chronicle of Morea: Historiography in Crusader Greece*, Oxford, Oxford University Press, 2009.

Sinclair, Thomas A., *Eastern Trade and the Mediterranean in the Middle Ages: Pegolotti's Ayas-Tabriz Itinerary and its Commercial Context*, London, Routledge, 2021.

Sinor, Denis, "The Mongols in the West," in *Journal of Asian History*, 33.1 (1999), pp. 1–44.

————. "Nekotorye latinskie istočniki po chanstvy Uzbeka," in *Zolotoordynskoe obozrenie*, 3 (2015), pp. 23–33.

————. "'Pray to God on my behalf that he give me such intelligence that I can learn fast and well your languages': Medieval Interpreters and Inner Asia," in *The Journal of Popular Culture*, 16.1 (1982), pp. 176–84.

————. "Un voyageur du treizième siècle: le Dominicain Julien de Hongrie," in *Bulletin of the School of Oriental and African Studies*, 14.3 (1952), pp. 589–602.

Skržinskaja, Elena Č., "Storia della Tana," in *Studi Veneziani*, 10 (1968), pp. 3–47.

Smith, John Masson, "Ayn Jālūt: Mamlūk Success or Mongol Failure?," in *Harvard Journal of Asiatic Studies*, 44.2 (1984), pp. 307–45.

————. "Hülegü Moves West: High Living and Heartbreak on the Road to Baghdad," in *Beyond the Legacy of Genghis Khan*, ed. Linda Komaroff, Leiden, Brill, 2006, pp. 111–34.

Smith, John M. and Frances Plunkett, "Gold Money in Mongol Iran," in *Journal of the Economic and Social History of the Orient*, 11 (1968), pp. 275–97.

Spinei, Victor, "Les Mongols dans Historia Ecclesiastica Nova de Tholomeus de Lucca," in *Archivum Eurasiae Medii Aevi*, 18 (2011), pp. 271–333.

Spinelli, Anna, *Dal mare di Alboran a Samarcanda. Diario dell'ambasciata castigliana a Tamerlano (1403-1406)*, Ravenna, Fernandel, 2004.

Spuler, Bertold, *Die Goldene Horde, die Mongolen in Russland*, Wiesbaden, Harrassowitz, 1965.

Stahl, Alan M., *Zecca: The Mint of Venice in the Middle Ages*, Baltimore, Johns Hopkins University Press, 2000.

Stantchev, Stefan K., *Spiritual Rationality: Papal Embargo as Cultural Practice*, Oxford, Oxford University Press, 2014.

Stark, Sören, "Türk Khaganate," in *The Encyclopedia of Empire*, ed. John MacDonald MacKenzie, Hoboken, NJ, John Wiley & Sons, 2016, vol. 4, pp. 1–15.

Stello, Annika, "Caffa and the Slave Trade during the First Half of the Fifteenth Century," in *Slavery and the Slave Trade in the Eastern Mediterranean (c. 1000–1500 CE)*, eds. Reuven Amitai and Christoph Cluse, Turnhout, Brepols, 2017, pp. 375–400.

Stewart, Donald A., *The Armenian Kingdom and the Mamluks: War and Diplomacy during the Reigns of Hetùm II (1289–1307)*, Leiden and Boston, Brill, 2001.

Stöckly, Doris, *Le système de l'incanto des galées du marché à Venise (fin du XIIIe-milieu du XVe siècle)*, Leiden and New York, Brill, 1995.

Stussi, Alfredo, "Un testamento volgare scritto in Persia nel 1263," in *L'Italia dialettale*, 25 (1962), pp. 23–37.

T'ovma Metsobets'i, *History of Tamerlane and His Successors*, trans. Robert Bedrosian, New York, Sophene Books, 1987.

*Ta'rìkh-i Shaikh Uwais: An Important Source for the History of Adharbaijan in Fourteenth Century*, ed. Johannes Baptist van Loon, Gravenhage, Mouton and Co, 1954.

Tafel, Friedrich G. L. and Martin G. Thomas, *Urkunden zur älteren Handels-und Staatsgeschichte der Republik Venedig. Mit besonderer Beziehung auf Byzanz und die Levante: vom neunten bis zum Ausgang des fünfzehnten Jahrhunderts*, 3 vols., Vienna, Kaiserlich-Königlichen Hof- und Staatsdruckerei, 1856–57, repr. Amsterdam, A. M. Hakkert, 1964.

Tangheroni, Marco, *Commercio e navigazione nel Medioevo*, Rome and Bari, Laterza, 1996.

*Tarifa zoè noticia dy pexi e mexure di luogi e tere che s' adovra marcadantia per el mondo*, ed. Vittorio Orlandini, Venice, C. Ferrari, 1925.

Thiriet, Freddy, *Délibérations des assemblées vénitiennes*, vol. 1, Paris, Mouton and Co, 1966.

———. *Études sur la Romanie greco-vénitienne, Xe–XVe siècles*, London, Variorum Reprints, 1977.

———. "Una proposta di lega antiturca tra Venezia, Genova e Bisanzio nel 1363," in *Archivio storico italiano*, 113.3 (1955), pp. 321–34.

———. *Régestes des délibérations du Sénat de Venise concernant la Romanie*, 3 vols., Paris, Mouton and Co, 1958–61.

———. *La Romanie vénitienne au Moyen Age: le développement et l'exploitation du domaine colonial vénitien, XIIe-XVe siècles*, Paris, De Boccard, 1959.

———. "Sui dissidi sorti tra il Comune di Venezia e i suoi feudatari di Creta nel Trecento," in *Archivio storico italiano*, 114 (1956), pp. 669–712.

———. "Venise et l'occupation de Ténédos au XIVe siècle," in *Mélanges de l'école française de Rome*, 65.1 (1953), pp. 219–45.

Tholomeus von Lucca, *Historia ecclesiastica nova nebst Fortsetzungen bis 1329*, ed. Ottavio Clavuot, in *Monumenta Germaniae Historica, Scriptores*, vol. 39, Hanover, Hahnsche, 2009.

Thomas, William, and S. A. Roy, trans., *Travels to Tana and Persia, by Josafa Barbaro and Ambrogio Contarini*, London, Hakluyt Society, 2017.

Thorau, Peter, *The Lion of Egypt: Sultan Baybars I and the Near East in the Thirteenth Century*, New York, Longman, 1992.

Tiesenhausen, Vladimir G., *Sbornik materjalov, otnosiaščikhsia k istorii Zolotoj Ordy*, vol. 1, *Izvlečenija iz sočinenii arabskich*, Moscow and St Petersburg, Akademija Nauk, 1884.

———. *Sbornik materjalov, otnosiaščikhsia k istorii Zolotoj Ordy*, vol. 2, *Izvlečenija iz persidskich sočinenii*, Moscow and Leningrad, Akademija Nauk, 1941.

Tognetti, Sergio, "Le compagnie mercantili-bancarie toscane ei mercati finanziari europei tra metà XIII e metà XVI secolo," in *Archivio storico italiano*, 173.4 (2015), pp. 687–718.

Trepavlov, Vadim Vincerovic, *Gosudarstvennyj stroj Mongol'skoj imperii*, Moscow, Nauka, 1993.

Tucci, Ugo, "L'impresa marittima: uomini e mezzi," in *Storia di Venezia. Dalle origini alla caduta della Serenissima*, vol. 2, eds. Gherardo Ortalli and Giorgio Cracco, Rome, Treccani, 1995, pp. 627–60.

―――. "La navigazione veneziana nel Duecento e nel primo Trecento e la sua evoluzione tecnica," in *Venezia e il Levante fino al secolo XV. Atti del I convegno Internazionale di Storia della Civiltà Veneziana (Venezia 1–5 giugno 1968)*, ed. Agostino Pertusi, 2 vols., Florence, Olschki, vol. 2, pp. 821–42.

Twitchett, Denis, and Klaus-Peter Tietze, "The Liao," in *The Cambridge History of China*, vol. 6: *Alien Regimes and Border States, 907–1368*, eds. Herbert Franke and Denis C. Twitchett, Cambridge, Cambridge University Press, 1994, pp. 43–152.

Udovitch, Abraham L., *Commercial Techniques in Early Medieval Islamic Trade*, Philadelphia, University of Pennsylvania Press, 2016.

Unger, Richard W., *The Ships in the Medieval Economy, 600–1600*, London, Croom Helm, 1980.

Uzelac, Aleksandar, "Echoes of the Conflict between Tokhta and Nogai in the Christian World," in *Zolotoordynskoe obrozrenie*, 5.3 (2017), pp. 509–21.

―――. "Tatary v Dunajsko-Dnestrovskom Meždureč'e vo vtoroj polovine XIV v.," in *Zolotoordynskoe obozrenie*, 7.3 (2019), pp. 416–33.

―――. "War and Peace in the Pontic Steppes (1300–1302)," in *Zolotoordynskoe obozrenie*, 2 (2015), pp. 65–80.

Vásáry, István, "The Beginnings of Coinage in the Blue Horde," in *Acta Orientalia*, 62.4 (2009), pp. 371–85.

―――. *Cumans and Tatars: Oriental Military in the Pre-Ottomans Balkans, 1185–1365*, Cambridge, Cambridge University Press, 2009.

Vasil'ievskij, Vasilij G., *Trudy*, 4 vols., St Petersburg, Nauk, 1908–30.

Vatin, Nicolas, "L'ascesa degli Ottomani (1362–1451)," in *Storia dell'impero ottomano*, ed. Robert Mantran, Lecce, Argo, 2004, pp. 47–94.

Venezia–Senato, *Deliberazioni miste. Registro XX, 1341–1342*, ed. Francesca Girardi, Venice, Istituto Veneto di scienze, lettere ed arti, 2004.

―――. *Deliberazioni miste. Registro XXI, 1342–1344*, ed. Claudio Azzara and Laura Levantino, Venice, Istituto Veneto di scienze, lettere ed arti, 2006.

―――. *Deliberazioni miste. Registro XXII, 1344–1345*, ed. Edoardo Demo, Venice, Istituto Veneto di scienze, lettere ed arti, 2007.

―――. *Deliberazioni miste. Registro XXIII, 1345–1347*, ed. Francesca Girardi, Venice, Istituto Veneto di scienze, lettere ed arti, 2004.

―――. *Deliberazioni miste. Registro XXIV (1347–1349)*, ed. Ermanno Orlando, Venice, Istituto Veneto di scienze, lettere ed arti, 2007.

―――. *Deliberazioni miste. Registro XXIX (1359–1391)*, ed. Laura Levantino, Venice, Istituto Veneto di scienze, lettere ed arti, 2012.

―――. *Deliberazioni miste. Registro XXX (1361–1363)*, ed. Ermanno Orlando and Andreas Kiesewetter, Venice, Istituto Veneto di scienze, lettere ed arti, 2019.

―――. *Deliberazioni miste. Registro XXXIII (1368–1371)*, ed. Andrea Mozzato, Venice, Istituto Veneto di scienze, lettere ed arti, 2011.

Verlinden, Charles, *L'esclavage dans l'Europe médiévale* vol. 2, *Italie, colonies italiennes du Levant, Levant latin, empire byzantin*, Bruges, De Tempel, 1977.

―――. "Le recrutement des esclaves à Venise aux XIV et XV siècles," in *Bulletin de l'Institut historique Belge de Rome*, 39 (1968), pp. 83–202.

Veselovskij, N. I., *Trudy po istorii Zolotoj Ordy*, ed. Il'nur M. Mirgaleev, Kazan, Fen, 2010.

Villani, Giovanni, *Nuova Cronica*, 3 vols., ed. Giuseppe Porta, Parma, Guanda, 1990–91.

Villani, Matteo, *Cronica*, ed. Giuseppe Porta, 2 vols., Parma, Guanda, 1995.

Vogel, Hans Ulrich, *Marco Polo Was in China: New Evidence from Currencies, Salt and Revenues*, Leiden, Brill, 2012.

Von Glahn, Richard, *Fountain of Fortune*, Berkeley, University of California Press, 1996.

Warner, Ernst, *Die Geburt einer Grossmacht, die Osmanen (1300–1481)*, Berlin, Akademie-Verlag, 1966.

Watson Andrew M., "Back to Gold—and Silver," in *The Economic History Review*, 20.1 (1967), pp. 1–34.

Weller, Anna Linden, "Marrying the Mongol Khans: Byzantine Imperial Women and the Diplomacy of Religious Conversion in the 13th and 14th Centuries," in *Scandinavian Journal of Byzantine and Modern Greek Studies*, 2 (2016), pp. 177–200.

Wheelis, Mark, "Biological Warfare at the 1346 Siege of Caffa," in *Emerging Infectious Diseases*, 8.9 (2002), pp. 971–75.

Wittek, Paul, *La formation de l'empire ottoman*, London, Variorum Reprints, 1982.

Yang, Bin, *Cowrie Shells and Cowrie Money: A Global History*, London, Routledge, 2018.

Yildiz, Sara Nur, and Andrew C. S. Peacock, eds., *The Seljuks of Anatolia: Court and Society in the Medieval Middle East*, London, Tauris, 2013.

Yudkevich, Jenia, "The Nature and Role of the Slave Traders in the Eastern Mediterranean during the Third Reign of Sultan al-Nāṣir Muḥammad b. Qalāwūn (1310–41 CE)," in *Slavery and the Slave Trade in the Eastern Mediterranean (c. 1000–1500 CE)*, eds. Reuven Amitai and Christoph Cluse, Turnhout, Brepols, 2017, pp. 423–36.

Zachariadou A. Elizabeth, *Romania and the Turks (c.1300-c.1500)*, London, Variorum Reprints, 1985.

# INDEX

## A NOTE ON THE TYPE

This book has been composed in Arno, an Old-style serif typeface in the classic Venetian tradition, designed by Robert Slimbach at Adobe.